Paving the Way

Paving the Way

New York Road Building
and the American State,
1880–1956

Michael R. Fein

UNIVERSITY PRESS OF KANSAS

© 2008 by the University Press of Kansas

Published by the University Press of Kansas (Lawrence, Kansas 66045), which was
organized by the Kansas Board of Regents and is operated and funded by Emporia
State University, Fort Hays State University, Kansas State University, Pittsburg State
University, the University of Kansas, and Wichita State University

Library of Congress Cataloging-in-Publication Data

Fein, Michael R.
　　Paving the way : New York road building and the American state, 1880-1956 /
Michael R. Fein.
　　　　p. cm.
　　Includes bibliographical references and index.
　　ISBN 978-0-7006-1562-9 (cloth : alk. paper)
1. Roads—New York (State)—History. 2. Roads—Political aspects—New York
(State)—History. 3. State-local relations—New York (State)—History. 4. Central-local
government relations—New York (State)—History. 5. Roads—Political aspects—United
States—History. 6. Central-local government relations—United States—History.
I. Title. II. Title: New York road building and the American state, 1880-1956.
　　HE356.N7F453 2008
　　338.109747'09041—dc22
　　　　　　　　　　　　　　　　　　　　　　　　　　　　　　　　2007043603

British Library Cataloguing-in-Publication Data is available.

Printed in the United States of America

10 9 8 7 6 5 4 3 2 1

CONTENTS

ACKNOWLEDGMENTS

Writing is not a solitary process. Over the past decade I have received help from many friends, scholars, and institutions. At Brandeis University, where I benefited from the support of the Irving and Rose Crown Fellowship in American History, Morton Keller and Michael Willrich offered expert guidance while this project was at an early stage. While on a year-long Fellowship in History, Public Policy and American Politics at the University of Virginia's Miller Center for Public Affairs, Brian Balogh, Sid Milkis, and Richard John gave generously of their time and introduced me to the scholarship of American Political Development. At Harvard Business School, David Moss, Walter Friedman, Meg Jacobs, Thomas McCraw, and Jason Scott Smith all offered their thoughtful perspectives on this project. Several historians at work in the field of American public policy guided my work at critical junctures: Julian Zelizer, Gail Radford, and especially Mark Rose, who again and again proved himself to be a model of scholarly generosity. The burgeoning international field of mobility history provided an unmatched forum for debating transportation policy. Special thanks to Gijs Mom, Laurent Tissot, Clay McShane, Ray Mohl, Tom Zeller, Mathieu Flonneau, and Alex Gall. The History and Society Division at Babson College offered generous support for conference travel. At Babson and in the Humanities Department at Johnson and Wales University, I have been fortunate to work with a supportive community of dedicated teachers, scholars, and staff. Librarians and archivists at Babson College; Brandeis University; Harvard University; the New York State Archives and Library; the Franklin D. Roosevelt Library in Hyde Park, New York; and Archives II in Suitland, Maryland, all provided essential assistance in locating hard-to-find materials. I am also grateful for assistance received through the Albert M. Greenfield Research Fellowship at the Roosevelt Library and the Larry J. Hackman Research Residency Grant from the New York State Archives Partnership Trust. My thanks go out as well to University Press of Kansas editors Fred Woodward, Susan McRory, and Susan Schott for the patience and care with which they shepherded this manuscript through its final stages. I also thank David Robertson, whose careful and constructive critique for UPK was much appreciated.

Many friends and colleagues improved this book through their constant support and willingness to comment on earlier drafts. My thanks go to Kevin Bruyneel, Clark Hantzmon, Brian McCarthy, Jeff Melnick, Emily Straus, and Jeff Wiltse, as well as to Rena Kirsch for her deft librarian's skills and to Ari Kirsch for his insights into contemporary public planning debates. My family, especially Matthew, Lisa, and Corey Fein; Maier and Sunny Fein; Joe and Sylvia Fein; Debra and Greg Harris; and Art and Eena Feld were unwavering in their love and support throughout this period. This book is dedicated to Marjorie Feld, who gracefully—and routinely—made personal and professional sacrifices on its and my behalf. She has lovingly illuminated not just my writing but every aspect of my life. This book is also dedicated to our infant son, Nate, and our two-year-old son, Izzy, a source of love, laughter, and (while his father was hard at work on a book about road building) boundless enthusiasm for "diggers."

Paving the Way

Introduction

On March 4, 1878, George Alston, Ransom Winchip, and David Buckbee, three upstate New York farmers who served as the town of Queensbury's highway commissioners, received a petition signed by forty-two of their neighbors. Among the signers were farmers, merchants, millers, stonemasons, and the principal of Glens Falls Academy. All agreed that "public convenience and wants" required that a new road be built from Queensbury to nearby Long Pond. Their petition set in motion a road-building process that had changed little since colonial times.

Using local landmarks—a butternut tree, a dwelling house, a stone set in the road—the highway commissioners surveyed the new road, marking its course "through mostly uncultivated lands" with a compass and a hundred-foot chain made of one-foot links. Measured according to the old English system, the road extended one and a half rods on each side of the centerline, leaving a fifty-foot right of way. Property owners whose lands were adjacent to the road, usually petitioners themselves, each received a dollar from the commissioners in return for waiving their rights to pursue damage claims stemming from the new public way. The road was then incorporated into the nearest road district, where residents maintained it, each laboring a few days a year under the direction of a locally appointed pathmaster. Road administration, finance, construction, and upkeep were purely local responsibilities that produced local roads in accordance with long-standing tradition.[1]

Three-quarters of a century later, the Queensbury commissioners had little say over road building: construction was no longer the organic product of local desires but the work of large, centralized, bureaucratic agencies. Experts in these agencies designed highways like the monumental New York State Thruway, perhaps the best example of a road-building program that had transcended local politics in its effort to serve broader regional interests. At 426 miles, the Thruway's mainline was the longest toll highway in the world when it opened in 1956, and its route was determined not by residents of the newly linked communities but by state and federal engineers.

The construction of the 15,764-foot Tappan Zee Bridge over the Hudson River completed the toll highway that joined New York City and Buffalo.[2] To mark the opening of this $60 million technological marvel, Governor Averell Harriman presided over a "daylong fete" on December 15, 1955. High school bands played, and hundreds thronged the toll plazas to catch a glimpse of the official cavalcade crossing the Hudson under the protection of its destroyer-escort, the U.S.S. *Rizzi*. During the day's speeches, Harriman and other officials promoted further state and federal funding for highways, praised the work of the engineers responsible for their construction, and trumpeted their potential to open up "boundless economic expansion and prosperity."

But not all were won over by the triumphant atmosphere and the tribute to heroic engineering. Nearly lost amid the pageantry were sixteen women whom the press described as housewives from the nearby communities of Piermont, Grand View, and Sparkill. Each wore a one-letter picket sign that together spelled out "S-A-V-E O-U-R V-I-L-L-A-G-E-S-!" Concerned that a proposed spur tying the Thruway to the New Jersey Turnpike would destroy their neighborhoods, they staged a silent protest on the ceremony's margins.[3]

The resistance of these sixteen women to highway development offers an important reminder of what had changed since Long Pond Road was laid out in 1878. In the intervening years, New York sparked a revolution in road building, the legacy of which is difficult to miss. The state led the nation in highway expenditures, improving 80,000 miles of public roads, including a 14,000-mile system of primary highways and the pathbreaking Thruway. Other states followed New York's lead; in the nation at large, the number of miles of hard-surfaced highways increased by a factor of fifteen during the first half of the twentieth century.[4] This ambitious construction program produced more than better transportation infrastructure. It also provided a critical stimulus to American Political Development. As highways emerged as a conspicuous and centrally important element in the built environment, road-building politics became a major site of public policy conflict and a decisive battleground in the struggle to define the modern American state.

Why Public Works?

This book examines road building in the state of New York and how it coincided with the development of American federalism. How public power has been apportioned among local, state, and national governments is one of the defining questions of American political history. Public works infrastructure turns out to be a crucial—and crucially overlooked—key to this problem. Recently, scholars have begun to explore the connections between shifting philosophies of government and the development of transportation and communication systems in the early nineteenth century.[5] Working at the intersection of political, legal, business, and transportation history, they have recast our understanding of the nation's first transportation revolution, the great wave of public and private investment that produced an extensive system of turnpikes, canals, and railroads. This study extends that analysis to the nation's second transportation revolution, exploring the links between road building and state building a hundred years later.[6]

Road building was central to the development of new ideas about the nexus of public power in America during the late nineteenth and early twentieth centuries. As citizens and policy makers sought to define the proper locus of road-building powers among the several levels of government, they set in motion a profound political evolution. Between 1880 and 1956, Americans embraced a richer, more vibrant array of public institutions; they also embraced a set of state-citizen relationships that promised more effective public administration but left them, as individuals, with less direct control over government activity. Scholars of American Political Development have emphasized the centrality of national administrative capacity in this transformation, linking the growth of federal powers to a wide range of subjects: the decline of political parties, military expansion, a developing welfare and regulatory state, and the concomitant growth of federal bureaucracy.[7]

This book deals with all of these themes but offers a significant corrective to the currently dominant narrative. It argues that the building of a new American state, including its crucial public works infrastructure, rested on the rise of a more complex American federalism that drew broadly on the governing powers of state and local governments even as the federal government expanded. It asks why local officials voluntarily delegated power to state governments, and how state governments, despite an upward shift in governance to the federal level, maintained a major policy-making role. In this regard, it is as interested in assessing the reapportionment of public power at the *subfederal* level as it is with traditional federal power-sharing arrangements between state and national institutions. Its focus is public works policy; in a larger sense, it is a history of the evolution of modern American government.

Road-Building Policy Regimes

To accomplish these tasks, I trace the evolution of New York road building through five policy regimes, each characterized by a distinctive locus of policy making, structure of highway administration, reliance on expert authority, and the system of intergovernmental relations in which it was embedded (see Table 1). These regimes help to mark out key transitional moments in the changing state of highway affairs across the period 1880 to 1956. Importantly, each regime did not materialize, fully formed, from the ashes of the former. Rather, these regimes were fluid and contested, gradually transitioning from one into the next. Despite the imprecision of these changes, the first regime was so dramatically different from the last that the entire process constituted a deep transformation of the political order.[8]

Simply put, the people of New York entered into a devil's bargain: to secure a system closed to localism and patronage, they bought into a system closed to all but highway engineers. This transition served the purposes of several key players—bicyclist and motorist associations, construction and real estate interests, politicians bred in patronage but seeking an alternate path to power, and the highway engineers themselves. Midlevel leaders of rural, suburban, and urban New York gradually let their control ebb as they saw local road-building control beginning to do more harm than good. Meantime, highway engineers, having been handed the opportunity to craft a new kind of politics, took full advantage of it. By the mid-twentieth century, a framework of highway administration rooted in communal governance had given way to a closed bureaucratic system. A thorough understanding of this evolution of New York highway affairs—and of the logic behind New Yorkers' calculated trade-offs—provides important clues to the making of this new political order.

My analysis begins on the eve of America's second transportation revolution, when New York roadways were administered under a *local policy regime* (1880–1898). Town highway commissioners and locally appointed "path-

TABLE 1. Road Building Policy Regimes

Road Building Policy Regime	Dates	Primary Locus of Policy Making	Dominant Structure of Highway Administration	Character of Intergovernmental Relations	Political Authority of Engineers
Local	1880–1898	Community	Town Highway Commissions and Pathmasters	Road-building power is decentralized and localized	Minimal
Subfederal	1898–1919	Subfederal, privileging local interests	State Highway Commission	State coordination of highways is voluntary and checked by local powers	Provisional, interested in transportation reform, but limited by demands of patronage politics
State-Centered Bureaucratic	1919–1931	Federal, privileging state-wide interests	State Department of Public Works	State highway coordination is mandatory Federal government offers aid and limited oversight	Relational, serving traffic needs, but limited by countervailing authority of state legislators and local officials
Nationalized Bureaucratic	1931–1945	Federal, privileging national interests	State Department of Public Works and New Deal Agencies	State highway construction operates under extensive federal aid and oversight	Relational, serving non-traffic needs and limited by pressures of unemployment relief
Consolidated Bureaucratic	1945–1956	Federal plus quasi-public agency, privileging state, national, and private interests	New York State Thruway Authority, State Department of Public Works, and Federal Highway Administration	State officials spin off the largest element of postwar reconstruction, the Thruway, to a public authority Federal government authorizes Interstate Highways	Consolidated, serving traffic needs, overriding citizen dissent through reliance on professional deference, and motorist-consumer rhetoric

masters" oversaw tens of thousands of miles of winding country roads that formed a critical component of New York's vernacular landscape. Meagerly financed and local in conception, they stood in marked counterpoint to the major transportation initiatives of the nineteenth century, such as canals and railroads. By the close of the nineteenth century, few New Yorkers failed to recognize the relatively impoverished state of their public roads. Chapter 1 examines the earliest challenges to "Old Ways": both the conditions of the old roads themselves and the politics of road building under the local policy regime. "Good Roads" advocates began to undermine this regime in the 1880s. Chief among these supporters of better highways was the League of American Wheelmen (LAW), a bicycling organization that formed a tenuous alliance with locally oriented machine politicians in their pursuit of road reform.

The first chapter thus introduces the first of the book's several themes: the inseparability of local consent from expanded state administrative capacity. The LAW's pact with urban machines secured the passage of a state aid road bill in 1898 that gave towns the option to draw on state assistance for highway improvement. It also proved to be an "opening wedge" to expanding state authority that was initially exploited by machine politicians operating out of the State Engineer's Office, an elected position geared to the demands of patronage politics. Significantly, the assumption of new road-building responsibilities by state officials was not a response to partisans of efficiency, who saw expanded state authority as the rational solution to a poorly managed highway system. Rather, it was the work of careful political compromise, sensitive to local interests who were willing to sacrifice a small measure of oversight in exchange for better local roads. The LAW, a well-organized interest group, abandoned plans for an ambitious state construction program and instead brokered a deal between political bosses and agrarian conservatives that jump-started a road improvement program while promising each the possibility of retaining their essentially localist road-building practices.

A *subfederal road-building regime* (1898–1919), the subject of Chapter 2, emerged in the aftermath of the passage of state aid road legislation. Under this regime, state and local road authorities operated under increasing tension as the voluntarist nature of this policy regime (and its susceptibility to corruption) made building a highway system difficult. Chapter 2 investigates how and why "New Ways" of highway administration took form during this period. Several factors were instrumental in the rejection of nineteenth-century, locally oriented road-building ideas and practices. These included the popularly supported creation of $100 million in bonded debt to finance the road improvement projects for which towns had petitioned, and the legislature's eventual rejection of the voluntarist principle that had left the state operating under essentially two separate highway codes. Most important, the state's political machines found themselves ill equipped to handle the politically divisive nature of constructing a state highway system.

Chapter 2, then, introduces a second theme: the political utility of administrative reform for hard-nosed politicians. Indeed, this story challenges what is often taken as an article of faith: that politicians relentlessly pursue ever more power.[9] The determination of route locations raised too many politically unpopular questions for locally oriented boss politics, and the State Highway Commission (created in 1909) found itself caught up in repeated graft investigations as its leadership struggled to respond to the competing pressures of patronage politics and systematic construction. Calls for the statewide improvement of the road infrastructure now pitted political bosses against engineers. Though they were political neophytes at the time, these engineers successfully highlighted the ineffectiveness of more parochial approaches to the demands of large public works projects.

Whereas the desire to preserve local control prompted the shift from the local to the subfederal regime, a lack of institutional capacity prompted old pols to concede the political utility of backing road reform and to drop their defenses of patronage-driven road building. Governor Alfred E. Smith, who proved to be as adept an administrative reformer as he was a ward boss, helped bridge the gap between this subfederal regime and the *state-centered bureaucratic road-building regime* (1919–1931), the focus of Chapter 3. This regime achieved full form under Colonel Frederick S. Greene, a U.S. Army engineer who administered New York's highways from 1919 to 1939. Smith was quick to recognize the political usefulness of reform, and he worked throughout the 1920s to reorganize state government by creating a powerful administrative branch of government under his own executive oversight. Part of building a more muscular governor's office entailed replacing the old Highway Commission (routinely tossed about in a game of political football) with a more robust Department of Public Works (DPW), led by a professional engineering staff and vested with critical map-making powers that had formerly belonged to the state legislature. Chapter 3, "Highways," explores the hot political battle this set up between engineers and professional politicians. Most legislators eventually yielded to Greene, recognizing the political capital they accrued through backing administrative reform and through passing off politically contentious issues to a governor's appointee.

Greene continued to have rocky relations with Old Guard Republican legislators, though, who resented both the loss of political power generally and Superintendent Greene in particular, as he was quick to castigate legislators as he parlayed his professional expertise into expanded political authority.

Chapter 3 builds on the themes of local authority and the political utility of subfederal administrative reform introduced in previous chapters, with a new focus on how engineers navigated these turbulent currents. By the end of the 1920s Greene had built a series of alliances with the governor, key legislators, and organized highway users groups, overriding scattered and localized opposition to his vast highway modernization project. Indeed, engineers enjoyed broad citizen support so long as Greene's department concentrated on improving existing routes for the state's growing number of motorists, evaded the scandals that had marked previous highway administrations, and left towns' and counties' countervailing road-building authority (such as the capacity to veto state projects) intact. Thus a bureaucratic road-building regime was in place by the 1920s, materializing first out of a desire to preserve local control, then through a calculated maneuver by reform-minded politicians to expand state administrative power, and finally through the work of engineers themselves in creating enduring networks that bolstered their provisional political authority.

Engineers' political expression of their bureaucratic authority continued to evolve over the next several decades. As Chapter 4 makes clear, federal responses to the Great Depression and World War II prompted the development of a *nationalized bureaucratic road-building regime* (1931–1945), placing road building in the service of unemployment relief and civil defense. At first, the enlarged federal role produced conflicts between New Dealers and highway engineers over the divergent goals of unemployment relief and highway modernization. But ultimately the new alliance between federal officials and state engineers emboldened the latter to further expand their own road-building powers. State–federal relations thickened during the 1930s, but of equal importance was the degree to which the New Deal affected the state–local power-sharing arrangements that had been cemented during the 1920s. Engineers argued that the principles of localism were increasingly out of step with such national demands as economic development and military preparedness. Chapter 4 explores how state engineers used the twin crises of depression and war to further their own bureaucratic autonomy and to "Clear the Way" of local obstacles to the Department of Public Works' highway modernization program.

After the war, a new generation of engineering professionals—Charles H.

Sells, Bertram D. Tallamy, John W. Johnson—secured the political gains that their predecessors had made over the previous decades in a *consolidated bureaucratic regime* (1945–1956). These highway engineers pursued a controversial postwar road-building program, the crowning achievement of which was the New York State Thruway. A 535-mile express highway linking New York's major cities to surrounding states and Canada, the Thruway was the culmination of half a century of state highway building and a precursor to the federal Interstate System. In order to accelerate construction of this colossal project, engineers backed the creation of the New York State Thruway Authority, a public authority standing outside of general-purpose government and charged with the planning and implementation of the Thruway.

Chapter 5, "Authority," takes as its focus the political, economic, and social implications of this new instrument of government that was so central to the consolidation of the bureaucratic road-building regime. Politically and financially autonomous, the Thruway Authority provided the wide compass of power that was critical to the speedy construction of the New York State Thruway during the 1950s. The benefits that accrued to motorists from the Thruway made it widely popular. But the day-to-day operations of the Thruway Authority revealed a widening gulf between engineers' visions of a new highway system and those of affected communities. Engineers stubbornly defended their vision, crowding out alternative transportation schemes and exercising authority with increased disregard for the nontraffic interests of ordinary New Yorkers. The growing chorus of road-building dissent—and the eventual end of deference toward the road builders in the late twentieth century—reveals that under the resilient and adaptive system of American federalism, the bureaucratic road-building regime never wholly supplanted the local.

Road Building, State Building, and American Political Development

The politically contested evolution of highway policy across five distinct road-building regimes offers several lessons for scholars of American Political Development. First, it recasts our understanding of postwar federal expansion, turning our attention to long duration transformations in subfederal politics as an essential precondition for later developments. Second, it foregrounds the grinding politics that helped elevate professional experts to positions of public power, and the means by which these experts then sustained and consolidated their power. Third, it reminds us of the continued importance of town and county governments, not simply as "vestiges of the past," but as essential players in America's "uneasy tension between center and locality."[10]

Federal and Subfederal Relations: Too often, historians describe the upward shift in the locus of authority from towns and villages to the federal government as a virtually inevitable process, driven by the pressures of new technologies, bureaucratic rationality, and modernization. This functionalist reading of the transformation of American federal relations, however, downplays the contested nature of this evolution and undervalues the work done by state governments.[11] As I will argue, the setting of transportation infrastructure policy, especially at the subfederal level, played an early and dominant role in the evolution of American intergovernmental relations and the limiting of national power.

The book's tale of New York highway politics calls into question the time-honored narrative of intergovernmental relations (IGR) that describes a shift from the "layer cake" federalism of the nineteenth century (in which local, state, and federal powers were clearly separated and defined) to the "marble cake" federalism of the twentieth (in which local, state, and federal governments produced a pragmatic admixture of authority exercised in various policy areas). This traditional interpretation positions the New Deal as the primary historical turning point in IGR analysis and sees the growth of the federal government in the 1930s as instrumental in shaping the flow of public power.[12] A close reading of New York highway policy suggests that this analysis is misleading in a number of ways. First, it disregards the important local-state struggles of the first three decades of the twentieth century that served as a critical rehearsal for federal expansion under the New Deal. Second, it fails to account for the effect of quasi-governmental state agencies, such as public authorities, that stand outside of general-purpose government. Third, it gives only cursory attention to the ways that local officials and ordinary citizens came to accept these shifts in power-sharing arrangements as legitimate. *Paving the Way* addresses each of these shortcomings in its attention to state-level highway policy debate, the creation of the Thruway Authority, and the growing level of New Yorkers' comfort with centralized bureaucratic expertise. Importantly, it dates the emergence of cooperative federal arrangements to World War I rather than to the New Deal.

Statistics bear out this interpretation of the restructuring of road-building authority among the various levels of government. Annual public expenditures for highway construction increased from $175 million in 1902—overseen almost entirely by local officials—to over $7 billion in 1956 (see

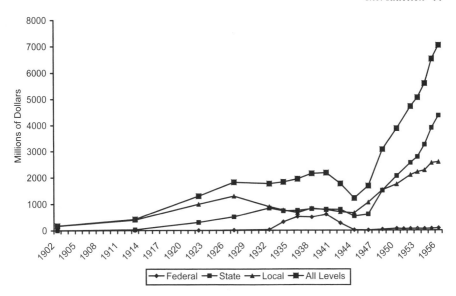

Figure 1: Federal, State, and Local Highway Expenditures, 1902–1956

Source: Compiled from data in U.S. Department of Commerce, Bureau of the Census, *Census of Governments: 1962,* Volume 6, Topical Studies, no. 4, *Historical Statistics on Governmental Finances and Employment* (Washington, D.C.: Government Printing Office, 1964).

Figure 1). As these sums increased, Americans sought a new balance among federal, state, and local governing powers. Figure 2 tracks the ebb and flow of highway expenditures at each level of government and is a good indicator of the timing of this reconfiguration of federal, state, and local arrangements. Road-building power had largely shifted from a local to a state responsibility by the 1920s. By 1924 highways were the largest cost item on the New York State budget after education, and in 1927 all state governments devoted on average an astonishing 36 percent of their public spending to highway construction (up from 7.7 percent in 1913). By the 1930s state governments were spending as much on highways as their local counterparts; by the postwar years, state highway expenditures outpaced local government by a wide margin. This shift in subfederal power relations was hotly contested. And it proved to be an essential precondition of the subsequent expansion of federal power and expenditures during the New Deal and the postwar Interstate Highway program.[13]

Political Authority and Expertise: The public's growing comfort with centralized bureaucracy was critical to this transformation of American federal relations, so it is essential to understand the way engineering expertise and professionalism entered into public administration. The story of the as-

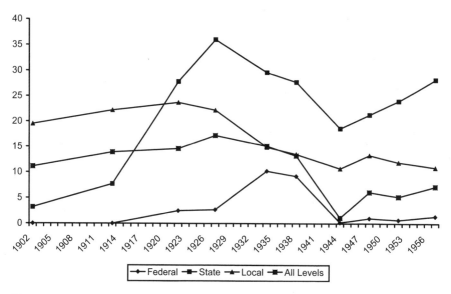

Figure 2: Highway Expenditures as a Percentage of Government Spending, 1902–1957

Source: Compiled from data in U.S. Department of Commerce, Bureau of the Census, *Census of Governments: 1962,* Volume 6, Topical Studies, no. 4, *Historical Statistics on Governmental Finances and Employment* (Washington, D.C.: Government Printing Office, 1964).

cension of experts into public life is a familiar one.[14] But often missing from that story is an awareness of the grinding politics through which citizens and local officials renegotiated their relationship with professional bureaucrats, whose own notions of their political power were also in flux. Unlike Robert Moses, the man most frequently associated with New York public works, the engineers who bureaucratized New York's highway program in the 1920s and 1930s—men such as Frederick S. Greene and Arthur W. Brandt—were not shrewd politicians, masking a grab for power with talk of rational planning and economic efficiency. Nor were they in service of private interests, such as the oil industry, cement producers, or automobile manufacturers. Rather, they were men who capitalized on the chronic abuses of machine politicians by translating their professional standing into a competing form of political expression.

Highway engineers rode into public office on a wave of Progressive Era aversion to patronage politics and support for administrative reform. In New York, the key figure was Al Smith, who endorsed one of Progressivism's central tenants: that public functions could be properly divided between the "political" (i.e., issues involving questions of social values) and the "administrative" (i.e., public tasks that were technical in nature and should thus be left to expert managers to efficiently handle).[15] In time, the politics-and-administration divide proved to be a false dichotomy, with engineer-administrators cloaking their value-based judgments in antipartisan, technocratic language. Over the next two generations, however, they effectively exploited this ambiguity in their efforts to realize their professional agenda.

Once highway engineers had assumed a policy-making role, they developed a more robust form of political expression. Through the 1920s, professional engineers offered a clear alternative to the pork-barrel politics of political machines and to the older, poorly coordinated system of local road administration. They managed to *sustain* their power, however, by carefully cultivating alliances with transitional politicians like Smith, for whom links to road reformers were politically useful, and with organized highway user groups who were persuaded by the advantages of framing highway politics as an administrative responsibility. Then, in the 1930s, engineers extended the reach of their power by using the crisis of the Great Depression to undercut long-held local road-building powers. When a new generation of highway engineers backed the creation of the Thruway Authority and a closed-system approach to highway engineering in the postwar years, it encountered little remaining countervailing road-building authority from citizens, local officials, or state legislators.

Engineers framed their decisions in the language of scientific rationality and professional expertise. But these were merely forms of political expression that advanced their traffic-service vision of highway planning. Though New York's road-building program predated mass automobility, engineers quickly seized on the phenomenon as a means of cementing their political legitimacy. Traffic censuses became the main foundational beam to engineers' authority, a scientific measurement of public demand for highways that was difficult to contest.[16] As long as state highway construction focused on the improvement of existing roads, dissent was weakly expressed. As engineering projects increased in scale, impact, and potential for controversy, resistance spiked. It was in the process of responding to increased opposition that strong tensions developed between engineers' service to their professional agenda (building a better highway system) and their responsibility to the public (balancing highway construction with other aspects of social development). These interests, once operating in tandem and instrumental to the engineers' rise to power, began over time to feed conflict and meet with cross-purposes. The engineers' solution to this problem was to stop treating motorists as citizens and start treating them as consumers, who paid "user fees" through motor fuel taxes and registration fees that were then dedicated toward the maintenance and expansion of the highway system. The adoption of this "motorist-consumer" logic suggests the extent to which highway engineers sought to crowd out dissenting political voices, diminishing the public nature of highways while interpreting the simple act of driving as an unqualified endorsement of the highway program.

Local Politics: A third area of inquiry, largely ignored in studies of the rise of bureaucratic power, is the role that local politics played in the "forging of bureaucratic autonomy."[17] Explaining why local officials voluntarily relinquished road-building power—and why ordinary citizens accepted this as legitimate, at least for a time—constitutes an essential corollary to the argument that engineers were making and shaping political choices. It is a central point of this book that the emergence of cooperative federal arrangements was not the inevitable consequence of "modernization," nor was it solely the work of a burgeoning class of engineering professionals and administrative reformers. It was contingent as well on the renegotiation of public authority, as local officials helped transform town and county bodies of road administration from autonomous departments to nodes within a relational system of governance. This political transformation mirrored localities' shifting infrastructural framework and reflected a growing comfort with a bureaucracy that, for a time, appeared to be the best solution to local road-building problems that were not effectively handled by town officials or political machines.

Through the end of the nineteenth century, road building was the province of local government, administered by town highway commissioners and pathmasters. Localities yielded control of their road-building environment to centralized authority for a multiplicity of reasons over the first half of the twentieth century. Greater state oversight was the price locals paid for state assistance in 1898; but the provisions of that landmark legislation were optional, and town residents could still tend to their roads the way their grandparents had if they so chose. In 1905 and 1912 New Yorkers endorsed a more robust state highway administration when they backed two referenda that put $100 million in the hands of state road officials. By the 1920s, local officials lent their backing to Governor Smith and Superintendent Greene's campaign to vest map-making power in the Department of Public Works in order to side-step the legislative log-rolling that had thwarted highway development in the prewar period.

Some of these decisions to relinquish road-building control to state agencies were devil's bargains: calculated maneuvers to sacrifice time-honored powers in order to secure the quick distribution of state resources to cash-poor localities. Others were made with the expectation that local checks on state authority would preserve some measure of town and county command over engineers' designs. Local officials put together a carefully balanced system of countervailing powers that lasted into the 1920s. But it soon came undone. The failure of towns to reconstruct narrow bridges or redesign dangerous grade crossings led state engineers to pressure localities to hand over those responsibilities to the state. The fiscal pressures of the Great Depression compounded towns' difficulties in meeting increased demands on local road systems, and, again, highway engineers framed these failures as a further justification for the expansion of state road-building authority. By the postwar years, ordinary New Yorkers began to recoil at the extensive powers highway engineers had garnered over the past half century. Though they still tended to back the road builders' consensus during the 1950s, their resistance to highway planners became more widespread.

The well-known antihighway protests of the 1960s and 1970s were bolstered by the environmental movement, new commitments to local control, and a deepening distrust of government. But their roots were visible in policy decisions made generations before, when New Yorkers first contemplated a road-building program that transcended local politics. This process raised important questions about the ability of experts and bureaucrats to measure community impact against broader economic needs and a burgeoning car culture against an awareness of its consequences.[18] Ultimately, it revealed that "local" voices, though muted, had never disappeared, and continued to be important in setting the terms of public policy debate.

New York State Highway Policy and American Politics

A few final words are in order about the choice of New York State highway policy to pursue this analysis. *Paving the Way* is a study in the evolution of American governance; it is as well a case study in how one state adapted to the coming of the motor vehicle. A transportation leader throughout the nineteenth century, the Empire State continued to lead the way (along with other eastern industrialized states) in the nation's second transportation revolution.[19] New York's diverse polity is a microcosm of the nation at large. Marked by deep partisan, urban-rural, and upstate-downstate schisms, its political and cultural cleavages embody national divides. New York's archetypal status meant that its experiences translated well to the national theater.

Former governors of New York occupied the White House for twenty-four years during the period 1893 to 1945. And leading actors in federal highway politics staged rehearsals in the Empire State: Roy Stone advocated for good roads in New York before he was called to head the newly established federal Office of Road Inquiry in 1893; Franklin Roosevelt studied road-building politics as a New York state legislator and governor before he inaugurated the nation's largest public works program during the Great Depression; and Bertram Tallamy left his position as chairman of the New York State Thruway Authority in 1956 to oversee the construction of the Interstate Highway System as the nation's first federal highway administrator. New York produced road builders well-suited to national leadership throughout America's second transportation revolution.

This revolution in motor transportation had enormous consequences for the built environment. But ultimately it affected more than the highways themselves, catalyzing a broad reconfiguration of the American political order. As roads pushed across local, state, and national borders, Americans drew heavily on the resources of centralized government. Yet the intrinsically local nature of roads—fixed in space, intimately related to community geography—meant that the politics of building them could never transcend the locales in which they were situated. The history of road-building politics thus speaks to a central question in American political history: how should public power be apportioned, especially when dealing with a policy issue that is national in scale yet state and local in implementation? In examining how every level of government confronted a massive infrastructural challenge, this book details the origins of the dynamic and interdependent local-state-federal arrangements that came to characterize twentieth-century American governance.

While historians and cultural critics have lavished enormous attention on American car culture, they have overlooked the political significance of the road revolution.[20] Only recently has the revitalized field of mobility history begun to press beyond the traditional automobile-centered concerns of transport history to open new vistas of scholarly inquiry. New work in this field takes a far more nuanced approach to evolving cultures of mobility, the consumption of space, the politicization of mass automobility, the transmission of engineering knowledge, and the connection between communities of experts and political power. This study operates in the same vein, recognizing that the revolution in road administration was the product of policy conflict and intertwined with political and cultural developments, rather than a technological inevitability.[21]

Importantly, the road revolution began well before mass automobility arrived in New York in the 1910s. Indeed, road improvement was one of the earliest policy areas to transition from a purely local responsibility to one enmeshed in complex federal relationships. Not just a pragmatic response to the automobile, the evolution of road-building authority was intimately linked to the emergence of a new set of federal relationships that overturned long-standing relationships between citizens and their governing institutions. In time, other traditionally local policy concerns—social welfare, education, criminal justice—would undergo a similar transformation.[22] But the state highway systems hold a special place in the history of American federalism. Too often obscured by the motor vehicle culture they serve, the nation's public roads were the product of—and a chief catalyst behind—a major overhaul in American governance. Their history highlights the extent to which public works infrastructure has been a dominant force behind the formation of the modern American state.

Old Ways: The Local Road-Building Regime in Late-Nineteenth-Century New York

The road-building practices of George Alston, Ransom Winchip, and David Buckbee's day persisted until the close of the nineteenth century. Though New Yorkers took advantage of major improvements in other areas of transportation and communications infrastructure—canals and railroads, the postal system, and the telegraph—public road construction had undergone no significant transformation in technology or administration. The local road-building regime responsible for this state of affairs was consistent with the economic interests and political ideals of nineteenth-century New Yorkers. Once the state legislature abdicated its road-building powers following the collapse of major turnpike construction during the first transportation revolution of the early nineteenth century, local highway officials were reluctant to again share their road-building prerogative.[1] Residents trusted a system that put them in charge of local roadways, allowed road-building disputes to be handled within the community, and, perhaps most important, was supported by a fiscally undemanding tax that was paid in labor rather than in cash.

The logic behind the local road-building regime faced its earliest challenges in the 1880s when Good Roads reformers lobbied the state legislature to put public road construction back on the state's political agenda. The Good Roads coalition would grow to include academics, industrialists, railroad corporations, well-off "gentlemen" farmers, and early motorists. But the first sustained action on behalf of improved highways came from a cyclists' organization known as the League of American Wheelmen (LAW). Spearheaded by the New York City Bicycle Club, the LAW was founded in 1880 at a meeting in Newport, Rhode Island, the posh resort destination for wealthy New Yorkers. This national organization of city cycling clubs pushed for an end to restrictive local ordinances aimed at limiting cyclists' access to public spaces. As cyclists grew in number and gained organizational clout over the course of the decade, they developed a positive agenda as well, lobbying for improved touring routes in state legislatures and in the U.S. Congress.

What began as a conflict between New York agrarians and urban cyclists led to a fundamental transformation in American intergovernmental relations. Sustained efforts by the Wheelmen and their legislative allies drew widespread attention not only to the condition of New York's public roads but also to the nature of local government and its limited capacity to embark on a major road improvement initiative. As it turned out, though, the modernization of New York highways and the centralization of highway administration was no easy feat. The success of the Good Roads campaign hinged on its fit with the interests of the state's most powerful political blocs: fiscally conservative agrarians and urban political machines. Both groups hoped to use the roads issue as a means of strengthening their predominantly localized politics rather than ushering in an era of administrative reform. Along with the road reformers, they struggled over how best to balance local and state authority. The legislation that emerged out of these debates—what one state senator described as an "entering wedge" to unprecedented public expenditure—was the product of hard-fought politics and the persistent appeal of localism rather than the allure of administrative rationality. By the end of the nineteenth century, partisans of road reform succeeded in undoing the old local road-building regime, but not the antipathy to centralized authority that undergirded it. Instead, they ushered in a subfederal road-building regime that traded away modest communal controls for the promise of better local roads. The history of this change in policy regimes suggests that the means by which local officials and ordinary citizens came to accept these shifts in power-sharing arrangements as legitimate are of critical importance, not only to the origins of the second transportation revolution but to the transformation of intergovernmental relationships as well.

The Origins of the Second Transportation Revolution

As urban cyclists cast their critical gaze in the direction of rural roads, they did not fail to comment on what they saw as a tremendous chasm between urban growth and rural stasis. Though often viewed through the lens of their own condescension, the gap was real: few things better highlighted the different trajectories of urban and rural life at the end of the nineteenth century than transportation improvements. Cities saw paved streets, wide boulevards, the first subway systems, and interurban railroads. Rural areas reaped real benefits from canals and railroads, but the implementation of these major traffic arteries threw the unimproved state of public roads into sharp relief.

Preachers of the "gospel of good roads" saw muddy and rutted roadways as just one more symptom of an agrarian society that was rapidly depopulating because of its failure to modernize. Keeping rural sons and daughters at home on the farm grew increasingly difficult during the late nineteenth century. Rural New Yorkers had been among the nation's leading agricultural providers until the 1850s. In later decades they faced declining incomes in the face of western competition, farm consolidation, mechanization, and overproduction. Of all the states in the nation, New York State suffered the greatest decline in rural population between 1880 and 1890. Across nearly five-sixths of the state, numbers in rural areas plummeted: a net loss of 150,000 residents, or about 10 percent of the rural population.[2] The LAW's advocacy of good roads may have been largely self-serving, but it was informed by this sense of rural vulnerability.

Reconstructing New York highways meant challenging a decentralized system of road administration that had been in place since colonial times. Town highway commissioners, pathmasters, and a residential labor force kept the politics of road building close to the ideal of community self-government. In its campaign for improved highways, the LAW faced the difficult task of convincing New York agrarians that their inherited system of local road administration was, as one convert to the Good Roads gospel put it, "the worst system for a civilized community."

Rural New Yorkers did not yield easily before the cyclists. They leveled strong attacks that derided the Wheelmen's condescending tone, pushed for local anticycling ordinances, opposed any new taxes that would support touring highways, and warned of inevitable corruption should the state political bosses add road building as one more wheel to their machine. As the league continued its publicity campaign into the 1890s, rural New Yorkers grew increasingly divided—based on economic interests, class lines, and ideological predispositions—over the issue. Poorer farmers dug in their heels with a strong antitax stand. Residents of New York's small towns and villages advocated moderate reforms, such as pooling town resources to purchase stone crushers and other road-building equipment. Wealthier "gentlemen" farmers, especially those with strong ties to the scientific agriculture movement, threw their support behind the Good Roads reformers and their promise to bring technological expertise to bear on road-building practices.

Any challenges to this system raised inevitable questions: could road building be modernized without resort to centralized authority? If centralized authority were required, did the financial and administrative capacity exist to embark on such an immense project? How would remote authority be insulated from the pressures of graft? Could engineering expertise be trusted to remain sensitive to local concerns? Which roads would be improved, for whose benefit, and by what means?

These questions had no easy answers; and they were complicated by the fact that the LAW's new brand of interest-group politics required alliances with multiple sources of authority: recalcitrant rural legislators, political bosses, engineers, and the federal government. Though the league was successful in putting road-building politics back on the state legislature's agenda, the earliest legislative achievements reflected members' often conflicting desires and the tension between urban and rural interests. Thus a tentative reform was born that foreshadowed the zigzag path that advocates of better roads followed toward the modernization of the state's highway system and the beginnings of the nation's second transportation revolution.

By the close of the nineteenth century, rural conservatives and urban machine politicians were still the dominant political forces in the state legislature. But for all their fiery attacks on one another, they proved to be two facets of the same waning political culture. Both were challenged by a new style of interest-group politics that rekindled a debate—begun during the early republic's age of internal improvements—over the proper role of elite planners and the appropriate balance between centralized and local authority. Though practitioners of this new politics presented their reform program in antipartisan language, they proved to be no less committed to a particular view of government than the proponents of the local road regime that they wished to displace. Likewise, they were no less interested in the exercise of political power than the state political machines, which were the organizations most likely to shape new road-building practices should the state legislature be pressed to take on the responsibility. Indeed, the challenge posed by this antipartisan, interest-group politics ultimately catalyzed a process that profoundly altered the location and character of public authority in New York State. During the last decades of the nineteenth century, however, New Yorkers only hesitantly embarked upon this transformation in policy regimes.

The Inherited Road-Building Regime:
The Agrarian Perspective

Why was the local road-building regime, in place since colonial times, so stubbornly adhered to until the end of the nineteenth century? Steamboats, canals, plank-road turnpikes, and railroads: almost every aspect of waterborne and overland transportation had witnessed technological innovation over the past century. And along with each came new forms of law, regulation, and administration. According to Good Roads advocates, no defense could be made for hewing to a road-building tradition that left roads muddy, rutted, and, for some parts of the year, impassable. But rural New Yorkers had good reasons to hold onto this regime even as managerial and technological revolutions transformed the organization and control of other parts of America's transportation infrastructure.

The local regime that dictated ordinary New Yorkers' road-building responsibilities had been born in England, nurtured in the American colonies, and matured in nineteenth-century New York. This regime emerged at a time when the heirs to revolutionary republicanism and Jacksonian democracy were suspicious of costly, expansive exercises of public authority. Rough country roads, like the one-room schoolhouse, were ubiquitous elements in the state's common landscape, features of time-honored patterns of rural life and governance. Local road administration had produced a vast, if particularistic, system of 80,000 miles of town and county roads while keeping public power close to the democratic ideal of community self-government. As the pressures of an organizational age bore down on New Yorkers late in the century, traditional road-building practices were a critical bulwark against destabilizing changes.

Certainly New Yorkers were aware of the possibilities of more modern road technologies. Many city streets had been paved in Manhattan by 1870, and snowy Buffalo was one of the nation's leading pavers by the 1880s. Other urban transportation initiatives, from broad avenues to subways, were also rapidly increasing the pace of city living. By the 1890s, a far-reaching system of interurban railways was under construction that extended cities' street railways into the countryside. The link between increased mobility and prosperity was not lost on rural New Yorkers. As one Rockland County road official put it, "Every community expects to see their village or district eventually become a New-York city and wants to provide wide roads to become wide streets."[3]

But there remained a general skepticism over public subvention of a more vigorous road construction program, rooted in an awareness of the problems that had beset other transportation improvements. Two waves of private toll road construction had collapsed under the panic of 1837 and the depression of the 1850s. Meantime, the state financing of the Erie Canal and the massive state subsidization of a rail network had led New Yorkers in 1846 to place significant constitutional constraints on the legislature's fiscal powers, which had been so critical to the development of a mixed economy in the early nineteenth century.

Anxiety over high taxes, mounting debt, mismanagement, and corruption led rural New Yorkers to endorse a system of public road administration that was not so much minimal as it was local. It was a form of self-governance that privileged communal control over centralized authority. At its most robust, this system—collective, participatory, self-determined, responsive to the popular sovereignty that undergirded it—proved to be a key pillar in support of what historian William Novak has referred to as a "well-regulated society," a vision of governance that enhanced local regulatory powers as a means of securing the public welfare and asserting power over public spaces.[4] The local road-building regime accomplished this by keeping the community at the locus of policy making. Town highway commissioners and their subordinate pathmasters were the principal road-building officials, and they owed their positions and their authority not to any particular engineering expertise but (especially in the case of pathmasters) to political geography.

New York State boasted some fifteen to twenty thousand road districts, town subdivisions that included thoroughfares that were typically shorter than two miles in length and that were maintained by a residential labor force under the direction of a pathmaster, or road overseer. Pathmasters, who were themselves residents of their road district, were appointed by the town highway commissioner to muster a road crew comprised of their neighbors and to warrant that their road work had been faithfully performed.[5] The work was seasonal, with weed and brush removal occurring in late June and late August, and loose stones removed regularly in all but the winter months. The number of days' labor to be worked was determined by an annual census of residents eligible for work: adult males between the ages of 21 and 70, excluding clergy, veterans, paupers, and the mentally infirm. Each was liable to "work out" his road tax at least one day a year; the remainder of the days was allotted (through a now-lost calculus) based on the value of assessed real and personal property. The average road district saw between thirty and thirty-five man-days of labor on it per year (see Table 1.1). All told, New Yorkers contributed roughly half a million workdays annually on their highways.[6]

This quasi-feudal system, imported from England and cultivated in the soil of rural New York, survived intact to the close of the nineteenth century. It achieved a minimal standard: highways were passable when the weather permitted; the labor tax kept the roads open, but rough. While no rural roads saw the sort of hard-surfacing that was becoming more common in New York's large cities, the condition of public ways could still vary widely, depending on the quality of work overseen by the pathmaster.

Typically, local pathmasters were farmers whose land bordered the road they were charged with supervising. But little else about the pathmaster was typical. Perhaps he was a respected figure in the neighborhood; in other instances he was the *only* adult male living in the district. Sometimes the pathmaster was a political aspirant, sometimes a recipient of political favor. Some were "progressive" or "scientific" farmers: those who read widely in the agricultural press and who had an interest in scientific ideas about modern farming practices and good road management. They adopted new road-building tools, such as the road drag, and encouraged the introduction of drains and sluices.[7] Others relied on traditional methods and were content with the results. There was no single pathmaster archetype, yet each was a fixture of local politics. Pathmasters and their neighbors set their own standards for the condition of public ways: from taking pride in a well-kept road to letting it fall into disrepair.

Though the quality of roads varied widely, it was clear that the system of road administration—in its design and implementation—was not intended to achieve an especially high standard of road maintenance. When pathmasters had little training in the principles of engineering—and this was often the case—maintenance work could often worsen the roads' condition. According to one aphorism, they did not do much more than "rearrange the dirt."[8] There was some truth to this: the principal source of road damage was rain, and the principal solution to this problem—heaping soft earth onto the center of the roadway—failed to address the problem of inadequate drainage.[9] Rain quickly turned fresh, loose-packed dirt into large pools of mud. Even when pathmasters had some basic knowledge of road engineering, they complained that they lacked the authority to use that exper-

TABLE 1.1. Oneida County, N.Y., Pathmasters, 1900

Town	Number of Pathmasters	Miles of Road	Days' Work
Annsville	81	90	1,500
Augusta	52	60	1,400
Ava	46	60	700
Boonville	62	200	2,084
Bridgewater	28	48	1,320
Camden	56	65	1,200
Deerfield	46	75	1,450
Florence	88	90	1,200
Floyd	47	60	1,500
Forestport	33	55	1,900
Kirkland	57	80	2,660
Lee	62	80	1,950
Marcy	43	60	1,700
Remsen	37	50	720
Rome	56	175	3,000
Steuben	66	70	1,527.5
Trenton	67	65	2,300
Vernon	64	85	2,272
Verona	111	175	3,000
Vienna	64	128	3,148
Western	62	60	1,850
Westmoreland	69	80	2,700
Whitestown	28	80	4,240
Total	1,325	1,991	45,321.5

Source: W. Pierrepont White, *Oneida County, New York, and Her Road Building* (Oneida County League for Good Roads, December 1900 [2d ed., January 1902]).

tise. The responsibility for roads of any length was diffused among many pathmasters and the residents they had at their command. And without an effective enforcement mechanism, even a diligent pathmaster could not fully ensure the quality of the work he had under his control.

Criticism of the local road-building regime increased toward the end of the century. Opponents of the system noted that the $10 fine for pathmasters who left loose stones in the road was rarely enforced, and that the highway commissioner who did not demand especially hard work from his pathmasters was the one who frequently got reelected. There appeared to be in many communities an understanding that the working out of the road tax ought not to be an especially "taxing" endeavor. Anecdotal evidence suggests that the very young and the very old—those least likely to be missed from other more important (and remunerative) tasks—frequently labored on the roads. An old man might put in a half-day's worth of less than rigorous labor; a young boy (perhaps substituting for a more mature family member) the same.[10] Familiar complaints were heard year after year in the late nineteenth century: "most men will not work at their road tax as they do on their own farms"; "no one expects to work hard on his road tax." By 1890 the social element of road labor had eclipsed the task itself: "working out" the tax was better characterized as "a neighborhood picnic."[11]

Limited town finance further complicated the matter. Since few towns and fewer road overseers could afford to invest in road machinery or equipment, men often provided their own tools, teams, and wagons. The town highway commissioner credited additional days' labor to the taxpayers for the loan of basic road-building implements. One Monroe County farmer complained that under the present system, thirty-seven man-days were allotted to his district's half-mile stretch of road. Eight men with teams drew a total of sixty loads of gravel over the course of two days, covering a sixteenth of a mile and completing their year's labor. By his calculation, it would take another eight years before they returned to the same patch of road, leaving a perennially dilapidated highway.[12] One New Yorker complained to the agricultural paper the *Cultivator and Country Gentleman* that "the present system in this state is about the worst that can be conceived for a civilized community, and stands as a bar to any improvement until it is overthrown."[13]

Toward the end of the nineteenth century, objections of this sort became a common refrain in rural New York. This was especially the case among the class of farmers who, whether by economic standing or personal inclination, favored the professionalization and systemization of the farming economy. But agrarian reformers had an uphill battle. The reluctance of less affluent farmers to adopt costly farming innovations is well documented; so too is the wave of agrarian discontent that led farmers to organize Granges and other cooperatives in an effort to bolster their political power.[14] So, despite the growing dissatisfaction of the rural reform element, most farmers and their local Grange organizations were unwilling to abandon traditional road-building practices. Keeping control of the roadways close to home meant that community members had a direct hand in maintaining and financing their public resources.[15] Though the inefficacy of the system earned it some detractors, it was still praised for reflecting agrarian ideals of democracy and self-sufficiency. And as long as residents were paying the road tax with their own labor, they could be certain that they got what they paid for. By contrast, rural New Yorkers' experience with nineteenth-century transportation initiatives had taught one lesson again and again: that when the state government or powerful railroad corporations set out to produce large-scale improvements, they occasionally redounded to the public's benefit; but they *always* cost something, and usually more than was advertised. The existing system of road administration suffered from weak and divided authority, but it was honest and it was cheap.

Urban Critiques of Rural Road Building

Though the local road-building regime had been damned by some farmers as "the worst system for a civilized community," it was clear that it still enjoyed local support. Thus, any significant reform of the system would have to be tremendously persuasive in order to uproot such a deeply entrenched system of administration. To some degree, this intransigence reflected local officials' reluctance to relinquish control of the public roads. But part of the problem was that the public roads themselves barely registered on the public consciousness as transportation improvements. State maps from this era depict railroads, canals, and rivers, but not local roads. Even those who recognized the inefficiencies of an administrative system that could not significantly improve a road system—despite the expenditure of half a million days' labor annually—were not optimistic about its reform. One midcentury agrarian assessed the situation: "That our system of doing the [road] work is an imperfect one—expensive and incapable—is very generally admitted; yet it is established and unlikely to be changed."[16] Even to its supporters, the system's failures were plainly obvious. Lodging road-building authority within town highway commissions produced a decidedly unsystematic web of roads. And relying on residential labor rather than hired road workers had proved ineffective.

To this growing chorus of rural discontent was added a new voice for road reform, and one with a distinctly urban accent. These Good Roads activists were city cyclists, and they lobbied extensively for road improvement through the aforementioned League of American Wheelmen, founded in 1880. It took less than twenty years for the league to grow from a small collection of urban bicycle clubs to a national organization of over 100,000 members. The LAW established itself as an association open to "any amateur white wheelman of good character."[17] The league's activities—extensive touring, parading in military dress, amateur racing, and the issuing of lofty declarations against professional racers—reflected the Wheelmen's Victorian beliefs in healthy outdoor activities conducted within the parameters of military pomp, gentlemanly order, and racial exclusiveness.

In its early years, the LAW confined itself to the setting of racing standards and providing a forum for cyclists' issues. But by the late 1880s, as cyclists sought the uninhibited use of parks and roads, the league became an effective and deeply politicized lobbying force. As Elisabeth Clemens has suggested in her study of the origins of interest-group politics, the "familiar organizational form" of a voluntary association, such as the LAW, was often adapted to new political purposes in the late nineteenth century.[18] At first, the LAW confined its political activity to campaigning against municipal measures such as the city ordinance that prohibited cyclists from riding in Manhattan's Central Park. Its New York State division vigorously opposed such measures and sent Rights and Privileges Committee chairman Isaac B. Potter to Albany to argue its position to the state legislature. Potter won, and the procyclist "Liberty Bill," which opened all public parks to wheelmen, was passed by the state legislature in 1887. Governor David B. Hill was pressured to veto the measure by a group of powerful Manhattan residents, led by Mayor Abram S. Hewitt, who were concerned that bicycles would endanger the safety of pedestrians. By this time, though, the LAW's effective political mobilization was well established, and when the group pledged to support Hill in his reelection campaign, he happily signed the Liberty Bill into law.[19]

The cyclists' group had the money, time, and motivation to organize on behalf of better roads. And as touring became increasingly popular, the leaders of the LAW shifted their attention from public spaces to public ways, circulating pamphlets that favored road reform. In 1886 the New York division became the first state unit of the league to make a political issue out of Good Roads advocacy. Members authorized the division to use league money to prosecute negligent road officials (an apparently unprecedented action) and to pressure them to act on laws designed to help cycling tourists, like those requiring road signs.[20] During the 1890s they pressed the New York State Legislature to centralize road-building authority in a state department, and they lobbied Congress to set aside federal funds for highway construction and for the collection of road data.[21]

How is it that the LAW came to play such a significant role in the reforming of road administration? In part, the Wheelmen's leadership position in road reform emerged from their worldview. Cycling gave these members of the urban upper and middle classes not only a wider acquaintance with rural roads but also a perspective on those roads that differed significantly from their rural counterparts. Members of city bicycle clubs touring the countryside were not simply feeling the pull of pastoral life. Rather, they were mapping their own ideas onto the rural landscape. Cyclists desired smooth touring routes that *appeared* natural but primarily reflected their desires for urban comforts. Moreover, they tended to gauge roads by their efficiency as passageways rather than by their usefulness to abutters. In this way, cyclists who sought to improve these roads for their own ends were engaging in what one cycling historian termed "recreational imperialism." Urban tourists in the countryside romanticized rural beauty while demanding that traditional road uses (such as grazing and animal-powered traffic) be subordinated to the cyclists' needs.[22] Thus the Wheelmen's perspective on rural roads put them at the forefront of a national debate over highway improvement, even as their view of the rural landscape as both romantic *and* antiquated fueled disputes with agrarians who resented this condescension.

Another factor that contributed to the LAW's leadership role was the facility with which it capitalized on its organization and membership as it stepped into the political arena. Its federated structure of local clubs, state divisions, and a national leadership was easily adapted to the pursuit of a broad range of Good Roads reforms. Meantime, LAW leadership recognized that the success of any state road improvement program depended on several things: its ability to convince farmers that better roads were in their material interests, its capacity to offset rural opponents who enjoyed strong legislative power as a result of rural overrepresentation, and its effectiveness in capitalizing on the internal divisions of rural dwellers. Above all, the New York Wheelmen needed to use their voting strength. They had already flexed their organizational muscle in their campaign for the Liberty Bill in 1887. By the 1890s, league members in New York numbered over 20,000, and cyclists in the state numbered in the hundreds of thousands.

When the movement's journal, *Good Roads*, urged members to cast aside party allegiances and vote instead for whichever candidate promised better roads, this presented a significant threat to both parties. Declaring in 1892 that "there is no room for a comfortable compromise on the question of good roads," the magazine's editors pushed their readers to think of themselves as a focused interest group standing outside traditional party politics. "If you are a Democrat," the editorial began, "make it clear that no candidate is a good enough Democrat for your vote who . . . refuses to take an active part in the movement to secure [good roads]." Likewise, the editorial warned, "if you are a Republican your time will soon come to repudiate every soft-headed, narrow-minded candidate who pretends to represent your party, and, if need be, to discard the party that foists him and his mental goods and chattels into the market of public favor."[23]

This was bold talk, but it was also savvy politics. The Republicans, out of all branches of state office in the early 1890s, were on the verge of recouping their losses to the Democratic Party. Not since 1882 had either party scored a margin of victory greater than 3 percent; the LAW's independent campaign had the potential to swing elections in an otherwise stable electoral environment. As New Yorkers considered ever more divisive transportation initiatives, the cyclists' potential to vote as a solid bloc grew in importance.[24]

Still, the LAW's urban core could be a political liability. Like other voluntary associations with large urban memberships, the LAW had to rely on "rural organizing drives" in order win over state legislatures in which rural areas were overrepresented. Thus the LAW represented a new form of political organizing that operated outside the traditional party structure, a form of organizing that could tap into the "calculus of interest" even while promoting an agenda that was framed in the language of the public good.[25]

Pulling off this rhetorical feat required the Wheelmen to induce the state's farmers to rally to the cause of road reform. Suspicious of state power and disinterested in improved touring routes, farmers posed the greatest obstacle to systematic road improvement. But they represented an important part of the voting base of the Republican Party, with whom the state's LAW division was allied; thus they had to be pacified. At the same time, the Republican Party could not ignore the LAW. It counted on independent, reform-minded interest groups, such as the LAW, to secure its primacy over a divided Democratic Party.[26] Regulars in both parties dealt with independent reform factions. But the Democrats' commitment to local government made it hard for them to square their governing philosophy with a platform that favored centralized road-building authority.

Unlike the Democrats, the Republicans were not ideologically disinclined to road reform. But they did struggle in reconciling the road reformers' agenda with that of the upstate farming communities, who were predominantly Republican. Certainly some rural New Yorkers found the logic of road reform persuasive. The LAW forged alliances with wealthy "gentlemen" farmers, who were tied more tightly to national markets and who supported road legislation that would help lower transportation costs. The organization was also aware of the fact that Long Island proprietors, for instance, found it more profitable to cater to well-heeled touring cyclists escaping the metropolis than to poorer truck farmers heading toward urban markets.[27] But for the most part, poor, fiscally conservative farmers who were served by more local markets greeted this newfound concern of upper-class city club members with skepticism. And as Good Roads advocates pressured state legislators to transform local highway administration, they provoked rural New Yorkers to defend their system of governance.

"The Good Old Democratic Way":
Rural Defenses of the Local Regime

The cyclists' critiques of road-building administration opened up a wider debate about the value of local government and its proper place within American federal and subfederal relations. At the root of the LAW's campaign for greater state involvement in road building was an effort to redefine town and county governments, long a repository of communal self-government, as inadequate to the tasks they performed. Yet the success of their new road program depended on its resonance with farming communities, and this proved no easy task.

Convincing agrarians of the need for improved roads put urban cyclists in the awkward position of appealing to farmers on their own terms, while at the same time drawing attention to the ills of country life. In an intense pamphleteering campaign, the LAW peppered rural districts with a variety of reasons to support road improvement. It argued that better roads would lower the cost of shipping goods to market and raise rural real estate values. The LAW contended that isolated farms could not compete with crops shipped by rail from the prairie states. Reformers preaching the "gospel of Good Roads" listed other benefits: efficient rural mail delivery, easier access to schools, a way to keep children home on the farm, a safety valve in times of unemployment, the elimination of disease supposedly transmitted by dusty roads, and the introduction of culture to the benighted hinterlands.[28]

This proselytizing easily dissolved into derision. From an urban elite perspective, the upstate farmers were mired in, as a *New York Times* editorial put it, "the whole soggy mass of rural conservatism."[29] Isaac Potter's "The Gospel of Good Roads: A Letter to the American Farmer," which appeared as the first article in the first issue of *Good Roads* in January 1892, exemplified the league's insensitivity regarding rural reluctance to support road improvement. Enumerating the "countless great improvements which were intended for our common benefit," Potter reminded the farmer "in all kindliness" that he had routinely opposed these things that "the lapse of time has placed in the highest niches of human achievement." Railroad subsidization, the telegraph, the mowing machine, the sewing machine, the thresher: Potter argued that "there is no great invention of commercial or agricultural value which was cheered at its birth by the warmth of your approval."[30]

Potter's patronizing letter won few converts to his cause. Indeed, a number of villages began to act out on their growing antipathy toward the cyclist-reformers by surreptitiously passing ordinances designed to "mulct the unwary cyclists by heavy fines."[31] Beyond such underhanded politics, rural New Yorkers responded to Good Roads campaigning with a wide range of defenses of their road-building system, based on a combination of economic interests and political ideology.

One objection to improved overland transportation hinged on the distinction between "market" economies, which operated according to the laws of supply and demand, and "moral" economies, in which the value of a product was related to the livelihood of its producer. Elisabeth Clemens explains that this division was at the heart of the rift between "gentleman farmers" who favored "the application of scientific and business techniques to agricultural marketing" and the "less affluent remainder, who comprised the membership of [farmers groups such as] the Grange, the Alliance, and the Society of Equity." According to Clemens, "throughout the nineteenth century, these two groups could be found opposing one another in many states, gentlemen farmers advocating 'scientific farming' to increase production, the rest calling for cooperative marketing, limited production, and the regulation of predatory corporations such as railroads and grain elevators." Poorer farmers harbored deep suspicions "that government programs were used to benefit classes other than needy or worthy agriculturalists . . . In an era where property rather than income was the primary object of taxation, farmers believed that they bore a disproportionate share of the financial burden of government."[32] Consequently, many New York farmers of lesser means were reluctant to support any program that raised taxes, removed administrative power from the towns, or threatened to undercut their local economies.

As market forces exerted increasing pressure on the struggling New York farmers in the late nineteenth century, opposition to road reform became a means of staving off further market expansion. One New York Granger wanted to know "what he would do with five or six tons of produce on his wagon if he had fine roads on which he could draw it?" He would still be unable to get the load from his barn to the main road, and once in Albany, he would "at once lower the price because of an over supply."[33]

Another defense of rural road administration blended fiscal conservatism and an ideological commitment to the sort of "direct democracy" that was implicit in the labor tax. One farmer objected to the proposed "revolution" in road administration. "If you abolish the road system, you add a large percentage, I think about twenty-five, to the already too heavy cash tax the farmer must pay. Now the farmer can pay his road tax in labor of self, teams, tools, and hired men, and when his crops are not suffering for work." Moreover, to remove road-building authority from local institutions "will increase the horde of engineers, superintendents, contractors, &c. After a little while, dishonest, lazy, incompetent inefficient men would do your road work even worse than is now complained of. We hard working, discouraged, overtaxed farmers want improvements but not revolution."[34] At this point in time, engineers were not seen as bearers of professional expertise. Rather, they were viewed as little more than an extension of the political machine that threatened to short-change farmers on their roads while undercutting their freedoms.

A Delaware County pathmaster agreed, warning that "the liberty of localities to perform their own functions in road-building and road-working is in danger."[35] Another pathmaster who had served the county for forty years was "profoundly gratified" by his efforts "to stop one of the greatest centralizing tendencies of the age." With clear Jacksonian overtones, he proclaimed: "Let not the State enter the business of road-making . . . The problem will be solved in the good old democratic way by each district working out its own highway tax."[36]

Despite these concerns about local liberties, it was clear that poorer districts lacked the resources to build roadways sufficient to the demands of a statewide system. Former New York Agricultural Society president James Wood addressed the problem in an 1892 essay on improving country roads. He thought that rural road districts, their surrounding villages, connecting railways, and distant cities all had "mutual" interests in local road improvement. Each received benefits in communication, passenger travel, and freight transport, and "each must bear its proper proportion of the expense of improvement." This would be "a matter of simple justice, if the rural districts were able to bear the entire expense, [but] as it is now that is impossible . . . To determine the proper proportions to be raised" by various units of government "requires the wisest consideration." "Not less important," Wood thought, was creating an "efficient administration" and protecting its work "against political jobbery and corrupt professional rings."[37]

Wood recognized that it was no "matter of simple justice" to balance the demands of statewide transportation development with the maintenance of local control. Rather, it required a significant realignment of public power. Rural conservatives and the urban machine politicians they so distrusted were the opposite poles that defined New York's political culture. How the sort of modern, "efficient administration" Wood envisioned was to emerge from the yawning gap separating these two extremes, he could not predict.

One thing was certain: most farmers of modest means were unwilling to accept the "revolution" in road administration that the cyclists advocated. To the extent that they showed any willingness toward change, it was for modest reform. This included the creation of county boards of highway supervisors that might consider broader, regional needs in determining which highways should be improved. It included as well the purchase of town road-building equipment such as stone crushers.

But even these efforts at modest reform proved controversial. Many New York towns appropriated money for stone-crushing equipment, which enabled them to maintain local control of the road-building process while bringing it in line with modern engineering principles. Laying crushed stone across the road bed in low-lying depressions, center drains, and side gutters could prevent highways from becoming mired in mud. But a crusher was still seen by many as an unnecessary expense. It cost almost $3,000 (roughly $65,000 in 2006 dollars), and a town might have to lay out $2,000 more a year to run and maintain it. The potential tax burden often led to fierce struggles over whether the town should commit itself to so expensive a road improvement program.

In one Dutchess County town, villagers supported the purchase of a crusher, and farmers (with higher property assessments and thus higher taxes) opposed it. The village's road reformers carried the crusher question with a slim four-vote majority. Its road supervisor, unwilling to commit the town to so divisive a purchase, chose not to buy the crusher, laid low for the rest of the year, and then retired. When the crusher project was renewed, and carried by the same thin margin, the new supervisor acted on his mandate. Annual appropriations continued to provoke debate, but the farming community was repeatedly voted down by the village bloc.[38]

Predictably, more radical proposals, such as the establishment of a fiscal tax to replace the ineffectual labor system, also met with meager success. Few farmers were willing to support a tax increase in times of financial distress. There had been a limited interest in adopting the money system of taxation earlier in the century. Cash (rather than labor) assessments had been made optional for the towns of Livingston County in 1838 following the collapse of the first turnpike boom; two Rockland County towns, Haverstraw and Clarkson, adopted money taxation in 1859 and 1862 after the failure of many plank road companies. Cognizant of the benefits the new system would confer, the state legislature passed a bill in early 1873 allowing any town the same option. But in response to dissatisfaction with the money tax—presumably due to a shortage of cash during the lingering economic depression—the legislature allowed towns to return to the labor tax if they wished in 1879.[39]

All in all, rural New Yorkers established an effective counterargument to the (at times condescending) logic of the Good Roads campaigners. Drawing on notions of moral economies, local liberties, and bottom-line economic self-interest, farmers of modest means forced Good Roads advocates to contend with their serious misgivings about centralized road-building authority. In the act of debating, though, they helped to keep road reform on the legislative agenda and kept the public's attention focused on the possibility of a better road system. This, as much as the actions of the road reformers, helped to turn the tide toward road reform.

"Everybody Admits It All":
Good Roads at the Crossroads

As rural New Yorkers stepped up their defense of the old road-building system, the League of American Wheelmen continued to refine its approach to road reform. In order to override rural resistance, the LAW began to disassociate cycling from road-building politics, forged tighter alliances with other groups interested in promoting road reform, and publicized road-building experiments taking place in other states. All of these efforts were designed to legitimize the road-building agenda as a product of public, rather than special, interests.

The LAW recognized that the Good Roads movement had wider implications than those originally envisioned by touring cyclists, and it soon was clear that the organization's involvement threatened to scuttle the campaign for better roads. Its elite status had become a hindrance as it pursued a major overhaul of road-building administration. Thus LAW officials encouraged their members to downplay their cycling interests when they discussed highway politics. Isaac Potter, now a high-ranking league official, helped organize the New York Road Improvement Association in order to distance the cause from supporters whom many viewed derisively as "the idle rich."[40]

But farmers had difficulty disassociating the Good Roads movement from its advocates. A Queens County resident observed, "There is altogether too much preaching on the part of the wheelmen . . . It is always easier to advocate the expenditure of other people's money than it is to put our hands into our own pockets."[41] An Onondaga County man echoed the sentiment: "Every one must concede the desirability of good roads. Not because manufacturers of bicycles advocate them however. In fact, I believe the more conspicuous they are in the advocacy of improved roads, the less enthusiasm the rest of the public will feel."[42]

As cyclists moved to publicly disassociate themselves from the Good Roads movement, they also sought to strengthen their alliances with other interest groups in order to gain strength and broader support. A handful of progressive academics argued for more centralized highway administration; railroad corporations sought better access between farms and rail junctions; motorists' groups (still quite small at this time) lobbied for better touring routes. All were united in their advocacy of reform, though each group had a different program in mind. Academics focused on the efficiencies of ending localized road construction and finance. The LAW had much in common with early motorist clubs: both groups emphasized the improvement of main routes for recreational purposes. Railroad executives, by contrast, sought to overhaul the secondary road system in hopes of expanding their markets. (Not for another decade would automobiles lose their character of an elite commodity; only after that loss of status did railroad corporations begin to see public highway construction as a threat.)[43]

Glossing over the often divergent objectives of this emerging Good Roads coalition, advocates publicized whatever pockets of reform they could discover. When Essex County, New Jersey (just west of Manhattan), began a coordinated highway construction program in conjunction with early suburban development, *Good Roads* magazine hailed it as the "birthplace of American Road Improvement."[44] It praised road work in Massachusetts, promoted by industrialists who wanted better intercity routes. North Carolina's Mecklenburg County, Iowa's Kossuth County, and Illinois's Monroe County were singled out as well.[45] But the diversity of wealth and transportation needs in New York State meant that some communities were clamoring for better roads while others were content with those they had. Under these conditions support for better roads emerged erratically, even in a state like New York, with a long-standing commitment to transportation improvement that had been well-evidenced over the past century by extensive turnpike construction, coastal trade, the Erie Canal system, and the New York Central and Erie railroads.

Still, by the 1890s it was clear that extensive Good Roads publicity was turning the tide. Though the Wheelmen served as advocates for a rural constituency whose needs they poorly understood, they sparked an important debate over the capabilities of existing public road administration. And though the cycling craze was too slim a reed to support a fundamental re-making of America's transportation infrastructure, its practitioners were effective in bringing the problem of bad country roads to light at a crucial moment. As one rural New Yorker observed, in the past "it was not so fashionable . . . to denounce the condition of our public highways"; now "everybody admits it all."[46]

"The Entering Wedge": Road Building on the Legislative Agenda

The Good Roads campaign carried on by the League of American Wheelmen and their allies evoked strong feelings in the New York countryside from the 1880s onward. But the movement for better roads reflected more than a clash between urban and rural mentalities at the close of the century. It also represented an early and important assault on the governing philosophies that underpinned the local road-building regime. As such, it drew public attention to the liabilities of this policy regime and sparked a debate over how best to balance state and local administrative strengths.

The LAW, by now regularly engaged in political lobbying, was the key actor in this effort to reapportion political authority. Year after year in the 1890s, the LAW pushed for a roads bill that would centralize road-building powers in a state agency. Each legislative session provoked intense deliberation over the value of the local road-building regime and the various administrative plans proposed to replace it. Strong support for existing arrangements—local control and minimal government—checked efforts to expand state administrative responsibility. Ultimately, the steadfast commitment to keeping highway politics at the community level was overridden as much by the appeal of administrative reform as it was by the careful refinement of legislation so as to retain important aspects of the local road-building regime. Thus the LAW successfully capitalized on its supporters' growing demand for a better transportation infrastructure only by capitulating to hard-bitten agrarian resistance.

The important debate over local control versus coordinated administration continued to shape highway politics over the next generation, even as the Good Roads movement gained in force and momentum. But a new challenge awaited. Once Good Roads reformers broke the logjam of rural opposition, they faced a significant obstacle in the patronage demands of machine politicians, who threatened to derail administrative reform.[47] State-sponsored public construction, such as enlarging the Erie Canal or building the palatial state capitol building, had always been a divisive political issue in New York.

Invariably some economic or geographic groups benefited from these projects while others suffered. But public works contracts were also politically attractive. They offered rich opportunities for the sometimes-legitimate dispensation of patronage and, occasionally, for outright corruption. As reform-minded politicians contemplated extending the state government's administrative responsibility to include public roads, they worried over what sort of highway system would emerge if it were administered within the culture of boss politics.

When a roads bill finally passed in 1898, New Yorkers made their first tentative steps toward the modern, activist state that would characterize twentieth-century governance. Agrarians continued to express concern that the price of improved infrastructure would be too high for both tax payers and local political officials. And indeed, the long-standing political traditions they supported—the delegation of powers to local bodies, limited state expenditures—mitigated this transformation. But the initial expansion of state road-building authority offered clear evidence that the old balance of local-state powers was tipping. Though highway legislation reflected the circumscribed possibilities defined by a political culture that was still devoted to localism and egalitarianism in public construction, it also reflected an emerging relationship between state and citizen that promised a better public works product in exchange for less direct control over the machinery of government.

Highway policy first received serious attention by the state legislature in 1890. In that year, Governor David B. Hill (Dem., 1885–1892) pushed for a consolidation of New York State highway law, securing the repeal of eighty-eight separate laws passed since 1832 and replacing them with a streamlined highway code. But the new law did little but affirm the old localized system of road administration. The town highway commissioner continued to divide up his town into road districts and apportion labor. Road improvements exceeding $500 per year were put to a town vote, as were motions to switch to or from a money system of assessment. The only expansion of centralized authority was a minor one: counties were authorized to assist overburdened towns with bridge repair.[48]

Soon after Hill's consolidation of the Highway Code, however, new proposals for centralized state action appeared.[49] Republican Senator William P. Richardson, a former pathmaster, campaigned on a road-improvement platform in his rural Mid-Hudson district, and in 1890 he proposed a bill that would create a State Highway Commission. The commission would be authorized to spend $100 million over the next eighteen years. Public improvements on that scale drew natural comparisons with the Erie Canal Commission. But that body, charged with overseeing the canal's expansion during the late nineteenth century, faced persistent allegations of canal fund mismanagement. These unpleasant associations made the bill an unappealing one, and it found little support in the legislature.[50]

Richardson introduced a modified version the next year, and the changes in the bill are telling. Under the new law, a bipartisan state highway commission would have control over the more modest budget of $10 million. It would be charged with the construction of 3,000 miles of state roads. Two roads would be constructed in each county, intersecting at the county seat and checker-boarding the state. Richardson's shifts were strategic: under the new bill, all counties would receive a pay-out. The 1891 bill was also more consistent with prevailing ideology than Richardson's original proposal. The new bill echoed the tradition of nineteenth-century public works initiatives, which were shaped by a geographical egalitarianism that distributed the state's money widely across New York's sixty counties. Evidence of this egalitarian impulse could already be seen in the unprofitable branch line canals secured by regions bypassed by the Erie's main line.[51] Similarly, under the proposed roads bill, every county—central or peripheral—would receive equal benefits.

The bill's distributive elements imbued it with the potential to succeed. Richardson had the support of urban Good Roads advocates, and he hoped to enlist the support of rural voters by arguing that under the bill's provisions the large cities would shoulder most of the road program's cost. He contended that New York farmers had unfairly financed canal improvements that worked to the farmers' disadvantage while serving urban, commercial, and out-of-state interests. Now it was their turn to receive the benefits of the state's purse.

Richardson's proposed highway commission, even its modified form, was a radical departure from traditional road policy. With a $10 million budget and the authority to engage the state directly in road building, some saw in it the seeds of a modern highway administration. But others thought that the commission would be used for political purposes: just another way for party bosses to dole out plum contracts. *Good Roads* magazine, which had long supported Richardson's drive for a centralized highway authority, admitted that the "curse of machine politics seems to have turned its withering breath against the Richardson bill."[52] Moreover, many believed that improving main roads was less important than upgrading the secondary farm-to-market roads that served the agrarian population. The state Grange denounced the bill as in the interests of bicyclists and pleasure carriages.

The combined reaction against both elite reform and boss politics doomed the commission bill. One contributor to the *Cultivator and Country Gentleman* thought "the big Richardson-Hill road scheme" nothing less than "pernicious." The *New York Times* dismissed "Hill's Pet Road Scheme" as one "which would add a good many wheels to the Democratic machine."[53] Richardson's 1891 attempt at road reform, which incorporated egalitarian principles, turned out to be as problematic as his 1890 effort, which relied more heavily on centralized planning. The Assembly defeated the bill by one vote in its 1891 session—the only bill supported by the governor to fail in a body that he solidly controlled.[54]

The fate of the Richardson bill revealed the growing tension—as well as the potential for alliance—between party regulars and reformers. Reform politicians like Richardson had little choice but to collaborate with the party machine. Though only a minority faction, the party organization depended on urban independents such as Richardson, who formed an important part of the coalition along with local political machines and small-town and rural voters. As a result, early road reform emerged from a blend of motives: public-spirited reform, interest-group demands, the appeal of administrative rationality, and the party pressures of resource and patronage distribution. But while this range of motives could produce a strong coalition in support of road reform, it was equally likely to feed conflict and cross-purposes.[55]

When Hill left Albany to become a U.S. senator, his hand-picked successor, Governor Roswell P. Flower (Dem., 1892–1895), favored the adoption of a county system. This would be "a golden mean" between "the two extremes of extravagance in state expenditures and stinginess in local expenditures for local improvements."[56] The argument for modest reform and fiscal restraint carried increasing weight after the onset of economic depression in 1893. The legislature gave towns the option to adopt a county road system, which would centralize road-building authority in a county department rather than leaving it dispersed among individual towns, and it would replace the labor system with professional road crews financed by a cash tax.[57] But opposition to change, and to new taxes and state expenditures in the midst of economic depression, was broad and deep.

John A.C. Wright of Rochester, secretary of the New York State Good Roads League, saw no hope for the passage of radical road legislation in the mid-1890s. According to Wright's "inside history of it," powerful politicians allowed the bills to pass in one house or the other so that, despite their reluctance to act, highway policy might stay in the public eye. Governor Levi P. Morton (Rep., 1895–1897), playing along in 1895, endorsed a special Good Roads commission to make a "pilgrimage" across New York and neighboring states. The commission was charged to study the advisability of state participation in highway administration, despite Wright's assurances that there was no more fact-finding to be done.[58] Nonetheless, the LAW arranged to bring several members of the legislative advisory committee on a special train to observe the success of New Jersey's road reform initiative in 1896. The Garden State had passed the nation's first county roads law in 1889 and state aid law in 1891. New York Good Roads advocates hoped their neighbor's example would prompt a new willingness to act.[59]

The highway advisory commission's report kept the roads question in the spotlight during the late 1890s. Especially compelling were new studies of haulage costs, commissioned by the advisory committee, which emphasized the aggregate savings brought by better roads. One study found that the rate per ton of produce dropped from 26 to 7 cents per mile when driven over a hard-surfaced road. That added up to a savings to New York farmers of $16 million a year, more than five times the amount assessed under the current labor tax system. This sort of economic data was widely touted by scientific farming organizations, such as the New York Farmers' Congress, which supported road improvement as a way of strengthening its position within an increasingly competitive agricultural economy. Given the vast potential for savings, the committee recommended that the legislature take positive action to foster better roads. The report recommended the appointment of a state superintendent of highways; state financing of highways upon the petition of road districts, town boards, or county boards; and the abolition of the pathmaster system in favor of the money system.[60] But alternate bills were offered up that aimed at bolstering the governing apparatus of the road districts, towns, or counties. An astonished agricultural press noted that "there seems to be no end to the number of good roads bills being introduced."[61]

This lack of consensus reflected the tremendous strain placed on the local road-building regime in the last decade of the nineteenth century. Already, the federal government had acknowledged the importance of road improvement, establishing the Office of Road Inquiry (ORI) in 1893 in the Department of Agriculture in order to investigate various experiments in road improvement and disseminate technical information on highway issues. Though the ORI had only a modest $10,000 budget, it still had the capacity to shape the debate over pending state legislation. General Roy Stone, the civil engineer at the head of the department (and a New York Wheelman as well), pressured the legislature to reject the existing road-building administration "brought from England 200 years" ago, which he considered to be "radically wrong."[62]

Though the presence of Stone and the ORI at legislative hearings lent road reform new legitimacy, opponents of road reform, such as Speaker of the Assembly S. Fred Nixon, disagreed with Stone's assessment that the time was ripe for rejecting an antiquated system. While acknowledging that wealthier counties might have interests in financing a road improvement scheme, Nixon believed the bill to be "in advance of . . . sentiment."[63] An Otsego County man echoed this opinion: "That there is a great need for change is beyond dispute," he argued, "but that the present is the time to make that change I have my doubts. Perhaps we had better obey and carry out the present laws a few years and see what they will do for us toward good roads; and when we get our capitol and nine million canal debt paid up and our present road machine worn out, we can wipe out all the present laws and begin anew on a right principle."[64] Cognizant of the social costs of poor roads, yet uncomfortable with the prospect of granting the funds or the authority necessary to address the problem, legislators proposed solutions that headed in all directions at once. The legislative committee expressed a special concern that in the midst of this cacophony, no farmers' group came forward to champion a particular bill.[65]

The absence of a clear mandate for radical reform tied up legislation in 1896 and 1897. The legislature undercut the efforts of Republican Senator Richard Higbie of West Islip, Long Island, to abolish the labor system and institute a money system, a move that entailed heavy costs and required the dismissal of tens of thousands of pathmasters. Higbie lacked rural support, and he faced vocal opposition from Republican Senate President and party insider Timothy E. Ellsworth. Ellsworth's Niagara County constituency opposed a tax increase during a depression; the Niagara Board of Supervisors passed a resolution opposing the measure. Ultimately, the bill was amended to death: its provisions would not take effect for a year, taxes due would not be collected for two years, and twenty-eight of the state's sixty counties were excluded. In its weakened state it hardly qualified as a state roads bill. Higbie, who had planned to introduce a more extensive roads program later in the session, withdrew his remaining bills from debate. The proposals supported by the highway advisory commission never emerged from committee, and the old town system remained firmly in place.[66]

Members of the LAW's New York State division continued to push for a statewide building program in 1897. Wright, who had emerged as one of the state's most strident Good Roads advocates, helped draft another bill. It was taken up in the Senate by Higbie and in the Assembly by Republican William Armstrong, a new legislator from Wright's Monroe County. (Armstrong, who had been elected in 1894 on his urban reform record, had introduced just one bill of note in 1896: requiring railroads to carry bicycles as baggage.) The new roads bill provided for a 50–35–15 cost apportionment among the state, counties, and towns; a three-member highway commission including one civil engineer; a 1/10 of a mill tax increase; and a distributive policy provision that no county would receive more than 5 percent of the total state appropriation. The bill had the support of the Wheelmen and won over some of the local farming associations, including the New York Farmer's Congress (which represented the wealthiest and best educated of the agriculturalists) and several county Farmer's Clubs and Granges.[67] The New York State Grange remained divided; its roads committee split 4–3 against any legislation. A mix of motives underpinned this broadening Good Roads coalition: the lure of state funds, the possibility of shifting the tax burden for rural road improvement onto urban taxpayers, and the growing appeal of modern administrative methods, even to rural communities, at the turn of the century.[68]

Despite the coalition's strength, controversial portions of the Higbie-Armstrong bill regarding debt financing, local control, and patronage politics contributed to its failure in 1897. The following year, the legislature reconsidered it in a modified form. While many features remained the same, changes in the structure of finance and administration took seriously the conditions and constraints necessary for communities to accept greater state coordination of highways. The bill specified that construction was to be financed through small-scale annual appropriations, not bond sales that would result in heavy public indebtedness. And importantly, local control was preserved by making the bill's provisions voluntary. No road would be built except at the county supervisors' or property holders' urging, thus placing a brake on runaway state spending.

Thus the Good Roads measure that was put forward in 1898 did not emerge out of the universal appeal of "rational" administrative reform. Rather, it developed out of a complex and prolonged negotiation among existing political forces, chief among them hard-nosed agrarians and local officials. Though the "pauper" counties were never won over by the fiscal logic of a state roads bill, other rural New Yorkers gave their assent. Wealthy "gentlemen" farmers had long supported the professionalization of road administration; farmers of middling means were, in time, won over by the promise of the redistribution of urban tax dollars to the countryside, so long as local control over their expenditure was assured.

The bill differed in another important way: it lodged the state's new construction powers in their traditional repository, the state engineer. This elected position, under Republican party control since 1893, offered a wealth of opportunities for the dispensing of patronage: surveying, construction, material, and maintenance contracts could all be directed to loyal supporters. Governor Frank S. Black (Rep., 1897–1899) opposed the creation of a new commission. An ally of party boss Thomas Collier Platt, Black had helped relax civil service requirements, and now he hoped to further support party regulars by bolstering the state engineer's power.

The strategic revisions to the Higbie-Armstrong bill reflected the persistence of a nineteenth-century style of governance in addressing what would become one of the twentieth century's most vexing infrastructural problems. Black hoped to maintain control of government by the time-honored tradition of patronage dispensation. This distributive style of politics had worked well when state economic policy consisted primarily of doling out privileges and public resources to one's constituency. By contrast, Good Roads advocates argued that the creation of a regionally integrated highway system involved exchanging the politics of promotion for greater bureaucratic control and technocratic expertise.[69]

This was not what Black had in mind. Placing the proposed highway administration solidly within the scope of electoral politics—and special interests—failed to enlarge state administrative capacity: instead it swelled the party machine. Fears of corruption contributed greatly to the strong rural opposition that had characterized the Good Roads debate during the early 1890s. The new roads legislation promised to buy off poor and middling farmers with the promise of redistributing state tax dollars to rural areas. But the buy-off was engineered not by road reformers but by the political machine, which proved to be tremendously protective of its patronage resources. Though boss politics and agrarian conservatism were frequently at odds with one another, they nonetheless combined to produce a roads bill that was consistent with prevailing political orthodoxy.

This should not suggest that the political machine had entirely displaced farming interests in setting state policy. Indeed, the only other viable roads bill to come out of the 1898 legislative session was a testament to rural New Yorkers' electoral strength. In 1898 Republican Senator Charles E. Fuller, himself a farmer, reintroduced the Fuller-Plank bill, one of the many attempts at reform that had been defeated several years earlier. This bill provided that the state match 25 percent of the amount raised under the money system of taxation to any town that switched to it from the labor system. Changing to the money system meant instituting a more efficient means of constructing and maintaining roads, and state aid would provide the impetus to take this step. Under the Fuller bill, towns could build inexpensive dirt roads and secure the cash subsidies to maintain them, while maintaining the town as the center of road administration.

Momentum gathered as the legislature actively debated the Higbie and Fuller bills during the 1898 session. For a number of reasons, it appeared likely that at least one of the road bills would pass this time. The Higbie bill had failed by only a few votes the previous year, and the new bill—which struck a more effective balance between city and country interests—had won over many converts. As well, the legislative hearings in 1898 had brought forth an impressive array of supporters, including officials from neighboring states who had already embarked on state highway programs. New Jersey State Road Commissioner H. J. Budd explained how rural Jerseyites had split on road building just as New Yorkers had: "the enterprising wanted the legislation; the conservative were opposed it." But now, Budd claimed, "no more enthusiastic class for good roads could be found than these same farmers."[70]

Still, rural communities who favored road reform were split over whether to support the Higbie or Fuller bills. The chief benefit to farmers from the Higbie bill was that the cities would bear the lion's share of the cost. But local governments still had to pick up half the tab, and many rural New Yorkers opposed any increase in taxes. The expanded power of the state engineer constituted another source of discord. Speaking before the legislature, one Albany County agrarian objected to investing this state official with road-building authority. "He told you that the canal improvements could be made for $9,000,000 [in 1895] and now they say it will take $7,000,000 more to finish it. It will be just the same with good roads." Another objected to the tax increase, arguing that dirt roads could be sufficiently upgraded with newly purchased town road scrapers. Moreover, the main county roads contemplated for improvement were less in need of repair than the secondary crossroads typically used by farmers.

Urban New Yorkers gave scant weight to these misgivings. Reformers regarded the rural opposition as misplaced at best; the *New York Times* thought it a "ridiculous display of ignorance."[71] But Republican Senator Hobart

Krum, hailing from a longtime farming family, issued the most prescient and penetrating objection to the Higbie bill when he described it as "the entering wedge to the greatest expenditure ever entailed upon the State. The combined expenses of the canal and the building of the Capitol would be nothing as compared to it." Indeed, the checks on spending and centralized control originally built into New York highway legislation proved to be quite weak. In time, public works policy would grow to become a major component of state government authority and expenditure.[72]

In a compromise move, the legislature passed and Governor Black signed both the Higbie-Armstrong and the Fuller-Plank bills.[73] The passage of the Higbie Act was a major victory for the road reformers, reflecting the ultimate success of the political alliances fostered by the LAW in the 1880s. And the Fuller Act, though it reflected the continued appeal of incremental local reform, was certainly no loss. Though the two acts embodied different approaches to road building—the Higbie Act created a new class of state-aid highways; the Fuller Act provided increased state assistance to towns—both carved out a new role for the state. Neither law mandated reform, but each gave communities the opportunity to begin the process of modernizing their road administration. Good Roads advocates counted on the fact that as isolated communities improved their local roads, the benefits would become apparent and demands for better roads elsewhere would grow. What, they thought, could better spread the gospel of good roads than state-built roads themselves?

But as Senator Krum astutely pointed out, new roads required money. Thus the real measure of the road reformers' success ultimately turned on the funds appropriated for construction. The legislature debated a substantial $500,000 appropriation bill in 1899. The high cost of much road construction, averaging $3,000 a mile, led many to argue that the sum should be at least $1 million. But the legislature settled on a pitifully small $50,000 appropriation. Actual state aid for 1899 totaled just $34,518.[74]

The legislation's provisions for selecting which roads to improve further hindered the creation of a modern, integrated highway infrastructure. Roads built in response to county petitions, on a first-come, first-served basis, meant that the new approach, like the old local system, would lead to highly segmented, decentralized road building. The State Engineer's Office optimistically predicted that through each county's pursuit of self-interest, a coordinated network of roads might emerge. That outcome was conceivable for a wealthy, densely populated, eager-to-build county like Westchester. But the fate of larger, poorer, rural counties' transportation system was less certain.[75]

Whether any rationally planned road system might emerge depended on the availability of increased funding. Between 1899 and 1904 the state constructed only fifty-nine miles of roads.[76] Petitions for 1,308 more miles piled up in the State Engineer's Office with no action taken on them. It was clear that the growing appeal for better roads far outstripped the state's capacity to pay for them, and the question of funding dogged the Engineer's Office during the early years of the program.

Small appropriations made sense for an untested program. But as the numbers of petitions continued to rise—compelling evidence of growing popular support for better public roads—road reformers renewed their appeal for increased funds. The Higbie Act created the potential for systemic change in the state's road administration by shifting the locus of road-building authority toward state government. This shift in the flow of money and power was a move with potentially profound consequences. But it also had the capacity to reinforce the existing brand of distributive politics by centralizing the means of allocating public resources and strengthening state party machines. The form of highway administration that might emerge from this uneasy alliance among road reformers, agrarians, and party politicians depended on which group, if any, could gain the upper hand.

The Fate of the Local Road-Building Regime

As the nineteenth century drew to a close, New Yorkers continued in their attempts to improve upon the pathmaster system that for so long had shaped their road-building experience. Their experiments initiated passionate debates over the rich possibilities of the American federal system, echoing deliberations not heard since the days of the early republic. Road-building authority had remained at the most local level since the resolution of those earlier debates, virtually untouched by the sort of innovations in technology and governance that characterized other improvements to the national transportation and communications infrastructure. New road-building legislation shifted the locus of policy making upward from local pathmasters and town highway commissioners to include a role for the state government. Its arrival augured the beginning of a new political era defined by citizens' new willingness to sacrifice direct control over community roads in exchange for a higher standard of transportation infrastructure.

And yet, despite the extraordinary nature of those policy changes, administrative reforms came haltingly, battered in the rough competition of the political marketplace. The new road legislation remained strictly voluntary: state aid was contingent upon the acceptance of state coordination, an exchange that was elective, not mandatory. This feature, a condition of the bill's reluctant rural supporters, meant that road-building authority remained decentralized and localized. Similarly, machine politicians' strong interest in protecting sources of patronage meant that the political authority of engineers remained minimal, despite the Good Roads campaign's interest in bringing technical expertise to bear on road improvement. And finally, the limited state expenditures authorized by a fiscally conservative legislature made the realization of the road reformers' vision of an improved highway network all the more doubtful.

As this chapter has shown, this era saw both rural conservatives and machine politicians grasping the mantle of road reform in attempts to strengthen their own political positions. Even the most progressive of rural New Yorkers was reluctant to completely relinquish local control of road building to the state. And party politicians, though more willing to entertain the use of state authority, hoped to employ it in the essentially local, patronage-driven interests of the party machine. While the League of American Wheelmen's lobbying energy propelled road reform forward, it could not keep the pressures of fiscal conservatism, local control, and patronage politics from blending with its agenda. The legislative record mirrors the complex interplay of multiple traditions entangled in the tentative alliance of agrarians, politicians, and road reformers. The paucity of new state roads testifies to the difficulties in advancing their divergent agendas.

However, as Chapter 2 will show, changes in state highway law contained within them enormous potential to up-end the very political philosophies that produced them. Machine politicians in time realized that their style of distributional politics did poor service to their party and the state's system of highways. Implementing a statewide road improvement program meant addressing a host of divisive, and thus politically unpopular, issues. Like rural conservatives in the final decades of the nineteenth century, party politicians would recognize by the early twentieth century that they too lacked the political capacity to affect broad infrastructural development through locally oriented politics. Each of these failures accelerated the search for institutional alternatives that drew more fully on state and federal units of government, while maintaining a high degree of local control over administration and expenditures. Policy choices designed to conserve local power in the late nineteenth century led to the emergence of a vibrant, active road-building state in the early twentieth.

Under this structure of governance, which I term a "subfederal" regime, local governments increasingly shared power with state agencies, and engineers gained a provisional authority, limited by the dominance of partisan politics. But as yet there were no system builders at the helm. A growing Good Roads coalition had spurred the New York State Legislature to accept greater responsibility for the creation of a coordinated system of improved highways, only to have road politics folded into the existing political system, driven by a mix of (predominantly local) impulses. This development set up the clash of views—over the state's role in road building, over the new framework of governance it entailed—that would dominate highway politics for the next generation. New York's method of road administration had clearly changed by the turn of the century, but reluctant innovation had so far led to only half-hearted reform.

New Ways: The Emergence of a Subfederal Road-Building Regime, 1898–1919

As I argued in the previous chapter, rural conservatives and machine politicians, though often at odds with one another, were in fact two sides of the same political coin. Each came to road reform slowly, and each hoped to press the Good Roads campaign into the service of an essentially local politics. In 1898, the year New York passed its landmark road legislation, rural advocates of the local road-building system could take pride in the fact that they had crafted a bill that ensured their interests would be protected. The voluntarism of the state-aid highway bill was to be the principal defense against runaway state spending. Likewise, machine politicians scored a major victory by ensuring that state highway construction would proceed under the direction of the elected state engineer. Plum road-building contracts could be directed toward the party faithful; the politics of public resource distribution would remain intact. Road politics and policy had been altered by 1898, but the foundational ideas and practices of nineteenth-century governance endured.

Twenty years later, few vestiges of the local road-building regime remained. The factors behind this transformation were many, but several challenges that drove road reform forward can be singled out. The first was financial: as petitions for new road construction poured into the State Engineer's Office, it soon became apparent that there were too few resources at hand to fund them. New Yorkers responded in 1905 with an unprecedented $50 million bond issue, followed by another $50 million in 1912, to fund the state's road improvement program. Growing popular support for state aid—as indicated by the enormous success of both referenda—overrode earlier commitments to fiscal conservatism.

The second involved public policy pressures: the voluntarism of the 1898 bill meant that New York's public roads were governed under two separate highway codes, one organized around the principle of state aid, the other around the old pathmaster system. As late as 1907, one-third of New York's towns still administered their roads under the labor tax. Growing concern over the bifurcated highway policy prompted a statewide investigation of highway administration practice, resulting in the creation of a State Highway Commission and the abolishment of the labor system of taxation.

A final factor concerned the nature of political authority: although the Highway Commission centralized the control of road building in a state-level institution, it was still influenced by the pressures of boss politics and was routinely mired in graft investigations. Moreover, machine politicians found it increasingly difficult to balance the demands of state party organizations and pervasive appeals for patronage appointments against competing demands (from engineers, political reformers, interest groups, and citizens) for the display of neutral competence in public construction. In time they recognized that despite the appeal of doling out road contracts, the politically divisive nature of state road construction could be a liability as well. As was the case with rural road-building officials, machine politicians recognized that policy demands had outstripped their political capacity. Once they acknowledged that the patronage uses of road building could be disadvantageous, old pols began to learn new lessons about the political utility of reform. And this created an opening for expert engineers to enter the fray and exert their own brand of political authority.

These three elements combined to bring about the ultimate rejection of the local road-building regime, and the nineteenth-century policy tools, governing institutions, and political philosophies that undergirded it. In its place emerged a subfederal road-building regime, a policy regime that differed from its local predecessor in the structure of highway administration, the locus of policy making, and the relative authority of politicians and engineers. Firmly in place by 1916, the subfederal regime reflected a significant reapportionment of public authority, in which state governments were empowered to exercise direct control over a critical governmental responsibility, the provision of public ways.

Congress's decision in that year to offer grants-in-aid to the states accelerated the centralization of road administration in New York State. Though financial assistance was contingent upon federal oversight, New York was already building roads that exceeded federal standards. The primary impact of the 1916 Federal-Aid Road Act, then, was to enlarge state road-building capacity by virtue of the influx of new funds into the recently established Highway Commission. Thus, by the end of the decade, highway politics, once the province of town governments, pathmasters, and residential labor, was now ensconced in a complex federalism that drew on the resources of all levels of government, while positioning the state government at the nexus of road-building authority.

"If We Get Fifty Millions It Will Build All the Roads We Want": Highway Users and the 1905 Bond Issue

Having gained an entering wedge by crafting a role for the state in highway administration, Good Roads advocates sought to enlarge and further centralize the state's system of road construction, administration, and finance. Petitions for new roads presented incontrovertible evidence of broad-based popular support for improved highways and modern road administration. But as the construction program expanded, it was an increasingly appealing target for the machine politicians who had formed a tentative alliance with proponents of road reform. How those interested in pursuing good roads could achieve the modern engineering feat they envisioned while at the same time keeping partisan forces at bay remained unclear. To this point, successful road legislation had been the product of neither boss rule nor reform politics, but of the complex interplay of the two traditions.

Soon after the pivotal legislative year 1898, the state legislature began to fine-tune its road policy. In 1900 the Higbie-Armstrong Act was amended to increase the state engineer's authority over the maintenance of town roads. In 1901 New York enacted the nation's first motor vehicle registration fee, a one-time, dollar-per-vehicle assessment. In 1902 the legislature increased its share of Fuller money—the matching grants offered to those towns that switched from a labor to a cash system of taxation—from 25 cents to 50 cents on the dollar; by 1909 it matched dollar for dollar. All these actions suggested a growing comfort with the state's role in road building. But from the reformers' perspective, two dilemmas remained: the town pathmaster system, and the vexing problem of road finance.

Though the Higbie-Armstrong Act provided for centralized road building—

county supervisors chose the main routes to be improved; the State Engineer's Office let the contracts, maintained standards, and oversaw construction— it was nonetheless an optional system. If they chose, towns could decline the state's assistance and continue to maintain their roads under the cheaper, localized pathmaster system. Reformers considered the voluntary provision, which maintained the town pathmasters' position, a major defect. But few were ready to mount a frontal assault on such a firmly established public post held by tens of thousands of New Yorkers.

Reformers had greater success in asking for larger road appropriations. Since the Higbie-Armstrong Act's initial passage, petitions for aid from the majority of counties continually exceeded the amount earmarked from general revenues. Responding to the growing number of petitions for new roads, the state legislature steadily increased annual appropriations, from $50,000 in 1898 and 1899 to $150,000 in 1900, $420,000 in 1901, and $600,000 by 1902. But despite improvements in road-building machinery, which bought more miles to the dollar, this increased spending did not cover demands. So Senator William Armstrong (the coauthor of the 1898 Higbie-Armstrong Act) introduced a bill in 1903 asking for a constitutional amendment to allow the state to issue $50 million in bonded debt for highway improvement.[1]

Like all proposed amendments to the state constitution, it would have to be passed by the next elected legislature as well before being submitted to popular referendum as a November 1905 ballot question. In order to exert pressure on the legislature to pass Armstrong's bill, Arthur Shattuck, president of the New York City–based Automobile Club of America (founded in 1902), teamed up with longtime Good Roads advocate William Pierrepont White. Shattuck had at his disposal a class of influential Manhattan motorists, ranging from the well-heeled William Guggenheim to the well-connected Democratic Assemblyman Charles F. Bostwick and Tammany politician George Washington Plunkitt. White, who headed the Oneida County League for Good Roads, had developed numerous contacts throughout the state among local road officials in favor of highway improvement. Shattuck and White had hoped Armstrong would introduce a $60 million road bond amendment but could hardly complain when he shaved it to an even fifty: "Fifty millions is as good as sixty," Shattuck wrote White. "If we get fifty millions it will build all the roads we want."[2]

Shattuck and White maintained daily correspondence as they shuttled the bill through its first stage during the 1903 session. White spearheaded a letter-writing campaign that asked 2,500 automobilists and 2,500 town supervisors to appeal to their legislators on behalf of the bill. Shattuck had faith in the power of interest-group politics, explaining to White that he should "just ask the [automobile club members] point blank to write their representatives and to get an influential friend to write also." Shattuck, a deft strategist, assured White that "I have my automobile people in good training." At the same time, Shattuck and White were careful not to reveal too much of the club's interest in good roads, adding a postscript to their appeal asking supporters to "not mention automobiles in your letter. Some statesmen do not like them." The campaign was successful, and Armstrong personally congratulated White for his work in securing the bill's passage.[3]

Though Governor Benjamin Odell (Rep., 1901–1905) spoke out against the amendment in 1904, insisting that an expenditure of $50 million constituted a "premature" investment in road improvement, the highway proposal was well received by the legislature when it came up again in 1905.[4] A number of factors account for the amendment's support. The first was timing. In New York State politics generally, and for Armstrong in particular, 1905 was an important transitional year. Reformers waged several campaigns against big business and the dominant political machinery, ushering in what one historian has called a "new political order."[5] Most spectacular was the 1905 investigation of corruption in the state's insurance industry, headed by Armstrong himself. The investigation energized the political atmosphere. Its revelations of corporate and political misdeeds tarnished the reputations of the Republican Old Guard and challenged the supremacy of the Republican political machine; at the same time, its thoroughness promoted a new faith in reform-minded politicians and in government's ability to police itself. The roads question received a new hearing in the aftermath of this political shake-up. Ironically, the increased clout of reformers—so critical of machine politicians' waste—placed them in an ideal position to lobby for vast increases in spending.[6]

Another factor involved a competing mode of publicly financed transportation improvement. The New York State Legislature had committed itself in 1903 to a controversial $101 million overhaul of the canal system; the new road improvement program was billed as a political offset. Republicans had split on the canal issue after Governor Odell relaxed party control on the vote, freeing upstate politicians to vote their counties' economic interests. Upstate residents, predominantly antitax Republicans who lived far from the canal, had opposed it in large numbers. Conversely, the canals had the overwhelming support of Democrats and residents of New York City and Buffalo, whose port cities would profit greatly.[7] Since the road bond authorization taxed urban areas heavily for the state's share of rural road construction, and since no roads could be constructed in cities or incorporated villages, the road bond amendment appeased rural Republicans who had been angered by canal expenditures.[8]

There remained lingering opposition to the bond issue from some urbanites (who would receive only indirect benefits from the proposed construction) and from some rural New Yorkers (who argued that the law would be "a good one for road contractors, but for nobody else").[9] And Governor Odell opposed it too, anxious about pursuing major policy initiatives such as the canal bill that spoke to New Yorkers' divisive economic interests, and thus diminished his ability to unify the Republican Party under his control. By contrast, the bond issue received overwhelming support in the legislature, which was quick to take Armstrong's lead after the repudiation of the Republican Party's Old Guard leadership.[10] These proponents of a reformed political order promised an overhaul of governance, and they were willing to spend considerable sums to do it.

The state constitution required that large bond issues be submitted to popular ratification, and the road bond was placed on the referendum ballot along with six others in the fall of 1905. Of all the referenda on the ballot (there were seven questions) the road bond issue passed by the widest margin (383,188 for, and 117,181 against). Only three farming counties rejected the bond proposal; seven rural counties gave it a slim majority. It received overwhelming support in the remaining predominantly urban and suburban counties.[11]

In light of the great reluctance to finance costly road improvements displayed by rural New Yorkers over the previous two decades, the success of the road bond requires some explanation. Part of the answer had to do with declining ideological resistance in the face of new public benefits. As the state assisted in the construction of improved roads, and as the economy continued to recover from the depression of the 1890s, farming organizations such as local Granges were increasingly persuaded by the value of good roads, and of their limited ability to provide such roads through local government alone.[12]

Of course, Good Roads advocates were aware that rural New Yorkers still needed to be handled delicately. During the debate over the bond amendment, White had advised Shattuck to keep figures on local road-building costs out of the public eye, since "some of the counties, if they saw how much money they would have to spend for roads, would certainly get cold feet." But few could ignore the fact that requests for hundreds of miles of new roads were rapidly outpacing state finances, and a solution had to be found.[13]

Significantly, widespread support for highway development preceded mass automobile ownership: state motor vehicle registrations totaled only 8,625 in 1905 (see Figure 2.1). Though Shattuck's Automobile Club was instrumental in getting the road bond amendment on the ballot, the hundreds of thousands of New Yorkers who voted for it in November endorsed a new public works program designed to address a financial shortfall, not drivers' demands.

Contemporaries and historians alike have commented on the general quickening of government during the Progressive Era, noting the expansion in both the scale and the scope of public activity.[14] Even in this context, the $50 million bond issue was a bold move, one that signaled a growing comfort with active state-level governance. No other state in the nation had ever adopted so substantial a measure for highway improvement. The 1905 amendment was the first indication that the original 1898 Higbie-Armstrong Act had indeed opened the door to a new policy regime. Fiscal conservatism, the first hallmark of the old, local road-building regime, had been decidedly rejected in a statewide referendum.

"The Most Perplexing Conditions": Reconciling the State's Highway Codes

The next stage in the transition to a subfederal regime occurred just two years later, as state officials wrestled with how to administer these new funds. Beginning in 1907, legislators engaged in a series of efforts to further centralize road-building authority. Two critical developments stand out: the empowering of the state engineer to create a system of state-funded primary highways, and the creation of a new State Highway Commission. Both moves furthered the process by which road-building authority was vested in state bureaucracies—and caught up in the machinery of boss politics.

Beginning in July 1907, the Joint Legislative Committee on Good Roads conducted hearings across the state to gauge public opinion on the revision of the highway law. The committee was in the hands of a party regular, Senator Jotham P. Allds. An Old Guard Republican, he would resign from the legislature after a 1911 investigation uncovered a record of bribery relating to state bridge contracts. But it also included Senator S. Percy Hooker, a roads advocate who, though no party maverick, allied with reform-minded Republicans.[15] Democratic state engineer Frederick Skene also attended many of the hearings, at which local road authorities and advocates of highway improvement voiced their opinions.

The committee concentrated on the changes in highway law over the past

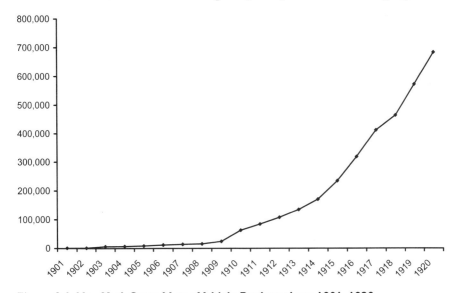

Figure 2.1: New York State Motor Vehicle Registrations, 1901–1920

Source: Compiled from data in William M. Curtiss, *The Development of Highway Administration and Finance in New York,* Department of Agricultural Economics and Farm Management, New York State College of Agriculture (Ithaca, N.Y.: Cornell University, March 1936), 59.

decade. As Allds saw it, allowing towns and counties to choose their system of road administration had created an incongruous set of laws. The existing highway code looked like the old English labor system with the benefits of a money system grafted onto it. Unless all towns adopted the money system (and by 1907 a third of them had not yet done so), the state was faced with the unpleasant prospect of dealing with two conflicting sets of highway law.[16]

What Allds discovered, however, was more than a disagreement between those who favored the labor system ("the shade tree element," in the words of its opponents) and those who favored the money system.[17] At stake was a fundamental debate over the nature of highway administration and, implicitly, the tension between local, decentralized control and those who argued for centralized road-building authority. A central engineering office might better coordinate the state's construction program, but at what cost? Erie County Highway Commissioner George C. Diehl warned that highway bureaucrats in Albany would be incapable of dealing with the needs of particular areas. He favored employing county engineers, who might be more receptive to locals' concerns. And he believed that land abutters should have the opportunity to review and advise upon the plans affecting them.[18]

Syracuse City Engineer Harry Allen disagreed. As the former head of

New York State's canal work, Allen had experience with large public works projects and was aware of the danger of allowing authority to spin outwards. "It would seem to me," he said, "that if the State is going into this business of constructing highways throughout its whole length and breadth, it would be well to centralize in some point in the government the power and authority to at least construct the road." Allen agreed with Diehl that localities should have some minimal advisory role, but he insisted that the state "ought to control [it] from top to bottom."[19]

The Allds committee concluded that prevailing opinion favored greater state control and limited local road-building authority. True, from some corners of the state came appeals for the continuance of the nineteenth-century system. The comments of one Jefferson County man, William P. Freeman, were a reminder that roads still had traditional uses. "In the olden times when the cows run the roads," Freeman explained to the committee, "they kept the bushes down; in certain places it is impossible to till the roads and keep them down except by cutting them, and the annual cutting will amount to about all we get from the State [in assistance under the Fuller Act]." Freeman wondered if instead a law might be passed to allow, at certain times, the herding of cattle in the highways. Worried that the committee might object to the slowing of motor traffic, Freeman had an answer: restrict grazing to "between the hours of five and ten A.M., before the automobilists get out of bed; [that way] we wouldn't trouble them."

Freeman's caricature of automobilists had the ring of truth. In 1906, William K. Vanderbilt Jr., grandson of Commodore Vanderbilt, and fellow aristocrats August Belmont and Harry Payne Whitney formed a corporation to build the Long Island Motor Parkway. The paved road, built almost entirely on private land and stretching sixty miles from Queens to central Long Island, was chiefly a product of Vanderbilt's ambition to race his red Mercedes without facing the perils of "grade crossings, dust, and police surveillance." But Freeman and Vanderbilt represented the extremes of New York road culture. The explosion of automobile ownership loomed in the distance, and automobilists still comprised only a small group of wealthy New Yorkers. But "the olden times when the cows run the road" had surely passed.[20]

Anxious to reform the highway code, though with little hope of satisfying either the Freemans or the Vanderbilts of the state, the Allds committee submitted its report to the legislature in 1908. It proposed the repeal of all existing highway laws and the creation of an entirely new statute—one that, among other things, abolished the labor system of taxation and suggested the establishment of a State Highway Commission to administer the new code.[21]

Growing private economic power, public health epidemics, labor crises, natural resource depletion, and a host of other late nineteenth-century problems had prompted the creation of numerous public oversight commissions in New York State. These bodies had significant investigative and regulatory powers. They were often confined, however, to analytical functions, like gathering statistics, or negative functions, like restricting certain private activities.

What made the Highway Commission different was its positive, constructive function. Unlike earlier commissions, the legislature charged the new Highway Commission with building and administering a public good. And unlike the State Engineer's Office, which was responsible for building the closest comparable public good—the Erie Canal—the new commission would function as an appointed administrative arm of modern government, insulated from electoral politics.[22]

State Engineer Skene objected to this transfer of power, which represented both a loss of party control and, to his mind, an unwarranted abridgement of local authority.[23] So too did Democratic political bosses, who relied on Skene to dole out contracts to favorite bidders.[24] But the Republican-majority legislature, unmoved by Skene's appeal and anxious to direct road contracts back to their own party faithful, approved a new, bipartisan, three-man Commission of Highways. S. Percy Hooker, former senator and a member of the Allds committee, chaired the commission, which began work in early 1909. Robert Earl, a Herkimer County banker and independent Democrat, was appointed to the minority position on the commission, but only after Republican governor Charles Evans Hughes—in consultation with legislative leadership and a committee of the State Grange—could settle on a nominee who would be sensitive to both upstate interests and the patronage demands of the Democratic Party. T. Warren Allen, an American road builder working in Puerto Rico and a political unknown, fulfilled the requirement that the commission have an engineer.[25]

No sooner had State Engineer Skene voiced his objections to the new commission when he and his administration faced accusations of graft and the mishandling of road contracts. He was eventually indicted on seventeen counts, including four counts of grand larceny. The gist of the charges was that the administration had increased awards on road work and then exacted campaign tribute from the contractors who did business with the state. The trial dragged on for weeks, amid much drama. A key witness suffered a nervous breakdown. Then Skene's confidential assistant testified against him. Eventually Skene was acquitted after his defense successfully argued that he was the victim of an elaborate Tammany frame-up.[26]

The Highway Commission was designed to keep this sort of partisan politics out of road building. But that was a difficult task. Even if the commission could keep the political machine at bay, choosing how and where the state would do its building was inevitably a political process. The official state map—approved by the legislature in 1907 in conjunction with county highway officials and the State Engineer's Office—had brought some coordination to the process of highway construction. But the program was dogged by the unevenness inherent in a system inclined to privilege local interests. This lack of balance was further exacerbated by the fact that road construction was initiated based not on need but on the order in which road improvement petitions were received from the counties.

Years after the bond issue had passed, disparities in construction were apparent. Whereas two counties, each with populations under 50,000, boasted over 2,000 miles of improved roads, Westchester County (population 283,055) had only 868 miles.[27] And many roads delegated as throughways pursued roundabout routes, wildly diverging to swing past small centers of population or looping through village centers, not unlike the winding nineteenth-century roads they were designed to replace.[28]

In response to this situation, the legislature created a new class of roads labeled "state highways" in 1909 (see Map 2.1). These consisted of 38 north-south or east-west through routes, totaling 3,600 miles and financed entirely by the state.[29] The basis of the early road network, the choice of their routes was complex and sensitive. Highway Commissioner Hooker acknowledged that "the question of determining the location of the State routes has been one of the most difficult of the problems with which the Commission has had to deal." According to the beleaguered commissioner, "the majority of cases" required the negotiation of "numerous conflicting interests," ranging from engineering dilemmas to the difficulties of picking routes that served the needs of both local and through traffic. This quandary was all the more complicated by the fact that the roads that communities were pressing the commission to improve were not always consistent with the route's intermediate and terminal points mandated by state law. All these factors "combined to create the most perplexing conditions" and necessitated "personal examination of each route by the members of the Commission."[30]

For over a decade, highway policy makers had sought to integrate new responsibilities for public roads into the framework of distributive politics

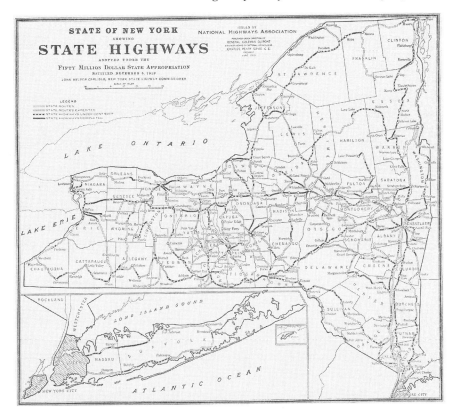

Map 2.1: 1912 Map of New York State Highways Adopted under $50 Million State Appropriation

Source: National Highways Association, held by Harvard Map Collection.

and delegated administration that had characterized state governance over the past century. When new road authority was first granted in 1898, it was quickly assimilated into the system of machine politics. But as Hooker recognized, the politics of broad resource distribution was of little assistance in the complex mediation among "numerous conflicting interests." By 1909 it was becoming clear that these nineteenth-century policy tools and governing philosophies were inadequate to the creation of a coordinated highway system, a paradigmatic twentieth-century policy challenge.

The Crisis of Distributional Politics (and the Engineers' Lament)

The passage of the 1905 bond amendment and the creation of the State Highway Commission dealt two serious blows to the local road-building regime. In the first instance, citizens lent their support to a more robust financing of public roads in order to act on the petitions pouring into the State Engineer's Office. In the second case, Republicans in the state legislature established the new commission in order to unify New York's highway code, while at the same time reclaiming party control over patronage resources. Both of these moves yielded a new set of policy tools and institutions that would serve as key elements of the subfederal road-building regime. Yet neither challenged the basic principles of local governance. The most enduring element of the old regime—distributional politics—was essentially a politics of localism, channeling public resources via the party machine to its loyal supporters throughout the state. Though Highway Commissioner Hooker had by 1909 realized that this sort of politics was ill-fit to the demands of a state highway system, local forces and partisan squabbling continued to determine the means by which road administration evolved. Before it was reformed, the Highway Commission had in store seven troubled years of political scandal and repeated charges of corruption.

The commission's work in the 1910s was complicated by an external factor as well: the democratization of the automobile. Increased auto traffic placed greater demands on the transportation infrastructure, forcing the commission to reassess the durability not just of existing roads but of those already improved. Still struggling with the initial task of laying out the state highway system, the commission faced a tougher struggle under these new pressures. Indeed, as public attention focused on the subpar quality of the highways and the dramatics of repeated highway investigations, road reformers, engineers, and politicians all sought new institutional solutions to the roads question.

Only 1,800 miles of highway had been macadamized during the first ten years of state road building (1898–1908), and these roads were constructed with loose water-bound macadam.[31] While fine for teams and wagons, the reverse thrust of automobiles' narrow pneumatic tires tore up loose particles, creating whirlwinds of dust and stripping the road of its top surface. In 1910 the Highway Commission focused its attention on resurfacing these roads before they degraded further in quality. Only after that did it shift its attention back to the primary system of state highways, though reconstruction and maintenance costs continued to play a major role in public road administration. Hoping to make up for lost time, the commission sped construction on these main routes, despite its original pledge to construct highways in the order in which petitions were received.[32]

No sooner had the Highway Commission settled into its reconstruction work when the 1911 victory of Democratic gubernatorial candidate John A. Dix generated new turmoil. Dix was the first Democrat to sit in the executive office since Roswell Flower departed in 1894. It fell to him to maintain an uneasy coalition of upstate independents and Tammany loyalists. This was a difficult task, made more so by the immense pressure to return state administration to the party after seventeen lean years for the Democratic faithful.

Dix would have liked simply to return road-building authority to the state engineer, but he found it politically difficult to eliminate the young and still untested Highway Commission. Instead he reorganized it along more favorably partisan lines. He made C. Gordon Reel, a Democrat with ties to Tammany chief Charles Murphy, superintendent of highways. Filling out the formerly bipartisan commission were two more Democrats: State Engineer John A. Bensel, who prepared plans and specifications for road projects; and Superintendent of Public Works Duncan W. Peck, who awarded the construction contracts. Bensel and Peck, who spent much of their time engaged in canal work, were *ex officio* members on the commission. It was widely acknowledged that highway administration was Reel's responsibility; Bensel and Peck simply ensured that the commission would remain firmly in party control.[33]

In what became an established pattern, Dix, as Hughes had before him, accused the previous administration of inefficiently handling highway construction and subjected the commission to partisan attacks. In early 1911 he instructed Bensel to hold up awarding contracts until they could be reviewed. Meanwhile, the *New York Times* accused the legislature of, in effect, giving Tammany $50 million to spend as patronage by returning state road building to the hands of the state engineer and the Democratic machine.[34] It is difficult to say whether the 1911 contracts were held up for fair review or simply to buy time while the cogs in the Tammany machine were set in motion under a new administration. In any event, under Reel's authority the Highway Commission almost doubled the amount of improved highway mileage in the state. By 1911 the state had 3,000 miles of hard-surfaced state and county highways, 3,000 miles of macadamized town roads, and 8,000 miles of improved gravel town roads. Forty thousand miles of the state's existing roads had been improved to some extent; 26,000 miles remained untouched.[35]

But Reel faced a dilemma. The rising cost of labor and materials; demands for a higher grade of construction to meet the needs of new automobile, truck, and bus traffic; and changes in the apportionment equation that secured greater amounts of state aid for poorer counties created a serious shortfall. With the $50 million bond issue almost exhausted, the state had completed less than half of its primary highway system.[36] It was evident by 1912 that a second bond appropriation was necessary. Some objected to renewed appropriations, arguing that the money would be wasted given the inconclusive experiments over the past six years to find a durable pavement for the automobile. Others worried that New Yorkers had gone "road crazy," especially after repeated investigations of the highway department exposed its corruptible nature.

Still, New Yorkers remained committed to financing an extensive highway program. Unlike urban mass transit, which was often portrayed as under the control of profit-hungry corporations, roads appeared to be unalloyed public goods. While mass transit was subjected to punishing political demands, public policies affecting highway construction and automobile use—policies that served both urban and rural transportation needs—tended to be flexible and supportive. Moreover, the number of motor vehicle registrations rose dramatically since the previous highway referendum: from 8,625 in 1905 to 107,262 in 1912. According to the *New York Times*, after the critical presidential and gubernatorial elections, Proposition No. 1, the road bond issue, was the most important on the 1912 ballot. In the end, the citizens of every New York county overwhelmingly supported (by a margin of 400,000 votes) a second $50 million bond issue.[37]

This new injection of funds highlighted the importance of safeguarding their expenditure. Unlike the first $50 million bond issue, which was apportioned so that each county received equal mileage regardless of need, the new appropriation was apportioned on a more demographically representative, tripartite formula: one-third would be divided by geographic area, one-third by population, and one-third by road mileage per county. The *New York Times* called the original mileage apportionment a "joker" that "played directly into the hands of the party 'grafters.'"[38] Despite the change, the Dix administration still faced accusations, this time from the *New York World*, that the Highway Commission padded costs and then exacted tribute from the loyal contractors. Costs per mile had risen from $8,000 in the Hughes administration to $20,000 in the Dix administration. Part of this jump was no doubt a function of inflation and the increased costs of a higher grade of construction. But the *New York Times*, ever wary of Tammany's influence, warned that "eternal vigilance" must be exerted when dealing with contractors.[39]

The Highway Commission was not prepared to meet these demands for administrative watchfulness. Reel ran the commission with a loose hand. He gave First Deputy Commissioner (and fellow friend of Tammany) Charles F. Foley complete control over that arsenal of political patronage, the highway maintenance department. Foley awarded hundreds of contracts worth several million dollars without competitive bidding. Reel's lax leadership created friction between him and several of his chief officers, and early in 1912 his chief engineer resigned. Troubles continued through the summer construction season, when Foley and Deputy Engineer Spencer Stewart faced an internal investigation for fraudulent highway work that led to Foley's resignation and the dismissal of 930 men from the maintenance department.[40]

Work ground to a standstill in late 1912, as the Highway Commission faced further charges of corruption. By October it ceased to keep official records of its proceedings, a sure sign of an agency in crisis.[41] When Democrat William Sulzer became governor in 1913 he made it plain—to the dismay of Tammany boss Charles Murphy—that there would be a thorough house cleaning and an investigation of highway graft charges. Independent Democrat John N. Carlisle, a Public Service Commission member and Albany lawyer, headed the investigation, which began in January 1913. By mid-March, Sulzer had dismissed Reel and appointed former journalist John A. Hennessy to take charge of the continuing investigation.[42] When Hennessy's investigative committee finally issued its report, it broadly condemned the Reel administration. Most damning was a 20 percent increase in repair contracts, the costs of which were easily padded when let through private bidding. C. R. Allen, an engineer formerly affiliated with the Highway Commission, claimed that contractors never had to give back a percentage of their contracts as campaign contributions. But if they did, he acknowledged in a moment of candor that would have made a Tammany man proud, it was no more than 3 percent.[43]

Former highway commission member and independent Democrat Robert Earl advocated the return of a bipartisan commission to assuage fears of mismanagement. But Sulzer favored a stronger, single-headed highway commission. He offered the chairmanship to Carlisle, the original highway graft investigator, who accepted the post. On assuming office he fired Division Engineer Stewart, who had been under internal investigation for highway fraud and now faced a review from an outside investigator. By September another division engineer had been indefinitely suspended in the face of fraud accusations.[44]

By the fall of 1913 the Sulzer administration had initiated a volley of investigations against corruption in all corners of government. Sulzer's lack of loyalty to the party machine did not sit well with Tammany chieftains. His refusal to appoint Jim Gaffney, a Tammany-sponsored candidate for highway commissioner, was the final straw that led boss Charles Murphy to engineer the governor's impeachment.[45] Even in those turbulent political times, the Highway Commission had seemed safe under former investigator Carlisle. Indeed, the engineering press credited him for making "an honest effort to establish the [highway] work on an efficient and economical basis."[46] But just days after Sulzer was forced from office, crusading investigator Hennessy ordered Carlisle investigated for fraudulent administration, accusing him of failing to root out pervasive corruption.[47] Carlisle emerged unscathed from Hennessy's investigation, though Hennessy indicted six Rockland County and three Buffalo contractors. In one instance, a Democratic committee member from Tammany Hall received $31,000 for a reconstruction project in which he skim-coated a highway with a quarter-inch of cement grout instead of four inches of concrete. Wyoming County's Democratic Committee chairman was arrested for paying party employees with highway funds during the 1912 campaign.[48]

The Highway Commission faced more negative publicity from Governor Martin Glynn's administration. Hoping to dispel the notion that Tammany would be immune from investigations under his watch, Glynn, a Democrat, had his new highway investigator, Jason W. Osborne, continue to target Carlisle along with former administrators Reel, Bensel, Peck, and Foley. District Attorney Charles S. Whitman also pursued the Highway Commission, helping to convict several former, low-ranking members as well as numerous contractors in 1914.[49]

By December, Carlisle—who had been both investigator and investigated—concluded that the political problems plaguing the department since the first $50 million bond issue needed to be resolved. In a long opinion piece published in the *New York Times*, he discussed the politics of highway construction in New York State. There had been seven different heads of state highway construction over the past decade and three major administrative reorganizations during the past five years. Successful administration, he concluded, required ending the game of political football.[50]

The engineering press, which over the years had taken a greater interest in state road building, agreed with Carlisle that partisan politics ought to be removed from public construction. An (admittedly self-serving) editorial in *Engineering News* on the New York State Highway Commission wondered, "After Investigation, What?" Though highway fraud investigations were part of "a necessary and salutary process," the journal regretted that "men who were compelled to participate in a system that they detested may have to suffer penalties, in injury to reputation and standing and in more serious ways, greater than they deserve." There was clearly "fraud and graft in plenty, as everyone knows," yet the important point "is that all this work of chasing criminals is . . . looking to the past rather than the future."

From the perspective of the engineering press, there was only one way of escaping from the cycle of fraud and misadministration, investigation and counterinvestigation: reorganize the Highway Commission along nonpartisan lines and rely on the supposed apolitical rationality of engineers. Restructure the commission in this way, the engineers argued, and competent experts would replace the political tools of earlier administrations. "When engineers can join a state engineering organization, with confidence that merit and not political pull will meet with reward, there will be plenty of competent engineers to take up road work. And with competent engineers in control, the questions of what types of roads to build and how to build them economically and efficiently will largely settle themselves."[51]

These questions were precisely the ones that had bedeviled Commissioner Hooker in 1909. Now, after five years of discontinuous leadership and uninterrupted investigations, the engineering community hoped to capitalize on the scandal and mismanagement that had plagued the commission. To be sure, this move was a strategic bid for power, but it emanated from a different motivating force. State and city political machines exercised control over highway officials to perpetuate party control over state resources. By contrast, engineers hoped to translate their technological expertise into a form of political expression that would allow them to direct public construction according to their economy and efficiency metrics, while bolstering their own professional standing.

But that was not to be. The partisan politics of the old regime were simply too deeply rooted to be brushed aside by the engineers' promise of administrative reform. District Attorney Whitman's crusade against highway graft helped propel him into the governor's office on the Republican ticket in November 1914. Once in office he pledged a "redemption" of the Highway Commission, and the political tide turned for the last time against Carlisle. At first he protested his removal. But Carlisle was persuaded to resign when a compromise was reached in February: he would go peaceably if the governor maintained a strong, single-headed administration and abandoned his plan to return to a weaker, Hughes-style, three-man commission.[52] Cortland County's former attorney general Edwin Duffey, a close friend and

Amherst classmate of Whitman's, replaced Carlisle. Duffey came into office in 1915 and, like his predecessors, overhauled the department, bringing in Republicans and sweeping out Democrats.[53]

As it turned out, Duffey would be one of the last of the old pols to head the state's highway administration. His tenure marked the beginning of the end of the distributive order and the new, subfederal road-building regime that had so recently come into being. Obeisance to the machine and its locally oriented, patronage politics simply generated too much bad press. Party members themselves began to doubt the usefulness of the Highway Commission as merely a supplier of state jobs, pet projects, and plum contracts. Not for another decade would self-proclaimed "apolitical" engineers be able to displace the political authority of the political machines with their own. But repeated scandal had taken its toll. The localism of the old road-building regimes, already weakened by the enactment of state-aid laws, the creation of the Highway Commission, and the passage of the twin bond amendments, was further delegitimized by highly publicized investigations into highway graft. Though the installment of Duffey as highway commissioner indicated that traditional political forces were still in operation, seven years of corruption had worked to cast the shadow of doubt over these older, localistic and distributive governing philosophies.

Yet for all its troubles—corruption, perennial changes in leadership, shortages of funds, increasing costs—New York's Highway Commission had overseen a substantial transformation of its rural road system. When Duffey took office that year, the state boasted some 6,000 miles of completed highways. To underscore this achievement, he had the highway department issue maps of the state highway system to the general public for the first time.[54] The maps confirmed a lesson politicians had been slow to learn: good infrastructure was its own political reward. It was a subtle admission, but one that would have a lasting impact on the relationship between politicians and engineers in the years to come.

One Eye on Washington: The Irony of Federal Aid

In the course of a decade, New York had made a solid start on a network of hard-surfaced state highways, standing head and shoulders above the rest of the nation in road construction mileage and expenditure.[55] Indeed, it was the nation's leading road builder: by 1916 one out of every three state road-building dollars was spent in the Empire State. With $100 million in authorized expenditures and the new Highway Commission to oversee them, road-building politics had shifted decisively toward a subfederal regime in which local officials—pathmasters, town highway commissioners, county supervisors—shared authority (if not political agendas) with party bosses and state administrators.

In the midst of this political flux, Congress contemplated new national road legislation that would have serious ramifications for New York State's highway program, offering critical support to the troubled commission. Proposals for federal aid had been circulating in Washington for several years, the result of a broad—and often internally conflicted—Good Roads coalition that drew on federal bureaucrats, motorists, road builders, auto makers, and agrarians. The diversity of political agendas behind these various groups made the crafting of federal road legislation challenging. But there was little doubt that as state-aid laws were passed not just in the densely populated Northeast but all across the country, appeals to the federal government would not be far behind.

The federal government's role in modern road building began in 1893, with the establishment of the Office of Road Inquiry (ORI) in the Department of Agriculture (USDA). From the beginning, the federal government drew on the experience of New York State leadership in highway affairs, drafting Roy Stone, a New York civil engineer and prominent League of American Wheelman member, to head the new department. With a modest $10,000 budget, the ORI was confined mainly to investigating various experiments in road improvement and disseminating technical information on highway issues. In the meantime, Stone used his close connections with the LAW to advocate for the adoption of state-aid legislation in New York (appearing at legislative hearings in 1897), as well as other states that had their own grass-roots interest in road reform, including New Jersey, Connecticut, Rhode Island, Michigan, Iowa, Kansas, and California.[56]

As had been the case in New York, the Department of Agriculture also found it difficult to keep partisan politics from dominating road reform. In 1899 the ORI was reorganized as the Office of Public Road Inquiry (OPRI) under the chairmanship of Martin Dodge, an Ohio lawyer and friend of President William McKinley. While Dodge's administration was still concerned with gathering and circulating engineering data, it now leaned more decidedly toward promotional activities. Dodge worked closely with Good Roads organizations, spreading the "gospel" of good roads, holding road improvement conventions, and drumming up local support for better highways.[57] This sort of work got Dodge into trouble. His direct lobbying for state legislation ran counter to the Department of Agriculture's dictum that the OPRI ought to provide disinterested scientific data and remain apolitical on road conditions. Dodge's other actions—such as endorsing patented construction methods, or building model roads in favored congressional districts—erased the already hazy line that the USDA intended to isolate the OPRI's technical expertise from political involvement and outright jobbery.[58]

When the department reorganized for a third time in 1905 as the Office of Public Roads (OPR), Congress insisted that a scientist sit at the helm. Logan W. Page, an engineer and former head of the OPRI testing laboratory, assumed control of the administration and guided the department through the next decade. His early administration was marked less by the political agitation favored by his predecessors and more by an emphasis on technical expertise. Under Page the OPR engaged in rigorous testing of road materials and construction methods, gathered detailed statistical information on road improvement, documented the economic benefits of hard-surfaced highways, set materials standards, and advised states and localities on highway administration issues.[59]

During these years the national road-building scene shifted dramatically, producing a stronger, more varied roads coalition. By 1909, twenty-nine states had state-aid highway laws, twenty-two had some form of state highway department, and five had designated a state highway system.[60] In 1911 the widely publicized construction of interregional memorial highways like the Lincoln Highway (from New York to San Francisco) and the Dixie Highway (from Michigan to Miami) put roads on the national political agenda. National automobile registrations, at 79,000 in 1905, had crossed the 1 million mark in 1912. Motorists were joined in their support of new road legislation by allied firms and organizations—auto makers, the American Automobile Association (1902), the American Road Building Association (1902), and, of course, the OPR. And while motorists were still tagged (as the cyclists had been in the 1890s) as "the idle rich," they were joined in their pursuit of federal road legislation by the National Grange, the nation's leading farming organization.

With the establishment of the postal system's rural free delivery (RFD) in 1896, and its expansion in the early years of the twentieth century, farmers (as had been the case in New York) turned in favor of road reform. RFD gave federal road reform a new legitimacy; even automobilists acknowledged that legislative success depended on approval from the Grange. Motorists and agrarians differed on which roads they wanted improved (main commercial and touring routes versus farm-to-market and rural post roads), but they agreed on the value of federal assistance. By July 1912, sixty new road bills had been introduced to Congress, and Page's influence had grown considerably.[61]

Proposals in Congress advocated a wide range of highway programs, from modest schemes for improved rural mail routes to a massive national construction bill that would have the federal government build a 51,000-mile highway system (larger than the existing system of interstate highways). After years of debate the Federal-Aid Highway Act, passed in 1916, hewed closely to the policy that Page and the OPR advocated: a $75 million cooperative program providing matching grants-in-aid to states to build improved highways in line with federal standards.

The act federalized highway practice, making state governments the administrative nexus and linking them to national and local units of government. It strengthened the role of administrative experts by requiring that all states have a strong highway department that met stringent OPR standards regarding engineering leadership, legal authority, and financial wherewithal. Emboldening state highway departments represented a compromise between those who wanted to nationalize highway construction and those who wanted only small-scale reform. And since the federal Bureau of Public Roads (renamed in 1918) was firmly in the hands of engineers as well, it provided further impetus for removing state highway departments from party control. The act was silent on which aspect of the road system was to be improved (primary automobile touring routes or secondary farm-to-market roads) and thus left it to the states to work out this thorny problem.[62]

Above all, the federal highway act capitalized on Congress's increased capacity, following the adoption of a federal income tax in 1913, to direct and redistribute national resources among the states.[63] Like other federal grant-in-aid programs, the act was designed to promote equity, direct national policy without top-heavy bureaucracy, and encourage coordinated development in traditionally state and local policy areas. States and localities in turn would draw on the superior capacity of the federal government to respond to problems on a national scale.[64]

Such power sharing, or "cooperative federalism," was a mixed blessing for New York State.[65] Congressional representatives of the nation's wealthiest state and leading road builder voiced strong objections to the bill. Only one New York senator and two of the state's thirty representatives supported the act. In contrast, opponents of the bill were vocal. Representative Walter Magee of Syracuse called it "a form of paternalism that ought not to be initiated nor fostered by the federal government." The hostility of Representative Edmund Platt of Poughkeepsie recalled traditional urban-rural tensions. He sarcastically asked that the act be put "on an honest basis," and he had the House clerk read a proposed amendment: "Page 1, Line 1, strike out the word 'agriculture' and the succeeding words to and including 'marketing farm products' and insert 'the manufacture and sale of automobiles.'" Declaring that there have been "more foolish things advocated for the benefit of the farmer than crimes committed in the name of liberty," Platt concluded the bill was no more than "hypocritical bunk."[66]

But New York opposition to the bill had less to do with political rhetoric than with the economics of redistribution within a federal system. The congressional roads appropriation depended on revenue from the recently established federal income tax. As the wealthiest state in the nation, New York State paid in $8.6 million of the $25 million collected annually and earmarked for highway aid. Were Congress to appropriate $25 million for highway improvement, New York would receive only $1.3 million (though still the second largest appropriation, after Texas).[67] Such a formula was not so different from the one New York used to redistribute the costs of road building among its economically diverse counties. But Representative Magee objected that after New York had boldly devoted $100 million to highway improvement, it was hard to fathom that Congress wanted the state to pay for roads in areas of the country as far as 3,000 miles away.[68]

Yet ironically, the Federal-Aid Highway Act of 1916 proved to be the salvation of New York's highway program. The act required that each state match federal appropriations. Unfortunately, New York's use of its $100 million bond issue was restricted, and it had to provide matching funds out of general revenues. New York was faced with a choice: decline the federal assistance (and further subsidize road building elsewhere) or accept it and increase its own highway expenditure beyond what had been agreed upon in the 1912 referendum.[69]

When Congress passed the federal aid road act, Commissioner Duffey was facing a serious shortfall. The year 1916 was the first in which the Highway Commission failed to meet its quota in road construction, building just over half the mileage finished the year before. Much of this had to do with the high price of labor at the time, the largest cost item in any contract. Upstate Cayuga County solved its labor problem by capitalizing on anti-immigrant sentiment. The county kept down costs by building roads itself rather than letting them open to contract. Cayuga's superintendent of highways underbid private contractors who paid competitive wages to immigrant laborers, banking on the attitude of the local native born "who would rather work for two dollars a day among their own people and friends than take a number and work among the Italians for a contractor who pays $2.50 per day."[70]

Measures such as these could not reverse the trend in costs, and the labor situation worsened in 1917. Duffey recommended a decreased appropriation until the price of labor stabilized.[71] After the United States declared war on the Central Powers in April, the legislature made no highway appropriations at all. The wartime emergency sharply reduced the supply of men and materials and limited the availability of transportation services. Highway work ground to a standstill. Completed mileage (primarily projects begun in 1916) totaled about a third of the peak 1915 mileage. No new construction was begun in the wartime year of 1918.[72]

When Duffey surveyed the situation, he concluded that the second $50 million bond issue would not be enough to complete the primary highway system under worsening economic conditions. With increasing maintenance costs and inflated wartime prices, each dollar from the bond issue built fewer and fewer miles. And increasing truck traffic during the war had made a costly demonstration of the perils of low-grade construction. To the surprise of few, the state took the federal money. Early federal appropriations to the state were small (about $250,000 in 1917; $500,000 in 1918), and the federal contribution per mile was capped at $10,000, even though the high-grade roads New York's Highway Commission advocated cost well beyond the $20,000-per-mile roads Congress envisioned. Still, it was enough to help keep the program afloat during the war years.

Thus, the passage of the Federal-Aid Highway Act of 1916, although it introduced a federal component to road building, served largely to cement the subfederal road-building regime that had been emerging over the past decade. With over a decade of experience with large-scale and high-quality road improvement, New York differed from states such as Texas, which, along with fifteen other states, was pressured into creating a state highway department in order to take advantage of federal road-building dollars. The key transformations for New York had less to do with inaugurating a new state-level agency than it did in bolstering the authority of an existing one. This task was accomplished in two ways: most immediately through the injection of new funds, but more importantly by firmly establishing the state Highway Commission as the critical nexus between local and federal authority. New York's state-aid road legislation of 1898 started a political conversation over the appropriate balance between local and state authority; Congress's federal-aid act legitimized the upward shift of political authority that had taken place over the subsequent two decades.

Neglected No Longer: The Highways of Prewar New York

The pause in construction during the war years provides a useful vantage point from which to view the important changes in road-building policy over the course of the preceding decades. After half of a century of passive road policy, New Yorkers began in the final years of the nineteenth century to advocate a new, vigorous system of highway construction, finance, and administration. Vocal interest groups, as well as thousands of local petitioners, called on the state to take an increasingly active role in highway construction after 1898. Voters twice endorsed the expansion of the highway program in 1905 and 1912 referenda, authorizing the expenditure of $100 million, a show of support for new road administration not lost on Old Guard politicians. By the war years, New York State had produced over 6,000 miles of improved highways and had outspent all other states combined by a margin of three to one.

Though the scope of state government's responsibility had been permanently enlarged, it continued to share the burden of public highways with local authorities, and concerns for better engineering and administrative reform still played second fiddle to patronage politics. But rural conservatism and urban bossism were really two aspects of the same waning political culture. Beneath the veneer of their divisions lay congruent assumptions about the importance of limited public expenditures and the values of local government. Despite the growing power of its central state leadership, the party machine's strength rested on patronage and resource distribution at the local level. Like their rural counterparts, cost-conscious urban bosses (for all the charges of public mismanagement) rarely rushed to support the reformers' expansive—and expensive—proposals.

Good Roads reformers, political independents, and engineers challenged this political duality and posed tough questions about the structure of government necessary to provide a modern statewide transportation infrastructure. Though they sometimes misunderstood the values of local government, they argued effectively that local road administration was no longer up to the task. How could New Yorkers reap the benefits of centralized authority and the state's financial power while maintaining local control over their public ways? This question played itself out again on a national scale in the 1916 debate over federal aid. How could New York State justify such redistribution of wealth to other states? Was it any different than asking New York's wealthy towns and counties to support state aid? The compromises reached—the voluntarism infused in New York's early state-aid system and the cooperative, federal-state approach to congressional assistance—reveal just how knotty these problems were.

Technological development accelerated this process of policy reform. Though the Good Roads movement and the big legislative achievements of 1898 and 1905 preceded mass automobile usage, by the war years the motor vehicle's impact on highway politics had greatly increased. Fifty million dollars far exceeded any sum ever spent on highway improvement. No one imagined that twice that amount would fail to secure the primary highway system it was supposed to achieve. Nonetheless, the change in highway policy was more than a functional response to the problem of more cars, delivered in the language of Good Roads progressivism. The automobile alone cannot account for the sweeping political changes that road reform entailed.

Scholars have looked to a wide range of factors in explaining the revitalization of the positive state in the early twentieth century: a burgeoning culture of Progressive reform, a major political realignment, a new emphasis on organization, the institutional-structural changes internal to the governing process, the impact of new technologies, the increasingly complex nature of economic arrangements, the fraying of "island communities."[73] All of these conditions and tendencies were evident in early efforts to rebuild the American system of public roads. But the most powerful legacy of this experience for modern American Political Development lay in the interplay of demands for improved infrastructure, the public-policy-making process, and the larger structures of government. A close analysis of highway policy making, driven by a mix of political concerns and motives, reveals how the handling of new infrastructural demands forced a gradual reassessment and rejection of nineteenth-century policy tools, governing institutions, and political philosophies.

The evolution of highway policy thus offers a unique window on the advent of the modern state. Grand plans for road reform did not appear fully formed. Rather, they emerged through a complex policy-making process that first sought to assimilate new demands into existing political structures. Local governments, tenacious in their embrace of road authority, began to share it only when it became clear that they lacked the administrative and financial resources to achieve systematic, statewide improvement on their own. Similarly, the party machine, once strong enough to bend reform to its patronage needs, eventually recognized the difficulties in applying distributional politics to the rigorous administrative requirements of an integrated highway system. Only when demands for more efficient construction outstripped the capacity of the existing system (and became a political liability for machine politicians) did they prompt profound, structural change.

The locus of road-building authority shifted dramatically in the thirty years before World War I. Once it was vested in individual communities. Now all levels of government—local, state, and federal—actively engaged in the maintenance and development of a state-built network of public roads. National in scope, but state and local in implementation, the building of the American highway system proved to be one of the twentieth century's earliest and toughest infrastructural challenges. In retrospect, America's resilient and adaptive federal democracy appeared adept at addressing this challenge. But at the time, many feared that the deficiencies of the subfederal regime might be as detrimental as nineteenth-century localism. Surely the fraud and mismanagement of the early highway commissions gave little cause for confidence, and highway administrators were harshly criticized. These criticisms, which continued into the 1920s, were delivered in a moral language that cited the individual failings of public men. But, in fact, they reflected a deeper systemic problem: the crisis of a political system struggling to adapt to the new policy demands posed by an extraordinarily challenging and immensely popular state construction program. Into this breach stepped proponents of a new bureaucratic road-building regime, engineer-administrators who were poised to embark on a highway construction boom of unprecedented magnitude.

Highways: State-Centered Bureaucracy and the Elevation of Engineer-Administrators, 1919–1931

Prior to World War I, politicians committed to a subfederal road-building regime shaped highway policy in New York State. Though state legislators had created a state-aid law, abolished the labor system of road taxation, and established a State Highway Commission by 1909, highway policy was still geared toward the service of local interests. County supervisors and town highway commissioners continued to play important roles in directing local road construction. State officials also tended to privilege local interests in highway matters, pursuing pet highway projects in home districts and directing patronage contracts to loyal party members. Federal aid, totaling just $750,000 in its first two years, had had only a minor impact on a state that had committed over $100 million to road building since 1905.

After the war, several related developments combined to shatter these older patterns of governance. The most significant was Governor Alfred E. Smith's (1919–1920, 1923–1928) appointment of an engineer, Colonel Frederick S. Greene, as highway commissioner. Engineers had served on the Highway Commission since its inception, but their authority had always been provisional, operating in the service of—and at the discretion of—the party machine. Smith elevated an engineer to the position of highway commissioner in 1919 and then enhanced his administrative authority in 1923 by creating a more robust Department of Public Works (DPW). These moves reflected his broader ambition to retool New York's governing machinery. A Democrat, Smith had long been hamstrung by the legislature's powerful Republican Old Guard and the sprawling government agencies over which it presided. Bred in patronage but seeking a more effective path to political power, he envisioned a streamlined framework of governance under his own strengthened command.

The old Highway Commission had moved beyond the "negative" investigatory and regulatory work typical of late nineteenth-century public oversight agencies by adding a "positive," constructive dimension to highway governance: innovating policy, building highways. But it remained mired in political partisanship and was plagued by constant changes in leadership. The DPW, by contrast, was designed to emphasize the common engineering problems faced by state construction programs rather than the patronage possibilities of public works. Drawing on broad public regard for the civil engineering profession, the new department promised to end the game of "political football" about which former Highway Commissioner John Carlisle had complained. Legislative opponents continued to resist Smith and Greene's effort to reclassify highway work as an administrative rather than a legislative duty, a move they interpreted as a blatant power grab. But the colonel and the Happy Warrior (Smith) soon overrode this dissent, reassembled a new governing coalition, and presided over an unprecedented highway boom during the 1920s.[1]

Support for this redistribution of political authority from legislators to engineer-administrators came from many areas. Organized highway user groups, such as the New York State Automobile Association and the Motor Truck Association of America, believed Greene and his cohort best able to provide the through routes they desired for intercity travel and short-haul commercial shipping. Real estate developers, especially in downstate counties that catered to Manhattan commuters, also favored this sort of construction. Well-established highway construction firms welcomed the DPW engineers who displaced party politicians as gate-keepers to plum contracts. Finally, other government officials helped to cement the authority of DPW engineer-administrators and their plans to privilege a system of primary highways: federal engineers at the Bureau of Public Roads pressured state engineers to expedite construction on the 7 percent of New York State highways that were dually categorized as part of the U.S. highway system; local officials, too, appreciated the DPW's capacity to redistribute resources, set safety standards, and facilitate traffic.

The state-centered bureaucratic regime that Greene ushered in during the 1920s rested on his capacity to translate the public perception of engineers as "apolitical" into a durable form of political expression. His efforts were bolstered first and foremost by support from Governor Smith, who was better positioned than anyone else in state government to straddle the worlds of machine politics and administrative reform. And he gained backing from the wide range of interest groups who established lasting links to the DPW, unmediated by traditional party organizations.

And yet, while the political authority of Greene and his engineering cohort was no longer provisional, neither was it absolute. Instead, it is best termed "relational": an independent political force, but nonetheless checked by the countervailing authority of state legislators and local officials who sought to offset Greene's centralizing tendencies. For instance, town highway commissioners continued throughout the 1920s to exert discretionary control over state-collected motor vehicle user fees, a system of local aid held in place by dissenting state legislators. And Westchester, a wealthy downstate county, embarked on a countywide parkway system (largely outside of the DPW's purview) that was without parallel in the nation. Thus local politics continued to play a significant role in highway policy, and Greene's department routinely adapted to the state's diverse political circumstances.

Though aspects of the subfederal policy regime persisted through the 1920s, there can be little doubt that Smith and Greene had steered the ship of state onto a new course. By 1931 a state-centered bureaucratic regime was firmly in place. Smith's work at strengthening executive governance and reorganizing the state's administrative apparatus gave newly empowered department heads such as Greene extensive managerial control over state construction. In a parallel development, Greene advanced his own political and professional agenda, one cloaked in the language of technical expertise and dedicated toward the advancement of a bold highway construction program that privileged the interests of organized highway users over communal concerns about road-building costs and unchecked development.

The impact of rising automobile use on highway politics during this period is hard to underestimate, as New York motor vehicle registrations doubled from one million to two million in the five years between 1922 and 1927 (see Figure 3.1). But the new road-building regime was not an automatic response to shifts in technology. Rather, it was politically driven and rooted in changing notions of government during the 1920s. Transportation interest groups, like state highway engineers, were political creatures, defined in relationship to the structures of governance in which they operated.[2] Both benefited from an expanded and reordered system of public ad-

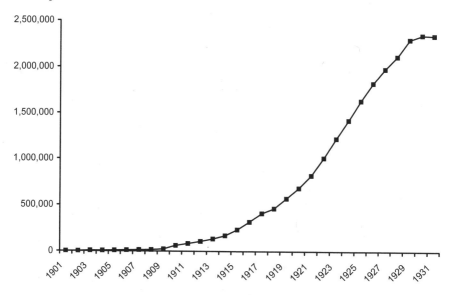

Figure 3.1: New York State Motor Vehicle Registrations, 1901–1931

Source: Compiled from data in William M. Curtiss, *The Development of Highway Administration and Finance in New York,* Department of Agricultural Economics and Farm Management, New York State College of Agriculture (Ithaca, N.Y.: Cornell University, March 1936), 59.

ministration that was available to meet the challenge posed by millions of new cars and drivers. Public services had undergone general growth following the Progressive interest in enlarging the state government's responsibility for health, education, and welfare. Less frequently noted, but just as important, was the subsequent expansion of public infrastructure. This was especially true for highways, which by the mid-1920s constituted the largest public cost to the state after education.[3] These vast sums were in the hands of state engineer-administrators, whom Governor Smith had put at the helm of a new bureaucratic road-building regime, and they moved quickly to secure their political power.

Frederick Stuart Greene, Al Smith, and the Appeal of Professionalized Governance

The creation of a state-centered bureaucratic road-building regime entailed a new style of leadership, one defined by its chief architect's technocratic expertise and professional standing.[4] This leadership came in the figure of Colonel Frederick Stuart Greene, a Virginia-born engineer who had built his first highways on the Western Front during World War I. Greene changed the political tone of the state's highway construction and oversaw a major expansion of its scale and scope. The key figure in the transition away from a subfederal road-building regime, Greene masterfully transformed his public claims to antipartisanship and neutral competence into a new form of political expression. In so doing, he made an end-run around traditional party organizational structures. During his two decades in office, Greene translated his reputation for professional integrity into a bureaucratic policy regime of lasting duration. Under this regime, the Highway Commission (and later the Department of Public Works) oversaw a remarkable expansion of the state's highway infrastructure while simultaneously enshrining the fraternity of civil engineers as a dominant force in state government. As Greene's work progressed, changes rippled outward, broadly affecting New York's system of public finance, administration, and federal/subfederal relations, its living and commercial patterns, the highway construction industry and labor force, and the landscape itself.

Frederick Stuart Greene was born on April 14, 1870, in Warrenton, Virginia. Raised in a war-torn corridor of the upper South, he may be presumed to have witnessed in his youth the steady rebuilding of his Shenandoah homeland. His father, Thomas Tileston Greene, a native Alabamian, held the rank of major during the Civil War and in 1864 served as first assistant secretary of the treasury to the Confederate States of America. Frederick's grandfather was a superintendent at the Virginia Military Institute, the institution from which he graduated with a degree in civil engineering in 1890.

Greene worked as a railway engineer in Georgia before slowly moving up the East Coast: first to Washington, D.C., working on rivers and harbors, and then to New York City, where he found employment as a dock engineer on Long Island Sound. In 1905 he accepted a position at the Waterproofing Company, a Manhattan firm that was active in the construction of the New York City subway and the Pennsylvania Railroad's tunnels under the East and North Rivers. He remained with the company for twelve years, rising to its vice presidency. Greene's talents extended beyond engineering: a prolific short-story writer, he had several pieces published in popular magazines and anthologies, including two in the *Best Short Stories* collections of 1916 and 1917.

In May 1917 American forces were being mobilized for the war, and Greene enlisted with the Army Corps of Engineers at the Plattsburg military camp. A year later he was in France, commanding the road-building efforts of the 77th Division's 302nd Engineers, B Company, during the Oisne, Aisne, and Argonne offensives. He attracted attention by orchestrating the construction of a three-mile railroad that allowed for the conveyance of hundreds of tons of ammunition to the front and the return of hundreds of wounded soldiers of the "Lost Battalion" during the battle of Argonne. After the November Armistice, he fell ill on a long, wet march back from the front and was sent home.[5]

Greene was recuperating in a Fort Dix military hospital when recently elected Governor Alfred E. Smith called on him to take charge of the Highway Commission. At first he balked at the governor's offer, claiming that the chairmanship of the Highway Commission was widely recognized as a political job and that he was not a political man. He considered himself an independent Democrat. The papers called him an "Al Smith Republican." Certainly he was no party regular.

As the story goes, Smith was persistent, explaining that he wanted a road builder rather than someone who would dispense patronage. He had seen the perils of politicized road building during his years in the New York State Legislature. Given Smith's close relationship with the Democratic political machine, he was well positioned to transfer highway authority to Greene while finding other ways to soothe the Tammany tiger. A good (and highly visible) road system, the reform-minded governor believed, would better serve his political needs than would an extensive patronage system. Greene's war record would bolster his public image; his rhetoric of efficiency was sure, in this age of machines, to win applause from the popular press. Greene would have the power to make all appointments—a free hand with which to build the best possible roads for New York. Disarmed by the governor's frankness, the colonel accepted the post and received Smith's unconditional backing over the next decade.[6]

Though Greene and Smith came from wildly different backgrounds (it is hard to imagine two more divergent institutions than the Virginia Military Institute and Tammany Hall), Greene's appointment to a commission renowned for its patronage potential reflected the governor's increasing commitment to administrative reform. The colonel was "a kind of poster boy of integrity in the Smith regime," in the words of Smith biographer Robert Slayton, and it is possible to trace the source of Smith's commitment to a man like Greene back to his early political education.[7]

Al Smith was raised in Manhattan's fourth ward, the old Bowery district that had become synonymous with urban poverty in the United States. His entrance into Democratic politics came in the usual way: a spoils appointment received in exchange for loyal electoral support. But his desire to turn his political career toward municipal reform was forged in the heat of the Triangle Shirtwaist Fire that claimed the lives of 146 sweatshop laborers in 1911. From that point on, Smith was determined to reform the conditions in which New Yorkers lived. Already he had begun to master the governing apparatus. He had grasped the fundamentals of legislative processes during his years as a state assemblyman. He had also learned how to operate the political machine with real finesse under the tutelage of Tammany boss Charles F. Murphy. Murphy presided over the hall's greatest period of stability (1902–1924), largely due to his ability to make strategic alliances with reformers while keeping lower-level political appointments rooted in old patronage arrangements. He taught Smith the political value of working with distinguished men and women who could lay claim to technical expertise or professional integrity. Smith's command of these varied worlds made him a political force of both subtlety and strength. When he was elected governor, he directed his political acumen toward a program of administrative reconstruction that would yield the political authority necessary to pursue his reform campaigns.[8]

A better highway system was one of Smith's goals, and he saw in Greene a man who could be instrumental in the establishment of a new road-building regime. Greene's early years as an engineer in New York City and elsewhere had brought him into contact with private developers, railroad companies, and the political realities of construction. By contrast, his wartime experience with the Corps of Engineers, where exacting standards and clear chains of command were vital, offered an appealing new methodology with which to transform the highly politicized Highway Commission. Greene's experience in industry ensured he would not enter public service naively; his military days would steel him against inevitable legislative assaults. Indeed, it was widely acknowledged that his "army training" resulted in an abrasive relationship with state politicos, who relied on much more fluid dynamics of power.[9] If Smith's vision of administrative reform was certain to put him on a collision course with the Old Guard Republicans in the state legislature, Greene was the man he wanted in the driver's seat.

"A Ditcher Who Became King": Greene and the Highway Commission

Though Smith had taken the unprecedented action of appointing an engineer to head the Highway Commission, Republican opponents in the state legislature still exerted an important check on Colonel Greene's authority. Thus the difficulties of Greene's duties were compounded. On one hand, Greene faced technical challenges in tailoring a road-building program to road conditions that were worsening under increased motor traffic during the 1920s. On the other hand, he faced political challenges as he encountered numerous sites of legislative resistance: over mapping power, the redistribution of funds to localities, and other efforts to keep road-building authority decentralized. Republican legislators and party bosses made Greene's first two years in office taxing ones, culminating in a brief two-year exile when a nationwide wave of resentment against outgoing President Woodrow Wilson cast Democrats (including Governor Smith and his appointees) out of office in 1920. But in time the battle with the Old Guard began to shift in Smith and Greene's favor. Smith's skillful politicking—and a growing sense that there was political utility to having an engineer head the highway department—resulted in a show of reluctant support by formerly intransigent legislators. This was another wedge moment, like the original state aid act of 1898, which opened the way to a new road-building policy regime built around a commitment to the idea that highway planning should be categorized as an administrative, rather than legislative, function.

Though Greene entered public service determined to oppose the machine politicians who had held sway over the Highway Commission since its inception, he was not so much "apolitical" as he was a new kind of political operator. Greene drew his political strength through publicity, through his ability to capitalize on the contrast between machine "grafters" and his own spit-and-polish image of professional integrity. Over time, Greene used these polarities to set new terms of debate: support for centralized road-building authority would emanate from respect for the "rationality" of technical expertise; opposition meant a return to Old Guard Republicanism and greasing the wheels of the party machine. (Tammany Democrats wisely threw their public support to Greene while quietly battling Smith over these same issues.) Though Greene scored some rhetorical victories early on, political ones were harder to come by. Even as the number of motor vehicles climbed to new heights and the engineering challenges inherent in modernizing New York's highway system grew increasingly complex, legislators showed little willingness to regard state road building as merely an administrative issue. Under the workings of the old subfederal regime, infrastructure was simply tied too closely to local politics to render it immune from legislative efforts to control its cost and direction.

Greene was nominated to the post of New York State highway commissioner in March 1919. While his appointment indicated the arrival of a new set of state-centered federal relationships in road-building affairs, resistance to this new policy regime was strong. Two decades of state involvement in highway construction had produced a subfederal regime that drew on state resources but did little to challenge the primacy of local control. This was evident even at Greene's confirmation hearing, which was held up until April. That delay allowed outgoing commissioner Edwin Duffey to make 900 appointments in the maintenance division, a choice area for patronage work. Greene protested that this delay also permitted the outgoing commission to direct new road contracts toward deserving party members. It was no coincidence, he observed, that one of these contracts affected property in which a member of the Senate Finance Committee, the committee responsible for moving Greene's confirmation along, had a personal interest. To make matters worse, this new road paralleled two already improved roads and was built without regard to the facts that much road work was left undone for the county's farming community and that it was not connected with the state highway system. Another new road apparently served a Republican assemblyman's Adirondack hunting lodge.[10]

Whether or not Greene correctly appraised the conditions surrounding his appointment, several things seemed clear to him. State road building remained firmly enmeshed in a system of patronage and partisan politics. And while important through routes had been improved, the state's road-building system would remain hopelessly uncoordinated without a map of proposed routes that met engineering standards. To remedy this situation, Greene pursued several courses of action. He "cleaned house," as all new appointees had in the past, though this time ostensibly in the name of efficiency rather than politics. He initiated surveys for a new state road map, established primary highway construction as a top priority, raised construction standards (building, as he put it, for "yearage," not "mileage"), and increased the building of concrete roads, which were more durable than asphalt ones.

But it was not a propitious time to overhaul the Highway Commission. That body had sunk into a deep state of inactivity during the war. Contractors abandoned current projects, the commission authorized little new construction, and problems stemming from deferred maintenance mounted. Meantime, New York's motor traffic had grown exponentially. Between 1909 and 1919, it increased by 1,879 percent, while horse-drawn traffic dwindled to about a third of its 1909 level. State motor vehicle registrations continued to grow rapidly after the war, more than doubling between 1919 and 1923.[11] And precisely at the time the commission needed them the most, its trained engineering staff began to seek more remunerative positions elsewhere.

The Federal-Aid Highway Act of 1916 required all states to have a centralized state highway department in order to be eligible for assistance. Prior to the act, several states besides New York had established highway departments that satisfied its terms, but sixteen had not: by 1919 every state had one.[12] Experienced highway engineers were scarce (the subject of highway engineering was taught at just a handful of schools). Often other states' highway departments lured away many of New York's most skilled engineers with the promise of higher salaries. New York's Highway Commission could not match its competitors' offers. It suffered a serious outflow of trained civil servants, losing almost a quarter of its staff in 1919 alone.

When Greene reported in early 1920 on his first year in office, he was not optimistic. Most of New York's prewar highways, designed for light motor and horse-drawn traffic, were just fourteen to sixteen feet wide and six to eight inches thick. Steadily increasing traffic placed ever heavier demands on the state's still weak infrastructure. And wartime constraints forced the commission to direct its efforts toward overdue repairs rather than new, high-grade construction.[13]

Managing staff shortages and overburdened highways was a task that sat comfortably within Greene's realm of expertise. Dealing with an intransigent legislature was more challenging. Greene may have been the first engineer to head the highway commission, but that did not mean legislators were ready to adopt his road-building philosophies in their entirety. In fact, he met resistance on many fronts: budgeting, mapping, and local aid. Each of these skirmishes reflected legislators' desires to promote fiscal conservatism and the decentralization of highway policy-making powers. Despite the creation of the state Highway Commission in 1909 and the concentration of road-building authority in Greene's hands, proponents of local control continued to shape road-building policy during the early 1920s.

Greene's doubts about his ability to have a "free hand" in running the Highway Commission were first realized when the Senate Finance Committee slashed Greene's proposed budget. With resources scarce in the midst of a serious postwar depression, he got only half of the $15 million requested appropriation. The high cost of labor and materials further limited the 1920 highway program. Less work could be done in 1920 with $7.5 million than had been the case in 1914, when the state appropriated $3.9 million. And Greene had to hold up new work out of fear that added competition among contractors might further drive up the price of labor.

Former Deputy Highway Commissioner H. Eltinge Breed criticized the legislature's budget cutting as an act of "false economy." "State governments," Breed insisted, "owe more to their citizens in providing satisfactory highways than formerly. Motor transportation is not going to stop." His observation was on point. Automobile registrations had climbed 150 percent since 1915. Of greater significance for highway maintenance costs, heavy commercial truck registrations increased 460 percent in the same period.[14] From Breed's engineering perspective, the great technological change that the automobile had wrought was indisputable; the commission's response, he thought, should be automatic.

But Greene's effort to centralize the planning of new highway construction revealed that not everyone accepted the fact that government's road-building obligations had to be so adjusted. Indeed, there was little consensus on how to divide road-building authority among the Highway Commission, the state legislature, and local governments. Greene wanted the commission's engineers to settle on a permanent map of proposed construction, prioritize routes according to their importance, and proceed without political interference. But Republican Charles Hewitt, the uncompromising chairman of the Senate Finance Committee, opposed Greene's plan to vest map-making powers in the commission. Instead he organized a legislative committee to do the surveying itself. In a related effort to undercut Greene's agenda, Republican Seymour Lowman, chairman of the Senate Committee on Internal Affairs and a strong proponent of local control, pushed through a county aid bill that returned millions of dollars a year to rural districts for local road construction.[15]

Despite legislative resistance to Greene's work, the Highway Commission managed a few notable accomplishments. One construction project in particular stood out: the Storm King highway, which shortened the Newburgh–New York City route by sixteen miles. This project attracted special attention for its daring engineering. Avoiding the roundabout route behind Storm King Mountain required cutting a bench into steep cliffs 400 feet above the Hudson River. Surveyors and excavators had to scale the mountainside or be lowered in baskets. According to one account, laborers (prior to Prohibition) demanded and got a shot of whiskey every hour to stiffen their nerves.[16]

In a less visible but perhaps more significant achievement, Greene diminished patronage control by revamping highway maintenance. Under the original Highway Commission, repair work was performed by the patrol system. Much like the pathmasters responsible for nineteenth-century roads, patrolmen often were recommended by local politicians, and were individually responsible for short stretches of road.[17] Greene replaced this with the foreman and gang system, in which a foreman and several laborers, selected on the recommendation of division engineers, covered a larger area. When the federal government donated a fleet of surplus wartime trucks in

1919, the Highway Commission assigned them to these modernized maintenance crews.[18]

For all this, the Highway Commission still was running in low gear. Matters did not improve when a wave of anti-Wilson revulsion sent Democrats packing in the elections of 1920. With Smith out of the governor's mansion, Republican Nathan Miller made it clear that he wanted his own man in the commissioner's chair, and Greene was forced out of office until his reappointment in 1922. Smith later wrote that Miller, in obeisance to the Republican machine, divvied up patronage positions among the "Big Four" Republican bosses of Albany, Rochester, Westchester County, and Erie County. Boss Fred Greiner of Erie got to select the highway commissioner, and he had Miller tap Herbert S. Sisson, a party regular from the Republican stronghold. Sisson was the state's excise commissioner, a position about to be abolished under former Governor Smith's reorganization plan. Miller called Sisson a "harmonizer"—though what interests Sisson was to bring into harmony was never made clear.

When outgoing Commissioner Greene reported on the commission's progress in early 1921, he sounded another "note of warning" and called for its administration to be put on a sound footing once and for all. The *New York Times* complained that Sisson's appointment meant a return to the old politics, characteristic of the past two decades. "A few years ago, the appointment of a man with no previous knowledge of road building would have occasioned no surprise." Greene, however, had ushered in a new trend in highway administration by promising to replace partisan dealings with the neutral competence of engineers. Miller's decision to appoint Sisson— and the repeated road-building entreaties he fielded from old party bosses— confirmed that that battle was far from over.[19]

Though the Highway Commission reverted back to Republican boss politics during the two years that Greene was out of office, it was impossible to return completely to the old road-building regime, marked by fiscal conservatism and decentralized control. Governor Miller, Commissioner Sisson, and state legislators continued to face thorny challenges in the administering of the highway system. Escalating costs demanded new sources of revenue; the federal aid law required close cooperation with engineers in the Bureau of Public Roads. Greene's departure—and the return of the Highway Commission to patronage politics—did not make these issues disappear.

State legislators confronted this reality when they were faced with the issue of motor vehicle taxation and license fees. Initially these funding mechanisms had stirred little interest. Modest fees had been imposed on Manhattan drivers and statewide commercial vehicles since 1901. New York City residents paid a $2 registration fee, and all New Yorkers paid a motor vehicle tax in proportion to their car's value. Commercial vehicles' fees rose with their weight. None of these fees and taxes, instituted before the takeoff of mass personal and commercial motor vehicle use, generated enough revenue to cover the escalating costs of highway maintenance. Nor did the fees discourage the operation of heavy trucks, a single one of which, at the wrong time of the year, could do (and did) as much as a hundred thousand dollars' worth of road damage.[20]

Legislators faced a conundrum. They had authorized the improvement of the highway system to encourage commerce; now they had to tax commercial activity in order to protect the state's investment. When they met in 1921, senators considered reworking the fee schedule with the aim of taxing heavy trucks off the highways. The *New York Times* worried that the trucking industry might be stunted in its infancy. The "ship-by-truck" movement allowed retailers and farmers to move their goods more cheaply than by short-haul trains. "Progress has to be both regulated and facilitated," it insisted. The truck, "an indispensable element" to the modern economy, was the public's "new ally."

But progress would not pay for itself. With 11,000 miles of state roads and maintenance costs running at $1,000 a mile, New York faced an $11 million price tag to keep its existing roads in good repair in 1921. The state levied a 40 percent increase on cars, a 50 percent increase on buses and trucks less than 3 tons, a 100 percent increase on trucks between 3 and 7½ tons, and a prohibition on trucks over 7½ tons outside Manhattan. To enforce this new rate structure, and to crack down on the practice of overloading, the Highway Commission sent out eight crews of inspectors armed with "loadometers" to weigh loaded trucks across the state. The first dragnet in Westchester produced 178 arrests in two months. And the increased tax rate, combined with a large growth in auto registrations, generated a 75 percent increase in motor vehicle receipts and the unprecedented sum of $9.6 million (though still short of $11 million necessary to cover maintenance charges).[21]

The state had another source of funds at its disposal, though not as rich as motor vehicle user taxes. The federal Bureau of Public Roads (BPR) had been subsidizing state highway construction since 1916, modestly during wartime and more extensively after Congress passed a revised appropriations bill in 1921. Secretary of the Highway Commission I. J. Morris complained that "New York gets only $4,000,000 where it would pay into the fund some

$25,000,000 or $30,000,000."[22] But even if the federal aid program represented a net loss for the state, it was a gain for the Highway Commission, which could count on the earmarked money.

Nonetheless, the BPR's bureaucracy aggravated state-federal relations and rankled New York State engineers. Machine politicians working under Sisson, such as the commission's acting secretary, Jeremiah C. Finch, detested the "inconvenience" of excessive federal reporting requirements and complained that "the 'red tape' got on my nerves."[23] Even the state engineers in the department, who were far more likely to share the BPR officials' mindset, found their materials standards to be "arbitrary" and a poor fit with New York's extensive road-building experience. Guy H. Miller, the federal district engineer for the region, had acknowledged that New York was "the leader in road matters" and hoped for its cooperation in leading "backward states into line and [in showing] them the light in highway improvement." But when the BPR tried to impose national standards on New York construction, state engineers balked. One of them shelved a BPR recommendation, noting tersely: "Our years of experience indicate that our method and the requirements of our specifications are satisfactory."[24]

Tension grew between state and federal administrators as New York struggled to accommodate new federal procedures after decades of working alone. One source of contention was the size of the primary highway system. In 1921 New York State's system constituted about 14 percent of the state's 80,000 miles of roads. BPR regulations stipulated that federal aid could only be applied to 7 percent of a state's overall road system: just half of New York's primary highways. New York maintained its larger state highway system, but did so with what Sisson called the "considerable hardship" of choosing which half to improve with federal aid, and which without.

Another problem: New York's Hewitt Act of 1921, which designated its primary highway system, required that construction proceed equitably among the counties. But federal aid projects, which favored interstate and inter-county routes over the even distribution of construction, already were under way. In order to comply with the Hewitt Act, many of these federal aid contracts had to be revised or withdrawn: a lengthy procedure laden with more bureaucratic red tape.[25]

By 1922 the Highway Commission's work showed signs of falling off, slumping under the heavy weight of an agency that had been plunged, in Greene's words, "back into the mire of Republican politics." Even Secretary Finch was forced to inform Governor Miller that there had been a "radical reduction in miles of pavement laid."[26] When Al Smith returned to the campaign trail that year, time and again he used the work of the Highway Commission under Greene as a testament to the potential of technocratic expertise and administrative reform. He staunchly criticized Governor Miller's appointment of Sisson as an effort by "the Old Guard . . . to take care of the faithful."[27] Indeed, New York's Republican Party had gradually given up the reform spirit of the early days of the Good Roads movement. Gone were the Republican senators—William Richardson, William Armstrong, and S. Percy Hooker—who shaped early road legislation and its administration. With the ascendancy of the Democratic Party and the devolution of the Republican Party into what one historian of New York politics called an "unimaginative standpattism" came a transfer of the mantle of road reform to a new coalition of progressives, professional engineers, and pragmatic political bosses.[28]

This group helped reelect Smith in 1922, and his decision to again nominate Greene reignited partisan wrangling over patronage and finance. Greene had been at odds with Republican state senators since his first confirmation hearing in 1919. During the intervening years he had publicly accused the Finance Committee of deliberately holding up his appointment so that several hundred road maintenance positions could be handed to loyal Republican foot soldiers. Clashes over highway finance, route maps, and patronage marred his two years in office, and Greene had not, during the Miller administration, suffered quietly.[29]

Greene had learned the value of publicity as a form of political expression during his first term as highway commissioner. In May 1922 he merged his political and authorial aspirations by recounting his struggle with state legislators in "Highways and Highwaymen," an anonymously published short story that appeared in the *Saturday Evening Post*. This morality tale, which was certain to arouse strong Republican opposition at his renomination hearings, was presented in stark terms as a conflict between the old and the new politics of road building. Greene's semifictionalized story depicted two warring parties: the "Property" Party (Republicans) and the "Poverty" Party (Democrats). The Property Party, the "highwaymen" of Greene's title, dispensed political favors while the Poverty Party governor sought efficient, economical reforms. Greene had nothing but contempt for one Property politician—apparently modeled after Senate minority leader Clayton R. Lusk—who committed "vicious" acts of bald corruption only to return to "his home town [where] he talks loudly of red-blooded Americans and on Sundays he goes to church."[30]

The ensuing partisan rancor testified to the high stakes for both sides.

Lusk was incensed when he discovered that Greene had authored the piece. A master of political dramatics, he complained that some of the senators to whom Greene referred were still sitting in the Senate and demanded that he testify under oath about the charges in his story. Greene arrived at the packed Senate nomination hearing in February 1923 to be greeted by great applause; Lusk derided the enthusiastic supporters, claiming that they were likely prospective job holders.

Greene readily admitted authorship of the article and testified to the veracity of his claims. Lusk argued that its description of Republican political machinations was biased, that such abuses were a thing of the past, and that Greene had raised old specters of corruption only to take credit for exorcising them. Recognizing that Lusk had to be appeased, and perhaps sensing that his story might have been drawn a little too boldly for dramatic effect, Greene backed down somewhat. He confessed that the article in its original form had been more evenhanded; the *Saturday Evening Post* had severely edited it and even changed the title from "An Amateur Job Holder" to the more sinister "Highways and Highwaymen." Nonetheless, Greene stood by his accusations and Lusk by his response. The only dissenter in the vote to send Greene's confirmation to the Senate floor and one of three senators to vote against his renomination, Lusk derided Greene's article as "untrue and defamatory."[31]

The cause of Lusk's opposition is clear. Seymour Lowman, who had pushed through the local aid law in 1920, had other reasons for opposing Greene. The highway department in peak season employed over 5,000 workers, and he regretted seeing "this army pass from Republican to Democratic control."[32] But this kind of hostility to Greene was growing increasingly exceptional. For the most part the legislature (which remained under Republican domination because of a skewed system of apportionment) sanctioned developing state highway policy.

Over the years, rural (and mostly Republican) New Yorkers, once the strongest opponents to increased spending, came to recognize the benefits of better transportation. They could see visible changes that resulted from improvements to their road system: rural free delivery, more efficient delivery of produce, access to centralized school districts, all-season roads. They also were ensured that they would receive paved miles out of proportion to their population, since no roads could be built in the cities or incorporated villages that were home to most New Yorkers. Still, rural communities were wary of the loss of local control and watchful of increased expenditures; occasionally they still complained of the difficulty of maneuvering horse traffic on new roads designed for motor vehicles. But so long as they were ensured a strong measure of oversight by a Republican-controlled legislature, their endorsement of the roads program appeared justified.[33]

When the Senate confirmed Greene by a vote of 31–3, Greene paid little heed to the conditional nature of his support and instead interpreted this development as a clear mandate for his vision of technocratic road administration. His readiness to dismantle patronage politics was evident after his return to the Highway Commission. He quickly restored the standards of engineering expertise that had characterized his earlier administration. He abolished several posts at the state office that he deemed "soft political berths." And he reinstituted the gang and foreman system of maintenance.

Road maintenance, new construction, future planning: these formed the core responsibilities of the Highway Commission, and Greene faced an uphill battle in transforming the agency's politics from one based on localism and the distribution of patronage to one based on the politics of expertise and bureaucratic autonomy. State road building had served Democratic and Republican machines over the past two decades in a time-honored exchange of political contributions, public works employment, and local improvements. Greene's effort to classify highway planning, construction, and maintenance as purely administrative functions, subject to bureaucratic practices and technocratic reasoning, represented a profound threat to old political relationships. And while legislators began to see the utility of keeping Greene as head of the Highway Commission, they were less than willing to cede him the powers that he so desperately wanted.

Maintenance was the first front on which Greene advanced. Sisson had allowed that department to revert to the old patrol system, whereby local political organizations rather than state engineers selected road crew workers. One critic thought patrolmen constituted "the largest political machinery any [Government] Body could work up . . . as they were always sitting beside the roadways drawing their salary for votes they could bring on Election Day" while the roads went "to pieces for lack of attention." Greene publicized the fact that under Sisson's control the commission had such a loose hand in employment decisions that it distributed official state appointment forms without names on them so that local political figures could fill them in.[34]

Greene also set out to eliminate the role of partisan politics in new highway construction. Sisson, he charged, had authorized too many new road projects, an old political tactic. New, highly visible construction indicated the sitting party's interest in a community, and it could be counted on to generate support at the polls. But heedlessly initiating new public works projects was impractical from both a financial and an engineering standpoint. Too many contracts drew on an already overtaxed labor pool, further inflating construction costs. And half-finished roadways obstructed traffic, created more road hazards, and increased costs each season they lay dormant.[35]

Sisson's policy of overletting contracts was compounded by a continuing labor shortage, which still dogged the commission as it entered the 1923 summer building season. Greene was forced to hold back $16 million in new highway contracts, about two-thirds of the total highway spending for the year, as the cost of labor rose. Contractors refused to submit bids during the labor crisis, even after the commission raised its cost estimates. Greene blamed "absurd immigration laws" that left the state with a dearth of "pick and shovel" workers. According to the *New York Times*, an abundant number of manual laborers had worked for 30 cents an hour just three years ago; now, even with wages of 60 cents an hour, there were too few immigrant laborers who would consent to work the roads.[36]

When work got under way, Greene wanted construction targeted at a highway system built according to the preferences of engineers. This meant removing the state road map once and for all from legislative control, and putting it in the service of perceived traffic needs. Greene had proposed a new map based on traffic census data during his first term in 1919. Not surprisingly, the legislature objected to the commission's usurpation of its deliberative power. Republican Senator Charles Hewitt instead formed a committee to create its own map, which the legislature adopted in 1921. Greene revised and resubmitted his map in 1923, only to have legislators further redraw routes in accordance with their own desires.

Greene's state highway map reflected an emerging traffic service vision of highway planning. It favored intercity traffic, regional through routes, and main commercial arteries. Of course, the analysis of origin-destination studies that underpinned the new map inevitably privileged this primary highway system at the expense of roads that served isolated communities. Thus Greene's map—and his politics of expertise—was entirely at odds with the intentions of state legislators who had their own constituencies to consider.

One might expect a Tammany graduate such as Governor Al Smith to have a great deal of sympathy for legislators who wanted to take care of their own. But when Greene asked Smith to reject the redrawn map, he did so with a forcefully worded veto. Like Greene, Smith had used the highway issue to advance his broader project of administrative reform. In his veto message, he declared "there can be no doubt" that "the engineers were brushed aside and that political influences dictated the location of certain roads on that map." The amended map was evidence "of the evil of political legislative tinkering with the road maps of this State." Smith justified his veto on the ground that legislative and administrative duties were fundamentally separate:

> The laying out of roads is an administrative duty. We have a corps of competent engineers who have been in the employ of the State for a great many years, and if the Legislature would leave them alone these engineers would give us a connected and a comprehensive State highway system that would be designed to meet the needs of the greatest number of our people; but as long as politics and legislative tinkering continue to dictate by a law to the Highway Department, we must expect the same chaos and disorder that grew out of the performance of this year's Legislature.[37]

It would be hard to find a clearer defense of Smith's campaign for administrative reform. Certainly there were political overtones to this: any transfer of authority from the legislature (which was predominantly Republican due to the overrepresentation of rural upstate districts) to a Democratic executive was hard not to view as a partisan assault. But Smith had more in mind than a variation on the old theme of patronage politics. Rather, he saw the division of legislative and administrative tasks as integral to his broader plan to retool the machinery of state government along what he termed "scientific" and "business-like" lines.[38]

Smith had grown to abhor the weak structure of government that had emerged out of a Jacksonian distrust of centralized authority and had been enshrined in the state constitution of 1846. This constitution had undercut the first transportation revolution in New York, devolving road-building authority back to local governments. It also created a political environment that spawned what Smith's biographer Robert Slayton termed "local chaos": a host of decentralized administrative offices that reported to the legislature without any meaningful executive oversight or interdepartmental communication. Under this system, which lasted into Smith's administration, the Republican-dominated legislature had control of 187 separate agencies, each with a secretaryship that offered a prime patronage appointment and each authorized to submit individual budget requests directly to the legislature. Smith thought this was folly, and he dedicated his time as governor to pressuring the legislature to adopt a system of governance that allowed him—and a cabinet of nineteen department heads—to directly manage state agencies and to have comprehensive budgeting authority.[39]

As a hard-nosed politician and a disciple of Tammany boss Charles Murphy, Smith's political education had led him to an awareness of the utility of expertise in ensuring political stability. As Smith understood the situation, the "old-time system" had worked when state expenditures were small and administrative duties minor. But the tremendous growth in state services that had occurred over the past decade changed all that. Economist Edwin Seligman noted that the cost of New York State government had grown by "leaps and bounds" between 1910 and 1919. And while inflation had contributed to this increase, its primary source was a general expansion of public services growing out of the Progressive interest in enlarging the state government's responsibility for education, welfare, health and, importantly, highways (which by the mid-1920s comprised the largest public cost to the state after education).

Under these conditions, the old machinery of governance had become a political liability. This was true for the citizens of New York, who suffered under its inefficiencies, but it was also the case for Smith himself, who had twice achieved the state's highest office and found that it was vested with only limited authority. Smith astutely recognized that he could wield political power far more effectively from an enhanced executive position. At the same time, he knew that it would be difficult for Republican opposition in the legislature to mount a persuasive defense of a system of governance that had primarily evolved through the slow accretion of bureaucratic sediment.

Smith's sweeping 1922 gubernatorial victory, in which he tallied more votes than any previous candidate for governor, gave him the political capital he needed to translate his populist appeal and status as a political insider into a mandate for administrative reform. He resuscitated an old plan for government reorganization that had gone down in defeat under the Republican leadership of Elihu Root and Governor Charles Evans Hughes during the 1915 Constitutional Convention. The 1915 reorganization amendments were victims of New York City Democrats' opposition to strengthened Republican control, and persistent anxieties (even among upstate Republicans) about centralized authority. But Smith was persuasive, appealing directly to the people and cajoling voters to support the plan, attacking Old Guard legislators in their efforts to protect the sinecures of office, even tapping

Hughes—an unassailable Republican and longtime proponent of reform—
to draft the final amendatory language.[40]

Smith doggedly pursued his restructuring program during the mid-
1920s, but it was a protracted process that did not meet with reward until
voters finally gave their support to the majority of amendments in 1926 by
a tremendous margin of 60 percent. Meantime, he made preliminary advances by consolidating the state's ten separate engineering agencies into
a single Department of Public Works (DPW). In the spring of 1923 the
legislature approved a consolidated DPW, including the former highway,
canal, and public building departments.[41] Greene supported the governor's
plan to break up and reassemble a governing coalition along reformist lines.
It meshed nicely with his own interest in achieving what political scientist
Daniel Carpenter has termed "bureaucratic autonomy," that is, the capacity
for public administrators to pursue their own agendas, even when they run
contrary to the wishes of elected officials.[42] Greene's years with the Highway Commission schooled him on how to capitalize on his own professional esteem as a means of securing policies that were at odds with prevailing legislative interests. His successes to this point had been small scale;
the expansion of the DPW's mandate held out the possibility of real triumph.

The convergence of Greene's pursuit of greater bureaucratic autonomy
and Smith's desire for administrative reorganization further cemented the
bond between the engineer and the old ward boss. But the particulars of
Greene's new role had to be worked out. The new office of the superintendent of Public Works carried a salary of $12,000, not large enough to attract
someone of the highest caliber. Smith hoped to induce General George W.
Goethals, the former administrator of the Panama Canal project, to take the
position, but he refused. Greene himself was left in a difficult spot: he could
accept the position of superintendent and move out of direct contact with
state highway work, or decline the job, take a pay cut, and serve as a "mere
bureau head" in an enlarged department.[43]

After months of fruitless searching by the Smith administration, Greene
agreed to take the top position. The *New York Times* praised Smith for choosing someone who would provide "the public a sense of security to know that
such a man is in charge of its estate." Reflecting on Greene's reputation and
the challenge he faced in overseeing the state's highways and waterways,
the editors thought he called to mind "a Greek poem written some two
thousand years ago which tells of a ditcher who became a king. If Colonel

Greene can make the ditch which extends across the Empire state of the fullest benefit for the people of this state . . . he will deserve to be remembered as long as that ancient ditcher has been."[44]

Under Greene's leadership and with Smith's unswerving support, the DPW established a form of state governance new in style and substance. It gained new clout in dealing with the state legislature, and it took a stronger role in dictating the terms of state-local and state-federal relationships. In the ensuing years, Greene revolutionized not only highway construction standards but finance methods, civil service requirements, and, most important, the status of engineers within the state administration. Through his persistence, a focus on regional infrastructure, as distinct from the distributional politics of building or the politics of localism, gradually emerged.

"Hellbent for Destruction"? Greene and the Consolidated DPW

The legislative flare-up over mapmaking powers had produced a crisis over the nature of road-building authority. Was it predominantly a legislative or an administrative duty? Should the state's highway map reflect the desires of legislators' constituents, or engineers' standard of enhanced traffic service? Governor Smith's veto and his establishment of a consolidated DPW suggested that he favored an administrative-executive model. But this governing framework was of questionable political legitimacy—even fellow Democratic politicos wondered whether Smith could long support his managerial paradigm. To gain the critical backing that Smith and Greene needed, they cultivated alliances with organizations that had strong interests in road building. And they worked to frame transportation policy choices in ways that privileged a traffic management vision. In this way, they forged a common ground—and a new basis of political support—around those who shared their planning-engineering mindset.

Superintendent Greene headed a consolidated organization that included the Bureaus of Canals and Public Buildings as well as Highways. But he remained most deeply involved with the Highway Bureau. For Greene and Smith, the new centralized authority that came along with the DPW was a considerable victory over the localism that had dominated earlier highway administration. Nevertheless, the new department continued to challenge entrenched political interests, leaving both men open to attacks not just by the usual Republican opponents, but from Democrats as well.

Putting the governor's consolidated public works plan into action meant the sudden elimination of 160 positions, as well as a reduction of the amount of rented office space, the size of the automobile fleet, and, above all, maintenance and operations costs. These moves trimmed the DPW's budget by more than $850,000. But Greene's blow for efficiency and economy threatened his and Smith's positions within the Democratic Party, which suffered the loss of many party-delegated posts: a "thinning out" of "fattening ducks." A political poster at an Albany press dinner reflected the Democrats' belief that Greene and Governor Smith could not long survive without paying their party dues. The image depicted Colonel Greene on a motorcycle speeding toward an open drawbridge, with Governor Smith clinging to Greene from behind, his hair streaming in the wind. The caption read "Hellbent for Destruction."[45]

Despite these occasional complaints over patronage, Greene enjoyed general legislative support. His strongest defense came from downstate Democrats who, whether Tammany loyalists or urban liberal progressives, were firmly in the Smith camp. Senator James J. Walker of New York City (later to be its mayor) praised him as one of the best engineers in the state. Brooklyn Senator William L. Love predicted that Greene's antipartisan methods might one day propel him to the governor's office: "He may be Greene," Love remarked, "but he is not as green as he looks." New York City Senator Nathan Straus Jr. believed that the state owed Greene "a great debt of gratitude" for his fine service and acknowledged that if he "scorns to play politics, he does know how to build roads."

The true test of Greene's acceptance was the unanimous vote cast in his favor after his appointment hearing for superintendent of Public Works, demonstrating a strong new faith in engineering expertise. In an editorial titled "Their Votes Anyhow Were Right," the *New York Times* chalked up predictable Republican criticism to political expediency. The Republicans' negative speeches put the responsibility for the department's actions on the Democrats; yet "the [yea] votes will allow the Republicans to claim some of the glory if Colonel Greene's administration . . . proves as successful as everybody with any knowledge of his qualifications confidently expects it to be."[46]

Despite the legislature's general endorsement of Greene, many of its members remained committed to the precepts of local control and patronage politics; they were not entirely willing to give Greene the free hand he wished. Last-minute amendments to the legislature's proposed highway map attached 792 miles of projected roadways, over half of which were parallel to existing highways, serving limited populations, or, as Governor Smith put it, "dead-end roads [that] start all right . . . but end no place." The cost of the new highways totaled over $40 million. As he had in 1923, Smith once again felt compelled—at Greene's urging—to veto the proposed map.

Smith and Greene had hoped to avoid a repeat performance by forming a committee of Good Roads advocates to review the new map. The committee reached out to a wide variety of interests likely to be more concerned with good roads than in "the politics of their location": the County Superintendents' Association, the New York State Automobile Association, the New York State Motor Federation, the Motor Truck Association of America, the New York State Association of Real Estate Boards, the Farm Bureau, the New York State Grange, and the Dairymen's League. Smith had close connections to a number of these interest groups already. He had worked with the Dairymen's League to settle the milk strike of 1919, and he had served for two years as president of the United States Trucking Company when he had failed to get reelected in the gubernatorial election of 1920. All these groups favored a "traffic-service" version of highway planning that would lower transportation costs and improve accessibility.

Greene and Smith cultivated the support of local public officials, transportation organizations, agricultural interests, and real estate developers in order to gain newfound legitimacy for their transportation policy agendas. These groups formed a new basis of political support in place of the old party organizations. Under the old regime, party bosses had successfully turned transportation policy into a means of serving local interests through employment opportunities and pet projects. Under the new regime, engineers and interest groups found mutual support for policies that promised to reduce traffic congestion, lower transportation costs, and raise property values—all unmediated by the party machine. With this new backing, Smith felt "unable to bring myself into a frame of mind where I should, by my approval of this bill, give countenance to the legislative log-rolling that succeeds in changing these maps after they leave the properly constituted engineering department and have the unanimous approval of those interested in a comprehensive State development of our highway system."[47]

Smith and Greene's persistence paid off. In the spring of 1925, when the legislature again convened, there was little fuss over the highway bill. After two successive vetoes, and six years after Greene had first pushed for a comprehensive highway plan, the 1925 highway map bill passed unchanged through the legislature. The system the DPW map proposed was significantly larger than had been envisioned in the aftermath of World War I. Totaling nearly 14,000 miles of roads, the new map built on a state highway system that had grown 20 percent since it was last formulated in the 1921

Hewitt Map. Reflecting the desires of the new political bloc of roads advocates, much of the new mileage was dedicated to providing through routes across the state, often bypassing major cities so as to allow truck traffic to traverse the state free of traffic congestion. Some of this mileage presumably included legislators' preferred highway projects as well. Of more lasting importance, though, was the fact that they had endorsed the DPW as the ultimate arbiter of route mapping.[48]

The triumph of an administrative conception of highway planning indicated the beginning of a process by which transportation policy choices were framed in a way that privileged engineers and organized highway users and their traffic management vision over the more localistic desires of state legislators and their constituents. As an engineer, Greene had never had any patience for the old political arrangements. Smith, who came of political age during the reign of the machine politician, also grew to reject their ways as an impediment to his vision of public service through administrative reform. By the mid-1920s these men had won more than rhetorical battles over the terms of the road-building debate; they had forged a new coalition of highway advocates that would back the greatest road-building boom in the state's history.

The Road Builders

Greene's vision of highway planning—and the traffic-servicing, state-centered, bureaucratic road-building regime that underpinned it—ultimately prevailed over the more locally oriented politics that had thwarted him since 1919. But beneath the political acrimony that characterized the previous six years there lurked a more significant problem that Greene and the DPW would confront over the remainder of the decade. By 1925, even as two-thirds of the state highway system had been improved to some degree, motor traffic—along with demands for new and reconstructed highways—was rapidly increasing. The DPW emerged from its political battles with the legislature only to face a two-front war over the building of the roads themselves. Increased traffic demanded both a major rebuilding program *and* the completion of entirely new heavy-duty highways. Failure to adequately reconstruct existing roads meant sacrificing the state's current investment and allowing its roadways to decay into an unsafe condition. Yet failure to proceed quickly with new construction would result in even greater congestion in and around the state's urban centers.[49]

New sources of revenue and new administrative tools were needed to finance and control an extensive program of highway construction and maintenance. This realization prompted Governor Smith to shift the state from a system of debt financing to one based on user fees. It was an important transition, marking the beginning of a roads program pegged directly to motor vehicle use. The highways' growing dependence on state-collected registration fees and, later, on a state gasoline tax, encouraged citizens to rethink the relationships among government, motorists, and public infrastructure. In the past they relied on local governments to tend to the roads; now they looked to a state agency. Moreover, they began to think of user fees not as general taxes, but as special payments reserved for better roads. In a subsequent transformation, DPW engineers—in an effort to protect the vast amounts at stake and to concentrate their own authority—exercised ever tighter control over local highway expenditure and administration.

These developments advanced three important shifts that had been under way for over two decades: an upward shift in governance from local to state authorities; a lateral shift in administrative powers from the New York State Legislature to the Department of Public Works; and a conceptual shift in state-citizen relations, from one rooted in local political forces to one based on the expectation that individual motorists could finance an improved highway system by channeling user fees directly into the hands of competent engineers. Though all these moves generated political resistance, the road-building boom of the 1920s was accomplished through the steady expansion of engineers' claims to political legitimacy. Once state legislators accepted Smith and Greene's argument that road building was an administrative rather than a legislative task, they grew increasingly willing to sign away remaining vestiges of town road-building authority in exchange for access to new highway revenues.

Highway construction was not the only state budget item to balloon in this period. The cost of state government more than doubled under Al Smith, rising from $90 million when he first took office in 1919 to $228 million when he left a decade later. Much of this increase reflected Smith's commitment to expanding social services: hospitals, schools, housing, parks, and other infrastructure. New roads formed a significant part of this new public investment, and though state spending rose across the board, highways constituted the second-largest state budget item by the mid-1920s. This transformation went hand in hand with changes in the method of financing public improvements. Highways were purchased through extensive bond issues until 1922. The state then turned to a "pay-as-you-go" strategy (see Table 3.1). Highways had a short lifespan compared to other elements of public infrastructure: prewar highways had been built and rebuilt several

TABLE 3.1. Sources of New York State Finances for New Road Construction (in $ millions)

Year	Total State Expenditures for New Road Construction …	Financed from Bonds	Financed from Current Revenues
1921	10.5	5.1	5.4
1922	15.3	6.7	8.6
1923	11.2	3.9	7.3
1924	10.6	2.7	7.9
1925	12.6	1.3	11.2
1926	12.4	0.7	11.7
1927	14.3	0.4	13.9
1928	19.0	0.4	18.5

Source: New York Times, June 14, 1930.

times during the life of the bonds. Under the Smith administration, they were to be constructed and maintained out of current revenues. Bond issues would be reserved for more permanent improvements such as hospitals and public office buildings.[50]

Under these conditions, the annual highway budget, about $25 million in the early 1920s, more than doubled during the decade. These figures prompted a reaction by fiscal conservatives who worried that the state's increased program would force local governments (because of cost sharing provisions) to overextend their constructive capacity. Republican Senator Seabury C. Mastick accused the Smith administration of adding to the burden of the state's taxpayers. "Primarily responsible for the existing situation are the roads and the schools. I am, of course, heartily in favor of good schools and good roads. Just as many good schools and good roads as taxpayers can build and maintain without too much sacrifice." Smith justified the increased expenditure in his 1928 annual message to the legislature: "The state does not grudge the money spent on its highways any more than [that] which it spends on schools or public health or the promotion of agriculture. It is part of the balanced program to promote the general business of the State and the highways are the arteries through which the life blood of the State must flow." With the highway program so essential, the state began looking for new resources to tap.[51]

State motor vehicle licensing fees provided a steadily growing flow of revenue. Fears of a registration "saturation point" proved to be unfounded. Though the licensing fee schedule remained substantially unchanged, the increase in New York motor vehicle registrations from 819,000 in 1921 to

2,000,000 in 1927 more than tripled public revenue from $9.6 million to over $33 million.[52] But given the mounting reconstruction costs, these fees were not enough. The New York State Tax Commission debated a gasoline tax as early as 1921; DPW officials began to lobby for it by 1925. Oregon had established the nation's first one-cent gas tax in 1919, and the practice quickly spread. By January 1, 1929, the one-cent tax had been replaced by taxes from two to six cents per gallon across the country.

These tax hikes, which were largely favored by organized highway users across the country, financed a nationwide highway boom that increased the mileage of surfaced highways from 387,000 to 694,000 miles. By the end of the decade, an estimated $400 million to $450 million would be collected nationwide, up from $5 million in 1921, ballooning state highway budgets from $430 million to $1.3 billion. New York, which still relied on license and registration fees (as well as general tax revenues and federal aid) to finance its own highway construction, remained the only state in the nation to have failed to adopt the gasoline tax, despite the fact that early estimates suggested it might reap $18 million per year on a two-cent per gallon gas tax. This figure was quickly revised upward.[53]

By the end of the decade, the state's Tax Commission, Real Estate Board, Dairymen's League, farming organizations, and chambers of commerce had joined the DPW in support of the levy as a proportional tax on road use, and one that would offset high property taxes. But motorists, truckers, auto dealers, and bus operators stood steadfastly against it, arguing that roads were public goods, properly financed through general revenue. Organized highway users in New York thus distinguished themselves from similar groups in other states, which had lobbied hard for the gas tax in order to support highway improvement programs elsewhere in the nation. New York had some of the highest license and registration fees in the nation, however, and highway users there refused to support a fuel tax unless these fees were lowered.

The gas tax received its strongest support from the new governor, Democrat Franklin D. Roosevelt, who entered office in 1929 and included the tax as a funding mechanism for his rural relief program. As Smith's chosen successor, Roosevelt continued his highway program and kept Greene in office. For the first time in the history of New York State, a change in governor did not mean a change in highway engineering leadership. Despite "temperamental" opposition from both Democrats and Republicans for his intransigent resistance to political patronage, Greene "had earned a sound reputation as a road builder," and Roosevelt felt he would be able "to sleep comfortably at night with the full assurance that in the Public Works Department 100 cents on the dollar is being honestly and usefully expended."[54]

Though Greene kept a free administrative hand under Roosevelt, the new governor affected the character of the DPW's work. FDR always lent Greene his public support, but he was somewhat less comfortable than Smith had been in yielding complete bureaucratic autonomy to the superintendent. On several occasions, Roosevelt chastised Greene for publicly criticizing administrative policy and requested that all dissent be discussed internally before going to the press. And at other times, Roosevelt pressured the department to advance small road projects as political favors. But on the whole, FDR was a staunch advocate of the state highway program, as he had been since his days as a state senator and as chair of the Taconic State Parkway Commission. When he moved into the governor's office he demanded that Greene send him a large sheet with all the state's construction projects. It was to be hung in his office and updated monthly, providing the governor with "some visible demonstration of how fast each project is going on." Throughout his administration, and indeed throughout his political career, FDR remained devoted to road building. His strong advocacy of public works, centralized planning, and rural assistance—all hallmarks of the later New Deal—influenced the development of New York State's highways in the late 1920s and early 1930s.[55]

The gas tax was the keystone of Roosevelt's rural relief program. The DPW's policy of concentrating on high traffic areas had neglected New York's rural secondary road system. And the traditional cost-sharing mechanisms, originally designed to preserve local control, were now a disservice to the state's poorest communities, left untouched by the decade's construction boom. Roosevelt recommended that the state pick up a larger share of the road-building burden in order to equalize construction. To do this required more money, so Roosevelt proposed pushing the costs onto highway users by enacting a two-cent gas tax. His Farm Relief Commission, headed by Henry Morgenthau Jr., recommended that towns be relieved of their $50 per mile maintenance charge and counties of their 35 percent contribution to highway and bridge construction, that the counties' share of grade-crossing eliminations should be further reduced, and that gas tax revenues should be redistributed to help the neediest counties.[56]

Roosevelt had difficulty pushing his 1929 policy agenda through the legislature but was successful in enacting the gasoline tax. The fuel levy won over Republican legislators as part of a broader effort to balance the state's budget and appeal to upstate Republican voters through rural tax relief programs. In so doing, FDR and state legislators rejected highway users' argument that roads were public goods to be financed through general revenue. Indeed, Roosevelt even pledged in a "gentlemen's agreement" not to direct these new funds toward nonhighway purposes. Though organized highway users' rhetoric was surely self-serving, the passage of the tax in order to defray the escalating costs of state government was an endorsement of the idea that roads should be supported by user fees. This development tended to mute the public nature of the roads and encouraged organized highway user groups (and everyday motorists) to think of themselves as consumers and the roads as private goods.

In its final version, half of the expected gas tax receipts—$13 million of $26 million—went into the state's coffers. A quarter was refunded to the counties. Twenty percent (a projected $5.2 million) went to upstate counties on the basis of existing dirt-road mileage—a good indicator of rural need. Five percent went to New York City. In return, the towns were relieved of their maintenance costs and the counties of their highway construction and grade-crossing elimination charges. Bridge construction still fell on the counties, since no appropriation bill was passed.[57]

Roosevelt's 1930 program offered real benefits to New York State's farmers, who had not shared in the preceding decade's prosperity and who were now hard hit by economic depression. He emphasized, as he had in 1929, the importance of assisting rural communities skipped by the previous decade's frenzied construction. "Every farm," Roosevelt declared, "should have a hard-surfaced road to market." He promised greater state aid for dirt-road construction on farm-to-market roads, for rural bridges, and for snow removal. Poorer towns had much to gain from Roosevelt's efforts to equalize state assistance: wealthy Rye, in Westchester County, was getting $1,500 per mile in matching state aid, while the least affluent towns received as little as $25 per mile. Under Roosevelt's new program, a $4 million appropriation would quadruple minimum aid to $100 per mile.[58]

Upstate communities eagerly supported Roosevelt's effort to "get the farmer out of the mud." They must have recognized that slogan as the one used to propel the Good Roads campaign decades earlier—with little real result for farmers, then the movement's alleged chief beneficiary. Now, a generation later, Roosevelt put that goal back at the top of the building agenda. One roads advocate, though, thought that Roosevelt's plan did not go far enough. William Pierrepont White of Utica, a longtime highway promoter who had been writing treatises for the Good Roads movement when Roosevelt was still a Harvard undergraduate, appealed to the legislature for a

$100 million bond issue so that the state might reconstruct 15,000 miles of farm-to-market roads. According to one report, 7 million acres of New York land had access to improved roads, while 23.5 million acres—and the rural residents who lived there—were still bound by mud. White and the Mohawk Valley Towns Association (MVTA) wanted to improve the "farm roads which have waited twenty-five years to have the previous $100 million bond issues expended on the main highways accommodating pleasure-seekers, tourists, and trucks."[59]

But the appeal for more bonds fell on deaf ears. Smith had moved the state, over the course of the past decade, to a pay-as-you-go approach to impermanent improvements such as highways. Nevertheless, the DPW was in agreement with White and the MVTA as to the extent of the problem. It would take $125 million to improve the approximately 50,000 miles of secondary and tertiary roads, more than half the total mileage in the state. Meanwhile, the DPW sought to develop an inexpensive yet lasting way to improve dirt roads that handled only light traffic. The high-grade concrete highways for high-volume traffic cost between $35,000 and $70,000 a mile. The DPW hoped to spend just $7,000 a mile on the new farm roads, using local materials. Enabling legislation passed in 1930 allowed the department to divert up to $100,000 of its maintenance budget to construct experimental third-class roads in each highway district.[60]

Well-documented as the rural road problem was, there remained little hope for the ten-year, $125 million program that the MVTA advocated. Under current law, only about $3 million was allocated each year to help towns construct and maintain their dirt roads. The DPW's highways bureau claimed that it was "not within the province of this division to work out the method of financing this cost" and put the onus on the state to devise some system of support. Its only criterion was that the money be spent by the counties and not the 933 town superintendents of highways.[61]

Along with "getting the farmer out of the mud," concern over the ineffectiveness of local road administration—so central to the previous generation of highway policy makers—picked up with renewed vigor during the Roosevelt administration. The governor's assistance, it seems, would come with a cost. In exchange for greater state responsibility for highways, local road officials would have to further sacrifice their already eroded road-building authority. By 1930, Roosevelt noted, state aid to local governments had risen to over $10 million a year for road work, but there was little evidence to show that it was being spent wisely. "The counties are governed under the same form, the same offices, and the same business methods as were established under the Duke of York in 1688," declared Roosevelt. "Most things have improved since then. Local government has not."

His primary concern was the problem posed by autonomous local officials such as the town road superintendent. This official, he observed, has "a considerable local independence" and "a considerable amount of money to spend each year." But it is "difficult to determine where his road-work leaves off and his distribution of petty patronage begins." One town official illegally contracted with himself to provide his own trucks, machinery, and team for local road work.[62]

Greene and Highway Bureau Chief Arthur Brandt were in agreement with Roosevelt's assessment of the town highway superintendents and supported the governor's quest for greater centralization in highway affairs. Brandt pleaded with the legislature in 1928 to place town and county aid under greater state supervision. He wanted to abolish the elective position of the town superintendent of highways. But, he conceded, that development was "a long way off."[63] At the very least he thought that the state's money ought to be dispensed by the counties rather than the towns. Brandt dwelled on the benefits of centralized administration: "The supervision by the state Superintendent of Public Works of fifty-seven county superintendents can be much more effectively carried out than can the supervision of 933 town superintendents." And the county engineer, unlike the town superintendent, was appointed from the civil service rolls.[64]

Revisions to the county aid law in 1929 revealed the degree to which the new road-building regime produced political winners and losers. Under the system established in 1921, the state's funds filtered down to the town superintendents, who constructed roads with the approval of the county board of supervisors. In practice, this meant that elected town superintendents decided when and where new county roads would be constructed. There was little regional or even in-county coordination, and short stretches of road might remain under construction for many years. To further complicate things, when a new superintendent was elected, the road program changed with him. The new law channeled both state aid and motor vehicle revenues into newly created state aid funds run by the counties. Expenditures were restricted to the construction and maintenance of highways on the county road maps, approved by both the town board of supervisors and the superintendent of Public Works. Contracts already under way would be completed before new projects were authorized.[65]

Despite the belief of Roosevelt, Greene, and Brandt that localism in road affairs was doing more harm than good, town highways remained outside of state coordination. Reporting was so spotty that the DPW could not precisely determine where and how the yearly $4 million of state assistance and $15 million in town tax receipts were spent. But what it did know brought little comfort. Some towns listed roads on which no work had ever been done as "improved." Many continued to construct new roads without the capacity to maintain them in the future. Others simply lacked the equipment and know-how to construct lasting roadways, and the state had no easy means by which to disseminate information to 933 separate bodies.[66]

During the early 1930s Greene and Brandt argued that town highways should be brought under DPW and county supervision. As they envisioned it, the town road system would become "a secondary part of the county road system . . . a preliminary step in the division of the road system into two general classes, the state and the county systems." Noticeably absent from this vision was the elected town superintendent. The several hundred million dollars the DPW recommended for improving these rural roads "should be under the supervision of men trained for that type of work."[67]

By 1931 centralizers like Greene and Brandt were able to complain about the absence of engineering capacity at the local level, and they had placed all but the state's dirt roads under the purview of their professional standards. They were also able to push for technocratic expertise within the DPW itself. During his tenure, Greene moved hundreds of positions out of the hands of political bosses and into the ranks of the civil service. In 1925, after successfully shifting the department from the patronage-based patrol system to the department-controlled gang-and-foreman system, he went a step further, putting almost 700 road patrol foremen on the civil service rolls. He declared that he would "put a stop to the pulling and hauling for jobs under political protection in this department." The Civil Service Reform Association praised Greene's move, the largest shift of state workers to a competitive basis since the adoption of the merit-based civil service system.[68]

As the state's maintenance force expanded to about 5,000 men, Greene continued to demand that these be trained workers rather than political appointees. During his tenure, almost the entire Department of Public Works came under the civil service. Only the extreme top and bottom of the department could be freely hired and fired: the highway bureau chief, his two deputies, and two secretaries on one end; the "pick and shovel men" on the other. Hundreds of engineers, inspectors, and foremen had to pass competitive examinations, a political move that helped Greene forge a department that could be controlled and sustained by his own professional ranks.

To some degree, this effort to remove road building from the province of local government had already been accomplished in the minds of New Yorkers. The experience of decades of road work—hard-surfaced roads, state maintenance forces, inevitable detours—impressed upon residents the idea that state agencies had a legitimate role in crafting transportation infrastructure. Moreover, they felt that it was the state, and no longer their communities, that owed them quality highways in exchange for the ongoing collection of state registration fees and fuel taxes. In a personal note to FDR's secretary, Greene commented that lately "a lot of people are writing the Governor relative to the condition of dirt roads in their towns." He dismissed their grumbling, deriding the complainants as those "who have not brains enough to understand that when frost comes out of the ground in the spring of the year, a dirt road is going to be bad and can't be anything else." But the volume of the complaints directed to the governor (rather than to local officials) reflected a deep transformation in the political order, one that had removed one of the most basic functions of governance from the localities and placed it within the domain of state government.[69]

By the end of the 1920s the politicized style of road building, firmly rooted in local government institutions, was on the defensive. Greene's DPW had pushed with increasing force during the decade for greater centralized authority in road building. New York's town governments had gradually allowed local control to slip away in the years prior to World War I. They did this in exchange for increased resources and out of a growing commitment on the part of the public to raise the standard of all New York's highways. But state policies favored through routes (the basis of the new road system) to the neglect of the secondary rural roads that served local needs. This meant that rural roads needed an even greater infusion of funds to bring them up to the new standards set by the DPW.

Unfortunately for rural New Yorkers, they were unlikely to receive the support to which they felt entitled. DPW engineers' antipathy toward town superintendents of highways and Governor Smith's efforts to move road work out of debt financing left rural roads more apt to remain mismanaged and underfinanced. New York's early policy choice to favor the funding of intercity routes, a policy seconded by both organized highway users' interests and the federal roads program's emphasis on intercity and interstate highways, was compounded by subsequent shifts in highway finance and administration. Along with highway planning policy, these changes in financial and administrative policy helped to bring about broad changes in the locus of public authority. In the process of funding and administering an improved system of public roads, Greene and other officials further concen-

trated their road-building powers, a move accomplished by the steady efforts to redefine road-building authority as fundamentally an administrative
rather than a legislative or a local task.

Local Ways: Road Building in a Diverse State

Though the expansion of administrative capacity at the state level entailed
diminished local control, the "local" never vanished entirely. Indeed its persistence serves as an important reminder of the continuing significance of
subfederal power during the twentieth century. Residents of New York's
communities had mixed responses to the expanding highway program of
the late 1920s, ranging from enthusiastic anticipation to outright hostility.
Greene and the DPW, in conjunction with regional park and parkway coun-
cils, sought to set down a modern transportation infrastructure throughout
the Empire State. But the sheer scale of this public works project made its
impact on individual communities difficult, if not impossible, to predict. For
all the DPW engineers' expertise, many aspects of highway-related development remained beyond their control, or outside the limits of their traffic-
service vision.[70] New roads reshaped living and commercial patterns in
countless ways, altering social and physical landscapes and presenting communities with new quandaries over how to plan for future growth.

These issues would affect the course of highway development throughout
the twentieth century. But in the 1920s, state and county governments were
primarily concerned with providing more and better roads; controlling the
impact of a car culture would come later. Suburban Westchester, situated
just north of the nation's premier metropolis, was the first county in the
country to fully embrace modern highway building, in the form of a regional
parkway system. Given its location and its large number of wealthy residents,
Westchester was uniquely positioned to take a leadership role in highway
construction and in adapting to its new imperatives.

Like Westchester's, Long Island's road-building experience was shaped
by its proximity to Manhattan. But differences in initial development, the
control of rapid growth, and the exercise of public leadership combined
to make Long Island's development a far more disruptive transformation.
Whereas Westchester had long encouraged transportation initiatives that
opened the county to suburban development, Long Island's "island" culture, rural economy, and exclusive social order offered strong resistance to
highway development.

Elsewhere in the state, where New York City's traffic demands did not
dominate highway planning, the DPW took a stronger lead in implement-

ing a highway system of uniform standards attuned to the needs of the state's general economic expansion. Compared to downstate parkways, upstate road construction tended to be less sensitive to regional interests, town officials, and community protests. Facing limited countervailing power in upstate localities, the DPW imposed systematic statewide improvements. In this way the state tackled a problem that local governments lacked the resources to do. But it did so in a way that paid less attention to local concerns regarding the effects of development. This legacy would have profound consequences for more than future highway policy. Ultimately, the failure to develop a bureaucratic regime that could reconcile conflicting technocratic and democratic demands constituted a critical weakness in the twentieth-century political order. As the following sketches of highway development in Westchester, Long Island, and upstate New York demonstrate, the authority of local actors and state-level engineer-administrators could intersect in a variety of ways.

WESTCHESTER

Westchester County's experience with road building during the 1920s constitutes an exceptional case in which a locality took a key leadership role with the development of a massive system of parkways. The Bronx River Parkway, contemplated as early as 1904 and constructed between 1913 and 1923, is generally acknowledged to be the first modern limited-access freeway. An outgrowth of the Bronx River reclamation project, Bronx River Park was a response to the high level of pollution in the river flowing past the borough's Botanical Gardens and the Zoological Society. Wealthy supporters, concerned about their local treasures, petitioned the legislature for assistance in cleaning up the area and eventually received its support for the development of a riverbank park and a recreational parkway running its length. Two of the three members who served on the Bronx Parkway Commission represented New York City, and one was from Westchester County, an acknowledgment that the parkway would have an impact beyond the city's northern periphery.[71]

Land rather than traffic management was at the heart of the Bronx River project. The commission secured over a thousand riverside acres, dredged the river, and landscaped the grounds. The parkway, which ran down the center of the elongated park, was four lanes wide, with the flow of traffic separated in part by a grassy median. Its limited-access nature was designed not so much to facilitate traffic as to provide entry to the area and to preserve its natural beauty. To the same end, commercial vehicles were excluded.

The parkway's winding curves reflected its origins in landscape design. As Herman W. Merkel, the German landscape architect responsible for the future Westchester parkway system, put it: "All around us in our cities we have straight lines and sharp angles. In our parks and parkways we need release from them. . . . After all, the natural rather than the artificial is our first love and we are getting back to it." Designed as a "recreational route," the Bronx River Parkway was based on the transverse drives that crossed Frederick Law Olmstead's Central Park, providing new traffic routes but in a decidedly leisurely setting. While innovative in construction, it was backward-looking in its reliance on nineteenth-century pastoral design. This decision had serious consequences when planners modeled the new thoroughfares surrounding Manhattan on the Bronx River Parkway's contours.[72]

The number of New York motor vehicle registrations increased nearly tenfold during the course of the parkway's construction. As it neared completion in 1923, Westchester County officials recognized that they needed more than just the Bronx River Parkway to handle traffic coming in and out of New York City. The Boston Post Road, a three-mile stretch of which ran through Rye, carried the heaviest traffic in the state: 50,000 vehicles a day by 1925. Westchester faced a real estate development problem as well. As a premier northern suburb and metropolitan conduit, Westchester property values climbed sharply throughout the decade. County officials worried that the region would be overdeveloped and lose its open spaces.

To manage these problems, the county established the Westchester County Parks Commission in 1923. Modeled on the Bronx River Parkway Commission, it too emphasized traffic facilitation within the context of land preservation. Composed of eminent citizens serving without pay, the commission met to plan a countywide system of parks and parkways dedicated to the "recreational, aesthetic, and ecological goals of the conservation movement."[73]

Within two years the commission prepared an impressive building program following its Bronx River Parkway predecessor's "road-field-and-stream policy." Making use of the area's natural endowments, county officials planned to add no fewer than seven north-south parkways, including ones along Saw Mill River, Sprain Brook, Hutchinson River, Mamaroneck River, Croton River, Hudson River, and Long Island Sound. To ease east-west traffic, the commission proposed the Cross-County Parkway, which cut across Westchester's southern border and intersected four of the proposed parkways.[74]

The county provided most of the financing for the parkway's land acquisition and construction, but it received continuous aid from the state. Governor Smith had expressed concern about New York State's parkland during his first administration and commissioned a study on the matter in 1920. In his second administration he focused on the need for a comprehensive program and pushed for a large appropriation in 1923. That year several regional park commissions joined a unified State Council of Parks; in the following year voters ratified a large park bond issue.

By 1927 Westchester had spent some $47 million and built 140 miles of parkways through 16,000 acres of parkland. To coordinate this massive project, larger than any other program of its kind in the nation, the county linked the half-dozen separate agencies responsible for regional road construction, including the state's Department of Public Works, the County Parks Commission, the County Engineer's Office, and several municipal departments of engineering.[75]

The parkway mentality, rooted in the aesthetics of landscape design rather than highway engineering, at first thrived under this new cooperative arrangement. The county residents who made up the original commission—men and women of wealth and taste—preserved their pastoral vision of parks and parkways through the rapid development of the 1920s. Fearing over-commercialization, the county denied motorists' demands for gas stations on the parkways. In part this fear was fiscal: as the areas surrounding the parks developed, land values rose and further land acquisition became more difficult. But beyond this lay the deeply held belief that the public could not be trusted to protect the natural beauty restored by the Park Commission. A 1930 report of the Regional Plan of New York and Its Environs blamed "public indifference" for the "desecration" of parkway roadsides. "People have a craving for nature," RPA officials asserted, "but when they get access to it, are inclined to destroy it."[76]

Despite efforts to control development, the massive parkway program encouraged unprecedented—and difficult to manage—growth. In 1927 Westchester issued more residential building permits than any other county in the nation. The city of Yonkers ranked seventh in the nation for building permits. Only four *states* (New York, Illinois, California, and New Jersey) issued more home building permits than Westchester *County*. In the first quarter of 1928 Westchester residential building was double that of all the major upstate cities (Albany, Buffalo, Rochester, Syracuse, Schenectady, Troy, and Utica) combined. And the county boasted more golf, shore, and country clubs than any other in the nation. Put simply, Westchester had become the nation's emblematic automobile suburb. As local real estate values doubled and tripled (even after the national real estate market began to decline), *New York Times* reporter Waldo Walker optimistically concluded that "Westchester has turned the threat of the gasoline engine into a leverage for community development."[77]

Thus, even as the road system began to take on its modern shape, Westchester's experience with parkway construction demonstrated that it remained tied to local politics and community needs. These developments had important consequences for future highway development. As highway engineers gradually integrated the parkway system into a larger statewide highway network, the county's role as parkway developer seemed increasingly anachronistic. When Westchester faced the double burden of mounting through traffic and heavy parkway debt during the Great Depression, the county sought relief from its encumbrance. But in the prosperous 1920s, Westchester's pioneering parkway program—and its record for producing social and economic growth—was one that other counties hoped to emulate.

LONG ISLAND

On the surface, Long Island and Westchester underwent similar transformations in the 1920s: a system of parks and parkways was rapidly conceived and implemented, while real estate values shot up accordingly. But unlike Westchester residents, Long Islanders displayed great resistance to parkway construction. Wealthy corporate magnates whose estates spotted the island's pristine stretches of shoreline or sat atop baronial hills, fishermen who worked the South Bay, farmers who labored on the wooded and rocky land that occupied much of the island's interior: few of these people (rich or poor) relished the idea of the urban masses pouring forth from the great metropolis at the west end of the island. An antiquated transportation infrastructure could be endured if it helped maintain a separate way of island living. Property owners who had a vested interest in maintaining their estates and their island lifestyle effectively stalled parkway development for years. Breaking the logjam of their resistance was not easy. It required a parks advocate with single-minded tenacity, self-assurance, and brass. That figure was Robert Moses.

Moses, who first served under Al Smith on the post–World War I Reconstruction Commission, had chaired the Long Island State Parks Commission since its creation in 1924. Beginning with a 200-acre area on Fire Island, Moses's commission accumulated 8,000 acres and over 100 miles of parkways by 1927, setting off the greatest real estate boom in the island's history. Construction began on the border between Queens and Nassau counties, where urban boulevards with an aggregate pavement width of 700 feet dumped their traffic into narrow streets totaling less than 150 feet. Governor Smith argued that "conditions of chaos would clearly develop" in western Long Island, as Manhattan and Queens continued their urban building program. "It is not unreasonable," he concluded, "that the entire future development of Nassau County and ultimately of Suffolk, and the preservation and orderly growth of communities, will be vitally affected by the way in which this particular traffic problem is handled."[78]

Smith's awareness of the problem did not translate into any comprehensive planning agenda. Construction moved apace, and by the end of the 1920s Moses and the Long Island State Park Commission, in cooperation with the DPW, had made substantial progress. The Southern State Parkway was nearly complete, as were the construction and widening of other important main thoroughfares: Merrick Road, Montauk Highway, Jericho Turnpike, Sunrise Highway (formerly Pipeline Boulevard, until an image-conscious Chamber of Commerce renamed it), and Conduit Boulevard (which, at $1.4 million for 16 miles was the costliest highway contract the DPW had ever let). Moses's parks had opened along the south shore, and the Jones Beach Causeway, Wantagh Parkway, and others now opened once-inaccessible shores to the overcrowded city. But with no effective state planning apparatus, a citizenry diverse in wealth, geography, and vision was unable to offer directed input into Long Island's transportation development.[79]

The state faced its greatest opposition over the construction of the Northern State Parkway, which was originally routed through some of the wealthiest estates on the island's "Gold Coast." Numerous "vigilance" committees fought to preserve the integrity of their private forests, meadows, and vast, rolling lawns. Wealthy Long Islanders including financier Otto Kahn managed to deflect the trajectory of the parkway to an eleven-mile detour southward around Wheatley Hills through Cold Spring Harbor farmland. Farming families there, with neither the wealth nor influence of their northern neighbors, had their land cut in two. Moses could not shape the north shore of the island as he had hoped. His vision of parks lining the meadows and beaches along Long Island Sound collapsed under the weight of wealthy communities' opposition.[80]

Unlike the north shore barons, real estate developers were unapologetically enthusiastic about the coming of the parkways. Local public officials were the next converts, as they realized that they could gain some control over who would profit from construction and development in exchange for dropping their resistance to the parkway plan.[81] Parkway and highway construction boosted real estate values along the new south shore routes. Large private estates were sold off and subdivided. Springing up in their place were inns and country clubs designed to meet the needs of the new wealth on the island. Soon after the Sunrise Highway opened up with a 300-car motor parade, a Miss Sunrise beauty contest, and a speech by Lieutenant Governor Herbert Lehman, one real estate developer predicted that it would "not be long before every bit of available frontage on the Sunrise Highway will be subdivided." Notably, smaller suburban homes were built to house the influx of fleeing ex-urbanites. Apartment complexes replaced single-family homes. And along with these new residences came a wealth of service structures: community centers, places of worship, schools, businesses.[82]

Local officials did manage to exert some manner of control over the coming of highways. As in Westchester County, new zoning laws were passed to preserve the natural-beauty aesthetic of Long Island's parkways. Cadman H. Frederick, the real estate mogul behind much of the island's south shore development, was concerned about what might happen after "the influx of the [metropolitan] crowd." He praised local government ordinances that prohibited "the motley aggregation of 'hot-dog' stands, service stations, garages, cheap bungalows, stores, restaurants, and other things that would not harmonize with the park environment." He warned against "cheap construction for mercantile purposes and untoward residential construction," which would yield congestion by "vehicles stopping here and there for a ginger pop, a sandwich or what not, the same as they do on Sunrise Highway or any other general traffic route." But along nonparkway land, development was harder to control. In as early as 1928 the *New York Times* concluded that what had taken place on Long Island was nothing short of a "great transformation."[83]

The rapid deployment of public road improvement programs in Long Island, as in Westchester County, triggered a great shakeup in the construction of social space. The upheaval of traditional Long Island country life—both agrarian and aristocratic—opened the way for the sort of suburbanization that would take off in the 1940s. Appropriately enough it was in Rockville Center, situated between the Southern State Parkway and the Sunrise Highway, that Abraham Levitt and his sons, the construction family responsible for the postwar suburban archetype Levittown, began work in 1929.[84]

UPSTATE NEW YORK

The proximity of downstate counties to New York City meant that local officials were the first to feel the pressure of addressing the impact of motor traffic. County planners in Westchester embraced this opportunity for the development of new transportation infrastructure, building a system of parks and parkways that was without parallel in the United States. Long Islanders accepted the influx of parkways with greater reluctance, eventually yielding to the wishes of powerful Parks Commissioner Robert Moses and the demands of eager real estate developers.

Upstate communities followed a third path. Here the DPW played the dominant role in shaping patterns of highway improvement. Regional park organizations played important roles, too, as did officials in prosperous Erie County. But for the most part the DPW faced limited countervailing power from local officials living in less-well-off upstate counties. They had only limited success in modifying the plans of DPW engineers, who, by the end of the 1920s, had begun to implement their emerging view of highways as integral to regional rather than community use, and servicing general rather than local commerce.

Highway and parkway development in upstate New York moved at an erratic pace, dependent on the idiosyncrasies of state and local public administration, community interest and wealth, and the priorities of the DPW. Since the acquisition of rights-of-way had always been a local responsibility, the wealth of downstate Nassau, Suffolk, and Westchester counties had hastened the construction of state roads. State funding was also crucial to quick progress. Without it, local projects could drag on interminably while land values along the route steadily rose. Thus regional parkway plans outside the downstate counties—funded in part out of the DPW budget and in part from state parks appropriations—developed unevenly.

Franklin D. Roosevelt, while chair of the Taconic State Park Commission, complained that his Hudson Valley parkways were being pushed aside to further Moses' work on Long Island. Moses had drawn up the laws creating the unified State Council of Parks, and then arranged to have himself appointed chairman with full budget drafting powers. His funding requests disapproved by the Moses-dominated Council of Parks, Roosevelt accused Moses in 1928 of playing "fast and loose with the Taconic State Park Commission." This conflict cemented the bad feelings between the two, and though Al Smith personally discouraged Roosevelt from resigning in protest, the Taconic Park and Parkway system remained sidelined.[85]

Moses's control over the state park system could help regional development as well as hinder it. Along with Nassau County, the Republican strong-hold of Erie County was the only other county to be singled out in the late 1920s for special emergency appropriations running into the millions of dollars for parkways, outer loops, and arterial highways. The maneuver served to forge an alliance between powerful Republican legislators, Moses, and proponents of Long Island's development. As governor, Franklin Roose-velt also acknowledged the political usefulness of special highway appropria-tions, resisting a proposal by Superintendent of Public Works Frederick S. Greene to merge Moses's Nassau County money into the general highway budget. The greater Buffalo area highway network offered local political op-portunities as well, in providing profitable contracts for loyal party mem-bers. A graft investigation that the local district attorney feared would lead to the board of supervisors bogged down Erie County road construction as late as 1930.[86]

While new parkways and boulevards relieved traffic on the urban pe-riphery of New York City and Buffalo, smaller centers of population in up-state New York had traffic problems as well. A 1924 survey of suburban plan-ning revealed that eleven of twenty-six upstate cities were dissatisfied with "main thoroughfares outside the city limits." They complained of inade-quate, narrow, and unimproved highways, and a lack of coordination with city roads.

For years political considerations had determined highway development, with construction spread broadly across the state. Not until the early 1920s did the DPW prioritize high-grade roads on the primary system. But even these roads were no longer up to specifications by 1930. As of 1919 the maximum width on state highways was 16 feet, and many of them had been constructed with inferior water-bound macadam. In the late 1920s the DPW raised construction standards for all main roads to include a 27-foot-wide high-grade base. In order to reclaim the 10,000 miles of roads that Deputy Highway Commissioner David Noonan described as being in "very bad shape," the DPW embarked on a major reconstruction program, con-centrating on the "L"-shaped route connecting New York City, Albany, and Buffalo.[87]

Acknowledging the uneven development of the state's transportation in-frastructure, DPW engineers took over two important new jobs: building and maintaining bridges and eliminating grade crossings. In so doing, it helped communities across the state cope with the challenges of growing automobile use. Prior to 1926, local governments were responsible for all bridges more than five feet in length. As traffic increased and DPW officials responded with their road-widening program, hundreds of bridges—some of them tagged as "death traps"—were deemed dangerously inadequate. A statewide survey condemned 198 bridges and found 514 more to be "unsafe." Under pressure to assume greater responsibility for bridge safety, the legislature authorized a $17 million bond issue for a four-year, 1,191-bridge reconstruction program.[88]

Even more dangerous were railroad grade crossings: places where train tracks and highways intersected on the same plane, or "at grade." The rapid proliferation of automobiles made these intersections especially dangerous. The Twentieth Century Limited's dramatic 1923 grade crossing collision with a stalled automobile in Forsyth, New York, prompted Al Smith to push for a $300 million bond issue to make the 4,000 dangerous New York crossings safer. In the record-setting year of 1924, a total of 835 grade-crossing accidents killed 190 people and injured 561 more—an increase of more than 21 percent over 1923 that prompted the state legislature to adopt Smith's proposal. As with bridges, safety concerns (and highly publicized accidents) served to link infrastructure and the public welfare in such a way that increased reliance on the DPW engineers' expertise.[89]

Grade-crossing accidents were the most vivid examples of two competing modes of transportation vying for control of overland routes. A less lethal (but in the long run more significant) instance was the competition between railroad operators and truckers over commercial shipping. Bureau of Public Roads Chief Thomas MacDonald insisted that trucks were a complementary rather than a competitive means of transport. MacDonald argued that trucks could more efficiently move the short-haul traffic that was costly for railroads and that was increasing along with the expansion of cities and residential suburbs. Railroad executives, who were forced to close down many unprofitable lines in the 1920s, found this logic unpersuasive. Nonetheless, engineer-administrators like MacDonald and Greene pursued a road-building agenda that favored the improvement of short-haul truck routes. In exchange, trucking organizations cooperated with efforts to limit truck size, ensure the use of wide tires, and crack down on overloading—all moves that would lower highway maintenance costs for the DPW.[90]

Demands for traffic facilitation enhanced the growing synergy between organized highway users and road officials and added to the DPW's institutional clout. This impulse could be seen in the construction of bypass highways, which were built in order to free the flow of general statewide commerce rather than aid a particular locality. Chief among this new construction was the Empire State Turnpike, a truck route from Albany to Buffalo paralleling the Mohawk Valley Highway but avoiding intermediate cities. Begun in 1928, the new 138-mile route detoured around every city and all but a few villages. Surveying got under way in 1929 for new routes that would avoid other major centers of population. The department predicted that belt-line roads would have to be constructed around "practically every city and congested village in the state whenever they are on main line routes." Captain Arthur W. Brandt, bureau chief of the Division of Highways, reported in 1930 that "radical changes in road building policy" were being implemented to relieve statewide traffic congestion.[91]

These radical changes had radical consequences for the state's economic development. As Brandt observed, "Engineers and State officials now look upon road construction from the standpoint of its value to commerce in general, as well as to local communities." The construction of bypass highways meant that lower transportation costs vied with community planning for top priority. The *New York Times* noted that early highways were laid out much like railroads in that they were "designed to pick up as many centres of population as possible. If any public official had suggested building one around a village or a town instead of through it, he would have been set down as a lunatic." But the "modern trend of engineering experience and regional planning" put more weight on lower motor vehicle costs than on the imperatives of local businesses. Harold M. Lewis, executive engineer of the Regional Plan of New York and Its Environs, agreed. "The day is gone," he observed, "when businessmen believe that their profits are directly proportional to the number of vehicles which pass their doors."[92]

The new through, belt, and bypass highways' impact on suburban development cannot be underestimated. Marginal land, distant from town centers but close to new highway junctions, became a more valuable part of the New York landscape. The state's rural nonfarming communities experienced the greatest population growth during the 1920s.[93] As a 1932 Cornell University Agricultural Experiment Station study concluded, "The suburban trend . . . was the most distinctive trend in New York's population during the decade 1920 to 1930." What brought this about was "the rapid development of hard-surfaced roads throughout the state, the widespread ownership of automobiles, cheapness of land and living outside of city areas, [and] the advantages of living in the open country."[94]

New circumferential routes, designed to relieve downtown congestion and free up general traffic, encouraged this growth, even when it ran counter to the wishes of local communities. As Superintendent Frederick S. Greene explained in 1930, his staff now obeyed "two cardinal principles in design:

1. The road should be located along the shortest practical route between two given points. 2. Centers of population should be by-passed wherever possible." This strategy was not always politically acceptable. But "in spite of the opposition which frequently arises, and is often violent, to one or both of these policies," he declared, "the Department will strictly adhere to and fight for these principles during the coming years."[95]

By 1931 engineers' traffic-service vision dominated highway planning and construction. Local and state officials and politicians had chosen highway routes in the past; now they yielded to the engineers. Likewise, whereas landscape architects once sculpted the early parkways as extensions of urban park projects, now technical specifications trumped aesthetics. In 1930 the world's first public parkway, which wound its way effortlessly through the Bronx River's natural banks, was retooled for modern highway use to eliminate the sinuous curves (now termed "dangerous") that had been its most prominent feature.[96]

The ascent of engineers in state highway policy opened the way to these important changes. Centralized public administration offered the possibility of statewide planning and the redistribution of scarce public resources, positive developments by most accounts. But it also displaced traditional forums for community control over public ways, especially when it came to the defining feature of the twentieth-century social landscape: suburban growth. Once designed to tap directly into centers of population, highways now avoided them and their traffic congestion. These bypass roads were significant not only for what they steered clear of but for their impact on the new terrain they traversed. They brought with them the beginnings of a new suburbia. They were not extensions of the street-car suburbs that surrounded urban cores in the late nineteenth and early twentieth centuries, but a new style of suburban development: a decentralized, peripheral growth that would fully bloom in the 1940s.[97] And though the key players in upstate highway development differed from those in Westchester County and Long Island, the result was the same: the implementation of a traffic-service vision of highway planning, broad suburban development, and ripe conditions for the further extension of engineers' bureaucratic authority.

The DPW and the Construction Industry

Mitigating safety concerns, facilitating traffic, and developing suburbia were three critical areas in which Greene's department excelled. And while his work occasionally generated local resistance, it helped him to forge new alliances with organized prohighway advocates such as motorists, truckers, and real estate developers. Greene required this sort of coalition building in order to generate the political support for his traffic-service vision of highway planning and the state bureaucracy that underpinned it. Another critical element of this coalition was the highway construction industry, which quickly adapted to a road-building regime defined more by administrative autonomy than partisan politics.

Under the old subfederal regime, highway contractors exchanged party loyalty for remunerative construction contracts. During the early years of state highway work, it was not uncommon to find Tammany assemblymen, such as Bart Dunn of the 18th Assembly District, heading up highway contracting outfits like the Dunbar Company. (Though Dunn's profiteering was so outrageous that he ended up serving a prison sentence on Blackwell's Island.) The more common arrangement involved kick-backs from favored contractors on the order of 5 percent, collected downstate by Tammany men or upstate by the notorious Democratic "bag man" Everett Fowler.[98]

As Greene moved the system of highway planning and construction out of legislative hands and under his own administrative watch, highway contractors had to find new ways to relate to state agencies. The DPW's increased reliance on private contractors to execute its plans quickened this evolution and, in a sense, called the modern highway construction firm into being. Turn-of-the-century road work was accomplished by pick-and-shovel and horse-drawn, bottom-dump wagons. Contractors required two things: a party "heeler" (public officials willing to arrange for a contract) and cheap and plentiful immigrant labor. By the 1920s, both of these were in short supply.[99]

Without the traditional patronage arrangements to facilitate the distribution of road-building contracts, a group of well-established New York highway contractors in 1926 organized a chapter of the Associated General Contractors of America (AGC) in order to protect their position within the industry.[100] The trade organization worried about new entrants to the field, hastened by "liberal" bankers who encouraged "the country cross roads store keeper [into] forming a partnership with some road foreman, and taking an excursion into the [road building] business."[101]

These "fly-by-night" contractors troubled the AGC, and its leadership asked the state to license contractors to protect its privileged position within the industry. Though the DPW refused to take on the bureaucratic nightmare of licensing a remarkably dispersed industry, it shared the AGC's interest in discouraging new entrants who too frequently failed to complete their contracts—or pay their laborers.[102] This reasoning was behind Greene's successful 1919 effort to get the state legislature to allow the DPW to self-insure on those contracts where the contractor could demonstrate experience and financial security. That provision benefited established contractors, who did not have to factor the cost of a surety bond into their bid, and it cemented the connection between key contractors and state officials.[103]

Greene wanted work undertaken by contractors who had the experience, equipment, and financial wherewithal to take on major construction projects. And with the rapidly expanding road-building program of the 1920s generating intense new competition, he was in an ideal position to foster the kind of industrial development that suited his department's needs. The state enjoyed increased public revenue with which to finance highway building. A widening pool of contractors kept bids low. New competition among contractors created a demand for new technology, which increased productivity. For its part, DPW officials came to recognize the mutual benefits of close and cooperative relationships between private contractors and bureaucrats now that, after a quarter century of state road building, the pull of patronage politics had been largely displaced by administrative protocols.

Engineering a State-Centered Bureaucratic Regime

In 1919 engineer-administrators such as Greene and his entourage were relatively new figures in New York. By the end of the 1920s they had become heroes. The ripe prose of F. P. Kimball's 1928 *New York Times* Sunday magazine article, "The Open Road of the Empire State," captures this transformation:

> The sleeping beauty of the New York State landscape has been delivered at last from its long thralldom of isolation. The Prince Charming who has affected the happy release is the road engineer. For thirty years he has toiled to lift the spell that hung over hills and vales, the lakes and streams of the Commonwealth, and now he has accomplished the seeming miracle.

It is difficult to imagine a more unlikely casting than the road engineer in the role of Prince Charming. The image suggests the important part now played by this professional actor, unknown a generation before.

Kimball was struck that "the countryside of the Empire State" had been transformed in just "one generation." In the thirty years since the passage of the first state road legislation in 1898, "the State has stepped into a new world as marvelous as the world that Alice found on the other side of the looking-glass." He was astonished by the physical transformation of the state by DPW engineers and highway contractors, who, "with titanic zeal . . . cropped off hills, bored through cliffs, and squeezed out macadam and concrete as from a mighty tube to spread a floor fit for civilization."[104]

Indeed, by 1928, thirty years after New York had embarked on its first experiments in state-assisted road building, highway construction in the United States had grown to be a $2 billion per year industry, engaging over a million workers. An industry official observed that "before the war, [these] figures . . . would have been startling, as prior to that time we seldom, if ever, talked in terms of 'billions' of dollars and 'millions' of men."[105] This development was closely related to the "enormous strides" made by the industry during the 1920s. Tight competition—fueled by an expanding state program and a decade of easy credit—forced contractors to organize, cooperate more closely with the state, and upgrade their equipment. All of this tended to raise the bar on highway contracts. In 1923 an exceptional contractor could lay one thousand feet of nine-foot slab in a day; by 1928 most contractors could accomplish twice as much in the same time.

All this paving had important social consequences, dramatically changing the ways in which New Yorkers perceived and experienced their landscape. An example: highway route signs. A decidedly nonuniform system of road markings prevailed before the mid-1920s. Early highway associations had marked maps with colored blazes, not unlike hiking trails. Motorists' guidebooks developed their own maps and route numbers. The state had always numbered its routes internally, and at several points renumbered major routes. But until the 1920s, rural roads were known by local names, typically by one of the two points the road connected, or by extensions of named village streets. Proposals for the adoption of uniform signage emerged out of a 1924 National Conference on Street and Highway Safety, organized by Commerce Department Secretary Herbert Hoover and attended by the usual members of the road-building coalition (transportation agencies, auto associations, truck and bus operators), as well as representatives of police officers associations, women's clubs, chambers of commerce, labor organizations, and insurance companies.[106] By the summer of 1925, New York had systematically marked its state highways with uniform route numbers. Every tenth telephone pole sported a route number painted on a yellow band with a black border. Over the next several years, metal signs appeared along the roads as well, black-and-white shields bearing numbers that signified the constructed reality of the highway engineers, but that bore no relation to the physical space they traversed or the communities they connected.[107]

More prevalent still were the billboards that quickly cluttered the roadside. Greene made it a personal crusade to rid the state's public ways of this form of advertising, which he viewed as both an eyesore and a dangerous distraction. When an outright ban failed, he suggested taxing advertisers for square footage of space. If the number of unauthorized signs reached an intolerable level, local residents often took matters into their own hands. Objecting to the overt commercialization of public space, the "Minute Men of Cherry Valley Turnpike" organized motorized patrols with axes and crowbars to dismantle ads mounted on U.S. Route 20. According to one account, "the spirit of battle seethed in the air while water boiled in the radiators." By morning huge stacks of signs littered the town common; at nightfall the Minutemen burned the collection in a public bonfire.[108]

By the end of the 1920s the paved highway was a prominent feature of New York's rural landscape. It remained a battlefield, and not just in the sense of conflict between locals and commercial advertisers. The death toll from highway accidents soared from about 10 per 100,000 people in 1920 to over 25 per 100,000 in 1929. Perhaps this was an inevitable consequence of the state's "swing[ing] into express-train speed." In the early 1920s local communities warned of dangerous curves and crossings. The Goshen Board of Trade posted a skull and crossbones on a stretch of state highway that was the site of repeated accidents. A four-mile stretch of state road in Schenectady earned the title "Death's Highway"—as well as two sheriffs deputized for the sole purpose of policing speeders.[109]

The dangers of the state's new highways were brought home to the Highway Commission in 1922 when Deputy Commissioner Fred W. Sarr was killed in an automobile accident. Highway Commissioner Sisson lamented that "since the organization of this department it has never been the sad duty of a commissioner to report the death of one of his deputies during his term of office." The duty was a "much sadder one" owing to "the fact that this death was the result of an accident on one of our state highways."[110] The mounting death toll prompted continual revision of the state's highway safety law. The legislature tightened the enforcement of drunken driving laws, provided for more "highway inspectors," and standardized the rules of the road. As part of its reconstruction program, the DPW aligned new highways on safer routes in order to eliminate sharp curves and areas of limited visibility, and erected thousands of warning signs on dangerous stretches of road.[111]

This new social scene—of fast cars and auto accidents, route numbers and road maps, billboards, gas stations, roadside hot-dog vendors, new suburbs, and an almost-completed system of state highways—was made possible by a new state-centered bureaucratic road-building regime. Importantly, this new regime came into being through a hotly contested political process rather than as an automatic response to technological changes mandated by increased automobility, or as part of an inevitable process of "modernization."

Governor Smith's appointment of Frederick S. Greene to the Highway Commission and the Department of Public Works paved the way for this transformation. Though the presence of engineering leadership in these agencies hastened the transition to the new road-building regime, it did not make it inevitable. Certainly Greene and his cohort worked tirelessly to transfer road-building authority from a locally oriented, patronage-driven, legislator-controlled system to one held in place largely by autonomous bureaucrats. But this was a necessary, not a sufficient, condition. Greene needed as well to successfully cultivate a broad range of political support—and political legitimacy. Governor Smith's unwavering support was bolstered by a range of organized highway user groups and other advocates including highway contractors, real estate groups, and government bureaucrats. Even town officials welcomed state assistance in allocating highway revenues to poorer communities, setting safety standards, and managing traffic congestion. Greene still faced pockets of local and legislative resistance to his centralizing tendencies, evidenced by such things as the persistence of an unimproved tangle of tertiary dirt roads, the lasting authority of town highway commissioners, and continued legislative support for unaccountable local aid. Even if the transition was not absolute, a definitive sea-change had taken place.

In addition to the support Greene received from this new coalition of roads advocates, the new road-building regime he advocated was bolstered by the broad program of public improvements inaugurated during the Smith administration. Major bond issues for permanent structures such as hospitals, prisons, office buildings, and parks, as well as the elimination of grade crossings, freed up current revenue for an ongoing program of highway construction and reconstruction. During these years the DPW's 14,000-mile state highway map, first contemplated by Greene in 1919, neared completion.[112] In 1931, even as the nation sunk into economic depression, New York contemplated the largest highway building program to date.[113]

Thus the highway program of the 1920s depended on—and helped bring about—a new frame of governance, one that rested on an expanded role for engineers, new sources and methods of finance, continued decline of local control, and the emergence of a public-private partnership between public road-building agencies and private contractors. This framework evolved out of countless moments of policy formation, dealing with issues as varied as mapmaking, grade-crossing accidents, bypass highway construction, and the hiring of maintenance personnel. Small-scale efforts to address the failings of an earlier, localized and patronage-driven form of highway administration added up to broad-based structural change.

The political system that grew out of this revolution in highway policy during the 1920s had little to do with the emergence of national administrative capacities or centralized statist planning.[114] Nor did it reflect the last gasp of local dominance in government—though certainly local and federal powers were dramatically transformed. Rather, the state-centered bureaucratic regime, brought about through a continuing evolution of highway policy, represented the creation of a more fully realized federalism, in which all levels of government worked in conjunction to tackle a national problem at the state and local levels.

It was a regime defined as well by the expanded authority of engineers, who struggled to establish bureaucratic autonomy in the face of the countervailing authority of state legislators and local officials. No single act aided this transformation more than Governor Al Smith's decision to place an engineer—a "systems builder"—at the head of the state's public works program, where politicians, bankers, and lawyers had been before. Smith, who rose to power through the ranks of Tammany, was uniquely positioned to effect this change. And though Greene's power was relational rather than absolute, he was effective in leveraging public regard for his professionalism against contrarian legislators. As was the case in the early Good Roads movement, road reform developed out of a tentative and pragmatic alliance, rather than a direct confrontation, with machine politics.

Indeed, as Greene once remarked to Franklin D. Roosevelt in 1928, this alliance led him to some surprising conclusions about the relationship between politics and engineering. Greene thought, for instance, that Herbert Hoover, though considered by most to be "a great engineer," was more accurately "an efficient promoter," since no one could "point to any great structure that he has ever built." "On the other hand," he claimed that Al Smith, the old ward boss, "has given more recognition to the engineering profession than any other Governor in this country, and, strange to say, he has an unusually good knowledge of engineering."[115]

Governor Smith's close relationship with Tammany allowed him to pacify the Democratic machine even while passing off road-building authority to antipartisan engineer Greene. In so doing, Smith endorsed the shift from an older style of road building based on distributive and egalitarian pressures to a bureaucratic regime that provided greater responsiveness to an emerging motorized economy. This closing off of road-building authority to localism and patronage was more than a functionalist response to automobility. It was a profound political shift, and one that was essential in securing a friendly environment in which engineers could increase their road-building power. This development would have a lasting impact on the structure of governance and the role of experts and allied interest groups in governing coalitions.

As Greene acted on his new mandate, changes in highway planning, finance, administration, and government-business relations further consolidated state engineers' control over road building. Local governmental units had been the dominant force in road building for generations. Now the federal government increased its grants to state highway departments and new state highway policy initiatives marginalized town officials by positioning New York's Department of Public Works at the nexus of road-building authority. This reapportionment of power between local and state governments—a reapportionment of subfederal power that left state bureaucrats with radically expanded abilities to make policy, amass resources, and direct vast public works projects—was one of the most significant alterations in American governance during the first three decades of the twentieth century.

There was as well a more immediate legacy. Engineers had picked up the standard of Good Roads progressivism and turned that vision into a built reality. Drawing on the popularity of the automobile, but more so on the resources of an enlarged state government, Greene and the road engineers found in the era of 1920s prosperity an ideal setting to implement their highway system. In sharp contrast, fifteen years of depression and war would produce a substantially altered New York road-building program, this one directed far more extensively by federal officials and the national demands of unemployment relief and civil defense. Yet even with the severe economic crisis and another world war—as well as the increased federal authority designed to cope with both—the bureaucratic road-building regime continued to shape the course of modern highway administration.

Clearing the Way: Depression, War, and the Nationalization of the Bureaucratic Regime, 1931–1945

By the close of the 1920s, engineers had emerged as the dominant figures in highway planning. State legislators and local officials still held some sway over the state's highway program, but they no longer called all the shots. After a decade of contentious debate, Frederick Greene, with the support of Governor Al Smith and an array of organized highway interests, had translated the colonel's technical expertise into real political authority, built around the bureaucratic autonomy of state engineer-administrators. At the same time, the state's Department of Public Works emerged as a critical nexus between local and federal road-building interests in New York State. Local interests could still shape the diverse transportation infrastructure of the state, and federal engineers at the Bureau of Public Roads offered critical support to state engineers, but the bureaucratic road-building regime of the 1920s was definitively state-centered.

This bureaucratic regime survived—even flourished—during the trying times of the 1930s and early 1940s, but it did not come through this period unchanged. The seminal events of the Great Depression and World War II put road building in the service of the national objectives of unemployment relief, economic development, and civil defense. The nationalization of Greene's bureaucratic regime did not disturb the centrality of the state DPW in the road-building universe so much as it entailed a new frame of reference for state-engineer administrators.

During the early 1930s, as the percentage of jobless New Yorkers reached as high as 40 percent in some areas and state and local governments faced major fiscal shortfalls, federal New Deal administrators quickly pressed road building into the service of unemployment relief. From strike actions by unionized road crews in Westchester to congressional battles over the legality of using gasoline tax revenues for relief purposes, it was clear that highway politics was deeply affected by the crisis of the Great Depression. And for a time, state engineer-administrators accepted the fact that their traffic-service vision of highway planning would take a back seat to more pressing concerns, even when this put them at odds with allied interest groups (such as automotive associations) that disapproved of any weakened commitment to serving motorists' desires foremost.

By the end of the decade, however, Superintendent Greene and his successor, Arthur W. Brandt, had seized on this malleable moment and directed highway construction toward their own self-consciously modern ideas. Highway modernization required the further centralization of road-building authority, and the public policy response to the depression (even as it downplayed the engineers' traffic-service concerns) hastened this process. New Deal relief agencies had shifted the center of the road-building debate from the local-state level (where it had been through the 1920s) to the state-federal level. Meantime, the collapse of local highway budgets during the depression was taken by state highway officials as further evidence of local officials' inability to bring about a modern road network. New interest in modern highways as an essential element of civil defense emerged during World War II, providing yet another stimulus to sweep away any remaining relics of the old subfederal regime in favor of a more bureaucratic one.

As state-level engineer-administrators worked to secure their control over highway planning, administration, and construction, new tensions developed between their professional agenda (self-defined as traffic management) and their responsibility to serve the public. Through the 1920s, when road construction was limited largely to the improvement of old highways, these obligations had operated in tandem and had been instrumental in conferring political legitimacy on engineers' road-building authority. Indeed, that authority had rested as much on agreement from below as it did on consolidation of power from above. But as DPW officials contemplated construction on a larger and an ever more complex scale—shifting from a locally oriented "parkway" to a through-traffic "superhighway" mentality—the controversial nature of this construction grew increasingly likely to feed conflict and meet with cross-purposes.

As engineers sought to modernize New York highways, they simultaneously worked to "clear the way" (as one official put it) of local obstacles to construction. This entailed a policy of undercutting local authority (especially in the area of right-of-way provisions) and expanding state control over a wider range of road work (such as urban highways). In the process, DPW officials began to consider localities as traffic nodes in a relational system, rather than as autonomous communities, with particularistic concerns in directing road building according to local needs. For their part, local officials, hamstrung during the fiscal crisis of the depression, regularly sought to hand off the responsibility (financial and otherwise) for local highways that they increasingly viewed as serving intercounty traffic needs.

The thickened federal-state alliances that emerged during the New Deal and World War II, the further abdication of local road-building authority, and public officials' increasing tendency to view road building as a solution to larger problems such as unemployment relief, civil defense, and economic growth: all these developments fit well with the state DPW's modernization program. Together, they produced an array of justifications for pursuing a traffic-service vision of highway construction and undermining the few (but important) remaining vestiges of local power. So it was that while industrial collapse and massive unemployment brought national objectives to the foreground, old road-building patterns—only transiently disrupted by the depression—were again under way by the late 1930s and early 1940s.[1]

"Hard Times Have Hit": Public Works in the First Years of Depression

It was not at all clear to Department of Public Works engineer-administrators what impact the gathering storm of the Great Depression would have on the state-centered bureaucratic road-building regime that they had brought into being over the past decade. Would it help or hinder Superintendent Greene's long-standing effort to relieve local politicians of their road-building responsibilities? In what ways would it transform state-federal relations, which had gone so far in cementing the authority of state-level bureaucrats? How would the road-building program itself fare under worsening economic conditions?

As it turned out, the Great Depression of the 1930s and the urgent need for public-sponsored work at first proved to be a boon to the DPW and to the highway contractors on which it relied. Rising unemployment led President Herbert Hoover to ask Governor Franklin Roosevelt to consider the role that New York's public works projects might play in stabilizing employment. Hoover's request was good news for the road-building business, which despite advances in technology still relied heavily on manual labor. Indeed, the more the political climate favored using public works to offset unemployment, the rosier the forecast for the highway construction industry. "There will be a great deal of public work to keep the business depression from getting you contractors," the upbeat Superintendent of Public Works Frederick Stuart Greene assured industry officials in October 1930. "It doesn't seem to me that hard times have hit the contractor as they have the fellows down in Wall Street."[2]

As the winter of 1930–1931 set in and the employment situation worsened, Roosevelt contemplated yet more serious action. He proposed a $200 million unemployment assistance plan, including $65 million to be spent on highways and $70 million for grade-crossing eliminations, sites where highways and railroads intersected on the same plane. He asked that $48 million be approved immediately in order to start construction as soon as the frost broke. Greene calculated that the sum would make possible the employment of 6,000 men under contract, 5,000 more through an expansion of state maintenance forces, and "a small army" in allied materials industries.[3]

The legislature expedited the approval of these funds, but Roosevelt worried that the DPW would be too slow in preparing plans and awarding contracts to get the work started quickly. He appointed a committee composed of DPW officials, legislators, contractors, architects, and laborers to expedite the department's plans and bring state policy "in line with modern business methods." "Careful safeguarding of state expenditures," the governor conceded, "will, of course, always make state construction slower than that undertaken by private enterprise." But with his new committee he hoped to "greatly reduce the disparity between the speed of public and private construction."[4]

The Republican leadership in the legislature blamed delays in getting work under way on "the failure of the department heads to prepare their plans rather than [on] . . . so-called governmental red tape or lack of appropriate legislation." To address this concern, Greene appointed an interdepartmental liaison to smooth the shuttling of plans between the various public offices. But other delays—like the counties' inability to quickly secure rights-of-way—were unavoidable. Local politics could still hamstring state administration. The most effective action in speeding the work along was Roosevelt's pulling the highway appropriation out of the general executive budget, thus securing its early approval.[5]

Roosevelt's decision to expedite highway construction reflected his pragmatic style of governance, a style soon to be exercised on a national scale. Seizing on a vigorous department and an expanding industry, Roosevelt substantially increased the public works program in the face of the mounting depression. By May 12, 1931, $30 million worth of construction was under way, twice as much as the previous year. By that June 18,000 workers were employed on 285 projects, the largest road workforce to date. A month later an additional 1,000 were employed, $37 million had been awarded in contracts, and the highway program had expanded to 950 miles (250 miles more than the previous year's program). Including federal aid, the state spent $58,250,000 on highways during the 1931 building season. Roosevelt claimed that this "constitutes a record for the whole nation."[6] It was as well an initial triumph for the advocates of a bureaucratic road regime, who displayed a singular capacity to accelerate their construction program in time with the exigencies of economic crisis.

"The Major Tilt": Labor Relations and the Westchester County Strike

The first clear sign of the Great Depression's impact on New York highway-building practices came in the busy summer of 1931, when hundreds of road workers protested wage cuts by walking off their Westchester County construction jobs. Such an action would not have been possible a generation before, when local residents constituted their own highway labor force. With the collapse of the labor system of taxation, road-building authority became more centralized and the work itself more professionalized. Hired workers gradually replaced local labor as the state contracted out more highway work. And as the highway construction industry grew larger, more competitive, and more complex during the prosperous 1920s, road building came to rely more heavily on the manual labor of recent immigrants.

By the time of the depression, this largely immigrant workforce was subject to the growing pressures of nativism, unionism, and communism. These complexities reshaped road-building practice, pulling it out of its local context and pitting native-born workers against immigrants, laborers against contractors, trade unionists against radicals. Under these conditions, the mass of unskilled, unorganized immigrant laborers who made up the bulk of the highway labor pool were left in a vulnerable position. Governor Roosevelt's effort to accelerate public works projects assured a steady flow of jobs on which contractors could bid. But as the depression wore on, and wages dropped in all sectors, the men on the road crews faced an uncertain future. What was certain was that New York's road-building program would be radically reshaped as it was drawn into the vortex of the nation's unemployment crisis.

During the record-setting year of 1931, Westchester contractors competed fiercely for public construction jobs. State contracts promised greater financial security than the private sector could offer, but large, out-of-state contractors threatened to underbid smaller, local firms.[7] In an effort to stave off cutthroat competition, the New York State Highway Chapter of the Associated General Contractors of America (representing over 100 contractors) agreed in May 1931 not to cut wages or to treat laborers unfairly. Reports alleged that contractors bid below cost for highway projects, then made up their losses by lowering or withholding wages or by running commissary rackets at labor camps. The contractors' association announced that it opposed "exploiting an already demoralized labor market" and pledged to avoid such activities. The association also promised to work with the state to discourage contractors from taking on more work than they could complete, in order to spread work and limit the number of defaulted contracts.[8]

Nevertheless, several of Westchester County's major contractors cut wages from 50 to 40 cents an hour in July 1931.[9] On Friday, July 10, after the pay cut, 200 workers from the Peckham Road Corporation went on strike, marching through the streets of White Plains and Greenburgh.[10] On the following day the North Castle police rounded up twenty-seven strikers who were encouraging other highway laborers to join them. They were lectured on the importance of orderly conduct, and the foreign-born among them were threatened with deportation. That night 400 strikers attended a meeting at Union Hall in White Plains, where they agreed not to return to work for less than $5 for an eight-hour day. The American Federation of Labor (AFL) offered assistance but was rebuffed by the more radical Construction Laborers' Union of Westchester County (CLUWC).[11]

The AFL–CLUWC rivalry was exacerbated by tensions already running high among Westchester's labor organizers. Westchester was the site of Brookwood Labor College, the nation's first school devoted to labor activism. The AFL had helped found the college in 1921, but at the end of the decade it attacked the school's increasingly politicized curriculum. A. J. Muste, the school's director, embraced increasingly revolutionary politics during the 1920s. He helped organize the Conference for Progressive Labor Action (CPLA) in 1929 in an effort to further radicalize the labor movement. Along with other communists and progressives, the CPLA challenged the AFL to drop its conservative stance on pure-and-simple trade unionism and adopt a broader social-justice critique of capitalism. As labor leaders battled for workers' loyalties, the highway laborers' strike went on not far from Brookwood's Katonah campus.[12]

The strike heated up when road contractors hired replacement laborers. A skirmish in White Plains on Monday morning, July 13, again brought police and strikers into conflict, as 500 union members harassed the new workers. One arrest was made that day by police brandishing tear gas guns and revolvers. Then the strikers turned violent, stoning 100 men who crossed picket lines to work on a sewer project in Valhalla, a wealthy, restricted residential area. By the day's end the strikers' numbers had swelled to 750, as 250 more men on an Elmsford job walked out on Petro Lucianno, one of Westchester's largest contractors.[13]

By the middle of the week tensions were high. Arthur Rose, an Italian immigrant laborer for the Peckham Road Corporation, was shot in the arm by patrolman Joseph McCue during an altercation, and two of his coworkers, Ecequiel Cuervas and Alvaro Gil, were arrested. Five wives of striking workers, including Manuela Laocus and Theresa Binon, stood with their babies in their arms and implored their husbands' replacements on the Valhalla sewer project to stop working: "We are starving"; "We cannot pay our rent." The commotion drew several wealthy housewives to their doorways. Shocked at the scene, they shouted at the women to leave their babies at home. Laocus and Binon were arrested.

Public officials reacted quickly. White Plains Mayor Frederick C. McLaughlin mobilized his reserve police forces, recalled Public Safety Commissioner John Generich from his Ocean City, New Jersey, vacation, and brought in two U.S. Immigration Bureau inspectors to "get rid of the agitators who are inciting the workers to fight." Police raids corralled 250 strikers, twenty of whom were held for illegal entry into the United States.

Civic leaders tried to negotiate a settlement, but union representatives instead pursued legal action. Louis Budenz, advisor to the CLUWC and executive secretary of the communist-led CPLA, spoke out against "the raids on workers' homes and mass meetings, and the use of the deportation threat," actions that the American Civil Liberties Union (ACLU) called the "most amazing and unwarranted exhibition of strike-breaking by public officers in recent years." Petitions to the Public Safety commissioner, Governor Roosevelt, the New York Supreme Court, and the U.S. Secretary of Labor all fell on deaf ears.[14]

A week after the initial walkout, 900 workers were on strike. Aware of the sizable impact the strikers' action could have on Westchester County's building program, Chief Engineer Jay Downer and Peter Doyle of the State Department of Labor met with the contractors to broker a deal. Meanwhile, the ACLU encouraged the union to assert its "legal rights" and resume picketing, which had ceased in the face of continual police harassment. Nineteen additional aliens had been removed to Ellis Island for deportation. Three strikers were arrested for harassing city employees; a fourth was shot at when he appeared to be sabotaging contractors' equipment.

After much negotiation, five of the smaller contractors agreed to the CLUWC's demands. But fifteen larger ones refused to move beyond restoring their original wages of 50 cents an hour. Striking workers agreed to return to work for the five small contractors, but that only accounted for a quarter of the laborers. Several of the larger companies were functioning at close to full efficiency by bringing in replacement laborers, many of whom were African American.[15]

After two weeks of striking, the union, now numbering 1,000, was in turmoil. Efforts to broker a deal with the remaining contractors had stalled. Dozens more striking workers were arrested when they assaulted newly hired laborers, including Henry Allen, a black laborer who was stoned and beaten before running home and returning with a rifle. Tensions flared again as the union struggled with its communist and noncommunist supporters. A late-night union meeting devolved into a riot when two members of the New York City–based Trade Union Unity League sparked an uproar, after which union president Sam Barber was ousted. No one was willing to take his place. While the police ransacked neighboring boardinghouses looking for alleged radicals, the leaderless union was reorganized as the Westchester County Construction Laborers' Union (WCCLU). Class, ethnic, racial, religious, and political differences heightened every aspect of the conflict. With the union in disarray, the large contractors stood firm in their demands. Thomas J. O'Connor, the strikers' beleaguered counsel, conceded that the contractors had "won the major tilt."[16]

In a last-ditch effort to force the remaining contractors to yield, the embattled WCCLU rejected its progressive and communist supporters. The CPLA, torn between its commitments to radical politics and straightforward trade unionism, could not shore up the fledgling union. And the AFL, more secure in its power base, saw no benefit in allying with the dissenting progressives of the CPLA. Caught between these vying organizations and their differing beliefs as to the aims of labor organization, the WCCLU gravitated toward the more powerful AFL and united with Local 60 of the Laborers' and Hod-Carriers' Union.[17]

Accepting AFL assistance dramatically changed the workers' position. In addition to the nearly 1,000 road laborers, hundreds of truck drivers, engineers, and other unionized workers agreed to strike in sympathy. On Wednesday, July 29, highway contractor Petro Lucianno agreed to a $5, eight-hour day after AFL intervention tied up his contracts. The AFL also tried to impose work stoppages on projects run by Will Peckham and Arthur Riegel, the two largest Westchester County contractors.[18]

By early August the AFL's intervention had paid off. Four principal contractors—A. Riegel & Sons, Paterson & Rossi, Fran Bracello Inc., and Miller Brothers—agreed to recognize the union, Local 60 of the AFL's Drillers, Blasters, Rockmen, Shorers, and Wreckers. They agreed to an arbitration committee and a new wage scale: $5 for an eight-hour day on all new contracts. Fifteen other contractors were ready to sign the settlement, and Contractors' Association Secretary J. Wallace Slewson predicted that the rest of the companies would fall in line.[19]

In the aftermath of the agreement, the Westchester County Board of Supervisors adopted new resolutions for county highway contracts. It authorized County Engineer Jay Downer to include provision for a $5, eight-hour day on all contracts and, in response to rising nativist sentiment, exclude alien labor from county work. The highway strikers jailed for disorderly conduct were freed when the contractors failed to show up in court. By mid-August most of the strikers had returned to work, though there were not enough jobs to take back all who had walked out.[20]

The Westchester highway laborers' strike of the summer of 1931 was a milestone in New York highway politics. Disrupting construction during the peak of summer work delayed over $3 million worth of public works contracts. Though a local labor action, the thousand-worker strike was a considerable stoppage. And given the severe nature of the economic depression, the leadership role that Westchester had played in the highway boom of the 1920s, and the proximity of the county to New York City's immigrant populations and their traditions of labor radicalism, it was no coincidence that the state's first major road workers' strike took place there.[21]

The strike's significance also lay in what it reveals about the changed nature of highway labor. Once communities turned from local residents to workers from foreign lands to maintain their roads, activities that were formerly purely communal were now tied to global currents, shaped by waves of immigration and international economic conditions. National responses to immigrant labor—nativism, restrictionism, antiunionism—were fully evident in Westchester.

But the most important aspect of the Westchester strike was what it portended for the future. After years of prosperity, the depression had quickly undercut labor's gains. The security promised by the highway contractors' 1931 agreement to maintain wages proved to be a slender reed upon which to rest worker security. When local wage rates collapsed, highway contractors, who were already facing stiff competition within the industry, could not make competitive bids and keep wages pegged at 1920s levels. For highway construction to continue, and the labor situation to stabilize, something had to change.

In past years, government officials had occasionally recommended small-scale public works projects to offset economic downturns. But concern over labor, other than its cost and availability, never dominated highway building policy. The 1931 Westchester strike and the county's newfound willingness to set highway wage levels made it clear that a new, closer connection between highway planning and the nation's unemployment crisis had come into being.

Highways and Unemployment Relief:
Federal Relations and the "Double Objective"

Just as the Great Depression transformed labor relations, so too did it transform the public works agenda and the set of federal relationships that underpinned it. During the 1920s the top priority of engineers in Albany (and Washington) had been the completion of the state highway system, which included 14,000 miles of primary highways designed to provide main travel routes of uniform quality throughout New York. Governor Smith considered such a system to be central to the state's economic development: highways, he claimed in 1928, were the "arteries" through which the "life blood of the state" flowed.[22]

But the economic crisis revised such sentiments. As the nation spiraled deeper into depression, the federal government took an increasingly active role in road-building politics and, in doing so, refocused the state's highway agenda. The Hoover administration initiated a limited program of federal public works projects, but not on a scale large enough to offset the rapid decline in capital spending by state and local governments. Under FDR the federal government, through a host of new federal agencies, embarked on an extensive, compensatory public works program that prioritized jobs and material purchasing programs over systematic construction.[23]

Highway construction—better funded than housing, conservation, and electrification projects—was a natural choice as the centerpiece of the New Deal's public works programs.[24] Driven in part by increased automobile use over the past decade, highways had become a modern imperative. The federal government's use of road work as a major element in its campaign against unemployment only reinforced this fact. Highway contractors and organized highway users, instrumental in supporting the shift to a state-centered bureaucratic policy regime in the 1920s, also welcomed the new spur to road building. But what was most notable about New Deal road building was its effect on the larger political system: the rapid thickening of state-federal relations, increased reliance on federal funds, and the corresponding growth of federal control over state policy. Thus the pressures of unemployment relief and the federal policy response formulated by New Deal administrators served to nationalize the bureaucratic policy regime that had come into being during the 1920s. In the process, federal officials recast the longstanding policy goals of engineer-administrators, dedicating large sums to further highway construction in New York State but requiring that traditional measures of productivity be subordinated to the demands of national economic recovery.

The Roosevelt administration targeted the twin problems of failing industry and massive unemployment in early 1933. To help revive industrial activity, FDR established the Public Works Administration (PWA) under the provisions of the National Industrial Recovery Act. Secretary of the Interior Harold Ickes first suggested that New York State Superintendent of Public Works Frederick Stuart Greene head the new administration.[25] But Roosevelt eventually settled on Ickes himself to run the PWA, the agency charged with stimulating the economy through the federal funding of large public works projects. The elaborate schemes contemplated by the PWA, with its $3.3 billion budget, required extensive planning and committed a large proportion of its funds not to unemployment but to the purchasing of materials.

To cope more directly with the unemployment problem, FDR tapped Harry Hopkins, who had run New York State's Temporary Emergency Relief Administration (TERA), to administer the Federal Emergency Relief Administration (FERA). Hopkins's FERA worked with the states to provide unemployment relief through direct federal grants. In the early years of the depression, FERA and TERA jointly administered work-based relief in New York State. The Civil Works Administration (CWA), also run by Hopkins, funded construction projects in the winter of 1933–1934, committing over half of its workforce to road building. The cost of the CWA was high, however, and Roosevelt feared that these direct (and generous) government relief measures would sap the national spirit and discourage private enterprise. The CWA was decommissioned in the spring of 1934. The next year, a reorganized and better-funded FERA assumed responsibility for all of New York's work relief programs under the new Works Progress Administration (WPA) but maintained the CWA's commitment to highways.[26]

WPA administrator Corrington Gill explained that the PWA and the WPA were "complementary, not competing programs. . . . They serve different functions: One is primarily a materials purchasing program designed to stimulate heavy industry, the other is primarily an employment program and a means of sustaining purchasing power."[27] Nevertheless, a rivalry between the two administrations developed, as each competed for funds and control over federal construction projects.

The FERA and WPA labor-intensive programs were roundly criticized as make-work or "leaf raking." But they could be implemented more quickly than PWA projects, and they moved larger numbers off the relief rolls at a faster rate. A $750,000 FERA grant in 1933 put 15,000 jobless to work on New York roads. The grant, coordinated by Hopkins, earmarked $600,000 to payroll exclusively. Employed on a staggered basis throughout the summer, men on the road crews earned $20 a week, widening and resurfacing roads in centers of unemployment throughout the state.[28]

Though slower to get going, in time the PWA provided more substantial assistance to New York's road-building program. By July 1933 the PWA had approved a modest eleven road and bridge projects. Like the WPA, the PWA set certain employment standards: labor was frozen at thirty hours per week, and minimum wages were prescribed. But the scale of the PWA projects had a bureaucracy to match, and the administration faced constant criticism for needlessly delaying construction. Still, New York voiced few objections. The first state in the nation to take advantage of PWA funds, it was ready the moment its $22.3 million appropriation was authorized. Contracts had been advertised in anticipation of approval, bids were received within four days of official authorization, and the first work started less than a week later. Within two months, seventy-six PWA projects worth $10.7 million were under way. Thirty-seven more, worth $4.9 million, had been advertised.[29]

Still, New York struggled to provide a large enough building program to contend with its exceptionally high unemployment rate of 40 percent in

1933.[30] As winter approached, Governor Herbert Lehman (1933–1942) and Superintendent of Public Works Frederick Greene responded to the state's dire economic straits by appealing to a broad array of federal agencies: the Public Works Administration, the Civil Works Administration, the Bureau of Public Roads (BPR), and the Reconstruction Finance Commission (RFC). Hopkins's CWA came through with a $5 million winter construction program, the BPR funded highway projects totaling $1.13 million, and the RFC debated a $45 million advance on future federal highway aid.[31] But this vast increase in federal assistance did not offset the decline in state appropriations. The DPW built fewer than 500 miles of new highways in 1933, compared to the record 1,000 miles constructed in 1931 (see Figure 4.1).[32]

When Lehman submitted his 1934 budget, Republican State Senator Frederick J. Slater noted the less than satisfactory treatment New York was receiving from Washington, despite the fact that its former governor was sitting in the White House. He thought that more aid might be garnered "by just calling up President Roosevelt." Lehman and FDR did in fact meet for a conference that year after the state's first PWA allotment had been spent. According to Lehman, the discussion consisted entirely of "relief and roads."[33]

As New York sought increasing highway aid from the federal government, state-federal relations tightened. In the process, traditional measures of productivity (contracts awarded, miles built) vied with new ones (workers employed, wages distributed). Greene, who resisted seeing public works projects solely as jobs programs, touted New York's ability to get "work under contract sooner and in greater volume" than other states. Contractors, too, chafed under the new regulations that established a thirty-hour work week and required that material expenditures and wages be pegged to federal ratios and that skilled and unskilled workers be drawn from the unemployment lists. Greene noted that the latter was particularly "discouraging to contractors. The thought of securing a man from the public relief rolls to operate a fifteen- or twenty-thousand dollar piece of equipment is not reassuring."[34]

Even under these conditions, relief agencies made significant headway in road building and jobs creation. The state-run TERA built or repaired over 3,000 miles of roads and 120 bridges while generating over two million man hours of labor in 1934. TERA road work was even tailored to white-collar relief, through important road use surveys conducted from 1934 to 1935—the first extensive traffic surveys in years. Largely due to the new standards set by the WPA, PWA, and TERA, public officials operating in New York

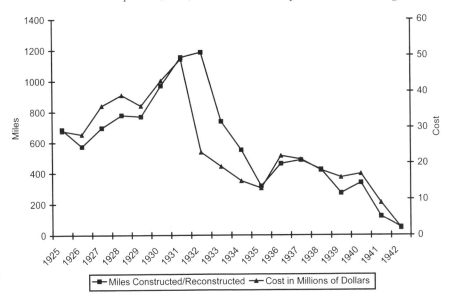

Figure 4.1: New York State Highway Program, 1925–1942

Source: Compiled from data in State of New York, Department of Public Works, *Annual Report,* 1940, 1942.

helped tailor its highway program toward job creation and industrial stimulation.[35]

Highway contractors hailed the use of road work in alleviating unemployment with great enthusiasm. In 1934 the American Road Builders Association (ARBA) pointed out that "high administrative circles" were attracted by highway construction's "universal application, its speed in getting underway, its great employment opportunities, its stimulation of capital goods industries, and its sound economic value." The ARBA thought it "reasonable to suppose that highway work will figure prominently in federal allocations." And it was correct: the following year saw a massive increase in federal funds.[36]

In January 1935 Roosevelt proposed an emergency employment program totaling $4.8 billion. The largest federal appropriation bill to that time, the Emergency Relief Appropriation Act (ERAA) of 1935 aimed to put 3.5 million of the unemployed back to work. In its immediate impact, the ERAA rivaled in importance the other great enactments of that year, the Social Security Act and the National Labor Relations Act. Road building was at the core of the program: Congress set aside up to $800 million of the $4.8 billion for highways and grade-crossing eliminations. In the first appropriation, New

TABLE 4.1. Project Funding under the Emergency Relief Appropriation Act of 1935

Type of Project	Statutory Limitation	Allocation as of December 31, 1936
Highways, roads, grade-crossing elimination	$800,000,000	$500,293,365
Civilian Conservation Corps	$600,000,000	$596,044,951
Rural rehabilitation and water conservation	$500,000,000	$272,492,810
Housing	$450,000,000	$109,504,483
Sanitation and soil erosion	$350,000,000	$227,791,871
Assistance for educational, professional, and clerical persons	$300,000,000	$110,978,692
Rural electrification	$100,000,000	$ 13,521,490

Source: Data cited in Arthur W. MacMahon et al., *Administration of Federal Work Relief* (New York: DaCapo Press, 1971 [1941]), 128.

York received a grant of $29 million for public works: $11 million for highways, $13 million for grade-crossing elimination, and $5 million for work on its barge canal (see Table 4.1).[37]

Governor Lehman sought to wring as much as he could from the federal coffers, but FDR was adamant about not giving preferential treatment to New York State. When Lehman pressed the president, Roosevelt's was a chilly response. "I have tried to make it perfectly clear," Roosevelt admonished, "that Congress has given me a specific sum of money and that I must put three and a half million persons to work out of this." The president had "no discretion" with regard to these funds, and he assured Lehman that "New York has and is receiving its equitable share of the total sum both in the number of men put to work and the dollars themselves. The federal government is discharging its obligations in New York State in the fullest possible manner."[38]

Roosevelt's reprimand was significant. The president intended federal relief grants to supplement, not supplant, state spending. Indeed, most programs, including the WPA and the FERA, required states to either match portions of the federal appropriations or face reductions in relief aid. Federal programs not only shifted responsibility for unemployment relief to the national level, they also spurred increased public spending at the state level. Comparable to New York's experience in shifting road-building authority from the local to the state level, the further centralization of policy (this time in national government) led to larger projects and greater budgetary outlays.[39]

The influx of federal money led Lehman to plan an expanded 1936 road-building program. Federal assistance was contingent upon the state's putting 8,000 people to work; Lehman thought a $27 million total highway construction program would be necessary to do that. With the $11 million federal highway grant and $6 million in matching federal highway assistance, New York needed only $9 million, or a third of the program's cost. After years of declining highway budgets—new construction expenditures dropped from $50 million in 1931 to $18 million in 1935—the DPW looked forward to the resurgence of building activity.[40]

As Ickes later noted, the $400 million earmarked for road building in 1935 "was the largest single allotment ever made by the government for highways." Approximately an eighth of the total ERAA appropriation, the sum clearly indicated congressional intent to place highways at the center of economic recovery.[41] According to Ickes, "the very extent of PWA's road program gave to both policy and effect a unique quality." Closing the highway system's gaps, eliminating hazards, improving rural roads and roadside landscapes, and providing "a large number of small projects designed to employ the maximum of human labor" added up to a new and invigorated construction program underwritten by the federal government.[42]

But the prospects for New York's highway system remained discouraging. The worst floods in a century devastated several Southern Tier counties in July 1935. Then early snows abruptly shortened the fall building season. The real problem, however, was systemic: years of depressed spending levels had placed New York's preeminent highway system in serious jeopardy. Highway Commissioner Arthur W. Brandt thought New York had slipped "away behind . . . due to lack of funds during the depression." Governor Lehman warned that "the State has in the past decades made tremendous strides in furnishing to its people . . . a good highway system. The State can ill afford to lower its standards." But in the crisis lay possibility: "We now have the opportunity of attaining a double objective," Lehman asserted, "one of the paramount duty of relieving the unemployment situation facing us today and the other of obtaining much needed permanent improvements."[43]

Achieving this "double objective" meant drawing heavily on the resources of the federal government. State-federal relations had gradually grown over the past two generations: the creation of the Office of Road Inquiry in 1895, the passage of the Federal-Aid Highway Act in 1916, the state-federal cooperative arrangements developed by the American Association of State Highway Officials during the 1920s. By the 1930s, state and federal roadbuilding officials were enmeshed in a long-standing, interdependent relationship built around their shared commitment to a traffic-service vision of highway development. While these existing networks were integrated into New Deal road building, the vast increase in federal funds and the new administrative agencies—none led by an engineer—also created a new set of road-building priorities. During the early years of the New Deal, traditional power-sharing arrangements were reconfigured in ways that threatened to displace the bureaucratic road-building regime of state engineers with national administrative concerns.

"In the Hole": Highway Tax Diversion and the Decline of the Citizen-Motorist

The new conditions imposed by the Great Depression transformed not only labor relations and state-federal relations, but also a third dimension of highway politics: fiscal policy. The Westchester strike illustrated the degree to which the old localistic style of road building had disappeared, and the unemployment crisis demonstrated the growing power of the federal government in setting public works policy. The challenge of creating fiscal policy during the 1930s, by contrast, highlighted the tensions state officials faced in their efforts to balance a national public works agenda with their own.[44]

As Greene's experience suggests, the rapid influx of federal dollars that brought about the nationalization of road-building policy set up a clash of agendas between engineer-administrators in the state DPW and the leaders of New Deal public works agencies. The subsequent diversion of state highway revenue (such as fuel taxes and registration fees) to relief purposes also strained relations between state highway engineers and longtime allies in the Bureau of Public Roads. During the 1920s, BPR engineers had lent real political legitimacy to Greene and his allies' efforts to classify road building as the province of experts. Now, the DPW-sanctioned siphoning away of highway funds appeared to them as a betrayal of their traffic-service vision of transportation planning and of their long-standing state-federal cooperative arrangements. BPR engineers (and their congressional backers) drew on a mix of cooperation and compulsion in order to pull New York's highway program back in line with federal expectations, suggesting the contested nature of nationalizing the bureaucratic road-building regime.

The ordeal of setting up a sound highway financing scheme during the Great Depression also opened up a fundamental debate over how to characterize the relationship between motorists and the public roads on which they drove. When the gasoline tax was originally approved, organized highway users had opposed it on the grounds that roads were public goods that benefited all citizens; therefore, they should be supported by general revenues.

State officials rejected this logic in 1929 and decided to shift the bulk of highway finance from general revenue to user fees (the only "fair" form of highway tax, according to Greene). In so doing, they supported the idea that motorists were less like citizens and more like consumers, paying the state for their use of the roads. It was a decisive shift, and one that tended to mute the public nature of the highways. By the time of the gas tax diversion battle in the 1930s, organized highway users had come to accept this new privatized classification. And though this change of heart was surely self-serving (once the tax was enacted, highway advocates wasted no time protecting it), the endorsement of this rhetoric had a profound and lasting impact on the discourse of highway politics.

The standoff between state and federal officials over the gasoline tax began in the early 1930s. When the tax was enacted in 1929, Governor Roosevelt had pledged in a "gentlemen's agreement" that the tax would always be used for highway purposes, and these revenues (along with vehicle registration fees) were deposited in the state's general treasury rather than a special fund. Since then, the fuel levy had generated at least $17 million annually for each one-cent tax per gallon. Appropriations from this motorist-generated revenue toward nonhighway purposes were minute at first, but as the depression worsened, the legislature authorized extensive use of this revenue for unemployment relief.[45]

The state's first widely publicized diversion of highway revenues came with the enactment of a one-cent emergency gasoline tax in 1932. By 1933 the state had diverted over $110 million from motorist-related taxes; $90 million had been siphoned off in the last two years alone. By 1934 the fuel tax was bringing in $71.5 million, while the state appropriated a mere $18 million for road work. Senator George Fearon, Republican floor leader and chairman of the legislature's Highway Committee, objected to this "stealing" from the state's motorists. He realized "that the State is hard up," but argued that it was important to "insure that we will not have to pay additional taxes next year for the reconstruction of roads at five times the cost of putting them in condition now."[46]

Democratic Governor Herbert Lehman's emergency fuel tax provoked heated legislative debate year after year. The Democrats argued that the levy was the best way to assure a solvent state while dealing with the unemployment crisis. But Republicans steadfastly opposed diversion. Robert Moses, the GOP candidate for governor in 1934, was a veteran supporter of public works, and his heading the ticket virtually ensured an antidiversion plank in the party platform.[47] And rural (and solidly Republican) communities had evolved into steadfast backers of better roads, who objected to any plan that would diminish highway resources in order to fund predominantly urban-directed relief programs. The party set its time-tested financial conservatism against what it considered to be the free-spending Democrats. The Republicans hoped that by withholding access to the gas tax receipts they could force Lehman's budget out of balance and keep him from running on a sound fiscal record.[48]

But these obstructionist tactics were hopelessly out of step with popular opinion in the mid-1930s. Most New Yorkers thought that the extent of the crisis warranted more pragmatic governance. The Republicans' plan failed, and the gas tax remained. In 1935 the Republican Old Guard was repudiated by the Progressive wing of the party, which advocated tapping the grade-crossing elimination fund (established in 1927) for more highway money rather than raiding gas tax receipts. Trying to put a Democratic governor "in the hole," as Republican State Committee Chairman Melvin Eaton argued, was a poor political strategy in a severe economic depression.[49]

But "in the hole" the governor undoubtedly was. Colonel William Chevalier, president of the American Road Builders Association, upbraided the legislature for resorting to highway fund diversion to balance the budget: "There is no defense in reason for using any part of the proceeds [of highway receipts] for any purposes, except that the State needs money. But with all due respect, that is the excuse of the embezzler and the pickpocket—they need the money."[50] Indeed, state legislators were having a difficult time as they tried to maintain the state's highway system while addressing the needs of New Yorkers suffering under depression-era conditions. Federal assistance provided tremendous help, covering two-thirds of the cost of new state road construction in 1936 (see Table 4.2).[51] But extensive as it was, it did not fully offset the decline in state appropriations for highways. Even as the state drew more extensively from the growing pool of motorists through registration fees and the gasoline tax, and the federal government took a more active role in supporting highway construction, financial pressures forced New York to reassess its highway finance policies.

In 1937 the emergency fuel tax was raised to four cents per gallon. Meantime, according to the New York Petroleum Institute, the amount of money diverted from highway use had risen from eight cents of every dollar in 1929 to fifty-nine cents in 1935. Road lobbyists did not mince words at a legislative hearing called to debate the issue in 1937. J. Mack Young of the New York State Automobile Association explained that the state's motorists "were through with this type of budget balancing."[52] Morris Braun, representing

TABLE 4.2. State and Federal Appropriations for All New York State Highway–Related Purposes (in $ millions)

Six-Year Period	State Appropriations		Federal Appropriations		State and Federal Appropriations	
	Total	Average	Total	Average	Total	Average
1926–1931	235.8	39.3	34.3	5.7	270.1	45.0
1932–1937	128.0	21.3	93.5	15.6	221.5	36.9
Increase/Decrease	-107.8	-18.0	+59.2	+9.9	-48.6	-8.1
Percent Change	-46%		+173%		-18%	

Source: Compiled from data in New York State, Department of Public Works, *Annual Report,* 1937.

Bronx filling stations, called the four-cent gas tax "a legislative knife between our ribs."[53]

Representatives of organized highway interests like Chevalier, Young, and Braun had long found common ground with state officials seeking to improve the state's highway system. They had lent their backing to the landmark state-aid legislation of 1898 and the twin bond amendments of 1905 and 1912. During the 1920s they had fought alongside Greene and Smith to strengthen the DPW's administrative power. But relations between highway advocates and state legislators were growing rocky: they had lost the battle over the enactment of the gas tax in 1929, and now they were losing the battle over the diversion of the revenue it generated.

Republican legislators split on the four-cent tax issue. Few wanted to further alienate the highway lobby. But the money had to come from somewhere, and many more thought it better to raise the (broadly imposed) motor fuel tax than to accept other proposed tax hikes that would hit wealthy New Yorkers harder. Measures on the table were in areas dear to the GOP's heart: the gift tax, the stock transfer tax, the inheritance tax. With the Republicans caught in a bind, Governor Lehman let them squirm.[54]

By the late 1930s New York ranked first in the nation in the collection of motor vehicle fees and fuel taxes but had dropped to tenth place in the allocation of highway funds. New York State Automobile Association secretary Elmer Thompson was furious over the fact that state motorists faced an increased tax burden only to be denied the benefit in better roads the tax was supposed to confer. On top of that, the federal government began issuing warnings that if states did not end the practice of diversion, which was contrary to congressional specifications, their federal funding would be in jeopardy. The Hayden-Cartwright Act of 1934, which authorized federal road-building assistance without matching grants from the states, included an antidiversion provision to ensure that states would not shift the burden of highway financing entirely onto the federal government.[55] In 1937 and 1938 two states had federal road-building dollars withheld on these grounds. Such a loss of federal money would be a crushing blow to the state, and Thompson vehemently protested against the "triple injustice"—higher taxes, diverted revenue, and loss of federal assistance—that New Yorkers might suffer.[56]

Though lobbyists from automotive groups staunchly objected to diversion, New York highway officials were more willing to concede the necessity of dedicating some motorist-generated revenue to relieving the unemployment crisis. They were keenly aware of the state's financial situation. Highway Commissioner Arthur Brandt had appealed to a number of congressmen to reject the wording in the Hayden-Cartwright Act that restricted federal road aid to those states that devoted motor vehicle fees and gasoline taxes to highways alone. He thought the provision "hastily conceived." "NO Highway Commissioner likes to see motorist revenues diverted," he argued, "but every Highway Commissioner and every motorist must recognize that our States are facing demands for money for relief purposes." States diverted user fees only reluctantly, "because they believe it to be absolutely necessary in the interests of the unfortunates who are unemployed." Though highway officials and highway lobbyists had often found common cause, and though the latter had provided instrumental support to Superintendent Greene during his early battles over the extent of his administrative powers, they did not always see eye to eye. Indeed, in cases such as this, Commissioner Brandt's role as a public official clearly ran counter to the lobbyists' hard-line highway advocacy.[57]

Though antidiversion language ended up in the Hayden-Cartwright Act, engineers at the Bureau of Public Roads helped shape this language in a way that favored cash-strapped state governments. BPR leadership quietly struck a compromise regarding diversion that would allow for modest diversion so long as it did not entirely derail the federal aid highway project. Under the agreement, if the state did not "divert more money in the years succeeding 1934 than [it] diverted in 1934," it would not be penalized. In exchange, the BPR expected that state highway funds would rise as motorist-generated revenue increased. Setting the base year of acceptable diversion at 1934 (rather than a predepression year) indicated a willingness on the part of the BPR to press for congressional verbiage that checked the most egregious instances of tax diversion, but it did little to roll back the emergency levies devoted to nonhighway resources.[58] This move suggested that the old, cooperative state-federal relationships were still operational, even as national political actors played a more direct role in shaping highway policy within New York State. State government officials complied with federal demands, but federal officials were careful not to set the bar too high.

Following the muscle flexing of Congress and the BPR, Governor Lehman curtailed the extensive diversion of the early 1930s, and the legislature authorized steadily larger appropriations for highways. Though the showdown between state and federal officials had been peaceably resolved, the consequences of the state's experiment with diversion were serious. First of all, the state highway system suffered for want of maintenance, and progress on the system of primary highways begun in the 1920s lagged considerably. The state legislature's Highway Survey Committee, created in 1934 to assess the troubled road program, warned in 1937 that "New York State is falling behind many of her sister states."[59] The precipitous decline in highway appropriations made it "most essential that this State adopt a highway policy which will adequately meet the situation with which it is confronted." Safe highways and efficient traffic service were the primary goals, and the committee members considered these to be among the state's top priorities. "The economic loss involved in the failure of the State to maintain an adequate highway system cannot be estimated."

In the previous year the committee had issued a report that called for the completion of the state, county, and town highway systems, and the widening and reconstruction of thousands of miles of bridges and highways.[60] Roads once had been a matter of local concern, the report concluded, but mass automobility "changed the whole picture. The advent of the automobile necessitated the development of a new system of highways, as revolutionary as the automobile itself." The creation of a new road network prompted a broad revision of state highway policy, affecting state aid to towns and cities, motor vehicle taxes, safety measures, the construction of sidewalks, the installation of highway lighting systems, and the development of uniform road markings. But no action was taken on the many recommendations contained in the 1936 report of the State Highway Survey Committee. Public relief measures assumed the highest priority, leaving little room in the budget for a system conceived in more prosperous times. There were simply too few resources at hand to initiate a major overhaul of the state's declining highway system.[61]

The challenges public officials faced in determining how to apportion motorist-generated revenue had other costs as well. Limited highway expenditures threatened to undermine the state's investment in its public roads. Beyond that, the rhetoric that surrounded the battles over tax "diversion" helped to perpetuate an emerging discourse surrounding highway politics and the concept of "user" fees. The notion of dedicated highway revenue first received sustained attention in the early 1920s, when the popular tax was sweeping across the nation. Superintendent Frederick Greene, supported by Governor Al Smith and several legislators, backed a fuel tax as the only "fair way to tax automobile owners," since they paid according to the "actual use" they get out of the road.[62] Though organized highway user groups elsewhere in the nation had supported the tax to supplement underfunded state highway budgets, the New York automobile lobby kept the tax at bay until 1929 by arguing that New York's already substantial vehicle registration fees provided adequate revenue. Moreover, they argued that roads were public goods that served not just motorists but property owners as well, and that they should be financed out of general tax revenues rather than special levies. This was self-serving logic, to be sure, but it did reflect a conception of highways as part of the larger fabric of society, the property of citizens rather than motorists. By contrast, the justification behind the fuel tax—that motorists should pay according to use—helped automobile owners to think of themselves as consumers rather than citizens, and roads as commodities rather than public goods.

When state legislators began to divert this revenue stream toward non-highway purposes during the depression, the highway lobby turned the logic of the gas tax proponents back on them. If motorists were paying "user fees" to the state, then that money should be earmarked for highway use alone. The passage of the gas tax, the antidiversion language in the Hayden-Cartwright Act, and the ensuing fight over diversion in New York State thus redefined the way highway users groups constructed themselves politically. From this point on, they saw themselves not simply as promoters of highways but as guardians of motorist-generated revenues. This shift in political discourse laid the groundwork for future developments into the twenty-first century: toll financing, the creation of self-financing transportation authorities, the emergence of the Federal Highway Trust Fund, and ongoing highway privatization schemes.[63]

The transformation of the discourse of highway politics came at a pivotal time. This was the moment of the democratization of automobile use. There were roughly three cars for every four households by 1930, a level of mass automobile ownership that appeared to endorse road building as an essential function of state government rather than as a concession to an elite group.[64] But what did widespread automobile usage mean in the context of motorist-generated revenue? Were these user fees to be controlled by the interests of motorist-consumers? Or were they public revenue, to be directed toward the interests of a more broadly conceived citizenry? Greene and Brandt's support of Lehman's emergency gasoline tax was one of the last times highway officials defended the idea that motorist-generated revenues belonged foremost to citizens rather than motorist-consumers.[65]

The official endorsement of the motorist-as-citizen did not last long. The pressures of Congress, the BPR, the highway lobby—even Lehman's description of the new levies as "emergency" taxes—ensured that the use of motorist-generated revenue for nonhighway purposes would be defined as a short-term "diversion" rather than a long-term statement of policy. Though New York did not go so far as the handful of states that placed antidiversion amendments in their constitutions, the rhetorical battle had been conceded. From then on, the gas tax was defined by all parties in power as a user fee, one that was vehemently safeguarded by organized highway users. The victory of the motorist-consumer had been accomplished, and the long process of diminishing the public nature of highways was just beginning.[66]

This process went hand in hand with the nationalization of the bureaucratic road-building regime. Federal relief agencies first pressed state highway policy into the mold of New Deal jobs programs; then BPR officials demanded that state engineers continue to adhere to their traffic-service vision of highway construction. As state officials found themselves whipsawed by conflicting federal demands, the old state-federal cooperative relations—so critical to expert engineers' claims to administrative autonomy—were placed under increased tension. But they did not break. Indeed, even as federal relief administrators and BPR engineers shaped and reshaped New York highway policy, they did so in a way that confirmed the position of engineers as the principal source of administrative authority in transportation matters.

Greene's Legacy: Engineers and the Politics of Highway Modernization

How did engineers solidify their position of authority so quickly and so thoroughly? Until the end of World War I, highway politics were firmly in the hands of machine politicians; members of the DPW and the state legislature were still bickering over the patronage uses of the highway department well into the 1920s. But by the late 1930s the engineers' role in highway planning had been secured, an event signaled by the continuity in leadership between Colonel Frederick S. Greene (who had directed New York highway construction since 1919) and his close associate, Captain Arthur W. Brandt.

In 1923, when Greene became the first superintendent of the expanded New York Department of Public Works, the *New York Times* praised him as "a ditcher who became a king." The appointment of an engineer to the post signaled the end of machine politicians' dominance and the beginning of expertise in charge of public construction, one of the state's most costly and pervasive activities. Greene's army training led him to take no truck from politicians seeking pet projects or personal favors. And though many had come to recognize Greene's political utility, there were some, the *Times* later declared, who would like "nothing better than to run one of his steamrollers over him." He had made few friends in the legislative chamber over the years.[67]

In 1939, on the twentieth anniversary of his service to the state, Greene's reappointment was enmeshed in the controversy to which he had become accustomed.[68] He had made what he later termed "some damn fool statement" about several (presumably paid-for) legislators' misdeeds in subverting his antibillboard program.[69] Senator Arthur H. Wicks, acting chairman of the Senate Finance Committee, took him to task at his confirmation hearing, and Greene made a tactical retreat—as he had after the publication of his "Highways and Highwaymen" exposé the decade before—in order to secure his reappointment. The old soldier had changed little.

But he had grown old. Greene was 70 in 1939 and was considering retiring when Governor Lehman called upon him to serve another four-year term as superintendent. Ever dutiful, he consented if "health permitted" to continue in office. He reneged on plans to move in with his son's family in Warrenton, Virginia, near his boyhood home; his wife Grace made the move without him. And he informed President Roosevelt of his decision to stay. FDR, whom Greene still addressed as "Governor," had been inquiring whether, given his "splendid record," Greene's services could be used "as a consultant" on the National Resources Committee, the precursor to the National Resources Planning Board.[70] As had been the case in 1933, Greene remained in New York, more interested in directing the state bureaucracy he had established than in joining Roosevelt's New Dealers.

Greene weathered his confirmation hearing and resumed his duties. But several weeks later he fell ill on a business trip to Washington and returned to the new family home in Warrenton rather than to Albany. He died on March 26, 1939, hailed by the *New York Times* as "not only an honest man, but a fighter, a tireless worker, a good engineer, and almost fanatically devoted to what he took to be the public interest. His name is written large across this State in good workmanship and stainless integrity." Roosevelt arranged for a state funeral at Arlington National Cemetery, with roses, a flag covering the coffin, and a soldier escort. Grace Greene thanked the president for his thoughtfulness and for his lifelong friendship. "Remember," she asked the ever-embattled president, "how [Fred] used to say that he had more enemies than any other person in public life?"[71]

Though Greene had been through many battles in his life, he left a legacy of harmony. The trouble-free appointment of his successor, Arthur W. Brandt, signaled that engineers had secured an uncontested place in the ranks of state government. Like Greene, Brandt was an engineer with military experience. A native of Wayne County, New York, he graduated from the Tufts College of Engineering in 1912 and immediately entered the New York State government, working on highways and canals. During World War I, Brandt served as a captain in the First Combat Regiment of Engineers. Following his discharge he returned to state service as deputy commissioner of highways under Greene. When Greene was promoted to superintendent of Public Works following the 1923 reorganization of the Highway Commission, Brandt took over the Highway Bureau.

Governor Lehman was pleased to replace Greene with someone who "rose from the ranks": Brandt had already clocked twenty-seven years of state service. And in a rare move, the state legislature approved the appointment without even bothering to pass it through committee.[72] Brandt did not share Greene's fiery, confrontational temperament—he didn't need to. The seamless installation of Greene's protégé confirmed that the engineer no longer had to fight his way. Greene's first decade of service yielded a new level of administrative autonomy in the state DPW; his second decade of work, in which he was the point man for relations with numerous agencies in Washington, further cemented his independence from state legislative interference. Public works projects still needed to be hammered out in the world of partisan politics, but Greene had won a large measure of bureaucratic autonomy for his corps of engineers.

The year 1939 offered an unprecedented instance of continuity in New York's engineering leadership. But in other ways it was an important transitional moment, marking a return to the old agendas that had been disrupted by the early response to the Great Depression. Brandt took the legislature's support for his engineering mentality as a mandate to pursue the program of highway modernization envisioned during the 1920s: classifying highway planning as an administrative duty, placing it in the hands of experts, privileging the construction of the state's primary highway system, enhancing state-federal relations, and, especially, diminishing town and county control over road building. Local officials had always held on to key road-building responsibilities, such as the provision of rights-of-way, not least as a way of preserving some role for community input. But national campaigns in the name of unemployment relief, national defense, and economic redevelopment helped hasten the continued decline of local road-building authority.

The years of depression and war provided a malleable moment, as the highway program was retooled to meet new goals. Once, roads had been a purely local issue: an archetype of the sort of "visible" politics town officials relied on to project an image of competent and responsive governance.[73] Now state officials, who had grown ever more comfortable in the use of state and federal bureaucracy to direct road building, worked to extricate highway policy from its local roots. By the late 1930s they began a protracted campaign not against the patronage uses of road building (the fiercest battles under Greene's administration) but against the perceived misadministration of local officials.

The political power of engineer-administrators was not simply imposed from above. They also gained political legitimacy through assent from below. Nowhere was this better displayed than in the World's Fair of 1939. The fair holds a special place in the American historical imagination, marking a shift in the national zeitgeist from the glum days of the depression to a new forward-looking optimism. Its centerpiece, General Motors' aptly titled "Futurama" exhibit, depicted the world of 1960 in all its high-tech glory. Tens of thousands of people visited the GM pavilion and walked out wearing buttons that read "I have seen the future." What they saw were highways.

Futurama, constructed under the direction of industrial designer Norman Bel Geddes, featured sleek transcontinental motor roads and streamlined, teardrop-shaped automobiles. A visionary extrapolation of the auto industry's emphasis on stylized design and of the expansive highway program begun under engineers such as Frederick S. Greene and Arthur W. Brandt in the 1920s, Futurama was a cultural artifact and technological prophecy, a utopian vision and blatant commercial appeal. Bel Geddes and GM saw America's commitment to automobility as increasing and unshakable.[74]

No major policy shifts came out of the Futurama event. Robert Moses thought it was little more than a "swell show" and dismissed it for failing to acknowledge the fact that "actual construction must be planned, financed, and done under all sorts of limitations."[75] But Futurama was important not so much as a policy doctrine than as a self-consciously modern affirmation of highways' roles in Americans' lives. And to the extent that it shaped a growing consensus that highways would form a major component of people's visions of modernity, it lent the engineer-administrators' quest for highway modernization increased political legitimacy. For all the political and economic constraints on maintaining and expanding public highways, the fact was that the Futurama exhibit resonated with its audience. Even after ten years of depression, the place of highways in the national imagination was more solid than ever. With the onset of World War II and its national defense imperatives, that popular devotion to highways propelled American road building to new heights.

"When the War Is Over": Highways, National Defense, and Postwar Planning

The military crisis of World War II, like the economic crisis of the Great Depression, both reinforced America's dedication to road building and moved it further from its localistic character. Once again, local administrative authority was subordinated to the imperatives of a national emergency. But unlike the depression, which embedded highway policy in the New Deal's work relief programs, the wartime civil defense initiative fostered the return to the older goal of improved traffic service.[76]

Though war needs prompted the state to renew its commitment to building a systematic road network, mobilization for World War II had mixed consequences for the highway program. The war diverted men and materials to the war effort, creating a shortage of resources for nonmilitary projects. And wartime restrictions impaired the highway program more than depression-era budget cutting had. But growing recognition of the highways' importance for national defense gave highway planners new support for their work. The "can-do" mood, first apparent in the World's Fair and bolstered during the war years, fostered a new vision of the postwar world. If it was still too soon to begin construction in the early 1940s, then at least plans could be made.

While stacks of ambitious blueprints piled high on the DPW's shelves and demand for a system of highways adequate to national defense grew, the legislature scrambled to find a new source of funds for military highways. Civil defense gave a critical impetus to the systematic rebuilding of public highways, a process thwarted by the depression. President Franklin Roosevelt instructed Federal Works Administrator John Carmody in June 1940 to begin making plans for a national system of defense highways, and by

1941 support for such a program was growing in Congress. Superintendent Arthur Brandt chaired a 1941 committee charged with coordinating the construction of military highways in New York. He contemplated a 3,200-mile system, which could be brought up to military standards at the cost of $52 million. These widened highways would include eleven-foot shoulders strong enough to support seventy-ton tanks. "Undoubtedly," thought Brandt, "most future highway funds" would support a road system geared toward civil defense.[77]

The release that same year of the final report of the State Highway Survey Committee also renewed interest in the roads question. Echoing many of the concerns voiced (but never addressed) by the committee five years earlier, the 1941 report catapulted the highway question to the top of the legislative agenda alongside national defense. "The time has come to face facts," the report's authors admonished. "Inadequate appropriations year after year, necessitating the deferment of essential construction and reconstruction projects, have taken their toll." Were it not for the continued diversion of fuel tax receipts and motor vehicle registration fees, "there would be far less serious problems today." The legislature had appropriated $47 million in 1940 for highways, but an "adequate highway program" would cost $110 million. A one-cent per gallon gasoline tax without diversion could bring in $17 million a year; a two-cent tax could finance $400 million in highway improvements over ten years. And the state would have to resort to new bond issues as well. With $40 million a year from bond receipts, plus user fees and state and federal appropriations, the highway system might be redeemed.[78]

These figures were devastating, dwarfing Brandt's suggested $52 million military highway program. Repair of the state's crumbling roads would be far more costly than lawmakers had imagined. The focus on combating the Great Depression allowed the 1936 Highway Survey Committee report to slip by unacknowledged. In contrast, the national defense issues of the early 1940s supported a growing consensus among engineers, state legislators, and federal officials on the urgency of new road building.

Though the early 1940s witnessed the familiar political sparring among Democrats and Republicans over how best to fund the rapidly escalating costs of highway development, there was a palpable change in the air. After years of depressing budget figures, the postwar outlook for New York's highways turned decidedly upbeat. Current spending was frozen—the legislature enacted wartime spending restrictions in 1942 and 1943—but the DPW looked forward to future surpluses as the war economy went into full throttle. And as everyone familiar with New York highway administration knew, there was plenty to do. "When the war is over," Republican Governor Thomas E. Dewey told the legislature in 1944, "the State must be prepared to undertake very extensive repairs, modernization, and new construction. . . . We must make ready now by clearing the obstacles that have previously hampered the proper development of our highway system."[79]

"Clearing the obstacles" was a potent phrase. During the 1920s this had meant ending the use of road building for patronage purposes and placing it in the hands of "system builders": engineers who laid claim to the neutral competence of technical expertise. Though close federal relations during the New Deal had bolstered engineers' authority, the exigencies of public works employment programs had derailed the highway modernization program. National defense needs put highway planning back on that track. By the 1940s, state engineer-administrators were thus emboldened in their quest to further centralize their authority, so that when new resources were freed up after the war, there would be little in the way of local resistance to their plans.

"Layers of Government": The Further Decline of Local Road-Building Authority

During the Great Depression, New York's state government moved from fiscal crisis to fiscal crisis, often relying on the assistance of the federal government. But town and county governments faced an even greater struggle as tax revenues and state aid sharply declined. Local governments focused on providing community relief, and road work seemed to many an unnecessary extravagance. Town obligations—the construction of sidewalks along highways, snow clearance in winter—became serious budgetary drains during straitened economic times. Likewise, counties frequently could not find the money to purchase the rights-of-way necessary to proceed with state highway construction projects. As local officials defaulted on established highway obligations, state engineer-administrators argued for the further centralization of traditionally local responsibilities.

Throughout the early 1930s, Superintendent Greene and Highway Commissioner Brandt pressured Governor Lehman to reduce the dollar-for-dollar matching grants the state government had paid to the counties since 1920. State-aid formulas (based on motor vehicle registrations) had locked the state into a fixed program of local assistance, even when the state highway program faced serious shortages during the 1930s. Towns and counties received over $22 million in local aid and emergency relief funds in 1934, funds that state officials doubted would be well spent. That same year, the state system, which had been funded at over $55 million a year during the period 1927 to 1932, had less than $28 million available. Under these conditions, Lehman decreased local highway aid by 86 percent over the course of the decade. Extensive local aid was not reinstated until 1943.[80]

New Deal programs also pulled local road building within the orbit of state and federal authority. In 1934 the state Senate agreed to devote two million of that year's $11.5 million federal aid highway grant to farm-to-market road construction. Three hundred miles of gravel road, costing from $5,000 to $7,000 a mile, would be constructed in fifty upstate counties. Though less extensive than some legislators wanted, the rural road improvement program was the nation's first of this kind and magnitude. Over the years, the WPA spent millions of dollars on rural road work, providing thousands of jobs in an effort to "keep farmers from being bogged on their farms."[81] As had been the case in the 1920s, organized highway users continued to back the further centralization of road-building authority in the hands of state and federal engineers. The American Road Builders' Association strongly supported the rural roads program, which its leadership thought "might as well be considered as an everlasting job."[82]

Farm-to-market road construction under the WPA took place within the context of the ongoing struggle by state engineer-administrators to cut aid to the town system of highways and undo the power of the town superintendents, who together spent $18 million annually.[83] As state engineers inserted themselves into traditionally local road-building affairs, they trumpeted their ability to reduce costs and increase efficiency were road-building politics removed from localities. Even state legislators—who were most likely to see the political utility of supporting local aid programs—found these arguments persuasive. Republican Senator Seabury Mastick, who chaired the legislative Tax Revision Commission and was charged with seeking out economies in depression-era budgets, felt that much could be saved if road work were carried out "under less layers of government."[84]

Mastick's conclusion reflected a growing awareness that the implementation of a state highway system had vast ramifications for New York's system of governance. By the late 1930s the nationalization of the bureaucratic road-building policy regime had given new impulse to an old set of ambitions: the continuing centralization of highway administration in the hands of engineers; a renewed commitment to a traffic-service vision of highway development. During the early 1930s these goals had been sidelined as highway policy was pressed into the service of national employment initiatives. By the close of the decade, state highway engineers had seized on this moment of economic and political flux and reenergized their long-standing commitment to highway modernization.

Nowhere was this process clearer than in the area of rights-of-way acquisition. Under the 1898 Higbie-Armstrong Act, counties had been responsible for acquiring the land for state highways. As the depression worsened, this arrangement became increasingly problematic. Statewide projects were held up for years while counties refused to appropriate money for the land. Highway officials hoped to transfer the costs of land acquisition from localities to the state, so as to cut costs and accelerate the construction process. But to do so required transferring not just the costs of obtaining the land but the authority to initiate and carry out eminent domain proceedings. Significantly, the acquisition of rights-of-way had long provided an important check on state action. Should a particular community want to block a state road, withholding land was a sure means of delaying construction—one of the last brakes on state road-building authority, and one of the few remaining voluntary provisions that had survived since the initial passage of the 1898 state-aid law.

Governor Roosevelt backed the DPW engineers' efforts to bolster the department's administrative authority over rights-of-way acquisition. But he was unwilling to transfer these high costs to the state without a corresponding diminution of local control over eminent domain procedures. Governor Lehman vetoed legislative attempts to transfer costs for similar reasons.[85] By the late 1930s, though, state road officials began to push harder for control over rights-of-way acquisition as critical to the advancement of their highway modernization program. As Highway Commissioner Brandt explained to Lehman in 1938, "Resistance to right-of-way acquisition is becoming more pronounced each year." He predicted that by the early 1940s "we will be having just as much difficulty in all upstate districts [as we are having downstate]."

Brandt's conclusions relied on an analysis of road work in the mid-Hudson region directed by District Engineer James Bixby, who "fear[ed] that we are reaching the end of right-of-way acquisition in the counties." His explanation of this shift is telling: "Formerly, highways took the farmer out of the mud and because of this were welcome everywhere for their benefits." But now, Bixby thought, "modern roads with high speed traffic are losing their popularity except with the business which serves motor vehicle traffic." As Bixby continued, he laid out a compelling narrative of what happens when property-service and traffic-service conceptions of highway policy collide. Whereas improving highways once entailed little more than laying a new surface on an existing road bed, new roads were widened and re-aligned, intended to carry increased traffic loads. "A better road means more cars, more speed, more danger, more accidents, more blood on the pavement; and home owners, while selfish, cannot be blamed for fearing such improvement." Rerouting traffic "disrupt[ed] farms or private estates" or took "vehicles away from established businesses." Both developments produced "determined opposition." Counties, which already had "to struggle to finance right-of-way acquisition," found that their "difficulties" were further "aggravated by local opposition." Bixby concluded that "property owners definitely do not want" the reconstruction of highways on new sites, "as it usually means damage rather than benefit." Ten Westchester road projects were indefinitely suspended in 1939 because of the difficulties in securing rights-of-way. As resistance to downstate construction increased, the DPW prioritized less-contested construction in underdeveloped upstate regions. But Bixby thought that this was "no solution [to] this developing problem."[86]

World War II was a more favorable context than the Great Depression for state highway officials to push for the transfer of rights-of-way powers. By 1941 military leaders and highway engineers were contemplating a system of military defense roads and expediting construction on key roadways. Nearly half of the state's $11.5 million highway construction program consisted of defense-related work, and plans were in preparation for a $100 million "strategic road system" laid out by the U.S. Army and designed to bring vital routes up to "minimal defense specifications." These defense roads linked military bases, war materials plants, and other tactical locations. But their fate was in the hands of near-broke counties. Thus civil defense concerns persuaded Lehman that he could no longer allow counties that had delayed road construction year after year to undermine national defense as the likelihood of war increased. State Highway Commissioner Harvey O. Schermerhorn thought that there was "no point in picking on any particular county," since the problem was endemic. Given this situation, he advocated that rights-of-way expenditures be charged to the state. He predicted that "costly condemnation proceeding[s]" would be eliminated once "all local influences are removed."[87]

In 1942 Lehman authorized the state purchase of rights-of-way, but only for military-approved purposes. State legislators hoped to extend these changes to general rights-of-way policy in order to relieve localities of the costs. But Lehman and his successor, Governor Thomas E. Dewey (Rep., 1943–1954), were reluctant to saddle the state with these new burdens. Dewey vetoed a general cost transfer bill in 1943 but agreed to study the measure further. County governments, he found, had avoided construction for years, in part because of the depression, in part because some hoped that the state would eventually agree to pick up the tab. When it appeared that the state administration was likely to take on the new costs, however, county officials objected loudly to their loss of local control. A compromise measure, one that allowed localities to protest route choices but reserved final veto power for the DPW, quickly gained favor in upstate communities. Objections came from downstate, too, where urban Democrats withheld support for a measure that would provide a significant windfall to rural communities at the expense of the cities (which were not a part of the state highway system). Only when the governor promised more aid to New York City parkways did this opposition fade.[88]

The forty-six-year-old rights-of-way policy was finally overturned in 1944, underscoring the gradual erosion of local prerogative over the previous half century. Dewey justified the new policy on the ground that the state's wartime highway program risked being "defeated" by the "unwillingness or inability of some counties to acquire the necessary rights of way." Just weeks after the announcement of the policy shift, the federal Public Roads Administration (PRA) issued a lengthy condemnation of New York's "obsolete land acquisition policy." The *New York Times* noted that while the objection came late, the PRA report served to second New York's "forward step" in highway policy, one that "other states may well follow."[89]

While the *Times* editorial celebrated the progress in further centralizing road-building authority, it failed to account for the larger implications of the upward shift of highway finance and administration. The rhetoric of military necessity and the reality of depression-era budgeting had combined to pressure county governments into yielding one of the last bulwarks of the subfederal road-building regime and its proponents' commitment to a highway system designed to serve communities of property owners rather than drivers. Under assault for over three decades now, that regime had slowly given way to the administrative authority of engineer-administrators. With the last of its defenses overrun, state engineers no longer faced any significant countervailing authority to their bureaucratic regime and traffic-service highway policy.

Drastic cuts in state aid had dried up a significant source of funds for struggling local governments. And the state's claims on traditionally local exercises of authority—building sidewalks, clearing snow, acquiring rights-of-way—further sidestepped local prerogatives. These policy initiatives were shaped by the exigencies of depression and war. But they reflected as well engineers' increasingly insistent and technocratic demands for a "modern" highway system, demands that made local consent an obstacle to, rather than a necessity for, development. Thus, at the very moment that highway construction was becoming more tightly connected to the national imperatives of unemployment relief and civil defense, communities were relinquishing important brakes on central authority. Under the cover of these emergencies, state engineer-administrators campaigned tirelessly into the 1940s to reapportion political authority in order to clear the way for the modern road network they envisioned.

"The Fruit of Many Years of Struggle": State Control of Urban Highway Policy

Urban highways constituted a key component of the modern highway system that state-engineer administrators sought. Whereas rural highways had been privileged under state and federal policy, urban streets had been denied state and federal aid under the original 1898 and 1916 legislation. This state of affairs made it difficult to bring city road work under the umbrella of state and federal authority, even though the economic crisis of the Great Depression required that road work be undertaken in centers of mass unemployment. The requisite policy shift was resisted during the early years of the New Deal. But engineers' plans for postwar reconstruction actively endorsed state- and federal-funded urban arterial highways, not only to create jobs and ease postwar economic "adjustment" but to meet the long-term demands of a modern transportation system. Much like right-of-way policy, in which national imperatives of unemployment relief and civil defense opened the door to the further expansion of powers, urban highway policy had been radically transformed by the 1940s. Once off-limits to state officials, city road work was increasingly geared toward meeting the highway modernization ideals that the bureaucratic road-building regime was designed to serve.

President Herbert Hoover's Emergency Relief and Reconstruction Act of 1932 authorized limited municipal highway construction and provided an entering wedge into new urban road work. But strict standards designed to spread work throughout regions of unemployment curtailed the size and duration of contracts, and these procedures annoyed state engineer-administrators. Leaders in the state DPW staunchly resisted this policy, which required the division of highway contracts into smaller projects and bucked the trend toward large-scale, technically complex public works. Highway Commissioner Brandt fired off a letter to a senior engineer at the federal Bureau of Public Roads, excoriating BPR Chief Thomas MacDonald for the effect his policies would have on New York's road-building program. Brandt thought that "Mr. MacDonald had better think this over pretty carefully before he makes any such decision" to limit project size, otherwise "this department is apt to be in a mess." According to Brandt, the plans they contracted out were the plans they had "in hand," and it would have been foolish to "waste time cutting them in two or three pieces." If MacDonald enforced his policy in New York, Brandt predicted that the state was "going to have a lot of broken down contracts next year."[90]

Federal aid for municipal highway construction again raised the DPW engineers' hackles when FDR proposed his National Industrial Recovery Act (NIRA) in May 1933. The act sought to tackle urban unemployment by expanding public highway construction in New York's cities. Superintendent Greene vehemently objected to the reversal of the established policy: the national government had restricted federal grants-in-aid to highways outside city limits since 1916. He argued that there was "no established basis" for the policy change, which would yield "endless complication and strife." Greene's own career began in urban construction, and he worried especially about "the confusion, political log-rolling, and delays inevitable in experimenting with a new and untried system." He acknowledged that NIRA money was "intended to be the first line of attack to conquer depression." But he thought that the difficulty of establishing effective oversight of an urban construction program would severely retard that work. Despite Greene's protest, Lehman was in no position to turn away funds for urban relief in 1933, and he endorsed the policy shift. That year's $22.3 million federal grant included for the first time funding for the extension of existing federal aid highways inside city limits, a pragmatic depression-era response that turned into a precedent-setting event.[91]

State aid to city roads was increased again in 1944. This time the policy shift was billed as a political offset to changes in right-of-way policy. Republicans considered state assumption of county land acquisition costs a victory for their upstate constituents; Democrats held up a final debate on that bill until they were assured support of increased state commitment to the funding of urban arterial highways. Some Manhattan officials, including Borough president Edgar J. Nathan, objected to the loss of city authority. Mayor Fiorello La Guardia thought that the creation of a state arterial highway system extending into New York City would do nothing except give the city "the privilege of paying for up-State arterial highways."[92]

Republican Governor Thomas E. Dewey paid little attention to these

Democrats' complaints and approved the construction of arterial highways in the state's cities in 1944 over their objections. Dewey supported the policy shift in terms that echoed depression-era concerns. Urban road work, he claimed, would be the "greatest public works contribution to post-war re-employment." But it was more accurately the product of long-term trends. Dewey thought that the new commitment to urban road work represented "the fruit of many years of struggle to obtain a modern system of highways in the State."[93]

By this time the resistance of state engineer-administrators that Super-intendent Greene had voiced in 1933 had faded. Once the long-standing pro-hibition on federal aid for urban road work had been overturned, Greene's successors worked to ensure that they would shape city highways to their own ends. Indeed, they expertly utilized the expansion of federal aid to mu-nicipal roads as a means of further centralizing public road-building au-thority in the state DPW. In the early 1940s New York's DPW leadership showed considerable interest in congressional plans to recalculate the ap-portionment of federal highway aid. Western lobbyists had long advocated a formula favoring the larger agricultural states. In exchange for their sup-port, New York and other eastern industrial states won an important con-cession: after 1944, the federal government would offset their loss of regular federal aid by appropriating special funds for the construction of urban ar-terial highways. This increase in aid came at a critical juncture. In the im-mediate postwar years, New York received over $100 million in govern-ment assistance, a greater proportion of total federal highway aid than ever before.

As had been the case with right-of-way policy, the utilization of congres-sional politics, federal funds, and national objectives was centrally impor-tant to the framing and implementation of New York's urban highway pro-gram.[94] For decades the authority of the state and federal government had been kept at bay. But in this new context, defined by economic depression, the expanded power of the federal government in combating urban unemploy-ment, and the traffic demands of the modern city, the long-held policy of ex-cluding urban highway work from state and federal control was overturned. In the process the power of state DPW engineer-administrators was further enlarged. Though depression and war enormously increased the federal gov-ernment's role in setting road-building policy, New York retained its pivotal position in shaping a new initiative in city construction: a massive, federally funded, urban arterial highway program for postwar New York. This was the major accomplishment of nationalizing the bureaucratic road-building regime. With the heightened importance of such national objectives as civil defense needs and postwar reemployment planning, DPW leadership was afforded crucial cover for its shift toward more ambitious public works planning.[95]

Cities, counties, and towns had all transferred critical elements of local road-building control to the state DPW during the 1930s and early 1940s. Once the bureaucratic road-building regime was placed in service of national interests, it became increasingly difficult to defend the maintenance of local authority. Urban autonomy, county acquisition of right-of-way, and extensive state aid to towns was hard to justify when localities lacked the resources to combat mass unemployment or interfered with the progress of civil defense initiatives. The fate of Westchester County's parkways offers a final example of how one of the last hold-outs of the subfederal regime eventually capitulated to the forces of bureaucratic centralization.

The State's "Stepchild": Westchester, Suburban Road Building, and the Fate of Local Control

If any county had local control to defend it was Westchester. Westchester County had distinguished itself as a national leader in road-building affairs during the 1920s, when it established an unparalleled system of parks and parkways. As one journalist of the time put it, Westchester officials had successfully used its parkway program to transform the threat of mass automobility into an engine for county development. But over the next decade they found it increasingly difficult to support extensive infrastructural improvement. The first signs of trouble came in 1931, when the county endured a protracted highway labor strike, one that indicated the enlarged role that labor relations would play in shaping new road-building conditions. By the late 1930s the county's concern for labor conditions was displaced by a more nagging problem: how to pay for its costly, overbuilt parkway system under depression-era conditions. Faced with decreasing resources and growing traffic demands, county officials called upon the state legislature to assume its mounting parkway debt, on the ground that intercounty traffic, which made heavy demands on the county system, was a state responsibility. When these demands were rebuffed, the county turned to charging tolls. But this was no simple return to the old turnpike days. Rather it was indicative of the realities of future construction costs and the limited capacity of small units of government, even relatively wealthy counties like Westchester, to sustain a commitment to large-scale public works projects. Westchester's fall from the pinnacle of road-building success illustrates how one of the last remaining elements of the subfederal road-building regime—and its locally oriented notions of parkway use, policy, and authority—was over-run during the national crisis of the Great Depression.

Westchester County was living in a "new era in road building," explained county chief engineer Jay Downer in a 1933 address to the American Society of Civil Engineers. "The pioneer Bronx River Parkway . . . has demonstrated dramatically the soundness of the bypass highway. As an outgrowth of this project, 160 miles of parkway have been laid out and acquired in Westchester County." Westchester's expansive parkway plan, which separated local from through traffic and commercial from noncommercial vehicles, was the nation's leading instance of parkway development. While other communities still believed that main highways ought to be routed through downtown areas, Westchester County's parkway program reflected its awareness of the perils associated with congestion in business districts. "Promiscuous marginal development and access" led to roads becoming "overburdened with a maze of local and through traffic, parking problems and traffic lights." The county's parkway system—an outgrowth of recreational interests—was now geared toward the principles of traffic management in one of the most heavily traveled counties in the state.[96]

But the parkways had not come cheaply. The county was saddled with $68 million in parkway debt, and the shock of the Great Depression made it almost impossible to maintain its roads while simultaneously paying down its debt, providing unemployment relief, and meeting other social service demands. The county faced rising expenses and reduced revenues. In a visible demonstration of this crisis, it darkened the lights on its prized parkways to cut costs.[97]

By 1933 the county could spare only a paltry $475,000 to maintain its parks and parkways. The following year it set aside no money for further improvement. The state, too, cut back on parkway development; in 1934 road work in the county was financed entirely by federal grants.[98] Soon the county sought other sources of relief. In 1936 it asked the state legislature to assume its $68 million highway debt. A $5 million debt assistance bill was introduced, but Governor Lehman, a Democrat, showed little interest in aiding a solidly Republican county and vetoed it on the ground that the measure would initiate an entirely new policy of the state bearing the costs of local improvements.[99] The county proposed a list of alternatives. The state could pick up the cost of maintaining Westchester's parkways; after all, the newly constructed Triborough and George Washington bridges were dumping more and more through traffic onto Westchester's roads. Or the state

TABLE 4.3. Gasoline Tax Refunds to Selected Counties, New York City and State, 1940

	Average Annual Gas Tax Refunds per Car
Westchester County	$0.45
Nassau County	$1.29
Erie County	$0.92
New York City	$1.80
Average of All Counties	$3.15

Source: Compiled from data in Westchester County Parks Commission, "The Needs of Westchester County Parkways from a Through Traffic Perspective," November 8, 1940, at New York Public Library, Science, Industry and Business Library.

could reapportion the distribution of gas tax receipts, which left Westchester short-changed year after year (see Table 4.3). Meantime, the deteriorated condition of the county's roads provoked repeated criticism from its residents. One disgruntled man insisted that the lights be reilluminated on the county parkways so that Westchester might stop "parading its poverty."[100]

In the late 1930s state and county officials entered into protracted negotiations to resolve the contest over the costs of parkway development. As a compromise measure, the state legislature offered in 1937 to purchase the Bronx River Parkway, the original jewel of the parkway system. The proposal to redevelop the parkway as a major traffic artery raised immediate objections from Herman W. Merckel, the parkway's designer and current superintendent of the Westchester County park system, who thought that redesigning a road built for leisurely pleasure traffic would entail "tremendous destruction." The plan collapsed when the county found out how little the state had planned to pay for the title—an offer that Gerard Swope, General Electric magnate and president of the Westchester County Parks Association, called no better than a "mess of pottage."[101]

Plans for a new parkway on the site of the recently defunct New York, Westchester, and Boston Railway also led to strife. A proposal for a commercial toll road met with strong objections from residents, who wanted the railroad line resurrected and were wary of a major truck artery to upstate and New England running through their neighborhoods. One spokesman argued that commercial activity in the community was based "on the natural supposition that trains would run indefinitely" over the existing route. In a rare confluence, wealthy Mount Vernon homeowners and the local Socialist Party joined forces to lobby for the resumption of commuter rail service.

Robert Moses, whose power extended beyond his Long Island base, suggested a compromise that soon gathered support: rather than tear up the railway tracks, situate a new road on the old Pelham-Portchester right of way, which the state had secured for just $6 million during the highway boom years of the 1920s.[102] One commuter wondered, to little effect, how Moses could "calmly" propose a $32 million parkway when it would only cost $2 million to revive the Westchester and Boston Railway. Swope pledged $5,000 to finance a commission to work out a compromise acceptable to all involved.[103]

Westchester moved from crisis to crisis during the late 1930s, and the range of conflicting interests soon left its construction program locked in paralysis. The parkways were repeatedly darkened to save money and then relit when accidents mounted. Rail commuters wanted "trains not trucks." Local motorists complained they were being pushed off the parkways by out-of-county traffic. At the same time, they objected to new toll roads, which they considered tantamount to "turning the calendar back fifty years." Others complained of the state's favoritism toward Robert Moses' Long Island parkways. "If we had a Moses to lead us out of the bulrushes," one thought, "we could get the state to build parkways for us." Even nature seemed to conspire: the county faced its worst floods on record during the "Great Hurricane" of 1938, and, then again, more reconstruction costs.[104]

Fed up with the state administration's lack of willingness to help the beleaguered county, Westchester public officials threw up their hands. "Through traffic," one concluded, "is a state problem," and he insisted that construction within the county be left to it.[105] But simply curtailing construction would not pay back Westchester's debt—"a yoke on our citizens," "a Frankenstein"—the amortization of which comprised 50 percent of the county's budget. (Of the remainder, 34 percent went to relief and 16 percent to operating costs.)[106] A 1940 traffic census confirmed what Westchester officials had been arguing for years: that the county had become a conduit through which Connecticut residents entered the city.[107] Still, Governor Lehman steadfastly refused to take over the costs of Westchester's parkway system. As one commentator put it, "The State follows the axiom of the street, 'Never give a sucker a break.'" County officials concluded that only tolls could pay for the county's costly parkways.[108]

This predicament put Westchester at the "storm center" of a national toll road controversy.[109] Several eastern states had begun contemplating the construction of multilane, limited access, express toll roads, financed by public authorities. The first such project in the nation, the Pennsylvania Turnpike, originally stretched 160 miles from Harrisburg to Pittsburgh and opened in 1940. Though the Turnpike was initially considered to be a singular exception to the general rule of free public highways, similar projects gained favor in other states.[110] But Westchester's problems, stemming from existing construction costs rather than future plans, had unique immediacy.

Westchester first collected tolls on the Cross County Parkway at the recently constructed Fleetwood viaduct, the site of nightmarish traffic tie-ups.[111] But the State Court of Appeals informed the county that it could not, under existing legislation, charge tolls on its parkways. Westchester County executive William Bleakley thought this distinction was inconsistent with the reality of the situation: "Our parkways are not paid for, State traffic is monopolizing them, and we are left to foot the bill." Yonkers town supervisor Jefferson Armstrong was infuriated to learn that Robert Moses, who had managed to sustain his impressive Long Island parkway program throughout the 1930s by securing special state appropriations, was merely "sympathetic" to the county's unfortunate position. Armstrong declared that he did "not intend to be blackjacked" into forcing property owners to support parkways for nonresidents.[112]

The *New York Times* agreed that Westchester was a "special, indeed a unique, case" and that there was no desire "to see a community punished for its pioneering spirit or its enterprise." But the paper's editors had their doubts about the return to toll roads and thought it better for the state to take over the parkways. Governor Lehman rejected both these options and again vetoed a proposed toll authorization bill, noting that "we cannot afford to retrogress to conditions prevailing in this country a century ago." The move prompted the *Times* to dub the hapless county the state's neglected "stepchild."[113]

By the early 1940s the county's roads had fallen into serious disrepair. In order to generate support for a new roads program, Swope and the Westchester Parks Commission produced a pamphlet, "The Needs of Westchester Parkways from a Through Traffic Standpoint." It detailed a $15 million improvement plan to eliminate bottlenecks on roads carrying twice their safe load.[114] Money for this new construction came in 1941, the first time since "the county purse strings were tightened on capital improvements a decade ago." But the war cut short hope of a revival. Shortages of funds and materials made non–defense-related work nearly impossible to complete. Gasoline rationing reduced not just traffic but gas tax receipts as well.[115]

New projects like the Pelham-Portchester Parkway plan were shelved until after the war. But when the Pelham-Portchester route reappeared as part of the state's postwar reconstruction plans, it was designated a mixed-use highway, not a noncommercial parkway as originally conceived. This revelation produced more public outcry, especially from the town of Harrison, situated on the proposed route. Supervisor Benjamin I. Taylor complained: "Building the road for trucks would do more harm to Harrison than any other thing could—except the county airport [built during the early 1940s]. All the doggone junk you can find you throw at Harrison." Another supervisor warned that the commercial road "will slaughter local real estate values." Taylor thought that "like most of our parkways, it would help build up Connecticut."[116]

By the mid-1940s Westchester's relationship to road building had been entirely upended. Once the nation's pioneer in parkway construction, it had successfully linked transportation improvement and community development in the 1920s. Now it suffered under crippling debt. Local officials, who had once supported parkway construction as an avenue to economic prosperity, now worried over the impact of these roads on real estate values. And Westchester residents, as district engineer James Bixby had observed in the 1939 debate over right-of-way financing, faced new threats (more "blood on the pavement") as their communities increasingly served as a corridor for traffic traveling between Manhattan and upstate New York or New England.

These new conditions—increased intercounty traffic, over a decade of neglected maintenance, growing local resistance to further highway development—were increasingly difficult for state officials to ignore. During the depression, toll authorization bills had been repeatedly vetoed on the grounds that roads were public goods. But proponents of the toll plan considered this a weak justification for denying the county the right to generate revenue from its parkways, as the state did by collecting "user fees" in the form of a gasoline tax. In 1944 the state legislature considered a toll authorization bill for the seventh time. Governor Dewey, as Lehman had before him, vetoed the act. But this time the Republican governor objected on different grounds. He explained that an agreement under the 1921 Federal-Aid Highway Act prohibited the use of federal aid on toll roads. The county had taken "small sums" for parkway construction—$2.5 million in 1933 and 1936—and was thus bound by the federal act's provisions. Westchester County executive Herbert Gerlach traveled to Washington to work out a deal, but the Public Roads Administration refused to yield on its long-standing policy. Not until

1945, when the state legislature agreed to reimburse the federal government for its capital outlay, did Governor Dewey finally authorize Westchester County to collect parkway tolls to pay down its debt.[117]

For Westchester County, winning the toll road battle meant losing the larger campaign to retain key elements of the old road-building regime: local control over public roads serving community needs. Local governments did not have the financial wherewithal to support major transportation initiatives, especially in an area with heavy interregional traffic.[118] Even a wealthy county like Westchester was eventually laid low by the large capital outlays required for construction and maintenance. The punishing demands of a costly parkway system forced Westchester to abdicate its leadership position in New York (and national) highway affairs during the Great Depression and World War II. Under the pressures of these national emergencies, the county's waning status helped solidify the gains of the bureaucratic road-building regime.

The affirmation of this policy regime by Westchester officials had two serious consequences for the highway politics of postwar New York. First, county toll collection enhanced the legitimacy of a user-financed road system (and thus generated new pressures to earmark highway revenue solely for highway purposes). This line of reasoning built on the belief, which first gained credence in the debate over gasoline user fees, that motorists were more properly understood to be consumers rather than citizens, and that to some degree, roads could be considered private rather than public goods. As the next chapter will demonstrate, engineers continued to embrace this shift in mentality and direct it toward their own ends. By midcentury, with the establishment of the Thruway Authority, the "client" relationship would come to dominate highway politics in New York State.

Second, Westchester officials' insistence in the 1930s and 1940s that through traffic was a state responsibility seriously damaged their ability to resist the DPW's increasingly controversial public works program. Once state officials began to respond to county leaders' persistent calls for state control of Westchester's parkways (as they did when the state reimbursed Congress for funds used on toll roads that had received federal aid), locals found it ever more difficult to pose objections to the wishes of state engineers. Tapping state funds meant, again, enlarging the mandate of DPW engineers, who pursued their traffic-service vision of highway planning with gusto during the postwar years. Nowhere was this more apparent than in the emerging design for a "superhighway."

From Parkway to Superhighway:
Big Plans for the Postwar Years

The local mentality that shaped Westchester's parkway development in the 1920s underwent a critical transformation in the 1930s. Certainly limited-access parkways, with their emphasis on serving through traffic, constituted a decisive shift away from the locally oriented, property-service construction of early state roads. But they retained a recreational design that still linked them to a community-service (as distinct from a traffic-service) vision of transportation planning. As parkway capacity was outstripped during the 1930s, DPW engineers began to apply the term *parkway* to expanded interregional routes, as they extended and linked previously disconnected parkways. By the late 1930s and early 1940s, highway planners envisioned modern expressways built on entirely new sites. In this way, the parkways of the 1920s served as prototypes—first emulated, then reworked, and finally rejected—for the postwar reconstruction boom of the 1940s. Significantly, the shifting standards of highway design reflected the political transformation that had taken place over the past several decades. During that time, highway engineers sought to centralize road-building authority and put it in the narrow service of smooth traffic flow rather than the broader array of local interests that roads previously served. Thus the transition from "parkway" to "superhighway" reveals the early flowering of an engineering vision—and a closed-system bureaucratic policy regime—that would reach full bloom in the Interstate Era.

World War II brought most state road work to a virtual halt. It also brought time to think and to plan. With new ideas about the extent of public responsibility and the reach of public authority, postwar planners began piling the shelves with blueprints of big new projects for a modern age: new rural highways, urban arterial routes, the New York State Thruway. This was not the fanciful world imagined by the creators of GM's Futurama exhibit, but a real world version of it: one that accepted designer Bel Geddes's traffic-service vision of mass automobility but that was hammered out on the anvil of politics, and bore the marks thereof.

Plans for superhighways had long been on the table. Good Roads advocates contemplated a system of national highways as early as the 1910s.[119] In 1932 the New York State Legislature entertained proposals for the construction of a cross-state "motor-speedway" costing $100 million and financed by tolls. Two years later Superintendent Greene advocated the widening of all through routes to four lanes. Special attention was shown to the completion of New York State Route 5, upstate New York's "Main Street," which linked most of the cities along the old Erie Canal route; and the Cherry Valley Turnpike (U.S. Route 20), which ran through "the hills and valleys in the backyard of central New York."[120]

During the late 1930s the DPW's parkway construction program concentrated on linking and extending existing parkway facilities. This work sparked debate over the often blurry line that distinguished parkways, designed for recreation and park access, from newer notions of express highways, designed to facilitate through traffic. The distinction was not lost on Robert Moses, whose "idea of futility [was] to build a beautiful parkway for speed demons who can't tell a flowering shrub from a bale of hay." But for a time in the late 1930s, new highway work drew on both design traditions.

In an address at a 1936 parkway opening, Governor Lehman reflected the gradual move away from the older parkway mentality. Following a Civilian Conservation Corps band's performance of the "Eastern State Parkway March" and the ribbon cutting by Commissioner Brandt's six-year-old daughter, Mary Linda, Lehman announced that the new parkway would be more than just a regional resource: "It is my sincere hope that we may be able to continue to build the parkway. I am looking forward within a measurable time to the parkway connection with the Albany-Boston highway, and then its northward progress perhaps into Canada." The Palisades Interstate Parkway, too, was billed as not only as "a genuine parkway" but also as a "superhighway."[121]

The half-way nature of this policy—extending parkways, rebuilding existing through routes—was evident in Greene's 1936 annual report, in which he informed the governor that "our main traveled routes should be straightened, widened and generally improved in order that they should become super-highways by 1950." He estimated that $300 million over the next thirteen years would do the trick. At this point, Greene himself was still locked in the parkway mentality, wedded to the idea that the state should focus its energy on improving existing roads—raising construction standards across the board as he had sought to do since his entrance into public service in 1919.

Further study, however, revealed the difficulty of turning old roads into superhighways, and by 1937 Greene had changed his tune. The main thoroughfares were "laid out more than three hundred years ago," built on narrow rights of way, and abutted highly improved property. Widening these routes would be costly, and limiting access was likely to involve an unconstitutional deprivation of existing rights of use. The new "superhighways" would have to be built on new sites.[122] Convinced of the importance of meeting perceived traffic needs and of the unassailable logic of his engineering expertise, Greene directed the DPW to begin planning for major new construction.

The high costs of such work led the legislature to propose the creation of an authority in 1938, empowered to issue $200 million in bonds to construct a new through route along the Hudson River. Reluctant to see the DPW lose any of its road-building authority, Brandt attacked the plan. Calling it "excessive," he boasted that the DPW "can build the highway for just half that amount. Give us all the money and we will build two highways, one on each side of the Hudson River, and throw in two bridges." President Franklin Roosevelt enthusiastically endorsed the plan and asked Greene to send him a map of the proposed highway for his close examination: "I will lay it out on the floor of the big room and crawl all over it on my hands and knees."[123]

Talk in Congress of an $8 billion federal highway program overshadowed discussion of the more parochial-sounding New York City–to–Albany superhighway. Cognizant of the shift in government power, a *New York Times* editorial jibed: "Surely Albany must be a misprint for Washington. Who nowadays ever goes from New York to Albany?" But plans for express highways, whatever their destination, appealed to builders and planners alike as they struggled through the lean years of the Great Depression. Assistant Commissioner of Highways E. C. Lawton explained to the Association of General Contractors that these new highways were imperative to address the traffic needs of the next quarter of a century. "Except for [the provision of] food, clothing, shelter, and life itself, such a program would provide the most useful work any form of government may undertake."[124]

Though Greene lobbied for express highways through the 1930s, depression-era budgets simply did not allow for new capital construction. Not until the early 1940s, when the state began to consider its postwar reconstruction program, did plans for the Thruway finally emerge.[125] In 1942 Assemblyman Abbot Low Moffat, chairman of the Ways and Means Committee, and Senator William H. Hampton proposed a bill to authorize the planning of an express highway along the lines of the Pennsylvania Turnpike. The New York State Thruway, with a 200-foot right of way and no grade crossings, would connect Buffalo, Albany, and New York City. The route would bypass the upstate cities and run along the west shore of the Hudson, accessible to 80 percent of the state's population. "It would seem the part of wisdom," explained the two legislators, "to place such a through system on the State map, thereby giving the seal of official approval to the project and that, when and if large public works expenditures are made, there will be ready a really worthwhile, greatly needed project affecting the entire State." Lehman approved the bill and made public a DPW memorandum that endorsed the construction of "a modern super-highway comparable to the one already built partly across the State of Pennsylvania" as "one of the best postwar projects under consideration."[126]

In 1943 the Post-War Planning Commission began to deliberate on the construction of the Thruway. Meanwhile, the legislature approved construction of a Berkshire Thruway extension from Albany to West Stockbridge, Massachusetts, and a New England Thruway running through the Bronx and Westchester into Connecticut. The New England Thruway proved to be especially nettlesome, since Westchester residents, after years of highway battles, were primed for a fight. One Connecticut resident of gentler perspective thought that New York's brawn was to blame for the bad community relations its highway politics engendered. The state, he thought, "which does things in a big and overpowering way," had "already ruined some of its lovely little towns."[127]

Indeed, as the New York DPW planned its postwar building program, it began to face public resistance to its work. The engineering, administrative, and financial demands of a modern highway system prompted new policies that steadily removed local control over ever more divisive construction. As state officials shifted their focus from unemployment relief to economic development, they envisioned vast superhighways, rather than regional parkways, as the great goal of public works. In their zeal to move the Thruway along in the postwar years, they paid little heed to community concerns. The decline of local prerogative, a process begun in the 1890s, was all but complete by midcentury. The elimination of "all local influences," as Highway Commissioner Schermerhorn put it in 1941, was deemed necessary to streamline the state's construction process and provide a more efficient and economical transportation system. As DPW officials planned an ever larger highway system, engineers downplayed any potential conflicts that might grow out of this shift from a "parkway" to a "superhighway" mentality, a move that rejected considerations of roads' aesthetic appeal or local service.

This was a time, it seemed, for action. When Westchester County Commissioner of Public Works Charles Sells (a Dewey appointee) replaced the ailing Arthur W. Brandt as state superintendent of Public Works in 1943, he "found a department stripped to the bare essentials." The depression had forced the DPW to run on a skeleton crew; voluntary enlistment in war industries further reduced its ranks. Now there was cause for optimism. In 1944 the legislature created a Post-War Reconstruction Fund to coordinate a massive capital construction program and direct future peacetime expenditures. Sells reported that "the shelf of completed plans ready for use in the postwar era is daily becoming more impressive." The scope of these plans—and their potential for controversy—was simply unprecedented.[128]

The outsized plans for postwar reconstruction only partly reflected the expanded public authority achieved during the heyday of New Deal politics. Of equal consequence were trends set in motion much earlier: the long-term maintenance needs of existing roads' physical infrastructure, public pressures to keep pace with the steady increase in automobile use, and engineers' efforts to create a system of public roads administration geared toward their traffic-service vision. After fifteen years of depleted resources (the "period of neglect," as DPW officials called the years between 1930 and 1945), there was no question in the minds of the road builders that more—more money and more miles—was needed.[129]

Conclusion

The public policy response to the twin crises of war and depression dramatically altered the existing highway order. New York's road-building experience during this time suggests the emergence of a new style of federalism, directly challenging the localistic notions embedded in highway politics. For decades, state and local authorities had struggled to renegotiate road-building authority. And yet, while the locus of road administration had shifted upward from the decentralized cluster of town highway commissions to the mandatory coordination of a state highway system, local officials and state legislators could still exert a powerful countervailing authority against DPW engineers. During the 1930s and 1940s, however, the national character of the economic and military emergencies shifted the policy-making focus from state-local to state-federal relations. In the process, older debates over the virtues of localism were muted, the shift toward centralized and bureaucratic administration gained new political legitimacy, and engineers consolidated their control over road-building politics.

The Westchester strike of 1931 was a signal event in depression-era road building, revealing a transformation of highway labor practices that had been under way for a generation. Compared to the calm, familiar waters once navigated by the local pathmaster and his residential labor tax, the labor unrest, nativism, and radical politics surrounding the road workers' strike were turbulent currents fed by strange and distant forces. Other developments—the use of public works to offset unemployment and, later, the prioritization of military defense highways—indicated bolder departures in the service of nationally directed objectives.

Yet the decline in importance of local road-building authority and the increased presence of federal agencies did not disturb the central place of the state administration within the road-building universe.[130] Ultimately it fell to state engineers and officials to mediate between local and national imperatives in road construction. The nationalization of the bureaucratic road-building regime did not place state actors in the service of federal ones, so much as it encouraged them to focus their attention on a more broadly conceived transportation agenda (including unemployment relief, civil defense, and economic development) that made local concerns over road building seem trivial by comparison.

Especially during the late 1930s and early 1940s, these national concerns closely paralleled state engineers' own desires for a traffic-service vision of highway planning and a bureaucratic road-building regime that would privilege that vision over local, particularistic claims. As Governor Dewey announced in 1944, a successful postwar road-building program was dependent on "clearing the obstacles" that "hampered the proper development of our highway system." With this, Dewey endorsed what had been the central goal of state highway officials during the late 1930s and early 1940s: the further constraint of local control in road building, more extensive reliance on federal resources, and a greater role for state engineers in setting rural, urban, and suburban highway policy. The nationalization of the bureaucratic regime had legitimized this process while hastening the transformation of the public's perception of public roads. With state and federal engineers squarely in the driver's seat, they effectively seized on these shifts (in the locus of public authority, in the public-private nature of highways) and shaped the discourse of highway planning toward their own ends. And with postwar budget increases looming on the horizon, the stage was set for a state road-building program the likes of which the modern world had never seen.

Authority: The Thruway and the Consolidation of the Bureaucratic Regime, 1945–1956

With the shift away from the imperatives of recovery and war in the late 1940s, and with a growing national consensus on the significance of transportation improvements to postwar economic development, highway engineers were poised to commit the resources of the state and federal governments to a vast program of highway modernization. By 1956 the Department of Public Works was spending on its postwar construction program more than twice what it had in the previous peak year of 1931. It produced hundreds of miles of new urban arterial highways, thousands of miles of rural roads, and the nation's longest toll superhighway, the 535-mile New York State Thruway.[1] The "Main Line of the Empire State" linked New York City, Albany, and Buffalo, and its connections extended to Pennsylvania, New Jersey, Connecticut, Massachusetts, and Canada. Largely completed by 1956, the Thruway represented both the culmination of a half-century of state highway construction and the prologue to the federal Interstate Highway System into which it was eventually incorporated.

A new generation of engineers took the helm of the State Department of Public Works in the postwar period, including Charles H. Sells (1943–1948) and Bertram D. Tallamy (1948–1954), who would go on to serve as the nation's first federal highway administrator. Both of Governor Thomas E. Dewey's Republican appointees had clocked years of public service and were well-schooled in the workings of the bureaucratic road-building regime ushered in by their Democratic forebears, Colonel Frederick S. Greene and Captain Arthur W. Brandt.[2] With the changing of the guard came a new set of political arrangements, most notably the creation of the New York State Thruway Authority, which served to strengthen and consolidate the bureaucratic autonomy Greene and Brandt had secured between 1919 and 1943.

As this chapter demonstrates, the establishment of a politically autonomous and financially independent public authority to direct the construction and operation of the Thruway revealed New Yorkers' great faith in the bureaucratic road-building regime, their comfort with remote authority, and their increasing deference to engineering professionalism. But once the Thruway Authority sprung into action, it became clear to local officials (who had yielded much of their countervailing road-building powers over the previous decades) that they were poorly positioned to influence the controversial plans that Thruway engineers had in mind. And as the Thruway came to dominate the state's construction program during the 1950s (two of every three New York highway dollars were spent on the project in 1953), highway engineers, who had few encounters with sustained dissent under previous decades of highway improvement, remained deaf to the growing chorus of resistance to their work.[3] Instead, they pursued ever-closer relationships with highway construction and real estate interests, motorist organizations, and Wall Street bond marketers. And they relied on traffic surveys as a mandate for their pursuit of extensive highway construction that promised to redefine social and economic life across a multitude of New York communities. By treating motorists as consumers, who cast unconflicted votes for more roads with their wheels alone, engineers downplayed the more complex concerns of motorist-citizens, who enjoyed improved highways but also sought a more honest reckoning of the impact of road construction on their lives.

This was a political world far removed from that of the late nineteenth-century pathmasters and the local road-building regime. It was also distinct from the early bureaucratic road-building regimes that came into being in the interwar years. Even when engineers such as Greene and Brandt directed state highway programs, localities still had a range of inputs that could shape transportation policy, most importantly the "veto" power they could exercise through the withholding of rights-of-way. With the culmination of the bureaucratic regime at midcentury, New Yorkers sanctioned a closed-system approach to highway engineering. And they endorsed a form of road-building politics that set the stage for the Interstate Highway System, which mirrored (and, of course, amplified) the Thruway in its enormity, expense, and ambition. The establishment of the Thruway Authority also foreshadowed the creation of the Highway Trust Fund, the legislation that ensured that all federally collected, motorist-generated revenue would be earmarked for highway construction. Ultimately, the consolidation of bureaucratic autonomy entailed the conscious diminution of the public's role in highway planning, an insistence on viewing motorists as consumers rather than citizens, and the single-minded dedication of highway revenue to perpetuate engineer-administrators' transportation visions. These developments capped off a deep transformation of the political order; they carried with them as well a set of hidden instabilities, rooted in its architects' intentional disregard for deliberative democracy.

"The War's End": Relief, Reconversion, and Reconstruction

With the cessation of hostilities in 1945, New York like the rest of the nation faced the daunting task of converting to a peacetime economy. The legacy of the past weighed heavily. Would America face a postwar recession as it had after World War I? Would it return to the depression-era conditions of the 1930s? Should the state administration foster New Deal–style jobs programs to provide work for returning veterans and ease the transition to peacetime? Or should it roll back the changes that depression and war had wrought on public works policy and resume a highway-building program that measured progress in terms of mileage rather than employment?[4]

These questions, informed by the experiences of the Great Depression and World War II, framed the immediate postwar response to highway policy. At the same time, the long-term pressures for highway development, present since the turn of the century, reemerged. As state officials responded to these pressing transportation demands, they gradually reoriented the framework of highway construction from employment relief to peacetime economic reconversion to postwar reconstruction. In the process, they set in motion important policy changes—the establishment of a Post-War Reconstruction Fund, the expansion of the Department of Public Works, and the creation of a Public Relations Bureau within the DPW—that emboldened state engineers to champion increasingly controversial projects such as extensive rural road improvement, a major urban arterial initiative, and the New York State Thruway.

New York highway policy continued to bear the imprint of New Deal politics into the mid-1940s. Republican Governor Thomas E. Dewey had successfully capitalized on the growing public distaste for big spending and big government in his 1942 bid for office. Dewey endorsed key aspects of the modern welfare state such as Social Security and industrial regulation. But he objected to Franklin Roosevelt and Herbert Lehman's haphazard administration of works programs and called for better management in public construction. With the war's end, he adopted a moderate Republican stance as he laid out the state's future building program. Careful not to sound too much like a New Dealer, he nonetheless encouraged visionary public works projects that would make a lasting contribution to the state's infrastructure.[5]

The immense wartime surplus gave Dewey the leeway he needed. The booming war economy had led to a vast increase in public revenue; by the war's end, the surplus amounted to $310 million. Dewey advocated its transfer to a Post-War Reconstruction Fund, designed to channel state revenue into long-deferred public works projects.[6] Dewey proposed a massive $840 million public roads program that could be financed on a "pay-as-you-go" plan. In the past, such a costly program would have required the state to go into debt to finance the project; now Dewey could play the big spender while appealing to fiscal conservatives.

Dewey stated flatly that "this program is not a relief project." But it appeared to some as emerging from the "pump-priming" and "make-work" mold of the Works Progress Administration, which had been given an "honorable discharge" in 1942. State Chairman Paul E. Fitzpatrick, a Democrat, chided Dewey for what he thought was a misguided plan. Dewey "takes a bow" on his highway program's ability to "employ the returning veteran," but "our boys have had their fill of digging fox holes and living in mud and mire without having to come back and be given the so-called generous opportunity to work with pick and shovel on the highway. They are not looking for a dole or a handout."[7]

While Dewey distanced himself from New Deal–style relief programs, he had learned the lesson of depression-era finance well: when large sums were available it was important to spend them, and spend them quickly. Most public officials feared a return to depression conditions following the war, and the DPW had been busily putting plans on the shelf during the war years to create work for returning veterans. According to Dewey, New York was "ready to go" almost immediately after V-J Day. "I don't believe any State in the nation, or the nation itself," he added, "was as ready as New York for the war's end. I am sure that none was ready to place its projects in the contract stage three weeks after the war ended."[8]

By 1946 the Post-War Reconstruction Fund amounted to nearly half a billion dollars. The fund was directed by the Post-War Public Works Planning Commission, a small, tightly integrated commission including the heads of the DPW and the Division of the Budget. It was, in Dewey's bold words, "an agency of action, not merely an agency of analysis and research."[9] The primary focus of the commission was the reconstruction of the state's highway transportation infrastructure, "the vital arteries of economic and social life," without which "our state would degenerate into a collection of isolated communities."[10]

Dewey's strident language echoed former Governor Al Smith's exuberant embrace of highways during the boom years of the 1920s. The DPW's annual reports of the 1930s and early 1940s had been glum reading: a collection of thin, despairing volumes. But the postwar reports offered a dramatic contrast. Thick, with pastel illustrations, and almost poetic at times, they exuded a zealous postwar enthusiasm. Along with Dewey's "agency of action," they set a new tone for postwar highway politics, characterized by renewed vigor, determination, and the ambition to tackle projects on a grand scale.

The 1946 report opened with an uncharacteristic meditation on the significance of the built environment by Superintendent of Public Works Charles Sells. "Just as the individual inherits from his forebears whatever legacy of worldly goods may be his," Sells rhapsodized, "so does society, with each passing generation, come into possession of the tangibles of yesteryear. Of utmost social and economic significance among these inheritables are those facilities which have come to be classified as public works."[11] Sells went on to make the case for the centrality of highways—those inherited, those yet to be built—to the postwar world. Now that the war was over, the DPW was free to envision a highway system of a new scale and scope.

The centerpiece of this program was the New York State Thruway, conceived as a six-lane, New York City–to–Buffalo express highway. Governor Thomas E. Dewey thought it "reminiscent of the Futurama," and his analogy is apt.[12] The General Motors Futurama exhibit at the 1939 World's Fair offered an early look at the postdepression world; the Thruway was its dream come true. In promoting the Thruway, DPW officials were doing more than just reverting to the old metrics of "miles built" in place of "numbers employed"; they were reenvisioning what new roads would look like. Rather than improving existing highways, the Thruway planners reinvented highways in a self-consciously modern way: the roads of the future were roads without pasts.

Sells's "idyll of the Thruway," sketched in the 1946 report, portrays the project as of yet a blueprint fantasy. He admitted that the six-lane "superhighway" might be "difficult for the reader to imagine," inured as he or she was to the "repeated bumpings" over long-neglected highways. "Fifty-mile-per-hour cars and thirty-mile-per-hour roads are no novelty to present day drivers. . . . But there will come a day, in the not too distant future, when both the new car and the completed Thruway will have become accepted parts of life in the Empire State."

Sells described a road trip free of "frayed nerves." Gone were the narrow lanes with cable guide railings "which seemed to be reaching for you as you tried to get by." Instead he depicted wide, uninterrupted lanes of travel. Bridges appeared with columns "smoothly curved and delicately proportioned, seeming to have grown naturally out of the ground for just the purpose to which they have been put." The bridge decks seemed "so smooth and sleek . . . in their attractive green paint" that it was difficult "to reconcile them with the usual appearance of structural steel members."[13]

Sells overplayed the naturalistic qualities of the Thruway-to-be, hoping to portray it as a high-benefit, low-impact structure. Indeed, Sells walked a fine line in his efforts to describe the highway's modernist elements without drawing attention to the controversial politics surrounding the construction of such a mega-project. Implementing this construction meant wrestling with questions of who would finance it, whose interests would it serve, and who would have authority over the structure.

Depicting the Thruway as in harmony with nature was one way of downplaying the politicized nature of its construction. And yet, the reality would be very different from the all-but-organic development that Sells described. To build the Thruway required a vast expansion of the DPW workforce. The number of engineers tripled in size with the addition of 1,500 new appointments in 1946, most of them returning veterans. Having outgrown the thirteenth floor of the Alfred E. Smith State Office Building in Albany, the DPW took over five more floors and parts of several other buildings.[14]

Of all the DPW's new units, the most noteworthy was the Bureau of Public Relations. The bureau hit the ground running; by the end of 1945, its first year of operation, it had generated 75,000 column inches of press. As much as postwar enthusiasm, public relations (PR) accounted for the dramatic difference in presentation in the 1946 annual report. The public relations industry experienced tremendous growth in the postwar years, and public as well as private institutions grew increasingly sensitive to their outward appearance.

Over time, much of the DPW's policy and public dealings was shaped by a PR perspective. Even the employment of highway laborers, so central during the Great Depression's unemployment crisis, was conditioned by concern over the public reaction to inefficient make-work. Thus the DPW justified a 1954 pay increase for its road crews on the ground that "our public relations would be much better" if more qualified (and presumably younger) workers were seen to be repairing the highways. Superintendent of Public Works Bertram Tallamy cautioned that "now we are running an Old Folks Home."[15]

In the triumphant years of postwar corporate dominance, the expanded DPW micromanaged public perception and information as part of its ever-more-businesslike style of management. A 1958 case study of the Dewey administration criticized "public relations work by government agencies" as "far too imitative of commercial procedures." Governmental public relations programs were in their infancy at this time, and these novice agencies faced tremendous challenges in adapting corporate PR techniques to state service.[16] Were PR men to provide objective information in the public interest, or to mold public opinion the way private enterprises did? Should they encourage citizen involvement in public decision making, or simply promote a government product? These questions had no easy answers. But DPW officials held an unshakable faith in the logic of highway engineering: that traffic surveys were the best reflections of motorists' demands; that motorist-generated revenue entitled highway users to improved roadways; that highway engineers were agents of modernity, hastening urban growth and economic development.[17] And this ideology made it easier for them to work amidst these contradictions.

"Like a Ton of Bricks": Postwar Highway Challenges

The promise of peacetime economic growth, the challenging new project of the New York State Thruway, and the support of an enlarged administrative and public relations workforce brought a new sense of its potential to the DPW. But Sells's 1946 analysis revealed some troubling figures. He thought it "interesting to reflect upon the legacy" of the inherited highway system, and what he found did not look good. "Fully a third" of the state's 14,000-mile highway system was a "carry-over" from decades ago, laid out upon alignments "selected in the horse-and-buggy days."[18] The future of New York's roads required updating its existing system at a faster pace, as well as constructing new, modern highways on entirely new locations. To meet this need, the DPW planned not just to build the Thruway but also to reconstruct much of the existing road system, to build major new urban arterials in all the state's medium and large cities, and to undertake systematic rural highway improvements.

Though the Thruway was to be the DPW's centerpiece project, highway rehabilitation had top priority. The state's highway building of the 1920s—the "so-called permanent type of construction," as Superintendent Sells put it in a 1947 special report to Governor Dewey—had produced roads with a twenty-year life at best. After that, they required total reconstruction or major repair.[19] Much of New York's modern highway system was constructed in the mid- and late 1920s, and extensive maintenance had been deferred during the 1930s and early 1940s. So a large percentage of the state system required immediate attention. In 1947 more than 5,000 miles (36 percent of the system) were over twenty years old; 5,800 more miles (41 percent) were between ten and twenty years old. Highways needed to be widened as well as resurfaced. It would take years to restore the old pavement, even at an accelerated pace. And each year, more miles of highway than could be reconstructed passed beyond the twenty-year mark.

To have kept up with the system's demand for continuous reconstruction, the state should have restored over 10,000 miles of roadway between 1930 and 1946. Because of economic depression and war, New York had reached about half that figure. According to the report's findings, to bring the system to "its peak of efficiency" by 1960 required the construction and reconstruction of 1,150 miles a year. Factoring in postwar inflation, that program would cost an estimated $143 million annually for the next fourteen years. The unprecedented $840 million postwar reconstruction program, now eighteen months behind schedule, was deemed wholly insufficient. In its place, Dewey and the DPW sought to increase it to an unprecedented $2 billion.[20]

As the Dewey administration contemplated ever larger highway budgets and ever grander construction programs, the policy orthodoxies of the past fifteen years—unemployment relief, peacetime reconversion, and highway reconstruction—appeared to offer little guidance for postwar road building. For the first time since the 1920s, highway officials prioritized the construction of modern transportation infrastructure over the series of ad hoc policy tools that had characterized the depression and war years. But in the years since the 1920s, postwar highway construction had increased in scale, complexity, and potential for political divisiveness. The discourse of postwar highway politics was distinguished by officials' heightened displays of confidence and ambition, and it continued to privilege the interests of the motorist-consumer who had come to dominate highway planners' thinking about roads and road use. But it was marked as well by difficult questions regarding financing and authority. Engineers' visions of "modern" highways often ran into conflict with postwar fiscal realities and raised public anxieties over the social and economic dislocation that accompanied new construction.

The emergence of a robust postwar DPW went hand in hand with the first major departmental reorganization since the 1920s. In 1944 the old DPW bureaus (highways, canals, public buildings) were abolished. In their place the DPW established three new divisions: construction, administration, and operation and maintenance. This restructuring reflected the triumph of engineering principles that emphasized the common elements of broadly defined functions rather than the particularities of isolated projects. The move made good business sense, allowing the DPW to make more efficient use of its personnel and to eliminate overlapping duties. But behind it was a mindset that conceived of engineering projects as closed systems, homogenous and reducible to basic elements. That approach reflected the way engineers had come to see their projects: through the narrow lens of engineering principles, removed from the diverse social and political contexts in which they were so deeply rooted.[21]

Of course, these engineering principles, while clothed in the apolitical rhetoric of neutral competence and statistical analysis, had always been a distinct form of political expression. Engineers had increased their bureaucratic autonomy during the 1920s by arguing that their professional expertise could better direct highway policy than, as they saw it, corrupt or self-serving legislators. The 1944 reorganization simply allowed engineers the capacity to exercise their autonomy more effectively. It also allowed them to better serve their self-described constituency of highway users, the road builders' satisfied "consumers" who lent the engineers political legitimacy.

Consistent with its effort to foster a more vertical, hierarchical organizational structure, DPW leadership continuously merged individual bureaus. Even as its authority expanded into new areas, the department developed an increasingly bureaucratic work culture, which paid little heed to the unique challenges posed by a varied and complex construction program. Thus the newly formed Bureau of Arterial Route Planning, created in 1946 after the state reversed its 1898 policy against constructing highways in cities, found a new home in the Bureau of Highway Planning. Despite the specialized knowledge required to address the mapping of urban arterials—especially the plotting of route locations through densely populated areas—the bureau took on this task alongside the surveying of new rural routes and the coordinating of federal-aid highway construction within the nascent Interstate System.[22]

In 1946 Deputy Superintendent Bertram D. Tallamy initiated a five-year, $119 million program to develop plans for urban arterial highways on a city-by-city basis. For the first time, the DPW made systematic surveys of urban traffic. A year later, plans were under way for highways in 80 percent of New York's cities. Forty cities participated in the state's urban highway program, and twenty urban area reports were finished by 1953. DPW planners translated origin-destination traffic surveys into new construction with astonishing speed during this period.[23]

The DPW's urban arterial highways were the first wholly new construction projects since the parkways and bypass highways of the 1920s. Like these earlier roads, the urban arterials were designed to ease traffic flow into, out of, and around urban areas. But the arterial program tackled urban traffic problems in a more comprehensive way than parkways had, promoting aggressive new construction in most of New York's metropolitan areas and privileging regional rather than local traffic.

The focus on eliminating through traffic congestion in highly developed urban areas made the program highly disruptive. Bottlenecks had developed where wide state highways merged into narrow city streets; these traffic jams were a fallout from the long-standing policy restriction against constructing highways in municipalities. As traffic congestion increased at these points of entry, real estate values dropped and the quality of life in the affected communities declined. When the DPW extended state highways (now termed urban arterials) through these impoverished areas, it opened the door to future charges from racial minorities and the working class of what would eventually be termed "transportation exploitation." A decade or more would pass before urban highway construction met with organized community resistance. But the seeds of the crisis were already evident in the union of new highway construction, the narrow engineering vision of highway planners, and the unintended consequences of past policy choices.[24]

When New York's urban arterial program broke ground in Buffalo in 1948, however, the response reflected older, more traditional concerns. When the Buffalo Chamber of Commerce worried that the city was not getting its "fair share" of state highway funds, Superintendent Tallamy was quick to offer assurances that while the city had about 20 percent of the state's upstate urban population, it was receiving close to a third of upstate urban arterial money.[25] And when critics decried the construction of a large, elevated express highway, Tallamy and his fellow engineers steadfastly defended the

DPW's plans. They argued that the new expressway would provide easy access to the city and facilitate through traffic, while at the same time avoiding the high costs of acquiring the right-of-way for a ground-level boulevard. But critics reacted sharply to the character and location of the design. Members of the Buffalo press and the Buffalo Chamber of Commerce objected above all to a stretch of elevated highway that nearly encircled Buffalo's downtown Memorial Auditorium.[26]

Constructed during the New Deal, the Memorial Auditorium had replaced Buffalo's aging Broadway Auditorium in 1940. The new structure was well-received, especially by the American Legion, which had been asking for a suitable war memorial since 1919. Now, less than a decade after its construction, the new route would mask the "Aud," a building that had become a source of civic pride. Tallamy assured critics that the highway would be "a handsome structure," one "of modern design" that "will not too much mar the beauty of the building." But his optimism could not hide the fact that the new highway dramatically altered Buffalo's cityscape. Though the express highway would have the sleek, concrete-and-steel functionalism of modernist construction, it lacked—and blocked—the auditorium's classic design and architectural grandeur. Beyond that, it separated the city of Buffalo from its waterfront, a move that would have serious consequences for urban development later in the century.[27]

Controversy in other urban areas followed as the DPW began to implement its arterial highway plans. Albany, Rochester, Syracuse, Binghamton, and other cities were to be the recipients of new highways designed to eliminate traffic bottlenecks about which residents had complained for decades. Tallamy's successor, John W. Johnson, faced the difficult task of defending the DPW work as it followed through on its bold new construction program. Soon after taking over Tallamy's post, Johnson confessed that myriad problems descended on him "like a ton of bricks."[28]

Chief among these problems was generating public support for the construction of urban arterials in large upstate cities, especially the "depressed" highways planned for large upstate cities including Rochester and Syracuse. Here DPW engineers planned to use old canal beds for the depressed arterial systems. But many objected to these moat-like highways; one critic of the DPW's Syracuse plan thought the proposed highway was more like "an open subway 20 feet deep."[29] Johnson told the critic that "travel over such a modern facility is safe, fast, pleasant and not even remotely related to a subway."[30]

Yet the comparison was apt. As was the case with Syracuse, Rochester's new arterial highway system ran along the old Erie Canal route, which had more recently served as the site of one of Rochester's subway lines. The subway had been in financial trouble since the depression, and DPW leadership positioned the agency to acquire the inexpensive right-of-way should the line be abandoned. Superintendent Johnson informed Assistant to the Governor Daniel Patrick Moynihan of the DPW's intentions. When Moynihan protested that thousands of subway riders would lose an important commuter service, Johnson assured him that the Rochester Transit Corporation had pledged to provide bus service along the new route.[31]

In truth the DPW considered support for mass transit systems a low priority. Charles H. Tuttle, chairman of New York City's Metropolitan Rapid Transit Commission, requested that the DPW integrate a commuter rail system into its plan for Manhattan's arterial highways. But Superintendent Johnson dismissed the request, claiming that the two transportation agendas were "separate and distinct." Johnson also had doubts as to the legality of diverting highway appropriations to purchase wider rights-of-way to accommodate commuter railways. Certainly it cut against his own belief that motorist-generated revenue "belonged" to the automobile owners and truckers who financed road construction.

More important, he thought that this form of transportation was inappropriate to the new realities of mid–twentieth century life. "The present and future arterial highway system in New York City," he concluded, "does not lend itself to the addition of rail transportation." The new highways "do not tap centers of dense population, but rather intercept traffic from an intricate street and highway system and carry it to river crossings where it is again dissipated over a large area." Johnson explained that decentralized residential development substantially transformed commuter patterns, and that the "arterial program meets an existing demand for flexible means of transportation which cannot be served by rail." Johnson recognized that commuter railroads serving metropolitan New York faced a "serious financial problem." But he believed that the rail system was simply not suited to existing suburban conditions and that it could not be supported by or integrated into the highway system. Johnson concluded that the problems facing mass transit and arterial highways "must be solved independently."[32]

The narrow mandate of the DPW under which Johnson operated— and the "user fees" logic that tagged highway revenue for more highway construction—cut against Tuttle's call for more comprehensive, multimodal transportation planning. Disassociating the problems of mass transit and urban highways had vast consequences for the future of New York City transportation. Johnson and the DPW's dismissal of the benefits of the rail system reflected a single-minded devotion to highways that remained largely unchallenged for many years. The urban arterial system was the product of the DPW's closed-system approach, a way of thinking that geared spending to traffic counts while relegating other issues—the impact of highways on the cityscape, the possibility of alternative forms of transportation—to the margin.

This tunnel vision reflected as well the engineering profession's commitment to its traffic-service model of highway planning, buoyed up by strong public support for the logic of "user fees." Throughout the 1930s, motorists, truckers, and the organized interest groups who represented them had backed the idea that fuel taxes and registration fees were there to build and maintain highways. An extension of this idea—that origin-destination surveys represented "demand lines" that must be responded to by the DPW—provided ample justification for the engineers' dismissals of any concerns about the impact of this new construction.

The pressure to respond to motorists' demands was felt not just in urban areas but in rural ones as well. Expanding suburbia, with its car-tailored sprawl, served as an escape from overcrowded cities at the turn of the century.[33] It was also a response to the pull of underutilized rural farmland, left vacant as the center of American agriculture shifted westward. While the DPW tried to deal with urban traffic snarls by constructing new, highly visible arterial highways, another less visible project was under way: the revitalization of secondary roads to meet the demands of rural communities.

In 1950 Senator Austin W. Erwin, Republican chairman of the state legislature's Temporary Commission on Agriculture, drafted a ten-year, $146 million town highway assistance program.[34] Support for town highways had long been a partisan issue. Since rural New York was predominantly Republican, assistance to town superintendents of highways sat well with that party. By midcentury, however, Democrats and Republicans alike could see the value in aiding town highways. The state could ill afford to assume responsibility for the 50,000 miles of town roads. But as suburban commuting increased and school centralization required extensive busing, support for increased aid to town highways became less contentious.

DPW officials backed this policy change, too. As Superintendent Johnson explained to DPW Director of Public Relations James E. Treux, bottleneck bridges on local roads were especially problematic, having "plagued the Department of Public Works since the '20s." Now he thought that "the pressure of publicity" might oblige the DPW to take greater responsibility for rural roads and bridges. Indeed, public relations considerations—and the careful maintenance of the DPW's reputation of infallibility—had become critical to every aspect of the state's postwar transportation program.[35]

Rural roads, like urban highways, had been hard hit by the budgeting crises of the 1930s and 1940s and the unabated increase in traffic. Despite the doubling of road maintenance and construction costs, state aid to towns had risen little since the 1930s. The Erwin plan provided greater town assistance in exchange for increased DPW oversight. State officials planned to renew 12,500 miles of secondary roads, roughly a quarter of the state's rural mileage and about half of what had to be rebuilt according to the DPW's assessment. It amounted to a sizable program. By 1952 DPW engineers had approved road modernization plans for 85 percent of the state, including 788 of the state's 932 towns.[36]

In contrast to the controversial urban arterial programs, which had a heavy impact on downtown areas, the rural highway programs ran through less-developed areas and were far less disruptive. In the two years following the passage of the Erwin Act, nearly two-thirds of the towns began to implement their road-improvement programs, constructing over 1,700 miles of town roads. A 1954 poll of road officials found overwhelming support for the expansion of rural road work: 48 of 57 upstate counties favored the development of these large public works programs. Even in 1956, a critical year for national highways, Superintendent Johnson assured the New York State Association of Town Superintendents of Highways that "in spite of the glare of publicity now being centered upon our great interstate and defense highway system, we will not overlook the county and town road systems, which are so important to the overall highway picture."[37]

Though the rural road improvement plan found many supporters, it was not adopted without debate. Changes in the apportionment of finance, planning, and responsibility for road construction tapped into age-old arguments. A group of prosperous farmers in Candor, New York, for example, wanted to know which roads would be improved, whose roads would be improved first, and who would pay for incidental costs such as the setting back of fences on the widened roads. But when it appeared that their potential quarreling might prompt the town board to reject the state assistance plan, they agreed to resolve their disputes amicably and pressured the board to accept the plan.[38]

Other rural New Yorkers viewed the burgeoning highway program with unmitigated antipathy. J. Sloat Welles was one of them. He worked the Elmira farm that had been in his family for five generations. As part of the postwar reconstruction program, the Welles farm lost crossing rights to State Route 17 (dubbed the Southern Tier's "milk route" because it provided dairy producers access to Manhattan). The state hoped to improve highway safety and make the highway more attractive for possible inclusion in the emerging Interstate System. But this came at the cost of the productivity of Welles's farmland, which was bisected by the highway. In an angry letter to Governor Averell Harriman, Welles informed him that "strong language is being used" among neighboring farmers who had lost their crossing rights, "even to the point of dynamiting the highway."[39]

Superintendent Johnson was quick to point out that this was not the first time the Welles family had had to make sacrifices in the name of progress: "Through the years, the Welles farm has been cut by the Canal bed, the Erie Railroad, the Delaware, Lackawanna, and Western Railroad, the original Route 17, and the grade crossing over Route 17. As it has survived all of these disruptions, we feel confident it will survive the present one." To soften the blow, Johnson bestowed upon Welles's farm the Century Award "as a tribute to the resilience and resourcefulness of those who have tilled its acres for a century or more." Angered by the injuries his family had endured by this long list of transportation revolutions, Welles turned down the honor.[40]

Johnson's catalog of transportation initiatives is an important reminder of the disruptiveness of all public works projects. Creative destruction has been a hallmark of American economic development since the early nineteenth century.[41] But Welles's rejection of the Century Award offers another lesson. New York's farming communities, well represented in the legislature, had been enlisted to support highway improvements since the turn of the century. But New York's agrarians rarely received the full measure of the state highway administration's attention. A half century after the start of the Good Roads movement, the majority of New York's farm-to-market roads was unimproved. Renewed efforts to get farmers "out of the mud" were viewed by Welles and others as costly, disruptive, and of uncertain benefit.

In a sense, the half-hearted commitment to rural road building was no different from that experienced by New York's cities. Policy restrictions limiting the construction of state highways in incorporated municipalities—logical in the context of turn-of-the-century politics—led to the uneven development of the state's transportation infrastructure. These restrictions, which continued through depression and war, assured that the eventual large-scale improvement projects would be that much more unsettling. The rebuilding of Route 17, like the construction of urban arterial highways, disrupted lives and landscapes.

These controversial construction projects reflected the uneasy balance between broad social and economic needs and the particularities of local conditions, values, and resources. And they illustrate the complexities of the evolving American system of federalism during the postwar years, when a new generation of engineers sought to consolidate road-building authority under their bureaucratic regime. Engineers had always recognized that political legitimacy and political power were instrumental to their success as professionals and to the successful implementation of their traffic-service vision of highway improvement. But the way in which that political power was exercised changed substantially between the 1920s (when engineers first began to dominate highway administration) and the postwar years.

Early state highway engineers, such as Colonel Frederick S. Greene, rose to power by leveraging the authority of professional expertise against the perceived inadequacies of existing road administrators: local officials and machine politicians. Though Greene and his cohort had defined their notion of public service in increasingly narrow ways (working on behalf of the "motorist-consumer"), their road-improvement program was largely a popular one, and, with the exception of Old Guard legislators, they rarely confronted hostile critics. Indeed, before World War II, opposition to road building was scattered and disorganized, largely because engineers were improving existing routes of travel rather than engaging in construction on new road sites.

As engineering projects increased in scale, impact, and potential for controversy during the postwar years, resistance to urban and rural highway plans spiked. In the process of responding to increased opposition, strong tensions developed between engineers' service to their professional agenda (building a better highway system) and their responsibility to the public (balancing highway construction with other aspects of social development). These interests, once operating in tandem and instrumental to the engineers' rise to power, began over time to feed conflict and meet with cross-purposes. It was left to a new generation of highway engineers, including future Chief Federal Highway Administrator Bertram Tallamy, to field these problems. Thus, at the very moment that Greene's successors were poised to consolidate the gains made by a generation of professionalized networking, their bureaucratic regime faced a wider chorus of challenges to its political legitimacy. These voices grew loudest in response to the construction of the New York State Thruway, a mega-project complicated by the fact that it included rural, urban, and suburban components.

"A Blueprint Dream": The Thruway from Paper to Pavement

The tensions of postwar road building peaked during the construction of the New York State Thruway. A decade had passed since Frederick S. Greene, the superintendent of Public Works who guided the department through the expansionary period of the 1920s, recommended the construction of a great superhighway across the state. The legislature put the Thruway on the official State Map in 1942, but World War II forestalled construction. On July 11, 1946, Governor Dewey finally broke ground on the first section of what he called "the greatest highway in the world."[42] At the ceremony he observed that "transportation has always been the cornerstone of the social and economic progress of any people." He added that New York's "greatness" depended in large part on its citizens' early interest in providing "relatively cheap, speedy, and safe transportation . . . from the days of the mule-drawn barge to the present motor car."[43] Drawing on this long-standing commitment to public works, Dewey's words were full of confidence and promise. But they veiled real troubles. Political differences, conflict over transportation priorities, financial difficulties, poor industrial conditions, and community opposition slowed progress on the Thruway. Many doubted its necessity and timeliness, as well as its projected cost and target completion date of 1951 (see Map 5.1).

Democratic Party leaders voiced a steady stream of objections to Dewey's "luxury boulevard," advocating traditional municipal and social welfare issues instead. Urban Democrats wanted aid to cities given priority over the cross-state Thruway. Bronx Senator Lowell H. Brown wanted the $202 million slated for Thruway construction to be redirected toward the rehabilitation of New York City's rapid transit facilities. Other Democrats argued that the money should go to affordable housing or new schools. Senate Minority Leader Elmer F. Quinn would rather have had "hospital beds than road beds." He could "not understand the social philosophy of the present Republican administration," a group that Democratic Chairman Fitzpatrick concluded "can only think in terms of gravel, cement, and macadam."[44]

When Dewey ran for reelection in 1946, his opponent, Senator James M. Mead, tried to capitalize on the governor's unswerving devotion to the Thruway. Though the political culture had changed dramatically over the

Map 5.1: Route of the New York State Thruway, 1960 (with official opening dates)

Credit: Benjamin Shaykin

past half-century, the rhetoric of early twentieth-century politics still lingered in Mead's accusations: the governor had stolen the war surplus from war veterans and turned it into a "Dewey slush fund" designed to "grease the Dewey machine"; the Thruway was a "postponable luxury boulevard"; the highway program was "the Dewey pork barrel."[45] Even the pro-Thruway *New York Times* thought that Dewey's estimation of the highway's costs and its potential economic savings were "on the optimistic side."[46]

Dewey saw the project quite differently. First of all, he found it rather easy to brush aside Mead's disparaging language of boss politics by citing the Thruway's technocratic origins. Beyond that, the Thruway represented for Dewey the achievement of a new kind of activist state: a big-ticket item financed in a Republican style. "The Republican party," Dewey argued, "has picked up the banner of liberal and progressive government from the faltering hands of the Democratic party." His support of the Thruway was consistent with postwar liberalism's embrace of public policies that stressed economic growth and minimized direct control over the economy. By using the wartime surplus rather than creating new public debt, his administration transferred tax revenues back into the hands of private-sector contractors. This strategy would, in Dewey's words, provide important public improvements while "lessening the burden of government."[47]

But the wartime surplus proved to be false security. As the DPW's general reconstruction program swelled from $840 million to $2 billion, the financial outlook for the state's transportation infrastructure became increasingly problematic. The year after Dewey's reelection, he candidly confessed to a meeting of the American Association of Highway Officials, surely a hospitable audience, "I don't know where the funds are coming from, but I do know it is our solemn duty to rebuild the highways." Public awareness of the deteriorated state of postwar New York roads was high, and in time Dewey grew more comfortable with the ability of highway needs to sustain voter support for his construction program regardless of looming financial shortfalls. In an address to New York City voters later that year, he declared, "We are entering the last half of a century with thoroughfares scarcely sufficient to serve the needs of the first quarter. . . . I have not the vaguest idea where the money is coming from, but if it is not expended on road projects, we are not going to get farm products into the cities in sufficient quantities."[48]

To address rising highway costs, the Dewey administration considered making the Thruway a toll road. As late as 1945 the governor informed the legislature that he was "not yet prepared to say that this special facility should be built at general state expense."[49] But thorny opposition from the state's automobile lobby made the toll proposal unappealing. Dewey authorized a series of traffic censuses to weigh the feasibility of a cross-state toll highway. William Gottleib, president of the New York State Automobile Association, mocked Dewey's indecision, stating that he "should be able to decide 'no tolls' without paying three sets of traffic consultants to make a study."[50]

Dewey saw tolls as preferable to large bonded debt, a depression-era style of finance that he denounced at the Thruway groundbreaking as "a spineless attempt to conceal the costs of government."[51] But toll roads, abandoned in the nineteenth century, had a decidedly retrograde quality to them. Moreover, a toll facility created a new set of knotty problems: the cost of toll collection, the resulting limitation of highway access, the effect on the traffic of parallel free roads, and the opposition of organized highway users who had long supported the highway engineers' efforts to bureaucratize roadbuilding administration. The Dewey administration optimistically agreed to a third choice: the Thruway would be a free road, financed on a pay-as-you-go basis through general revenues and the Post-War Reconstruction Fund.

Things did not go as the administration had hoped. Industrial conditions continued to hamper Thruway construction during the late 1940s. Federal restrictions, linked to the Marshall Plan, created serious steel shortages, which led to a projected 30 percent decline in New York's road construction for 1948. "Within these ceilings," Superintendent Charles Sells complained, "it has been practically impossible to award work involving large quantities of steel or structural concrete." Federal steel rationing left New York with an "unbalanced program" including "critical gaps . . . principally bridges." The steel shortage was especially problematic because it coincided with the growing demand for better bridges to handle both the Thruway crossings and the increase in school busing, a product of the school centralization movement.[52]

Though over $200 million was spent on the Thruway between V-J Day and 1948, little progress had been made. J. R. Crossley of the New York State Automobile Association thought the whole road program was a "blueprint dream," a project that "limps pitifully behind the original timetables established in 1946." Given the realities of Thruway construction, the DPW's proposed $2 billion program seemed chimerical. "How can we talk of a ten-year program," he asked, "when the present [$840 million] program now is just about physically impossible to fulfill?"[53]

Crossley had a point. As cost estimates were revised upward to account for postwar inflation, it became clear that the Thruway would match (if not surpass) the cost of the state's general non-Thruway highway program. New rural and urban projects needed funding. And the existing state highway system—overused and understaffed—remained vulnerable: in the winter of 1945, heavy snows shut down 4,000 miles of upstate highways. Conditions were so bad and road crews so underequipped that the National Guard was called in to use dynamite to clear snow. Milk deliveries were cut by 40 percent, and city fuel shipments were drastically curtailed.[54]

By the late 1940s DPW officials began to bump up against the limits of their road-building logic: that traffic service meant increasing lanes and mileage along established demand lines. Sells acknowledged that demand might always outpace infrastructure, regardless of economic conditions: "Highways are not keeping pace with motor traffic volume. They never have and probably never will. . . . It takes much longer to construct or reconstruct roads than to build motor vehicles." Dewey seconded the thought: "You can't pick highways out of a Sears-Roebuck catalogue."[55]

The governor's consumer-tinged allusion was telling. Since the Great Depression, political economic thought had shifted decisively: now underconsumption rather than overproduction appeared to be the central economic problem for the government to address. Consistent with this development, politicians began to promote a new politics of "growth liberalism" that relied on government spending to foster economic growth in the form of corporate expansion, suburban development, and mass consumption.[56] The automobile was central to this new politics of consumption, with the car itself one of the costliest consumer durables. But widespread automobile ownership had vast indirect effects as well. The car opened the way for the explosion of suburban development and home ownership (also subsidized by a wide range of local, state, and federal policies). And it stimulated demand for a host of motor-related businesses, including tourism, motels, roadside advertising, fast food, and suburban shopping.[57]

In this light, the lagging road network became a major policy concern. As Superintendent of Public Works Bert Tallamy explained, the highway problem had "its roots in the simple fact that, from the outset, America has devoted more money and more attention to its motor vehicles than it has to the roads upon which they operate." The failure to provide roads adequate to the demands of the developing automobile culture—now so central to national economic prosperity—was a public responsibility. "We have stuffed the boy with growth promoting food," Tallamy told a group of New York businessmen, "but have neglected to keep him in pants that are big enough to cover him."[58]

Tallamy and other highway advocates remained unwilling to concede the fact that more money and more miles of highway would not address the problem that Sells had acknowledged already: that road construction generated greater demand for more highways, and that car and truck manufacturing consistently outpaced road construction. This proved to be one of the great blind spots generated by the political culture of growth liberalism. Privileging sustained economic growth fostered a road-building mentality that produced a costly highway network that was itself tremendously difficult to sustain.

Despite the note of growing urgency that Tallamy sounded on behalf of Thruway construction, less than thirteen miles of the express highway had been constructed by 1950. The *New York Times* wryly noted that the "highway of the future" was "a description which had its special ironies now."[59] To accelerate the pace of construction, Dewey hoped to secure funding from unspent grade-crossing bonds, first approved in 1927. The balance of the fund, amounting to $60 million, had been transferred to general highway construction in 1941, but spending was deferred during the war.

The move toward bonding did not sit well with Democratic Party leaders, who happily recalled Dewey's remarks at the groundbreaking ceremony about the "spinelessness" of going into debt for public improvements. "We will pay as we go," Dewey had said, "without plunging the state into a debt to be paid by our grandchildren." Chairman Fitzpatrick was so incensed by the policy reversal that he wanted the whole Thruway project suspended and investigated. Republican Party chairman William L. Pfeiffer thought Fitzpatrick's idea was "not only silly, futile, unnecessary, and time wasting, but thoroughly in keeping with the Democratic effort in this state to sabotage post-war rehabilitation."[60]

By 1950 the Thruway had become an intensely partisan issue. More than that, it became a touchstone for postwar political debate. Few public projects were so directly connected to the policy choices made during the previous half century. The heightened status of experts and engineers, the early and sustained commitment to an expansive program of highway construction, the complex system of highway finance maintained through fluctuating economic circumstances, the centrality of automobiles to American economic prosperity, the new relations among local, state, and federal units of government: these shaped the political environment in which public officials responded to the transportation challenges of the mid-twentieth century.

The Thruway, now a top policy concern, was one of the most significant products of this postwar environment, an embodiment of the postwar political ideal of economic growth through public investment. Yet by 1950, only 3 percent of this "highway of the future" had been built. Political bickering and inaccurate cost estimates hampered construction. And the lack of public resources waylaid the Thruway's arrival as well. The Dewey administration never expected that the postwar surplus would be inadequate to meet the full range of postwar transportation improvements. Yet there simply was not enough money available to implement the highway rehabilitation program (necessary after fifteen years of deferred construction) and make real headway on the Thruway.

The Dewey administration and engineers in the Department of Public Works were at a crossroads. All the partisan wrangling and creative financing of the late 1940s had done little to advance the agenda of the bureaucratic road-building regime that had steadily consolidated its power over the last generation. During the 1920s, engineers had displaced state legislators and machine politicians as the primary force behind transportation policy. By the late 1930s, they had overridden much of the old town and county systems of road administration as well. With the depression and World War II behind them, they had initiated a range of new rural road-building programs and urban arterial highways. But the Thruway—a statewide mega-project of unprecedented scale—brought them up against intense partisan controversy, severe financial shortfalls, and, ultimately, the limits of the existing structure of highway administration.

Having framed the wartime neglect of the highway program as a "major error" and the construction of the Thruway as "indispensable" to national economic growth, Tallamy successfully leveraged his own expertise into billion-dollar highway budgets. Though Governor Dewey had declared these figures beyond the state's capacity to pay, he too was a committed member of the highway consensus and would not renege on his "solemn duty" to refurbish the state's highway system. It was in this context that Dewey took the ultimate step in the consolidation of the bureaucratic road-building regime's political power: the creation of the New York State Thruway Authority.

Authority: The Motorist-Consumer and the Bureaucratic Regime

Once the Thruway had been elevated to a top policy initiative, Dewey and the DPW engineers made the critical decision to spin the Thruway off to a new governing body—the New York State Thruway Authority—that would finance the Thruway's construction by collecting fees from motorists. The DPW had the resources to advance the reconstruction of rural roads and urban arterial highways. But Dewey was persuaded by a committee, including Superintendent of Public Works Tallamy, bond attorney Lewis Delafield, and consulting engineer M. J. Madigan, that the Thruway required fresh political and financial management.[61] This decision had enormous consequences for New York State. Road politics had grown increasingly contentious since the late 1930s, as evidenced by ever-more-divisive public construction, the aggressive use of public relations management, growing public resistance to rural road improvement and urban arterial construction, and the short shrift given to mass transit. The creation of the Thruway Authority heightened all of these tensions.

The new means of planning, administration, and finance developed to build the Thruway sparked a revolution in the political order on the scale of the initial 1898 decision to expand state road-building power: it was an "entering wedge" to a profound political transformation.[62] But unlike that earlier revolution in highway policy, which preceded the rise of engineers in highway politics, the creation of the Thruway Authority was the ultimate step in the consolidation of the engineers' bureaucratic regime. A certain level of officiousness had always characterized the ways in which engineers pursued their traffic-service agenda since Frederick Greene became state highway commissioner in 1919. But until 1950, engineers' power remained relational, subject to the countervailing forces of local politics, the legislative budgeting process, and executive accountability. With the creation of the Thruway Authority, the construction of the nation's longest toll superhighway had been removed from direct public oversight. Highway engineers' support of this shift reveals the distance they had traveled from the reformist, antipartisan politics of the 1920s to the rawer exercise of political clout in the 1950s.

The creation of a public authority to finance, construct, and maintain the Thruway was Dewey's grandest stroke to jump-start the stalled project in 1950. Construction of the superhighway would be expedited by a $400 million bond issue. This appeared to be another stunning policy reversal from the governor who had formerly balked at the idea of foisting the costs of present construction on future generations. But now Dewey argued that without bonding, Thruway construction would forever plod along behind schedule. The saving grace was that the Thruway would be self-liquidating. Tolls would be charged—or special flat-fee license plate permits could be purchased by New York residents—and receipts would go toward retiring the bonds.[63]

This move was in part a natural extension of the trend toward earmarking user fees for highway purposes that had been so instrumental in the consolidation of engineers' bureaucratic autonomy. But public authorities themselves have a long history.[64] These institutions proliferated in the United States after the creation of the Port of New York Authority (PNYA) in 1921. The bistate Port Authority was the product of progressive reformers' long-running effort to modernize the world's busiest port. Its leadership successfully overcame intense local rivalries in the metropolitan region and constructed a complex system of harbors, bridges, and tunnels. In the process, the PNYA became a model for a number of other New Deal–era authorities. New York alone created fifteen state-level authorities devoted to power, transportation, and housing between 1933 and 1935. The most notable federal counterpart was the Tennessee Valley Authority (TVA), created in 1933. As of 1945, over a hundred other such quasi-public corporations were partly or wholly owned by the federal government.[65]

These bodies were designed to replace narrow and often short-sighted politics with the expertise needed to address a single, complex, and costly construction problem. But administrative autonomy and financial independence had their costs. While the TVA survived a series of bitter court battles in the 1930s, its design was not imitated elsewhere in the country.[66] The popular consensus that had developed in support of the PNYA by 1950 gradually eroded after midcentury.[67] Like the PNYA and the TVA, the Thruway Authority faced its share of troubles, largely stemming from the inherent tension between the goal of economic efficiency and the American democratic tradition.[68]

Although the Thruway Authority operated outside the state's formal budget, it was closely tied to the administration. DPW Superintendent Bertram Tallamy, appointed to a nine-year term, chaired the three-member Authority and was its chief executive officer until his departure for Washington in 1956. A civil engineer who began highway work in western New York during the 1920s, Tallamy was a senior partner in a private engineering firm and chief engineer of the Niagara Frontier Planning Board before he rose through the DPW ranks in the late 1940s. Early DPW superintendents Frederick Greene and Arthur Brandt drew heavily on their military experiences; Tallamy's years in the private sector proved as decisive in shaping his public career. Indeed, his casual bridging of the public and private sectors was emblematic of the blurring of these two categories under the Thruway Authority.

Burdell Bixby, the governor's executive assistant, received a six-year appointment to the Thruway Authority, thereby ensuring close relations between it and the Dewey administration. The Authority was rounded out by Manhattan civil engineer David Martin, who took a three-year post. A close associate of New York City Mayor William O'Dwyer, Martin was critical in securing the backing of downstate Democrats.[69] This choice split New York's Democratic Party, with O'Dwyer in support of the Dewey administration and upstate Democrats opposing the new agency that they termed a "supergovernment."[70]

The Thruway Authority's close government ties were furthered by state credit backing of Thruway bonds, a move that the governor's Thruway committee saw as essential. This arrangement, which required consent by public referendum, vastly lowered the interest rate on the bonds, and thus the cost of the Thruway and its tolls. When an enabling constitutional amendment was put before the people in November 1951, Tallamy explained that "in simplest terms, Thruway users have the unique opportunity to vote themselves lower fees."[71] Paul Fitzpatrick thought the amendment, which extended New York's credit to a body outside of legislative control, was an "evasion of the state's rightful responsibility." But the amendment passed by a ratio of over four to one, revealing widespread, popular support for the state's highway program and granting political legitimacy to Tallamy's motorist-consumer rhetoric.[72]

Prior to the amendment's passage, Tallamy explicitly connected the referendum to New York's early (and precocious) support of highway construction. "There is a parallel here between a current problem and one back in 1905. At that time, New York State voters looked ahead to a better highway system for the whole state. We feel sure that such foresight has not been lost, and that the public will realize that in building the Thruway today, we are avoiding traffic troubles tomorrow."[73] But unlike 1905, now there were far fewer checks on the state's road-building authority. Towns no longer petitioned as to which roads to improve; counties could no longer veto construction plans by withholding rights-of-way. State road builders had grown ever more powerful over the past half century, to the point of casting off the constraints of public control. The Thruway Authority, a heavily capitalized public corporation with a powerful public relations machine, seemed less like a government entity than a big business.

Certainly the Thruway Authority managed its extensive capital resources with the sophisticated financial acumen of a large corporation. When the first of the Authority's bonds were issued, they carried a record-low interest rate of 1.1 percent. Tallamy thought it "doubtful if any other authority was ever able to float a loan on such favorable terms." But the Authority was not content simply to secure a low-interest loan backed by state credit. Before the money was channeled to the contractors responsible for building the Thruway, it was reinvested at a higher rate of return. The Authority repeatedly increased its resources through its close relationship with Wall Street investment firms, with Tallamy (sounding less like an engineer than a CEO) talking about "doing business" with "a few top-notch men on the Street."[74]

This was an unprecedented new presence in New York highway construction. The Wall Street connections and aggressive marketing of highways reflected the vigorous exercise of public power by the DPW and the Thruway Authority in highway projects unique in their scale, complexity, and potential for controversy. Despite the uncertainties surrounding these new arrangements, there was sense to it all: Wall Street saw the Thruway as a profitable, low-risk investment; the Dewey administration appreciated the road's promise of fostering economic growth; DPW engineers valued its ability to handle increased traffic. All were well-served by the Thruway Authority's assertive financial management and public relations.

Though critics later questioned the Authority's troubling alliances with private interests, the conventional wisdom of the 1950s emphasized the benefits of privately managed public works projects, freed from the sort of fiscal constraints that made construction so difficult during the depression and war years.[75] The successful management of other public authorities, like the Triborough Bridge and the Port of New York authorities, furthered this belief.[76] Nevertheless, as the Thruway Authority commenced its work, the crucial differences between the Authority and the governmental departments that had previously administered public roads revealed themselves time and again.

Perhaps the most evident of these changes had to do with the Thruway Authority's public relations arm, which appeared in full force during the enabling amendment campaign. To bolster support for its passage, the Thruway Authority authorized a mass mailing of pro-amendment brochures announcing that "saving money is the object" and that a "'Yes' vote is a vote for lower Thruway costs."[77] The cost of the mailings, it was thought, would barely register against the huge savings from the lower bond interest rate. A Manhattan resident objected to the Authority's use of "public" funds, a practice he equated with mailing campaign materials in support of a candidate by a sitting administration. But Authority officials were not so constrained and, given the significant sums at stake, were willing to flex the agency's power.

Public road-building officials were now partnered with Wall Street financiers and actively lobbying for themselves in ways that many found out of accord with Thruway Authority engineers' claims to neutral competence. By the 1950s members of the New York press, who had been content in years past to faithfully report DPW news releases, began to investigate Thruway politics more thoroughly. This was made difficult by the department's effective information management. H. Floyd Burd, editor of the Wyoming County *Times*, criticized *Life* magazine for being "taken in by Dewey's publicity staff" when it published a glowing piece on the Thruway. William M. Ringle, the editor of the Rochester *Times-Union*, charged Superintendent Johnson with running the DPW "in an atmosphere of secrecy and gag-rule."[78]

An interview with Associated Press reporter Richard Hunt cast light on the Thruway Authority's style of guarded public relations and sophisticated financial management. Director of Public Relations Bob Monahan fielded questions by Hunt on the structure of Thruway tolls, a conversation he later relayed to Chairman Tallamy. At one point Hunt raised the issue of the "breakage fee"—the rounding off of distance-based tolls to the nearest dime, which over time added a considerable amount to commuters' costs. Monahan explained to Tallamy that he told Hunt that "we don't have odd cents because people don't carry pennies around and—he caught me—I didn't realize the breakage was the nearest ten cents instead of the nickel." Hunt had asked, "Why didn't you make it the nearest nickel?" When Monahan admitted that "we do get the benefit," Hunt retorted, "You're darn right you do!"[79]

These nickels and dimes formed the financial basis of a complex administrative entity, one that relied on the careful management of public information. Such actions made it difficult to determine how the Thruway Authority related to the people of New York: as a state to its citizens, or as a corporation to its customers. That the Authority gleaned extra cents from motorists does not suggest fiscal indiscretion, only that the administrative independence of the Authority left uncertain the appropriate balance between its obligation to treat the public fairly and its compulsion to maximize income and economic efficiency.

From the Thruway Authority's inception, it remained unclear whether its purpose was to respond to the public interest or actively shape it. Public opinion had always affected highway policy: first directly, under the old pathmaster system, and later through elected officials and election-day referenda. But the Thruway Authority's independence weakened those old ties. Abandoning the public deliberation central to the legislative budgeting process, the Thruway Authority was beholden instead to its major sources of revenue: motorists and the private bond market.[80]

This consolidation of the bureaucratic road-building regime under the Thruway Authority raised profound questions about the nature of mid-twentieth-century highway politics. As road administration evolved in New York, the pathmaster system had been dismantled and replaced first by the Highway Commission and then the Department of Public Works. In each phase, highway administration increasingly privileged bureaucratic over local knowledge and the benefits of statewide development over the cost of community impact. The Thruway Authority, which supplemented the DPW and outspent it during the 1950s, furthered this trend. But unlike the DPW and its predecessors, the Authority relied on its own profitability rather than legislative appropriations to support itself. By creating an independent Thruway Authority, New Yorkers chose an approach that offered clear advantages for the speedy construction of a large project but closed off a critical forum for public debate.

Several developments prefigured the rise of the Thruway Authority and its emphasis on pleasing a narrowly defined constituency of motorists: the emergence of "user fee" rhetoric in the 1920s, the antidiversion campaigns of the 1930s, and the toll battles in Westchester during the early 1940s. But the creation of the Authority took this to a new level. Had the express highway remained within the control of representative government, elected officials might have been able to better assess New Yorkers' complex responses to highway construction: acknowledging their praise for better roadways but responding to their anxieties over community impact. Instead, the Thruway Authority adopted a grossly oversimplified perspective of the electorate, viewing the everyday action of driving on the Thruway—and the successful bond referendum—as unqualified votes of support for road building. The Thruway Authority relied on private economic indicators (toll revenues and the bond market) to gauge its success. And its leadership worked harder to convince the public of the Thruway's benefits than it did in listening to its concerns. With the creation of the Thruway Authority, the transition from citizen-motorist to motorist-consumer was complete.

Engineer-administrators in the Thruway Authority and the DPW pushed hard to sell the Thruway as something that would benefit all New Yorkers. It made a special plea to the state's news organizations, asking them "to throw the weight of your newspapers" behind the Authority if they found its policy to be "sound and equitable."[81] And it courted New York's Southern Tier communities, a region not serviced at all by the Thruway. As construction sped up in 1951, the DPW announced plans for the construction of a "Quickway" paralleling New York's Route 17, the "milk road" that linked the Southern Tier with New York City. Tallamy was quick to point out that the passage of the Thruway bond amendment would free up DPW money for this needed construction.[82]

Construction firms also became a target of Thruway Authority publicity, as Chairman Tallamy emphasized to industry leaders the years of steady work that the new highway would provide. The four-year building program included a construction payroll of $168 million. "This adds up to an impressive volume of purchasing power that will be virtually constant. . . . The road building industry has historically been an industry of economic ups and downs. For the next four years, at least," Tallamy claimed, "it promises unprecedented stability in New York State."[83]

The Korean War gave the Thruway military importance, another impetus for its speedy construction. At the opening of the Catskill-Saugerties section in July 1950, just weeks after President Harry S. Truman authorized the use of U.S. forces, Governor Dewey took the opportunity to talk down those Thruway opponents who had "fought it to the end" four months earlier. "I do not mean to be an alarmist," he maintained, "but it is the business of the government to be prepared, as many people are now realizing. If anyone ever does drop a bomb on New York City, you won't hear any more arguments about whether New York City needs the Thruway."[84]

Although the Thruway promised to help channel funds to Southern Tier road work, aid the flagging construction industry, and bolster New York's civil defense, its primary beneficiaries were motorist-consumers and the businesses that served them. As work accelerated (140 miles were finished or under construction in 1952), Authority officials continued to try to persuade New Yorkers, especially business owners, of the Thruway's merit. Authority member David Martin told the New York State Chamber of Commerce that the Thruway would be a "shot in the arm and every limb of the state's economy." Harold A. Evans Jr., Tallamy's executive assistant, sought to convince downtown businesses of its benefits: "Non-buying traffic will be siphoned away, thus encouraging the prospective motorist-consumer to come to the central business district to shop. This reduction in non-buying traffic also facilitates pedestrian movement and will make for greater safety in downtown areas."[85]

This was what city shopkeepers had been arguing for years. Early in the century, business interests sought improved highways in downtown areas; in time they saw there was something to be said for siphoning off through traffic on bypass highways. But central business districts, with their perennial parking problems, were not able to attract the motorist-consumer. Despite its prodowntown rhetoric, the Thruway actually drew motorist-consumers outside of downtown areas and created an entirely new commercial environment geared to their needs.[86] Shopping centers and office parks (all with large, adjoining parking lots) sprang up along its route. In much of upstate New York, the coming of new industrial and commercial outlets was welcomed. But where this new growth came at the expense of existing commercial activity, the Thruway's detractors were heard. They grew louder when they realized that this new economic development was not merely the natural outcome of an improved transportation infrastructure but something courted by the Thruway Authority itself.

Never Say "Impact": The Authority, Economic Development, and Public Resistance

As the Thruway opened section by section, officials in the Thruway Authority along with the DPW and the Dewey administration repeatedly reaffirmed the worthiness of that massive public works endeavor. Public relations director Bob Monahan choreographed each event, peppering speeches with data on the cost-effectiveness of the highway of the future, its low cost-per-mile compared to other toll roads in the Northeast, and its general economic benefit. A cavalcade followed the speeches, with prominent places for members of the Automobile Old-Timers Club and an "appropriate descendent of DeWitt Clinton," the primary force behind that New York public works archetype the Erie Canal. By this blend of ancient and modern, the administration hoped to portray the New York State Thruway as the natural consequence of two centuries of enlightened transportation policy making.[87]

When Thruway Authority Chairman Bert Tallamy spoke at the opening of the 57-mile stretch connecting Buffalo and Rochester, he devoted much of his speech to "the new industries and enterprises" that were opting to construct facilities alongside the Thruway. "They are selecting their sites," Tallamy explained, "for the identical reason that so many businesses picked locations beside the Erie Canal more than a century ago. . . . The State's newest transportation artery promises more profit, a better and more extensive market, a more expanded supply for material, and a more coordinated delivery system, all to the benefit of everyone." The Thruway, New York's greatest public project since the Great Depression, was nothing short of "an economic lifeline."[88]

But an economic lifeline for whom? The state Democratic Party continued to be skeptical of the project. Chairman Richard Balch thought the theatrics at one opening were no more than a "typical Dewey political maneuver designed to delude the people in an election year."[89] And the administration's public relations strategy, however consistent with contemporary business and political practices, did raise questions as to whose interests the Thruway Authority, free as it was from direct public oversight and accountability, would serve.

Gone was the public works egalitarianism of the first decades of the twentieth century that had spread transportation improvements broadly across the state. Gone as well were many of the local checks on state road-building authority that had been given up since the 1920s. Instead, the public works paradigm of the 1950s was geared toward serving the motorist-consumer, a politically disempowered entity whose presence on the roads was interpreted by engineers as support for their traffic-service vision of highway construction, but which was otherwise stripped of political clout and the capacity to shape transportation policy. Indeed, the bureaucratic road-building regime that depended on the motorist-consumer for its political legitimacy was accompanied by a series of filters between the public and the highway administration: not just an elaborate private bond market and an extensive public relations machine, but also a new emphasis on economic development as the primary criterion by which to judge the work of the Thruway Authority. Downplaying citizens' objections to changes in the economic and social life of communities wrought by the proposed Thruway, the Authority attracted a wide range of critics who claimed that it served as a handmaiden to commercial interests alone.

Aware of opposition from those communities that the Thruway would disadvantage, the Authority campaigned doggedly for its speedy construction. As this public relations campaign intensified, so did local resistance. The Thruway Authority assured Cherry Valley Turnpike (U.S. Route 20) business owners, who operated on the main highway parallel to the Thruway, that their business would not be siphoned away. Experience, it claimed, showed that after the construction of the Pennsylvania Turnpike there was more, rather than less, traffic on adjoining routes.[90]

But there was little the Authority could say to pacify the Yonkers North Broadway Citizens' Association, which engaged in a protracted (and unsuccessful) legal battle after the Authority claimed a stretch of storefronts for the Thruway's New York City approach. The Yonkers group petitioned the courts to relocate the Thruway's route and accused Tallamy of, among other things, "sneering at questioners of his God-given insight." But the State Supreme Court rejected their petition, arguing that the Thruway Authority had operated within its mandate in selecting the route and that the choice was "in essence an engineering and policy question."[91] The court's narrow, legalistic interpretation of the Citizens' Association's complaint sidestepped the larger question of whether ordinary New Yorkers had any role at all to play in the setting of transportation policy, especially policy decisions that promised seismic shifts in local economies. By affirming that the Thruway's route selection was an engineering question, the court also affirmed the engineers' progrowth, traffic-service priorities.

Some years later, in correspondence with another highway official, Superintendent of Public Works John W. Johnson summed up the DPW's position on economic impact:

It is our feeling that the construction of these expressways must be carried on and that they will result in greater business activity in the area traversed. As in the case with every new highway we build, whether expressway type or not, there are bound to be some individuals who are inconvenienced and will actually lose business. This is one of the costs of progress, and we know of no way to avert these individual problems.[92]

This view made sense from the perspective of the state's general commercial needs. When the Thruway passed through undeveloped land, economic prosperity often followed at little cost. But when geography or density of population forced the rerouting of traffic through highly developed areas, outraged communities bitterly protested. And they resented transportation officials' assertions that economic losses should best be understood as isolated sacrifices made by individuals in the name of the public good, rather than systemic social and economic transformations.

Such was the case in Suffern, formerly a sleepy Rockland County tourist destination, which now lay on the main interstate traffic route to New Jersey. The town sat in a narrow gap in the Ramapo Mountains, and it already channeled the Ramapo River, two highways, and a railroad. To squeeze the Thruway through this narrow corridor, the DPW planned to divert the Ramapo River by 200 yards. The river's new course would flow over three of Suffern's reserve wells and potentially pollute its water supply. Responding to these fears, the Suffern police ordered construction workers to cease making test borings. Soon after, the workers resumed drilling, only to be stopped again by John C. Petrone, a village trustee who took it on himself to patrol the area. Flummoxed by the local opposition to their work, one driller cried out, "Why, we represent the State of New York!" Petrone shot back in language that recalled the local highway resistance of the early twentieth century: "I don't care who you represent. Get out of here! Governor Dewey isn't king of New York State yet!"[93]

Similar problems plagued the village of Fultonville in Montgomery County, situated on a narrow stretch of the Mohawk Valley between a steep elevation and the Erie Canal. The village was literally bisected, the Thruway splitting its main street in two. Raymond A. Donaldson, the sixty-eight-year-old town clerk, lamented the changes to his hometown: "The public today is a good deal different. They don't know where the trees were. They don't know about the skating on the canal, the fishing and the row boating. So to me this is a black eye, but I don't like to say that. It's progress—and I won't be here forever."

Fultonville soon came to epitomize the casualties in the name of New York's transportation progress. Economic prosperity was pursued with single-minded zeal and varying degrees of regard for community impact. A year after the Thruway tore through Fultonville, Tallamy declared in proud defense that despite the changes lamented by Donaldson, the village was in its "soundest financial position in history."[94] This pursuit of prosperity at the expense of community was not so much the result of callous disregard for the values of small-town life as the predictable outcome of a political system designed to subordinate the narrower politics of localism to a broader program of economic development. Over the course of a single generation, the increasing disruptiveness of construction placed new strains on the road-building consensus. The new roads of the 1930s and 1940s were wider, safer, and afforded faster travel, but they could be harmful in other ways: clogging cities, cutting through productive farmland, increasing traffic (and traffic-related injuries) in the suburbs. By midcentury the Thruway Authority proposed even more divisive construction: bisecting villages, threatening public water supplies, and diverting consumers away from central business districts.

Nowhere was the difficulty of charting the Thruway's course more contentious than in Westchester, which for decades had been a focal point of highway innovation, road crew strikes, and political wrangling. By the 1940s the county had won a campaign to shift the burden of its costly parkway system to the state. In yielding to the state the authority to direct highway development within its borders, Westchester validated the premise implicit in the Thruway Authority's mandate: that a distant, autonomous administration would serve New York's transportation needs better than one rooted in local politics.

Densely populated and already riddled with commuter and interstate traffic along its extensive parkway system, Westchester County felt a desperate need for another traffic artery. But it could scarcely spare the space to build it in the 1950s. The Thruway Authority employed Westchester engineer and former state Superintendent of Public Works Charles Sells as a highway lobbyist to negotiate this thorny problem. Dozens of alternate routes were considered, their merit weighed against engineering considerations and the displacement of businesses and residents. Each time the proposed route shifted to skirt one community, another was up in arms over the Thruway's running through *its* backyard.

Westchester Commissioner of Public Works James C. Harding astutely recognized that residents were in for a "disagreeable dose" when they learned that the Thruway route was to cross the Hudson and enter New York City through their county. The Greenville city council objected to the route transfer, but county executive Herbert Gerlach could not do much to soften the blow: "Additional motor vehicle routes must be provided," he explained, "but they cannot be suspended from the clouds." There was little he could do to pacify critics who worried about the "backwash" of trucks onto residential streets, still less for those who hyperbolically complained of an "atom bomb" attack on local merchants in the form of colossal new shopping centers.[95]

When the time came to vote on yielding the county's right of way to the Thruway Authority, Westchester's board of supervisors supported the proposal 32 to 9. Some objected to the creation of more "obnoxious speedways," but few could argue against the creation of new express lanes in a county that had experienced a 65 percent increase in traffic between 1946 and 1951.[96] As Thruway Authority engineers deliberated on the final route, the politics of construction heated up. Chairman Tallamy assured Westchester residents that all possibilities had been "fully explored from the standpoint of engineering feasibility and local impact." Still adamant, those communities that stood to lose the most from the route choice sought assistance from the county in fighting the Authority's decision.

But the county board was loath to insert itself between its towns and villages and the Thruway Authority. The county—having finally paid down its depression-era highway debt—worried over the DPW's unspoken policy of directing resources toward uncontroversial road work in thinly populated areas of the state. James C. Harding explained that his "greatest fear" was that the county, if it opposed the Authority's route choice, might risk losing funding for the desperately needed Cross Westchester Expressway "to some welcomed project upstate." Furthermore, the county had long argued that its traffic was interregional rather than local, and it encouraged the state to assume a greater role in Westchester road building. As the county board of supervisors put it: "For many years the county has insisted that the state assume the duty of handling this [construction] problem. If the state is now ready, our wholehearted cooperation is certainly indicated." Westchester officials manifestly accepted the gradual reapportionment of public power going on over the past several decades.

Community resistance increased, with "cities, villages, school boards, neighborhood groups, and powerful political leaders" urging Westchester to back one route or another. In the face of this vocal opposition, the county pursued a deliberate "hands-off policy." County executive James D. Hopkins told Westchester residents that the Cross Westchester Expressway, a vital link between the proposed New York State and New England Thruways, was "a state project and the selection of the route is an engineering problem for Bertram D. Tallamy. . . . As a county, we realize that the expressway is essential. . . . We want it built. We hope that the route causing the least harm to homes and other buildings is chosen. But we do not intend to be on the side of one community in opposition to another."[97]

With Westchester County officials unwilling to pick and choose among towns and villages, local communities were left to battle the Thruway Authority on their own. The Authority's piecemeal construction had the effect of further dividing the opposition. By unveiling the final route choice one stage at a time, Thruway Authority administrators isolated unrest at the neighborhood level and prevented antihighway sentiment from gaining mass and momentum. Opponents came to view the Thruway as no longer just a highway, but a living, malicious entity: in the words of one critic, "an ugly, creeping thing . . . burrowing its way from Buffalo."

As word of the final route spread, residents reacted sharply to the threat to Westchester's community life. Many saw in the coming of the Thruway the loss of the county's elite status, transforming it from the "Beverly Hills of the East" to a "hub for interstate traffic." Other longtime residents could not bear the loss of familiar places. The Hein sisters, Lisa and Margaret, simply refused to accept the state's taking of their property. Unwilling to evacuate their house, they remained in it even as blast debris shattered their windows.[98]

Westchester's fate was further complicated by the construction of the Tappan Zee Bridge crossing the Hudson River between Nyack (Rockland County) and Tarrytown (Westchester County). The new link would tie Westchester's extensive parkway system to Route 17, the state's major Southern Tier highway.[99] In its location, design, and cost, the bridge was one of the Thruway Authority's most controversial undertakings. The Tappan Zee was a clear symbol of engineering confidence: it crossed the Hudson at its widest point. Three miles long, it was supported by a unique design structure consisting of eight floating concrete caissons that supported the bulk of the bridge's weight. And it was expensive: an estimated cost of $80 million. Paul Windels of the Regional Planning Association considered the Tappan Zee a "basic error": "costly," "unsightly," and of "freak design."[100]

Tallamy justified the construction of the bridge, whose location was chosen by "placing the general public interest above local interest."[101] Design engineer Emil H. Praeger, a former U.S. Navy captain and dean of Rensselaer Polytechnic Institute, seconded the point: "It's not the width of the body of water you want to cross but the number of people who want to cross there." Another less-publicized reason for the bridge's location was a state pact with the Port of New York Authority that required that the bridge be far enough north of the George Washington Bridge so as not to interfere with that structure's profitability.[102]

The Tappan Zee link prompted a general reordering of economic life, a pattern that recurred along the entire Thruway system. The west-shore city of Kingston virtually moved from the "wrong side" of the river (that is, the side furthest from Manhattan) to the "right side." The city underwent a terrific "boom," according to the Kingston planning commission. Land values shot up by an average of 50 percent—and by a factor of ten in some instances. New industries like IBM, which opened a new plant and promised 5,000 new jobs, were attracted to the site, now "within 90 minutes of the [New York City] market."[103]

Superintendent Tallamy proclaimed the benefits of the Thruway to east-shore communities as well. He told a Westchester businessmen's organization that "everyone is aware that shopping habits have changed since the auto came of age." Highways were "the molders of your community, for that is the actual fact. . . . The highways in your community have shaped and will shape the whole pattern of your growth." The Tappan Zee in particular "will make neighbors of the thousands of people who rebel against leaving their own backyards to shop."[104]

The shortened distance between cross-Hudson communities opened up a wide range of new commercial ventures, like the unprecedented suburban bank merger in which the White Plains County Trust Company, capitalized at $234 million, absorbed the smaller National Bank of Tuxedo in Orange County. Bank acquisitions were not new, of course, but this was the first instance in which a suburban bank acquired a bank across county lines—and across the Hudson.[105]

Not all economic change was a straightforward "market response" to the improved highway system. State and county agencies actively promoted the construction of new suburban shopping centers at the expense of central business districts. The mammoth Cross County Shopping Center was the work of the Westchester County government, the DPW, the Thruway Authority, and private developers—but local Yonkers officials were left out of the loop. In this complex deal, the state DPW assumed the cost of realigning part of Westchester's original parkway system, the Cross County Parkway. The $1.5 million project eliminated a dangerous curve in the road, but it also yielded valuable land for commercial development along the old right-of-way. That land was given by the county to Cross Properties Inc., which built a $30 million shopping center. In exchange, the developer offered the Thruway Authority $116,000 worth of Central Avenue frontage property to facilitate the construction of the Thruway through the city of Yonkers.[106]

Though the DPW and the Thruway Authority aggressively pursued this real estate transaction, Superintendent Tallamy suggested in public statements that it was simply the natural economic effect of the new transportation infrastructure. At the ribbon-cutting ceremony at the Yonkers barrier connection to the Cross County Parkway, he directed the crowd's attention from the Thruway-parkway link to the Cross County Shopping Center, which he described as "another of those concrete and steel reminders of the tremendous economic effect this new superhighway has exerted upon our State's economy." Rather than reveal the behind-the-scenes deals that secured this "showpiece" of economic growth at the expense of Yonkers' central business district, Tallamy simply explained that "the developer of this new facility . . . told us that he would not have considered this site if it had not been for the Thruway."[107]

Tallamy's speeches drew attention away from the negative consequences of the actions of the Authority and the DPW. Thruway Authority Public Relations Director Bob Monahan coached him carefully, instructing Tallamy to emphasize the positive aspects of construction, like the rising real estate values along the Thruway route, which served as "an economic lesson for all of us." Monahan advised him never to use the word "'impact' . . . because it bears a connotation of serious disruption." As he explained, "Our job is to build, not destroy."[108]

Highway officials repeatedly trumpeted that motto: in Syracuse, where a new industrial park lifted the local economy; and in Buffalo, where the Thruway Super Plaza, costing $2.5 million and providing parking for 3,000 cars, became the largest retail outlet in western New York. The shopping center was further proof that the "suburban movement is taking a new tack" in Buffalo. Observers noted a "moderate slowdown of residential construction in the close-in suburbs—accompanied by a marked speed up farther out." The decisive shift from first ring to peripheral suburban construction was vastly accelerated and actively promoted by the Thruway Authority.[109]

The Thruway fostered economic development consistent with the progrowth goals of postwar economic liberalism. At the center of this policy was a desire to meet the needs of the near-universal category of "motorist-consumers," a term that had, in practice, replaced "citizens" in the political rhetoric of highway administrators. But the blurring of these categories masked implicit assumptions about whom the built environment and public funds should serve. Thruway engineers, whose authority, according to the State Supreme Court of New York, rested on the basis of neutral competence and nonpartisan decision making, now promoted a distinct brand of social and economic development. This became most evident when the Thruway Authority and the DPW arranged to sacrifice Yonkers' downtown shopping district in exchange for the development of the Cross County Shopping Center.

By the mid-1950s the engineers' insistence that their goal was to "build" rather than "destroy" could not conceal the fact that road building generated intense political controversy. Certainly the highway work engineers had promoted since the 1920s was political in nature, and increasingly geared toward the interests of their constituency of motorist-consumers. But never before had a state transportation agency exerted its power on this scale, with such little regard to local concerns and in the face of such little countervailing authority. The Thruway's route had immense consequences for Westchester's communities, and the seismic economic shift that ensued—the virtual evisceration of the Yonkers central business district—was not simply the result of "natural" market forces. Both developments were political in nature, despite the Thruway Authority's effort to promote its decisions as politically neutral. This is not to suggest that the Thruway Authority acted conspiratorially—all political decisions have winners and losers—but that it masked its politics with the veneer of incontestable rationality. That public image was in large part a reflection of how highway engineers saw themselves. Seeking to balance their roles as experts and public servants, members of the Thruway Authority and the DPW sought to provide public leadership, and they dismissed public reaction to their work as narrow-minded (and thus inconsequential) carping.

"The Obviously Sound, Moral, Ethical Way": Politics and the Engineering Profession

In the course of the building of the Thruway, the engineering profession, which had a near iconic status since the 1920s, came under attack as increasingly politicized, biased, and indifferent to community opinion. As the DPW and the Thruway Authority expanded to meet the challenge of an enlarged construction program, highway engineers and officials faced new challenges to their authority. The Thruway Authority's ambiguous mandate—to produce a public good while remaining isolated from public input and subservient to private financial markets—obscured the distinctions between public and private interest. The close relationship between public works projects and the private engineering firms called on to design them further undermined the engineers' claims to neutral competence.

Despite increased hiring after the end of World War II, the DPW struggled with a recurrent personnel crisis. Civil service requirements, which had helped to professionalize the department in the 1910s and 1920s, now limited the advancement of new hires, many of them veterans without engineering degrees. And tight staffing budgets made it difficult for the DPW to offer salaries competitive with private engineering firms. As the DPW and the Thruway Authority took on more work during the postwar years, they relied increasingly on outside consultants.

Consultancy raised its own set of problems. Private engineering companies, like other highway contractors, worked for profit. But unlike pavers and excavators, engineering firms directed the design process and exercised an exceptional degree of control in decisions that would affect the public at large. To ensure a sense of fairness and economic efficiency in the dispensation of these public contracts, former executive secretary of the American Society of Civil Engineers (ASCE) Colonel William N. Carey proposed that engineering firms bid on a competitive basis. But this was a minority viewpoint and ran counter to the engineers' professional ethos, which frowned on competition within the engineering fraternity. The ASCE's Code of Ethics asserted that it was "inconsistent with honorable and dignified bearing by any member of the ASCE . . . to advertise [their services] in self-laudatory language, or in any other manner derogatory to the dignity of the profession." Tallamy thought the code, which rejected competitive bidding in favor of merit-based awards, was the "obviously sound, moral, ethical way" to distribute engineering contracts. Tallamy and other engineers rejected attempts to sell their skills on an open market. He wondered if Carey would "advertise for a doctor's service to remove his gall bladder if it had to come out."

Competitive bidding not only ran counter to Tallamy's sense of professional identity but also seemed inappropriate to such important projects. Tallamy wondered how the DPW would protect itself against incompetent firms. Contracts would have to go to the lowest bidder, he felt, or the superintendent would be "on the defensive in every quarter. Talk about accusations of favoritism—he would certainly be up against it then. In addition he would be subject to law suits in which he would have to prove that the low bidder was not qualified to perform the work, and that would be something!"[110]

In the face of strong opposition, the DPW continued to contract with engineering firms on a merit basis. But as its work became more controversial, reliant on private contractors, and distant from public oversight, the department was subject to charges of favoritism. A newspaper columnist wrote a series of Thruway "memoranda" accusing the DPW of playing patronage politics. One memorandum revealed that the Thruway Authority gave preferential treatment to engineering firms that had contributed nearly $50,000 to the Republican State Committee by purchasing ads in its journal. No engineering firm had so advertised prior to the 1950 establishment of the Thruway Authority; the thirty-three firms purchasing ad space between 1950 and 1954 received $27 million worth of engineering survey contracts in noncompetitive bidding during that period.

Other memoranda pointed to instances in which the engineers' supposed apoliticism appeared to be compromised. One noted that Tallamy's former engineering partner, Harold J. Senior, had received $830,000 in highway contracts. Another criticized the hiring of the engineering firm Madigan Hyland. M. J. Madigan had served on the original committee that recommended the establishment of the Thruway Authority and later was the chief advocate for the construction of the Tappan Zee Bridge. There was an apparent conflict of interest in his firm's receipt of a multimillion-dollar contract to design the bridge he had recommended.[111]

The DPW and the Thruway Authority worked in the postwar years under a load of incongruous combinations: engineering professionalism and patronage politics; disdain for self-laudatory language and a growing dependence on public relations management; a continued obligation to public service and increased reliance on corporate-style administration. But there was consistency amid these incongruities. Proponents of postwar economic liberalism linked economic development to national welfare and in the process blurred the line between the public good and private interests. The Thruway Authority endorsed this liberal economic model, promoting new construction with little concern for its broader impact.[112] More so than ever before, engineers working under the auspices of the Thruway Authority were pursuing a form of "creative destruction," making political choices that privileged suburban residential and commercial development at the expense of older town and city centers.

New road construction in the prewar period had always helped some New Yorkers while disadvantaging others. But as the Westchester case and other examples in this chapter suggest, the singularly transformative nature of a newly built express highway threatened existing social and commercial arrangements on a much grander scale than had been the case in earlier decades. At that time, state and county transportation agencies concentrated on the widening and straightening of existing roads and the construction of a small number of comparatively shorter recreational parkways. From the 1920s onward, towns and localities had yielded tremendous powers to state-level engineer-bureaucrats in hopes of hastening the improvement of the state's highway system, and diluting the power of local interests that undercut the engineers' vision of through traffic service. Thus, by the 1950s communities no longer had the political clout or institutional authority to challenge the increasingly controversial plans that engineers in the Thruway Authority were pursuing. The overtly political decisions that Thruway Authority engineers were making presented the strongest challenge to their reputation of neutral competence. Impartiality had been the hallmark of their profession—and the basis of their claims to political legitimacy—since the turn of the century. Now, convinced of the validity of their traffic-service vision of highway construction and bolstered by the perceived mandate of the motorist-consumer, they embraced the politicized subjectivity that had once been their profession's antithesis.

"If You Don't Build, You Die in This Modern Civilization": The Road-Building Consensus

While public reaction against road building and its impact on social and economic development would fuel a future highway crisis, highways' celebrants remained the dominant voices of the mid-1950s. When community opposition to the New England Thruway caused construction delays, citizens of New Rochelle countered with a "reverse protest." They wanted the Thruway Authority to take a *larger* role in financing and coordinating the construction of the new express links in Westchester—the New England Thruway, the New York State Thruway, and the Cross Westchester Expressway.[113]

In 1949 like-minded highway advocates, including representatives from real estate organizations, the financial sector, chambers of commerce, and the highway construction industry, formed the New York State Good Roads Association (NYSGRA). They elected as their director former superintendent of Public Works Charles Sells (who later served as the Thruway Authority's negotiator for the Westchester section of the Thruway). The NYSGRA took its name from the Progressive-era Good Roads movement of a half-century earlier. Like the original movement, this latter-day version sought to promote highways in the face of strong opposition. But the new group had a more confrontational edge. Its forerunners had fostered a culture of road improvement through publicity; the NYSGRA aimed to root out the opposition. According to Westchester Public Works Commissioner James C. Harding, its mission was "to combat groups that fight required highways, want unnecessary traffic lights, and demand ridiculous speed limits."[114]

Even staunch highway advocate Thomas E. Dewey found himself on the wrong side of a NYSGRA issue, such as the diversion of highway revenue. The NYSGRA supported an amendment to the state constitution that would earmark all highway revenue (including motor fuel taxes) for road improvement. Highway lobbyists in New York had been pushing for such an amendment since the 1930s, when they had bought into the idea that motorist-generated revenue should properly be considered "user fees." Twenty-five other states had accepted this logic and adopted antidiversion amendments. But like his predecessors, Governor Dewey saw this as little more than a grab for political control of a major revenue stream, and he steadfastly opposed what he called a budgeting "straight jacket." It was a "stupid" plan to so limit the state's financial flexibility: "pretty soon all revenue from alcoholic beverages will be earmarked for the benefit of drunks." This disagreement caused a rift between Dewey and Sells, who weakly argued that "even a stupid plan" was better than none.

That New York State diverted highway revenue (a popularly held notion for many years, supported by the federal Bureau of Public Roads in the 1930s) was, according to Dewey, "one of the largest fictions in the history of the state." Two studies, one by a private firm in 1951 and another by the state budget office in 1953, revealed what highway officials had always argued: that when local aid was factored in, the state spent far more on highways than it received in user revenue. The labyrinthine finances of New York's general treasury fund made this a difficult puzzle to solve, however, and the federal Bureau of Public Roads continued to seek clarification from New York on the diversion issue into the 1950s.[115]

Though Dewey and Sells squabbled over the details of highway finance, they joined in support of a broad construction program that expanded on the original Thruway. To this end, Dewey and DPW officials agreed on a 1954 public works plank that recommended the construction of four new express routes. Two were to run from south to north: one from the Pennsylvania state line to the St. Lawrence River (now I-81) and the other from Albany to Canada (the Northway). Two would run from east to west: one across the Southern Tier (the Quickway), the other across Long Island (the Long Island Expressway).[116]

These new express highways evoked sharp reactions. The Long Island Expressway (LIE), which linked Wantagh and Oyster Bay, turned out to be especially controversial. Since it ran through some of the state's most developed land, the DPW sought to expedite work on the LIE before rising property values prohibited further building. But aggressively pushing construction stirred greater community opposition. As controversy surrounding the LIE project turned uglier, Johnson sought to stem the tide of bad publicity. "I believe we have taken a 'pasting' on this whole area long enough," he told DPW public relations director James E. Treux, and implored him to "see if we cannot, for a change, obtain favorable comments for the department."[117]

The Northway, though it ran through far less developed country, also had its opponents. Senator Herbert Lehman, who had been instrumental in developing New York's highway system as governor during the 1930s, now negotiated on behalf of Adirondack residents and business owners with Superintendent Johnson over the proposed express highway. The U.S. Route 9 Improvement Association appealed to Lehman to oppose the Northway, on the ground that it would siphon traffic (and business) away from their road, which they preferred to have widened. It was typical of DPW policy at this time that Johnson dismissed the protest, explaining that he had to consider the Northway's effect on all the citizens of New York and not just one interest group.[118]

Thinking broadly about general economic development rather than the impact on a particular community helped the state highway administration justify its dismissal of significant community opposition. As Governor Dewey put it: "If you don't build, you die in this modern civilization."[119] This was a melodramatic statement—though certainly the rising number of highway fatalities, and the effort to make the Thruway one of the safest highways in the nation, lent a rationale to his life-or-death rhetoric. But Dewey's dictum reflected most of all the pursuit of a new transportation infrastructure geared to a motorist-driven economy.

Again and again, highway officials bore witness to the automobile's claim on America and its inevitable consequences for the nation's road-building program. Tallamy told a group of business editors that the highway construction boom of the 1920s was "a smashing success":

Passenger vehicles are no longer *luxuries*. They move people to and from their work. The almost universal ownership of cars has fostered mushrooming Suburbia far removed from industrial centers. Highway transport has decentralized industry as well. The plant which produces everything under one roof is a rarity now. In brief, our whole economy has become entirely dependent on the motor vehicle and the highways over which it rolls.[120]

He said the same to Congress: everything the individual "eats, wears, or uses" moves by motor vehicle, from the source of raw materials to finishing plants to retail outlets:

> Downtown areas in cities and villages are no longer the only shopping areas. New shopping centers developing in outer areas are almost entirely dependent on trade brought in by motor vehicles. More and more homes for city workers are being built outside congested areas and the commuters travel to work by car and bus, and in some areas by train. People want more elbow room and they are pushing out along or adjacent to good highways.

Given these developments, Tallamy could only conclude that the "American way of life is irrevocably geared to the motor vehicle."[121]

Of course those trends—the growth of a suburbia dependent on improved highways and increased automobile use—had been under way for decades. Good Roads advocates at the turn of the century argued that better roads would provide an outlet to overcrowded cities; city planners in the 1920s contended that a new decentralized style of suburban development was made possible by infrastructural advances in transportation (roads and cars), communication (radios and telephones), and power (electric grids). During that early period of highway development, the costs, calculated in financial terms, and benefits, measured in the safety and ease of travel, appeared plain.[122]

But by the 1950s it became increasingly difficult to gauge the success of new construction. Express highways like the New York State Thruway had the power to reshape social and commercial life on a grand scale. They were expensive, complex, and the products of deft financial and political maneuvering. This made them at once marvelous feats of public works engineering and all but immune to public control. Opponents of the Thruway objected to its impact on communities, though with little effect. The shift in the locus of road-building authority toward a centralized, tightly run bureaucracy thwarted the Thruway's foes. They were even more alienated by the Thruway Authority's slick deals, which capitalized on the deliberate blurring of public-minded and private entrepreneurial motivations.

Thruway supporters, by contrast, had little but praise for the work of

DPW and Authority engineers. The Ford Motor Company thought the cloverleaf pattern of the Thruway's interchanges was nothing less than "a symbol of modern civilization."[123] And DPW engineers never doubted themselves, for they had their own way of tallying votes of support: before the Syracuse section of the Thruway was officially opened, the DPW received reports that crowds of motorists were making illicit use of the highway. To get a sense of the roadway's early appeal, they set an automotive counter across the roadway that registered thousands of cars a day.[124]

To officials in the DPW and the Thruway Authority, this was incontrovertible evidence of the validity of the highway program. Well aware of burgeoning community resistance, they nonetheless chose to interpret highway use as the only reliable measure of public opinion. State highway officials had grown increasingly isolated from the broader forum of political debate, a critical consequence of the consolidation of the bureaucratic road-building regime. Now they appeared incapable of appreciating the complexity of New Yorkers' responses to the transportation revolution they were witnessing. When these complexities were thrown into sharp relief during the highway bond referendum of 1955, the road builders were stunned.

The Referendum

Though there had always been diversity of opinion in New York road politics, the Thruway polarized debate in the mid-1950s. It became increasingly difficult to parse out the mix of support and antipathy directed toward the Thruway in particular and the state's road-building program in general. Clearly engineer-administrators in the DPW and the Thruway Authority had made their share of friends and enemies as their work became deeply involved in the state's postwar economic and social reconstruction. So when the citizens of New York had the opportunity to vote on a highway referendum in 1955, they were offered the first clear chance since the twin $50 million bond authorizations of 1905 and 1912 to voice their opinions on half a century of public road building.

In that year the Temporary State Highway Finance Commission (popularly referred to by its chairman's name as the Diefendorf Commission) issued its final report.[125] After three years of deliberation, the report reiterated the DPW officials' recommendations of 1952: a $2.8 billion, ten-year program, financed by a $750 million bond issue and the revenue from a two-cent per gallon gasoline tax increase. Dewey had originally rejected bonding as an appropriate means of financing the state's general highway program. But now, with 56 percent of the state's highways listed as below a tolerable level, his administration backed bonds as the only means of accelerating the construction program.

It fell to the Democratic administration of Governor Averell Harriman (1955–1958) to implement the Diefendorf Commission's report. Harriman was initially silent upon its release, reluctant to support the findings of a twelve-member commission, ten of whom were Republican stalwarts. But given the condition of the state highways, Harriman eventually signed off on the commission's plan. The legislature approved the proposed bond amendment and sent it to a popular referendum in November.[126]

By the summer of 1955 there was ample reason to be pleased with the state's achievement. The Thruway was doing spectacularly well—it had taken in over $300,000 in its first month—and boasted a safety record of just 2.44 fatalities per hundred million vehicle miles traveled. (The Pennsylvania Turnpike had a fatality rate of 4.2; the overall national average was 6.5.) And for all the community unrest that had marked the Thruway's construction, this was a year of openings: not just of the final sections of the Thruway and the three-mile-long Tappan Zee Bridge, but new industrial plants and retail shopping outlets throughout the state.[127]

In a celebratory mood, the Republican-dominated legislature passed an act to rename the new Thruway in honor of former governor Dewey. Harriman would have none of it. While generally supporting the legislature's highway-related agenda, he thought that "there was no precedent for naming a state highway for an individual, no matter how renowned." Republican Party chairman L. Judson Morhouse found Harriman's opposition "amusing." "There is no precedent," he retorted, "for building such a superhighway in this state either."[128]

The November referendum was widely seen as an opportunity for the public to assess the state highway program and all that it had done, especially in the decade following the war. Highway officials looked to the bond issue as a sign of public approval, a green light to continue their building program and reconstruct the state's weakened prewar transportation infrastructure. There was much activity in Washington centered on the creation of a system of interstate highways, but the Diefendorf Commission urged that "until the federal program has been defined by Congress . . . the state's program be continued as it has been planned and started." Given the extent of the commission's prohighway sentiment, it was profoundly dispiriting to highway supporters when New Yorkers resoundingly defeated the measure in the fall of 1955 by a margin of 3 to 2.[129]

What led voters to reject the bond proposal? Those looking for evidence of a strong antihighway movement have a hard case to make.[130] Most contemporary observers agreed that the amendment was scuttled by the New York State Automobile Association, which campaigned vigorously against its passage. For years the auto club had bitterly complained that the state diverted highway user funds to nonhighway purposes. Now it sought to punish the state by making the highway bond contingent upon the passage of a constitutional amendment (already adopted by twenty-five other states) earmarking highway revenue for roads. The 1955 bond authorization amendment had only nonbinding constraints on revenue from the gas tax increase.[131]

The road lobby's public relations campaign effectively linked the amendment in the public's mind with New Deal–style emergency fuel levies, which taxed motorists but left the roads in bad conditions. This opposition was bolstered by a general public reaction against an increased gasoline tax. In the same year Congress raised the federal gasoline tax to support the nascent Interstate Highway System, a move that had a "seriously adverse effect" on the state's bond amendment, itself tied to a two-cent tax hike. In this context, the odds were stacked against the highway bond's success. Nevertheless, the referendum marked an important departure: for the first time since the end of the war, voters rejected more spending bills than they approved.

When Robert Moses was asked about the defeat of the bond measure, he expressed "astonishment and chagrin" but held that it was "no more than a setback." Ardent highway champions like Moses were undeterred by the public's disapproval of the bond measure, confident that the legislature's failure to dedicate highway revenues to the highway program, rather than popular antihighway sentiment, was responsible. The defeat of the proposal forced the DPW to scale back its 1956 program, but next year the legislature again submitted a modified bond amendment to the people. This time the proposal was for $500 million and a one-cent gasoline tax increase. The tax hike, as well as 60 percent of present gas receipts, would be earmarked for highway use only. That provision—part of a growing trend toward the dedication of highway revenue that would soon be codified in federal highway policy—made it acceptable to the road lobby, and the smaller sums involved appealed to tax-weary voters. The amendment passed by a margin of 2 to 1.[132]

The turnaround between 1955 and 1956 revealed the degree to which American life had become, as Thruway Authority Chairman Bert Tallamy told Congress, "irrevocably geared to the motor vehicle."[133] Many objected to the turn the DPW and the Thruway Authority had taken in the late 1940s and early 1950s. The perceived indifference of engineers to community concerns, the clear preferences road officials had for new forms of suburban commerce, the trend toward earmarking highway revenue, the way highway users had become "consumers" and targets of sophisticated public relations campaigns: all of these developments were products of a long political evolution and precursors to the later antihighway response to parts of the Interstate Highway System.[134] But as yet, highway protests were scattered, discontinuous, and no match to the pressures of a broadly supported car culture. It would take more than a decade for these fissures in America's highway consensus to develop into deep schisms. When work began on the Interstate System in 1956, the support for road building was as strong and vibrant as ever.

The Federal Interstate System and the Culmination of the Bureaucratic Regime

The federal government's role in highway construction expanded steadily through the first half of the twentieth century. But it had always maintained a cooperative relationship with the states. Though federal grants-in-aid came with important guidelines, the states directed construction within their borders. Even with the growth of federal power during the Great Depression and World War II, the states, and especially New York State, took center stage in their own road building.

New York's position as a leader in highway affairs enabled it to sidestep federal Bureau of Public Roads directives with little fear of reprisal. Local BPR agents assigned to monitor New York road work were treated with a general air of dismissal. As late as 1955, while the Interstate Highway program was being debated by Congress, New York district engineers noted that while "frequently Federal Bureau men were overruled," they agreed that "it would be generally good practice to let them come in and that it be voluntary rather than to send for them."[135]

While regional BPR officials folded under pressure from New York's influential highway administration, officials in Washington eagerly sought the state's advice in national road affairs. Starting with the first serious contemplation of national interstate highways by the Roosevelt administration in 1938, the White House, Congress, and the BPR looked to New York for leadership. The New Dealers' 1938 proposal was for an $8 billion federal jobs program designed to construct a network of toll-financed superhighways. But road analysts vigorously objected to the plan, arguing that a national system of toll roads was financially unsound. It threatened as well the established position of state and federal road-building authorities. New York

Superintendent of Public Works Frederick Stuart Greene staunchly objected to what he termed a "crackpot bill." After working for twenty years toward a road-building consensus, he was averse to seeing it upset by the federal government's employment goals. He told Bureau of Public Roads Chief Thomas MacDonald that one of its "worst features" was "that it by-passes all existing, experienced agencies such as your Bureau and the several state departments."[136] MacDonald, who had been instrumental in sustaining this system of cooperative road building, agreed, and the plan was abandoned.

As in New York, the wartime construction hiatus offered federal highway planners the opportunity to contemplate postwar projects. Roosevelt appointed an Interregional Highway Committee in 1941, which in three years produced a lengthy report tying federally sponsored express highway development to an extensive postwar revitalization program. But the administration's involvement in the war effort prevented it from giving much attention to the committee report. In 1944, when Congress turned to highway policy, it focused on a more narrowly defined traffic-management bill supported by the American Association of State Highway Officials. Though the bill called for the designation of a 40,000-mile system of interstate highways, it did little to alter the basic contours of federal highway aid practice and allocation formulas, which remained in place during the next decade.[137]

While New York developed and implemented its pathbreaking Thruway in the postwar decade, the Truman administration came up with few highway policy innovations. A wide array of interests—truckers, farmers, road engineers, urban planners, motorists—sought to tweak the federal highway aid program in their favor. But none succeeded in putting forward a new set of road-building arrangements that would support the construction of the interregional, high-volume express roads that later made up the federal Interstate Highway System.

By the early 1950s the same considerations that fueled New York's highway program—the centrality of highways to economic growth, their consistency with national defense aims—suggested that the time was ripe for another attempt at a federal highway system. Anxious to break the deadlock that had frozen the existing model of federal aid, the Eisenhower administration gave first priority to the Interstate Highway System in 1954. Yet deep divisions persisted. Some saw road building from a broad perspective, linked to national economic planning. Others thought of road building in strictly local terms. Some wanted to centralize the construction program in a National Highway Authority; others wanted to preserve the existing cooperative structure. Road users, legislators, and engineers from around the country differed on how funds ought to be apportioned among rich and poor states, large and small states, states with vast urban populations and larger rural ones. Perennial financial differences remained: over tolls, the taxation of commercial trucks, motor fuel taxes, and the dedication or diversion of highway revenue.

New York continued to play a prominent role during the interstate debate. President Dwight D. Eisenhower invited Bertram Tallamy and Robert Moses to the White House in 1954 to help draft legislation and to offer advice based on their long years of experience in the construction and maintenance of a large, integrated highway system. In a confidential letter to BPR Chairman Francis DuPont, Tallamy tendered a detailed proposal for a national highway plan, covering everything from the intricate workings of public finance and credit to the minutiae of snow removal, roadside gas stations, and police patrols.[138]

During the final revision of the federal highway bill in 1956, New York highway officials again provided guidance. Superintendent of Public Works Johnson corresponded with chair of the Senate Public Works Committee Dennis Chavez (Dem.) and New York Senators Herbert Lehman (Dem.) and Irving Ives (Rep.) and convinced them to delete a provision that would have provided for public hearings on bypasses in populated areas. Reflecting New York's streamlined politics of secrecy and public exclusion, Johnson believed that such a stipulation would unduly complicate construction.[139]

After two years of intense pressure from the White House, a proposal emerged that was satisfactory to competing interests. The Highway Revenue and the Federal Aid Highway Acts of 1956 provided record sums for farm-to-market roads, urban express highways, and interstate trunk lines, financed through an increase in motor vehicle taxes. The new financial and administrative heft of the federal government was evident in the 90–10 funding ratio for interstate highway construction.

The legacy of the Great Depression—and the 1955–1956 New York highway referendum battle—could also be seen in the act's provision that highway revenues be earmarked in a Federal Highway Trust Fund to preclude diversion. The adoption of the Highway Trust Fund signified, above all, the growing public comfort with relinquishing political and financial power to distant authority. A system of federally funded highways had been practically unthinkable—and politically nonviable—in the early 1900s.[140] Years of experience with state highway construction led New Yorkers (as it did their fellow Americans) to accept with little unease extensive political and financial autonomy in public works endeavors: this time a massive roads project, 90 percent of which was funded by federal gas tax receipts earmarked by the Federal Highway Trust Fund.

Importantly, state highway departments continued to direct Interstate Highway System construction and other federal-aid highway work. The success of the cooperative system of federal road work (and the rejection of a centralized National Highway Authority) suggested that the power of the state highway administrators and the bureaucratic road-building regime that they had founded were firmly entrenched. But more than calcified bureaucracy kept the cooperative system intact. Two generations of state-directed highway construction had created a rich store of road-building experience and a deeply rooted network of engineer-administrators, state officials, and organized highway user groups. Most important, state administrative agencies were uniquely situated to mediate between the inherently local nature of highway construction and the broader scope of the Interstate Highway program. New York's experience was particularly important. There is no better indicator of the state's preeminence than the selection of Thruway Authority Chairman Bertram D. Tallamy as the nation's first federal highway administrator.[141]

The New Political Order

New York provided an important model for the nation's Interstate Highway System. Its experience in executing public works projects on a grand scale was instrumental in opening the way and setting the standards for the federal interstate highways. At the same time its centrally managed, closed-system approach, developed during the first half of the twentieth century and adapted to the building of the interstates, bred popular discontent.

Frustration with New York highway politics peaked in the postwar years. The establishment of the Thruway Authority was the latest stage in a long political evolution that since the late nineteenth century had gradually separated road-building authority from local communities. Much as the DPW had done since the 1920s, the Thruway Authority privileged bureaucratic over local knowledge. But the Authority's political and financial autonomy took this a step further. By supporting the removal of highway politics from legislative accountability, New Yorkers endorsed a political organization that aggressively courted public opinion, reshaped New York's economy, and never questioned its faith in better living through rational engineering.

Above all, it muted citizens' complex responses to road building by regarding them solely as motorists, who tendered unqualified votes for roads with their wheels alone.

Still, the building of the New York State Thruway was a fundamental expression of the new political order that had developed over the previous half century. A complex federalism emerged during these years, catalyzed by the policy response to demands for improved highways. This complex federalism, which drew on the resources of local, state, federal, and quasi-public agencies, was not the inevitable consequence of "modernization." Rather, it was contingent on the contested renegotiation of public authority, as "governing generalists" in the state legislature yielded power to expert administrators, and as local governments (and locally oriented roads) were repositioned as nodes in a relational system.[142] Highway engineers played a key role in bringing about this transformation. During the early decades of the twentieth century, they helped New Yorkers learn a series of important political behaviors—deference to engineers' professional authority, faith in bureaucratic decision making, and comfort with distant authority—that appeared to offer the best solution to local road-building problems that were not effectively handled by town officials or political machines. Without these lessons, it is impossible to imagine the construction of the Thruway, much less the federal government's Interstate Highway System into which it was incorporated. These massive investments in transportation infrastructure were the most important products of the bureaucratic road-building regime. And the political legitimacy of this regime, in turn, rested as much on consent from below as it did on the consolidation of engineering authority from above.

Significantly, even the creation of the federal Interstate Highway System did not challenge this model: though the trajectory of twentieth-century political development tended toward increased federal powers, state governments remained important mediators between the national government and local communities.[143] In time, broad-scale, locally organized opposition (like that faced by the Thruway Authority) would check the expansion of the Interstate System in urban areas and call further highway development into question.[144] But even in this context of growing public distrust, the states retained their pivotal role in directing road-building affairs. For if the long age of public road building was drawing to a close, the changes it had wrought on the American political system remained as durable as ever.

Conclusion

An effective steward of the Empire State's highway modernization project for many years and a leader in national highway politics, Federal Highway Administrator Bertram Tallamy saw the nation through the first crucial years of its interstate highway construction. In 1958 he brought Bob Monahan, public relations director for the Thruway Authority, to join him in Washington. Tallamy served until 1960, when the position, a political appointment, was given to a Democrat by President John F. Kennedy. But during his years heading the interstate program, Tallamy started the nation down a path that, like preceding transportation revolutions, fundamentally reshaped not only America's built environment but its federal arrangements as well.

At 41,000 miles, the Interstate Highway System was without precedent in the sheer scale of its undertaking. It was developed at a critical stage in the nation's political evolution, when the powers of state and federal engineers and the road-building consensus had reached their pinnacle. But that power soon crested, as highway engineers faced louder and better organized critics. Road-building authority had been in a state of tremendous flux for seventy-five years, and it continued to be so. The so-called golden age of road building that produced the interstate highways lasted no more than a decade, undone in the late twentieth century by a broad coalition of citizen activists and public officials who sought a better equilibrium between the authority of professional experts and advocates of local control.[1]

Antihighway groups began to oppose the expansion of the nation's highway system by the late 1960s. As transportation historians Mark Rose and Bruce Seely note, "large, vocal, and politically savvy" groups expressed a diverse set of "social, local, ecological, or economic development concerns." Rose and Seely admit that "perhaps a portion" of this opposition "spilled over from other urban and national developments, such as racial conflicts and the war in Vietnam."[2] Technology historian Thomas P. Hughes goes further, arguing that a distrust of "large-scale technology" can be attributed "in no small part to the counterculture values that spread in the 1960s."[3]

But the cultural explanation alone is not sufficient to explain the antihighway movement, any more than it can account for the suburbanization of Westchester County, which was determined as much by decisions made by engineers in Albany as it was by affluent homeowners. Both the early road-building consensus and the later critical response to it were rooted in far-reaching *political* changes that took place between 1880 and 1956, during the nation's second great transportation revolution. During this period, New York and the nation built a vast network of state highways, designed to connect communities and integrate markets, develop industry and an expanding suburbia, and especially to serve the motor vehicle. As New Yorkers of all kinds—bicyclists, farmers, merchants, motorists, engineers, public officials—set about to build a better road system, they gradually recast their system of highway administration. As they worked out a new balance between the often competing goals of democracy and economic efficiency, road-building authority drifted away from citizens who had once worked their own roads and toward a more technically adept but less responsive bureaucracy comprised of state and federal engineer-administrators.

The overturning of old ways—the old politics and practices of road building—was contested at every stage by a diversity of groups: tax-weary farmers, urban cyclists, construction and real estate interests, local officials, political bosses, hard-nosed legislators, an ever-increasing number of motorists, and, most of all, an emerging cadre of engineer-administrators. By midcentury, these engineers had fought and won many bitter battles: against fiscal conservatives who worried about the expense of a modernized road system; against machine politicians who hoped to use road building for patronage purposes; against town and county officials who sought to check the highway system's expansion into their communities. Each time, engineers successfully framed these disputes as conflicts between expertise and the narrow politics of conservatism, bossism, and localism. Their successes brought them new authority in the setting of public works policy. But they also blinded them to the legitimacy of alternative political interests. The consequences of this were foreclosed opportunities to place engineering expertise in the service of a broader agenda that included local and environmental concerns alongside highway modernization and economic development.

The Thruway Authority extended this trend. Politically autonomous, it trumpeted its claims of neutral competence over the muted voices of community opposition. Financially independent, it took its cues from motorist-consumers, the private bond market, and real estate developers rather than from citizens, town and county boards of supervisors, or the state legislature. Of course, autonomy and independence are relative terms. The Authority owed its existence to Governor Dewey and Republican legislators who backed a plan that gave engineers a free hand in constructing the Thruway and in overriding local political opposition, but that also freed themselves from the burden of funding the highway through general revenue. Thruway officials' sovereignty was most secure when the direction of influence of the dominant players (state politicians, interest groups, and engineers) all pointed in the same direction.

The Thruway Authority's construction of the New York State Thruway—the nation's longest express toll highway—marked the apex of America's second great transportation revolution. As the preceding discussion suggests, this revolution was contingent upon a fundamental alteration of federal relations. The reordering depended not only on engineers' claims to professional expertise but also on town and county officials' (often grudging) compliance in relinquishing long-held local road-building powers, and the public's growing (but occasionally wavering) comfort with centralized bureaucracy, expertise, and professionalism. Each of these developments offers an important clue to more clearly understanding modern American state-building.

As this book has shown, when the politics of setting transportation infrastructure policy is given due weight in the emergence of the modern American state, old explanations about the evolution of intergovernmental relations break down. The conventional narrative of modern federal arrangements posits a practically inevitable upward shift of authority from towns and villages to the federal government, and from the "layer cake" federalism of the nineteenth century to the "marble cake" federalism of the twentieth. In this traditional account, the key turning point is the New Deal, and the key policy initiatives are social welfare programs and economic regulation.[4]

A close examination of New York highway politics reveals a different story. Public works policy cannot be dismissed as simply a functionalist response to technological changes or as inexorable obedience to engineering rationality. Rather, it evolved through a deeply *politicized* process that pitted against each other advocates of conflicting sources of road-building authority: residents, road users, pathmasters, local officials, political bosses, state administrators, and professional engineers. New Yorkers had been experimenting with alternatives to the local road-building regime of pathmasters and town highway commissioners since the late nineteenth century. But a bureaucratic regime did not emerge instantaneously, or without conflict. First, a subfederal regime traded one politics of localism (agrarian conservatism) for another rooted in machine politics. Not until party bosses had left the State Highway Commission mired in multiple graft investigations did engineers effectively capitalize on the chronic abuses of the commission and translate their professional standing into a form of political expression that favored a traffic-service vision of highway construction. With the passage of the Federal-Aid Highway Act in 1916 and the emergence of the state-centered bureaucratic road-building regime during the 1920s, a new, cooperative federalism was in place to guide transportation policy through the following decades.

Struggles over public works policy during the first three decades of the twentieth century played out largely on the subfederal level, between representatives of the local road-building regime and competing sites of authority within the state government: the governor's office, the legislature, the Highway Commission, and the Department of Public Works. These confrontations constituted a critical rehearsal for the expansion of federal powers during the New Deal. Early experiences with increasingly distant, isolated bureaucracies also proved essential to the consolidation of bureaucratic road-building authority during the postwar years, including the establishment of the Thruway Authority, the formation of the Interstate Highway System, and the creation of the Federal Highway Trust Fund.

In contrast to traditional interpretations of the evolution of intergovernmental relations, then, the New Deal itself was not, in the case of public works, a watershed event.[5] Certainly the public policy response to the Great Depression and World War II led to the nationalization of the bureaucratic regime during the 1930s and early 1940s, as road building was put in service of national objectives. But thirty years of administrative evolution had produced both widespread public comfort with nonlocal authority and a deeply entrenched state-level bureaucracy. The locus of policy making for most key transportation decisions remained at the state level, in states' Departments of Public Works and quasi-public agencies such as the New York State Thruway Authority. Even the construction of the interstate highways left this system intact. Though financed predominantly by the federal government according to standards set by federal engineers, the all-important route choices were chosen largely by the states' various transportation departments, which continued to direct construction within state borders.

New Yorkers' growing comfort with the centralized bureaucracy—so important to this transformation of federal relations—rested on three essential elements: the triumph of engineers' political authority, the willingness of local officials to voluntarily relinquish road-building power, and the conferring of political legitimacy on this transfer of authority by ordinary New Yorkers. Significantly, these last elements—the conference of political legitimacy on the bureaucratic road-building regime by citizens and local authorities—was an essential corollary to engineers' work in "forging" their own bureaucratic autonomy.[6]

Colonel Frederick S. Greene and Captain Arthur W. Brandt were two of the first highway engineers in New York to enjoy this autonomy. Once they had parlayed their reputation as transportation reformers into policy-making positions in the 1920s, they worked to secure their newfound political power. They built a professionalized network of engineer-administrators, supported by well-organized highway user groups. Together, they promoted their shared traffic-service vision of highway construction and pressured legislators to hand over jealously guarded mapmaking powers to engineer-administrators. Then they undercut local officials' preexisting road-building authority by appealing to a range of arguments: the economic efficiency of centralized coordination, the professional expertise of engineers, and the appeal of state assistance, especially during the cash-strapped years of the Great Depression. Local officials were, predictably, more willing to accept state aid than they were to surrender authority, and some vestiges of the old localized road-building regime (like county control of rights-of-way) persisted well into the mid-twentieth century. Engineers, most notably Herbert Hoover, may have been lionized during the 1920s, but their scramble for power was protracted.

By the early 1940s a new generation of New York engineers was ready to take the wheel: Superintendents of Public Works Charles H. Sells, Bertram

D. Tallamy, and John W. Johnson. These men inherited the bureaucratic regime of their predecessors and quickly began to consolidate their power and extend it into new areas of highway development, such as an improved rural road network, urban arterials, and the New York State Thruway. As they pursued ever more controversial construction, they stopped thinking of motorists as citizens and began to conceive of them as consumers. Superintendent of Public Works Brandt was still arguing during the Great Depression that motorist-generated revenues belonged foremost to citizens rather than motorists. But by the 1940s, leading highway officials accepted the idea that automobile use constituted the only legitimate metric for gauging the public's feelings on highways, and that motorist-generated revenue constituted "user fees" that should be dedicated solely toward the construction of more highways. Most New Yorkers bought into this way of thinking, endorsing state backing to the Thruway Authority's bond as a means of lowering fees on the toll road. But since town and county officials had already yielded significant countervailing road-building authority to state administrators, dissatisfied citizens had few platforms left from which to stage a protest against unfolding highway development. By the time the Thruway Authority began blasting in Westchester County (and other areas across New York State), highway engineers' public and professional agendas were clearly working at cross-purposes. Engineers had always been making political choices, but they had also traveled a great distance from the reformist, antipartisan politics of the 1910s and 1920s to the rawer exercise of political clout in the 1950s.

Agreement from below had been as important as consolidation of power from above for expert engineers' powerful new role to come into being. With the construction of the Thruway, citizen frustration with New York highway politics intensified, and this political legitimacy, conferred on highway engineers by ordinary New Yorkers during the previous half century, was increasingly called into question. The sixteen women, described at the beginning of this book, who protested the 1955 opening celebration of the Tappan Zee Bridge with picket signs reading "S-A-V-E O-U-R V-I-L-L-A-G-E-S-!" were an early indication of the dissatisfaction with the bureaucratic road-building regime that had been consolidated during the postwar years.[7] Compared to the freeway revolts of the late 1960s, in which demonstrators blocked bulldozers with their bodies, this small-scale, Not-In-My-Back-Yard (NIMBY) protest seems both quaint and of doubtful effectiveness.[8] Indeed, Governor Harriman took the wind out of the protesters' sails when he invited the women to join him on stage.

But there were other warning signs from within the planning community, new dissenting voices, suggesting that the politics of localism was never wholly supplanted by the bureaucratic road-building regime. Hugh Pomeroy, director of the Westchester County Department of Planning, recognized that NIMBY protests such as those at the Tappan Zee opening should not be dismissed as narrow or inconsequential opposition. Taken in aggregate, he said, hostility toward the Thruway in Westchester "added up" to "an unbroken wall" of resistance "from Long Island Sound to the Hudson River."[9] Pomeroy saw in this opposition the seeds of the sort of antiplanning mentality that was articulated by citizen groups in Lewisboro, which persuaded the town board to adopt a resolution limiting highway planning only to those projects slated for immediate construction.[10] Though Pomeroy thought that the rejection of a master plan was folly, he was sympathetic to the loss of local power. Pomeroy maintained that "the manner in which some turnpikes have been laid out [and] officiously presented" was not in accordance with "the American way of doing things." He challenged highway officials to engage in an "honest process" with local representatives. "This is tough to do," he acknowledged, "but so are many things in a democracy."[11]

Pomeroy thought that "deeply rooted citizen participation" would not only embody "full democratic participation in the planning process" but also provide "the only . . . conclusive means of settling local controversy."[12] The toughening up of local government would be a good thing for state highway officials: "a mean fox," he told them, would be "a better customer to deal with than a dumb ass."[13] Others disagreed. As late as 1987, Bertram Tallamy, former chairman of the New York State Thruway Authority and the nation's first federal highway administrator, complained that with the current "red tape," it was nearly impossible to initiate new road work when "everybody wants to stick their nose in it."[14]

By the final decades of the twentieth century, highway engineers had lost much of the sweeping powers that they had accumulated in the years since Frederick Greene rescued the New York State Highway Commission from endemic political corruption in 1919. By the 1970s changes in the federal government prompted a major devolution of highway authority to state and local governments. The Intermodal Surface Transportation Efficiency Act of 1991 furthered this trend by investing significant decision-making powers not in state departments of transportation, but in local political bodies such as metropolitan planning organizations, which were far more responsive to communal pressures.[15]

Along with this devolution of road-building authority, the late twentieth century saw a broadened range of inputs into highway policy making. At one time traffic surveys alone shaped highway planning decisions. Now they are supplemented by environmental and economic impact statements, efforts to preserve ethnic and historic neighborhoods, and a wide array of other nonhighway concerns. Highway engineers continue to receive a strong measure of deference as the voice of technical expertise. But the pressures to operate with greater transparency make it increasingly difficult to overcome highway opponents' politics of delay and severely limit the kinds of construction projects that can be completed in a reasonable period of time. Nowhere is this trend toward "open-system" rather than "closed-system" planning more evident than in Boston's Central Artery/Tunnel project, the nation's largest extant public works endeavor. Under way for decades and plagued with multibillion-dollar cost overruns, the "Big Dig" has come to embody the messy complexity—and the long time tables—necessary in any large project that forgoes centralized planning in favor of an open design process.[16]

A competing tendency—toward the privatization of transportation policy making—is visible as well. Though the $15 billion price tag for the Big Dig has been largely attributed to the high costs of "mitigations" (the practice of mollifying critics through a seemingly endless variety of accommodations), Big Dig officials have also been criticized for privatizing the management of the project. Cost overruns, unsafe construction practices, and questions surrounding liability for a fatal tunnel collapse in 2006 have led to a power struggle among the State House, the Attorney General's Office, the Massachusetts Turnpike Authority, and the joint venture contractors Bechtel-Parsons Brinckerhoff. In these debates over the benefits and drawbacks of politically insulated public authorities, one hears echoes of earlier public anxieties over the creation of the New York State Thruway Authority.[17] The tendency toward privatization is visible elsewhere in the United States, evidenced by the recent decisions by the Indiana and Illinois state legislatures to transfer ownership of the Indiana Toll Road and the Chicago Skyway to private, multinational corporations through 75-year and 99-year leases. Other smaller-scale toll road privatization schemes have been tried around the country since 2000, and public-private partnership talks were on the table for the New York State Thruway and the Tappan Zee Bridge in 2006.[18]

As *Paving the Way* demonstrates, the origins of twenty-first-century conflicts—between open and closed planning systems, between the devolution and privatization of road-building authority—can be seen in tensions that began to build decades earlier. These were evident in the great political transformations that had taken place between 1880 and 1956 as a localized road-building regime was displaced first by a subfederal regime and then, in turn, by a state-centered, nationalized, and consolidated bureaucratic regime. Such a complete overhaul of road-building administration constitutes what scholars of American Political Development call a "durable shift in governing authority."[19] So it is that the same prediction that Governor Thomas E. Dewey made for the New York State Thruway can be equally applied to the governing system that was created to produce it: both were destined to "effect a quiet revolution on all our lives."[20] And as Americans continue to wrestle with how to balance their taste for automobility with their distaste for what cars and roads bring with them, so too do they wrestle with the tensions between local and centralized control, between democracy and efficiency.

Still, a few things seem clear. When transportation policy is understood as a set of political choices rather than an inevitable, functionalist response to technological and cultural imperatives, Americans' mid-twentieth-century decisions to continue to sideline deliberative processes in favor of engineering protocol suggest a dangerous lack of faith in democratic institutions. Unless Americans are willing to make difficult decisions—insisting on openness and transparency in transportation planning while remaining willing to support bold but costly projects—American infrastructure, and American democracy, will remain locked in old and vexatious patterns. In this regard, the history of public works is inseparable from the history of public power and its exercise by citizens, experts and nonexperts alike.

NOTES

Abbreviations

AWB	Arthur W. Brandt, superintendent of Public Works
BDT	Bertram D. Tallamy, superintendent of Public Works
CCG	*Cultivator and Country Gentleman*
CG	*Country Gentleman*
DPWAR	Department of Public Works, *Annual Report*
FDR	Franklin D. Roosevelt
FDRGP	Franklin D. Roosevelt, Governor's Papers, FDR Library, Hyde Park, New York
FDRNYSS	Papers of Franklin Roosevelt as New York State Senator, FDR Library, Hyde Park, New York
FDRPPF	President's Personal File, FDR Library, Hyde Park, New York
FFHCP	Correspondence Files of Division of Highways Regarding Federally Funded Highway Construction Projects, 1917–1933, New York State Archive, Albany
FSG	Frederick S. Greene, superintendent of Public Works
GR	*Good Roads*
HLP	Herbert Lehman Papers, Governor's Correspondence, New York State Archives, Albany, New York
HRPC	Hugh R. Pomeroy Collection, 1926–1966, Series 21, Westchester County Archives, Elmsford, New York
JWJ	John W. Johnson, superintendent of Public Works
NMP	Governor Nathan Miller Papers, "Highway Commission," New York State Archives, Albany, New York
NYT	*New York Times*
ORI	Office of Road Inquiry
RCH	*Report of the Commission of Highways*, State of New York
RSCH	*Report of the State Commissioner of Highways*, State of New York
SPW	Superintendent of Public Works, Correspondence and Subject Files, 1943–1964, at New York State Archives, Albany
TPCF	New York State Thruway Authority, Press Clippings File, New York State Archives, Albany
TPIF	New York State Thruway Public Information File, New York State Archives, Albany
TPRPF	New York State Thruway, Public Relations and Planning Files, New York State Archives, Albany

TSNRF   Thruway Speech and News Release File, New York State Archives, Albany

USDA   United States Department of Agriculture

Introduction

1. Town of Queensbury, *Highway Commissioners' Minutes*, 1850–1927, New York State Archives, Albany; *Gazetteer and Business Directory of Saratoga County, N.Y. and Queensbury, Warren County* (Syracuse, N.Y.: Hamilton Child, 1871).

2. Another three miles of nontoll road from Yonkers to New York City, the final stretch of the Thruway's main line, opened in August 1956.

3. *NYT*, December 16, 1955.

4. The United States had 154,000 miles of hard-surfaced roads in 1904, the first year the federal government began collecting such statistics. Fifty years later, the mileage had increased to 2,228,000. Bureau of the Census, *Statistical Abstract of the United States from Colonial Times to the Present*, Transportation, Series Q 50–63, 710 (New York: Basic, 1976).

5. On transportation, see John Lauritz Larson, *Internal Improvement: National Public Works and the Promise of Popular Government in the Early United States* (Chapel Hill: University of North Carolina Press, 2001); L. Ray Gunn, *The Decline of Authority: Public Economic Policy and Political Development in New York, 1800–1860* (Ithaca, N.Y.: Cornell University Press, 1988); William J. Novak, *The People's Welfare: Law and Regulation in Nineteenth-Century America* (Chapel Hill: University of North Carolina Press, 1996), especially ch. 4, "Public Ways: The Legal Construction of Public Space." On communication, see Richard John, *Spreading the News: The American Postal System from Franklin to Morse* (Cambridge, Mass.: Harvard University Press, 1995); John, "Recasting the Information Infrastructure for the Industrial Age," in *A Nation Transformed by Information: How Information Has Shaped the United States from Colonial Times to the Present*, edited by Alfred D. Chandler Jr. and James W. Cortada (New York: Oxford University Press, 2000), 55–105; John, "The Politics of Innovation," *Daedalus* 127 (Fall 1998): 187–214.

6. On the term "transportation revolution," see the pivotal study by George Rogers Taylor, *The Transportation Revolution, 1815–1860*, vol. 4 of *The Economic History of the United States* (New York: Holt, Rinehart & Winston, 1951). Harold U. Faulkner described an early twentieth-century "revolution in transportation" in *The Quest for Social Justice, 1898–1914* (New York: Macmillan, 1931) and in *The Decline of Laissez-Faire, 1897–1917*, vol. 7 of *The Economic History of the United States* (New York: Holt, Rinehart & Winston, 1951).

7. The widely held view that state building entails, above all, the growth of national government is best represented by the work of Steven Skowronek. See especially *Building a New American State: The Expansion of National Administrative Capacities, 1877–1920* (Cambridge: Cambridge University Press, 1982). "New institutionalist" scholars in history and the social sciences (Skowronek, Theda Skocpol, Margaret Weir, and others) have long focused on the evolution of the federal government, neglecting important changes at the state and local levels and relying on a set of assumptions about the decline of localism rooted in the work of Robert Wiebe. Theda Skocpol, *Protecting Soldiers and Mothers: The Political Origins of Social Policy in*

the United States (Cambridge, Mass.: Harvard University Press, 1992); Skocpol, Ann Shola Orloff, and Margaret Weir, eds., *The Politics of Social Policy* (Princeton, N.J.: Princeton University Press, 1988); Robert Wiebe, *The Search for Order* (New York: Hill & Wang, 1967). For critiques of these assumptions, see Thomas Sugrue, "All Politics Is Local: The Persistence of Localism in Twentieth-Century America," in Meg Jacobs, William J. Novak, and Julian Zelizer, eds., *The Democratic Experiment: New Directions in American Political History* (Princeton, N.J.: Princeton University Press, 2003); Jon C. Teaford, *The Rise of the States: Evolution of American State Government* (Baltimore: Johns Hopkins University Press, 2003); and Martha Derthick, *Keeping the Compound Republic: Essays on American Federalism* (Washington, D.C.: Brookings Institution, 2001); Derthick, "How Many Communities: The Evolution of American Federalism," in Derthick, ed., *Dilemmas of Scale in America's Federal Democracy* (Cambridge: Cambridge University Press, 1999), especially 130–135.

8. Karen Orren and Stephen Skowronek would call this a "durable shift in governing authority," which they see as the essence of American Political Development. Orren and Skowronek, *The Search for American Political Development* (Cambridge: Cambridge University Press, 2004), 123.

9. The lust for power is a central theme of Robert Caro, *The Power Broker: Robert Moses and the Fall of New York* (New York: Vintage, 1975 [orig. pub. Knopf, 1974]), probably the most widely read book on the politics of New York transportation infrastructure.

10. Sugrue, "All Politics Is Local," 301–302.

11. A notable exception to this trend is Jon Teaford's *Rise of the States*. Teaford's work was praised in the *Journal of American History* for opening up the history of state governments to historians who otherwise would have labored under the erroneous belief that state governments were "curious anachronisms in the American political system, squeezed between vigorous cities and a growing national government." Gerald Gamm, review of *Rise of the States* in *Journal of American History* 91 (September 2004): 676.

12. Deil Wright, *Understanding Intergovernmental Relations* (Belmont, Calif.: Duxbury, 1978).

13. U.S. Department of Commerce, Bureau of the Census, "Census of Governments: 1962, Volume 6, Topical Studies, Number 4, Historical Statistics on Governmental Finances and Employment" (Washington, D.C.: Government Printing Office, 1964). See also John Joseph Wallis, "The Birth of the Old Federalism: Financing the New Deal, 1932–1940," *Journal of Economic History* 44 (March 1984): 139–159; Wallis and Wallace E. Oates, "The Impact of the New Deal on American Federalism," in Michael D. Bordo, Claudia Goldin, and Eugene N. White, eds., *The Defining Moment: The Great Depression and the American Economy in the Twentieth Century* (Chicago: University of Chicago Press, 1998), 163–171.

14. See especially Brian Balogh, *Chain Reaction: Expert Debate and Public Participation in American Commercial Nuclear Power, 1945–1975* (Cambridge: Cambridge University Press, 1991); Bruce Seely, *Building the American Highway System: Engineers as Policy Makers* (Philadelphia: Temple University Press, 1987); Kenneth Finegold, *Experts and Politicians: Reform Challenges to Machine Politics in New York, Cleveland, and Chicago* (Princeton, N.J.: Princeton University Press, 1995); Eugene Lewis,

Public Entrepreneurship: Toward a Theory of Bureaucratic Political Power: The Organizational Lives of Hyman Rickover, J. Edgar Hoover, and Robert Moses (Bloomington: Indiana University Press, 1980).

15. Robert H. Nelson, "The Economics Profession and the Making of Public Policy," *Journal of Economic Literature* 25 (March 1987): 49–91.

16. Paul Barrett and Mark Rose, "Street Smarts: The Politics of Transportation Statistics in the American City, 1900–1990," *Journal of Urban History* 25 (March 1999): 405–433. Dwight Waldo explains the link between scientific management and public administration by noting that bureaucrats tend to adopt the "scientific maxim . . . that measurement 'solves problems.'" Waldo, *The Administrative State: A Study of the Political Theory of American Public Administration* (New York: Ronald, 1948), 58.

17. Daniel Carpenter, *The Forging of Bureaucratic Autonomy: Reputations, Networks, and Policy Innovations in Executive Agencies, 1862–1928* (Princeton, N.J.: Princeton University Press, 2001).

18. On the tension between high-modernist, top-down models of construction and more open-ended models that rely on flexibility and local knowledge, see James C. Scott, *Seeing Like a State: How Certain Schemes to Improve the Human Condition Have Failed* (New Haven, Conn.: Yale University Press, 1998); Morton Keller, "Looking at the State: An American Perspective," *American Historical Review* 106 (February 2001): 114–118; Thomas P. Hughes, *Rescuing Prometheus* (New York: Pantheon, 1998); Donald Worster, *Rivers of Empire: Water, Aridity, and the Growth of the American West* (New York: Pantheon, 1986).

19. New York was home to the Erie Canal, the Erie and New York Central Railroads, and over 4,000 miles of turnpikes. On New York's transportation leadership, see Gunn, *Decline of Authority.*

20. Most work on the early highway system pays scant attention to the connection between state building and road building, stressing instead the link between highway development and the emergence of the automobile. See, among others, John B. Rae, *The Road and the Car in American Life* (Cambridge, Mass.: MIT Press, 1971); James J. Flink, *The Car Culture* (Cambridge, Mass.: MIT Press, 1975); Flink, *The Automobile Age* (Cambridge, Mass.: MIT Press, 1988). Highway studies also appear in a range of works of cultural criticism, from Helen Leavitt's *Superhighway-Superhoax* (New York: Doubleday, 1970) to Jane Kay Holtz's *Asphalt Nation: How the Automobile Took Over America and How We Can Take It Back* (New York: Crown, 1997).

21. On highway development and the new mobility history, see Gijs Mom and Laurent Tissot, eds., *Road History: Planning, Building, and Use* (Neuchâtel, Switzerland: Alphil Editions, 2007). For works that are more broadly attuned to the evolution of early twentieth-century urban road policy, see Clay McShane, *Down the Asphalt Path: The Automobile and the American City* (New York: Columbia University Press, 1994); Paul Barrett, *The Automobile and Urban Transit: The Formation of Public Policy in Chicago, 1900–1930* (Philadelphia: Temple University Press, 1983). Though it focuses primarily on engineers at the federal Bureau of Public Roads, the best general work on the politics of early twentieth-century state highways is Bruce Seely's *Building the American Highway System.* The standard history of interstate highway

politics remains Mark Rose's *Interstate: Express Highway Politics, 1939–1989* (Knoxville: University of Tennessee Press, 1990, rev. ed.).

22. Michael B. Katz, *In the Shadow of the Poorhouse: A Social History of Welfare* (New York: Basic, rev. ed., 1996); Patrick McGuinn and Frederick Hess, "Freedom from Ignorance? The Great Society and the Evolution of the Elementary and Secondary Education Act of 1965," in Sidney Milkis and Jerome Mileur, eds., *The Great Society and the High Tide of Liberalism* (Boston: University of Massachusetts Press, 2005); Rebecca Mary McLennan, "Citizens and Criminals: The Rise of the American Carcereal State, 1890–1935," Ph.D. diss., Columbia University, 1999.

Chapter One. Old Ways: The Local Road-Building Regime in Late-Nineteenth-Century New York

1. The state constitution of 1846 placed significant limits on debt, special incorporation, and state-subsidized internal improvements that had been critical to the turnpike booms of the early nineteenth century. An 1874 amendment specifically forbade passage of local road-building bills. L. Ray Gunn describes the constitution of 1846 as a victory of the "traditional American principle" of direct democracy over the desire for a more efficient and "rational" system of public administration. Gunn, *Decline of Authority: Public Economic Policy and Development in New York State, 1800–1860* (Ithaca, N.Y.: Cornell University Press, 1988), 184–188, 188 n53, 196–197.

2. *Eleventh Census of the United States, 1890*, vol. 1, pp. lxvii–lxx; Paul W. Gates, "Agricultural Change in New York State, 1850–1890," *New York History* 50 (April 1969): 114–141.

3. *The Cultivator and Country Gentleman*, October 17, 1878, p. 667. *The Cultivator* (founded 1834) and *The Country Gentleman* (founded 1859) merged in 1866 to form *The Cultivator and Country Gentleman*, until 1898, when the journal reverted to simply *The Country Gentleman*. Part of upstate New York's burgeoning agricultural press, these journals "probably circulated more thoroughly among the rural folk of Western New York than any other paper." Whitney Cross, *The Burned-Over District: The Social and Intellectual History of Enthusiastic Religion in Western New York, 1800–1850* (Ithaca, N.Y.: Cornell University Press, 1950), 141. On the agricultural press, see Donald H. Parkerson, *The Agricultural Transition in New York State: Markets and Migration in Mid-Nineteenth-Century America* (Ames: Iowa State University Press, 1995), 16–17; Margaret W. Rossiter, *The Emergence of Agricultural Science: Justus Leibig and the Americans, 1840–1880* (New Haven, Conn.: Yale University Press, 1975), 8–9. While the editors of these journals often spoke for proponents of scientific farming, the papers' wide readership guaranteed that a broad cross-section of rural New York would be represented in the letters and opinion pieces, which form part of the evidentiary basis for this chapter.

4. William J. Novak, *The People's Welfare: Law and Regulation in Nineteenth-Century America* (Chapel Hill: University of North Carolina Press, 1996), especially 10–11.

5. The historical record offers some conflicting data as to whether the position of pathmaster was an appointed or an elected one, but it appears that in most instances pathmasters were appointed positions, rotating among abutting landowners and occasionally reflective of social status.

6. On the labor system and road districting, see W. Pierrepont White, *Oneida County, New York, and Her Road Building* (Oneida County League for Good Roads, December 1900 [2d ed., January 1902]), 4–5, 13–15; the comments of former governor Roswell Flower, reprinted in the *Albany Argus*, February 17, 1896; *CCG*, October 17, 1878, p. 667.

7. The road drag—a split log drawn over the road by a horse—was a cheap but increasingly popular road grading tool. See Malcolm Gladwell, "Clicks and Mortar," *New Yorker*, December 6, 1999.

8. Wayne E. Fuller, *RFD: The Changing Face of Rural America* (Bloomington: Indiana University Press, 1964), 179.

9. The principles of basic nineteenth-century road engineering included opening sluices, digging ditches, grading and crowning the surface, filling mud holes, leveling ruts, and removing stones. Failure to accomplish all of these maintenance jobs led to the roadway's quick decomposition. But ultimately, without hard surfacing or at least a base level of crushed stone, such repairs were only stop-gap measures.

10. One source suggests that children as young as twelve served the road tax. *CCG*, January 26, 1888, p. 66.

11. *CCG*, October 17, 1878, p. 667; February 19, 1880, p. 115; June 12, 1890, p. 466.

12. *CCG*, November 14, 1889, p. 855. See also the 1883 road account book of S. F. Shaw, Series 745, Rare and Manuscript Collections, Kroch Library, Cornell University, Ithaca, New York.

13. *CCG*, September 15, 1892, p. 685.

14. Roy V. Scott, *The Reluctant Farmer: The Rise of Agricultural Extension to 1914* (Urbana: University of Illinois Press, 1970); Elisabeth Clemens, *The People's Lobby: Organizational Innovation and the Rise of Interest Group Politics in the United States, 1890–1925* (Chicago: University of Chicago Press, 1997), 178; Lawrence Goodwyn, *Democratic Promise: The Populist Moment in America* (New York: Oxford University Press, 1976).

15. Paula Baker, *The Moral Frameworks of Public Life: Gender, Politics, and the State in Rural New York, 1870–1930* (New York: Oxford University Press, 1991), 43–44, n52, citing records of the New York State Grange.

16. *CCG*, January 6, 1859, p. 378.

17. Philip Parker Mason, "The League of American Wheelmen and the Good Roads Movement, 1880–1905," Ph.D. diss., University of Michigan, 1957, 44; Gary Allan Tobin, "The Bicycle Boom of the 1890's: The Development of Private Transportation and the Birth of the Modern Tourist," *Journal of Popular Culture* 7 (1974): 838–849. On the proliferation of federated associations like the LAW, see Theda Skocpol, Marshall Ganz, and Ziad Munson, "A Nation of Organizers: The Institutional Origins of Civic Voluntarism in the United States," *American Political Science Review* 94 (September 2000): 527–546.

18. Clemens, *People's Lobby*, 44, 84, 279.

19. Mason, "League of American Wheelmen," 52–56.

20. Though these laws were on the books, there is little evidence that litigation was widespread. For an early example of the threat of prosecution, see "Remove the Roadside Weeds," *Rochester Union Advertiser*, August 13, 1881.

21. Bruce Seely, *Building the American Highway System: Engineers as Policy Makers* (Philadelphia: Temple University Press, 1987), 11–16.

22. On traditional versus modern uses of city streets, see Clay McShane, *Down the Asphalt Path: The Automobile and the American City* (New York: Columbia University Press, 1994). For interpretations of cyclists' motives, see Richard Holt, "The Bicycle, the Bourgeoisie, and the Discovery of Rural France, 1880–1914," *British Journal of Sports History* 2 (September 1985): 127–139; Gary Allan Tobin, "The Bicycle Boom of the 1890's: The Development of Private Transportation and the Birth of the Modern Tourist." *Journal of Popular Culture* 7 (1974): 838–849; Richard Harmond, "Progress and Flight: An Interpretation of the American Cycling Craze," *Journal of Social History* 5 (1971–1972): 235–257.

23. Editorial, *GR* 1 (May 1892), 283.

24. Richard L. McCormick, *From Realignment to Reform: Political Change in New York State, 1893–1910* (Ithaca, N.Y.: Cornell University Press, 1981), 24–25. See also Clemens, *People's Lobby*.

25. Clemens, *People's Lobby*, 44, 84, 279.

26. McCormick, *Realignment to Reform*, 41–43.

27. *NYT*, July 28, 1895.

28. See, for example, "What Good Roads Mean," *GR* 2 (November 1892), 247; "How to Keep the Boys and Girls on the Farm," *GR* 4 (July 1893), 46–50. On mail delivery, see Daniel Carpenter, *The Forging of Bureaucratic Autonomy: Reputations, Networks, and Policy Innovations in Executive Agencies, 1862–1928* (Princeton, N.J.: Princeton University Press, 2001).

29. *NYT*, February 22, 1898.

30. Isaac Potter, "The Gospel of Good Roads: A Letter to the American Farmer," *GR* 1 (January 1892), 3.

31. *Albany Argus*, April 24, 1897.

32. Clemens, *People's Lobby*, 178.

33. *Albany Argus*, February 18, 1898.

34. *CG*, August 31, 1891, p. 694.

35. *CG*, April 14, 1892, p. 284.

36. *CG*, May 12, 1892, p. 365. On Jacksonian democracy and the reaction against state public works, see Marvin Meyers, *The Jacksonian Persuasion* (Stanford, Calif.: Stanford University Press, 1957, 1960), 268–270.

37. *CG*, April 7, 1892, p. 266.

38. *CG*, April 28, 1892, p. 324. The author of the article suggested that the vote might have been tipped by laborers who needed work.

39. William M. Curtiss, "The Development of Highway Administration and Finance in New York," Department of Agricultural Economics and Farm Management, New York State College of Agriculture (Ithaca, N.Y.: Cornell University, March 1936), 23.

40. Mason, "League of American Wheelmen," 76, 87–88.

41. *CG*, January 12, 1893, p. 26.

42. *CG*, September 22, 1892, p. 704.

43. On nineteenth-century leisure fads, see Dwight W. Hoover, "Roller Skating Toward Industrialism," in Kathryn Grover, ed., *Hard at Play: Leisure in America, 1840–1940* (Amherst: University of Massachusetts Press, 1992), 61–76; Frederic

Paxson, "The Rise of Sport," *Mississippi Valley Historical Review* 4 (September 1917), 143–168; John Higham, "The Reorientation of American Culture in the 1890s," in John Weiss, ed., *The Origins of Modern Consciousness* (Detroit: Wayne State Press, 1965). On the attitude of railroad corporations toward road reform, see Bruce Seely, "Railroads, Good Roads, and Motor Vehicles: Managing Technological Change," *Railroad History* 155 (Autumn 1986): 35–63; Stephen B. Goddard, *Getting There: The Epic Struggle between Road and Rail in the American Century* (New York: Basic, 1994).

44. *GR* 3 (June 1893), 313.

45. Charles L. Dearing, *American Highway Policy* (Washington, D.C.: Brookings Institution, 1941), Appendix A; *GR* 2 (December 1892), 327; *GR* 4 (August 1893), 68.

46. *CG*, January 19, 1893, p. 44.

47. On the lack of "smooth functional fits" between state agencies and social actors, see Terrence McDonald, "Building the Impossible State," in John E. Jackson, ed., *Institutions in American Society* (Ann Arbor: University of Michigan Press, 1990), 217–239, especially 235.

48. See McCormick, *From Realignment to Reform*, 26, 104–105; Herbert J. Bass, *"I Am a Democrat": The Political Career of David Bennett Hill* (Syracuse, N.Y.: Syracuse University Press, 1961), 51–56; Chap. 568, Laws of 1890, constituting Chap. 19, General Laws of New York; Curtiss, "Development of Highway Administration," 46–47. Subsequent court proceedings noted that the law was "not strictly a consolidation since new provisions [for county funding of bridge repair] were engrafted on the antecedent law for the purpose of improving the highway system." *People ex rel. Root v. Board of Supervisors of Steuben County* (1895), 146 N.Y. 107.

49. On the general late-nineteenth-century trend toward enlarged state public responsibility for social and economic conditions, see William R. Brock, *Investigation and Responsibility: Public Responsibility in the United States, 1865–1900* (Cambridge: Cambridge University Press, 1984), chs. 1–3.

50. The first canal commissioners were appointed under a limited mandate in 1810. But by the mid-nineteenth century the commission's powers to control canal contracts had vastly increased. On the expansion of the Erie Canal and the continuous investigation into its management during the late nineteenth century, see Noble E. Whitford, *History of the Canal System of the State of New York*, vol. 1 (Albany, N.Y.: Office of the New York State Engineer and Surveyor, 1906), 10–14, 131–408; *CCG*, January 22, 1891.

51. On the promise and problems of egalitarianism in public works, see Harry Scheiber, *Ohio Canal Era: A Case Study of Government and the Economy, 1820–1861* (Athens: Ohio University Press, 1969), especially ch. 4; L. Ray Gunn, *The Decline of Authority: Public Economic Policy and Development in New York State, 1800–1860* (Ithaca, N.Y.: Cornell University Press, 1988), especially chs. 4–5; Carter Goodrich, ed., *Canals and American Economic Development* (New York: Columbia University Press, 1961), 1–66.

52. *GR* 1 (March 1892), 164.

53. *GR* 1 (January 1892), 45; *CG*, January 30, 1890, p. 91; *CG*, January 22, 1891, p. 65; *CG*, April 20, 1891, p. 673; *NYT*, February 27, 1890, p. 2:1; *NYT*, January 22, 1890, p. 3:2; *NYT*, April 22, 1891, p. 3:1.

54. Bass, *"I Am a Democrat,"* 278 n57. Reintroduced the following year, the bill went down by a wider margin.

55. The complex interplay between "bosses" and "reformers" has received substantial attention in the field of urban political history. See Terrence J. McDonald and Sally K. Ward, eds., *The Politics of Urban Fiscal Policy* (Beverly Hills, Calif.: Sage, 1984), especially McDonald and Ward, "San Francisco: Socioeconomic Change, Political Culture, and Fiscal Politics, 1870–1906," pp. 39–68, and M. Craig Brown and Charles N. Halaby, "Bosses, Reform, and the Socioeconomic Bases of Urban Expenditure, 1890–1940," pp. 69–100. See also Kenneth Finegold, *Experts and Politicians: Reform Challenges to Machine Politics in New York, Cleveland, and Chicago* (Princeton, N.J.: Princeton University Press, 1995), 1–67.

56. Quoted in *CG*, January 19, 1893, p. 50.

57. Chapter 333, Laws of 1893. The text of the law is reported in *CG*, May 25, 1893, p. 405; Curtiss, "Development of Highway Administration," 38.

58. Speech of Hon. J.A.C. Wright, at the International Good Roads Convention, 1901, in U.S. Department of Agriculture, Office of Public Roads, Bulletin 21 (Washington, D.C.: Government Printing Office, 1901), 29–34.

59. New Jersey had a long history of road reform. In the 1860s, Essex County, jealous of Manhattan's Central Park and Brooklyn's Prospect Park, contemplated its own urban improvement. A group of residents, organized as the Essex Public Road Board, suggested that the county improve its roads instead. The board constructed arterial roads emanating out from Newark to the county line. These roads, and similarly improved ones in nearby Union County, formed the nucleus of New Jersey's early improved road system by the 1880s. See *GR* 3 (June 1893), 313–320.

60. Another study reiterated the stylized fact, long bandied about by shipping companies, that it cost more for farmers to transport their goods from their farms to a rail junction than it did to ship the same goods 3,100 miles from New York to Liverpool. *CG*, January 23, 1896, p. 70, and February 13, 1896, p. 130; *Scientific American* 99 (December 1908): 451.

61. *CCG*, February 13, 1896, p. 130.

62. Seely, *Building the American Highway System.*

63. *Albany Argus*, February 26, 1897.

64. *CG*, April 23, 1896, p. 323. USDA, ORI, "State Laws Relating to the Management of Roads Enacted in 1894–95," (Washington, D.C.: Government Printing Office, 1895), 76.

65. *CCG*, January 30, 1896, p. 90, and February 6, 1896, p. 110.

66. *CCG*, March 26, 1896, p. 250; April 30, 1896, p. 351; and May 7, 1896, p. 370.

67. C. S. Walker, "The Farmers' Movement," *Annals of the American Academy of Political and Social Science* 4 (March 1894): 94–102.

68. On the transformation of rural communities and the acceptance of modern public administration, see Jacqueline Swansinger, "From Farmers to Businessmen: The Transformation of Elites in Fredonia, New York, 1898–1907," *New York History* 73 (January 1992): 43–63. *CCG*, March 11, 1897, p. 186; February 11, 1897, p. 106; April 6, 1897, p. 264; and April 18, 1897, pp. 264–265.

69. McCormick, *From Realignment to Reform*, 21–22.

70. *Albany Argus*, February 18, 1898.

71. *NYT*, February 18, 1898; February 21, 1898, and February 22, 1898.

72. *NYT*, March 4, 1898, and March 11, 1898.

73. Chaps. 115 (Higbie-Armstrong Act) and 351 (Fuller-Plank Act), Laws of 1898.

74. *CCG*, March 31, 1898, p. 246; March 24, 1898, p. 227; April 25, 1898, pp. 326–327; and March 23, 1898, pp. 226–227.

75. "State Highway Management, Control, and Procedure," *Public Roads* 1 (February 1919): 51–56.

76. The first road improved under the Higbie-Armstrong Act (ch. 115 of the Laws of 1898) was the Troy-Schenectady Road. "Road No. 1" was two miles in length, cost $14,590, and came in at $10 under budget. The road was accepted and turned over to the county on July 27, 1899. Record of Contracts for the Improvement of Public Highways, New York State Archives, Albany.

Chapter Two. New Ways: The Emergence of a Subfederal Road-Building Regime, 1898–1919

1. *NYT*, February 12, 1903. Since the ratification of the constitution of 1846, all public improvement projects requiring large debts had to be authorized by law, limited to a single objective, and approved at a general election. See L. Ray Gunn, *The Decline of Authority: Public Economic Policy and Development in New York State, 1800–1860* (Ithaca, N.Y.: Cornell University Press, 1988), 184–185. Armstrong introduced a similar bill in 1902, calling for a $20 million bond issue, but it was not approved. *Harper's Weekly* 45 (July 6, 1901): 689; *Harper's Weekly* 46 (April 5, 1902): 426.

2. Arthur Shattuck to William Pierrepont White, January 10, 1903. William Pierrepont White Collection, Division of Rare and Manuscript Collections, Kroch Library, Cornell University, Ithaca, New York. On the importance of organized interest groups as lobbyists for bond referenda, see R. Rudy Higgens-Evenson, *The Price of Progress: Pubic Services, Taxation, and the American Corporate State, 1877–1929* (Baltimore: Johns Hopkins University Press, 2003), 62–63.

3. Arthur Shattuck to William Pierrepont White, March 30, 1903; Shattuck to members of the Automobile Club of America, March 30, 1903; William W. Armstrong to White, April 4, 1903; John B. Uhle, President of the Highway Alliance, to White, February 13, 1903, William Pierrepont White Collection, Division of Rare and Manuscript Collections, Kroch Library, Cornell University, Ithaca, New York.

4. *NYT*, January 28, 1904.

5. As Richard L. McCormick writes, "After 1905 politics and governance in New York State differed in fundamental respects from what they had been throughout most of the nineteenth century." McCormick, *From Realignment to Reform: Political Change in New York State, 1893–1910* (Ithaca, N.Y.: Cornell University Press, 1981), quoted here and above, 219. On the investigative culture of 1905, see Morton Keller, *The Life Insurance Enterprise, 1885–1910: A Study in the Limitations of Corporate Power* (Cambridge, Mass.: Harvard University Press, 1963), ch. 15.

6. M. Craig Brown and Charles N. Halaby debunk the myth of the "costly boss and the cost-efficient reformer" in "Bosses, Reform, and the Socioeconomic Bases of Urban Expenditure, 1890–1940," in Terrence J. McDonald and Sally K. Ward, eds., *The Politics of Urban Fiscal Policy* (Beverly Hills, Calif.: Sage, 1984), 71.

7. On the canal improvement controversy, see McCormick, *From Realignment to Reform*, 160–161; R. Rudy Higgens-Evenson, *The Price of Progress: Public Services, Taxation, and the American Corporate State, 1877–1929* (Baltimore: Johns Hopkins University Press, 2003), 56–58.

8. *NYT*, July 31, 1905, and October 28, 1905.

9. *NYT*, July 31, 1905.

10. Only two senators cast dissenting votes.

11. *NYT*, December 29, 1905. About 500,000 voted, or approximately one-third of the typical turnout for a gubernatorial election in a nonpresidential election year. Three farming counties rejected the amendment: Orleans, Yates, and Schuyler in western and west-central New York. It received slim majorities in the counties of Columbia, Delaware, and Schoharie (mid-Hudson and Mohawk Valley), Genesee and Wyoming (western New York), and Steuben and Tioga (Southern Tier and south-central New York). "Facts and Figures Arranged from Official Records Concerning Highways in New York State" prepared by William Pierrepont White, 1906. In "Roads" pamphlet collection, New York Public Library, Science, Industry, and Business Library, Manhattan. On the rural categorization of New York's counties, see W. A. Anderson, *Population Trends in New York State, 1900–1930* (Ithaca, N.Y.: Cornell University Agricultural Experiment Station, 1932).

12. Paula Baker, *The Moral Frameworks of Public Life* (New York: Oxford University Press, 1991), 108.

13. Shattuck to White, March 3, 1903, William Pierrepont White Collection, Division of Rare and Manuscript Collections, Kroch Library, Cornell University, Ithaca, New York.

14. Clarence Heer, *The Postwar Expansion of State Expenditures: An Analysis of the Increase between 1917 and 1923 in the Cost of State Government in New York* (New York: National Institute of Public Administration, 1926); Edward Taylor Bullock, "Financial Aspects of Highway Development with Special Reference to New York State," Ph.D. diss., Harvard University, 1926; McCormick, *From Realignment to Reform*; Morton Keller, *Regulating a New Economy: Public Policy and Economic Change in America, 1900–1933* (Cambridge, Mass.: Harvard University Press, 1990); Jon C. Teaford, *Rise of the States: Evolution of American State Government* (Baltimore: Johns Hopkins University Press, 2003).

15. On the Allds investigation, see Robert F. Wesser, *Charles Evans Hughes: Politics and Reform in New York, 1905–1910* (Ithaca, N.Y.: Cornell University Press, 1967), 276–287; and Harold F. Gosnell, *Boss Platt and His New York Machine* (Chicago: University of Chicago Press, 1924), 157–159, 245–256. On Hooker, see Wesser, *Charles Evans Hughes*, 120, 138.

16. New York State Legislature, Joint Legislative Commission on Good Roads, *Hearing Testimony*, 1907, 23a, in New York State Library, Albany.

17. Ibid., 313.

18. Ibid., 5f, 12.

19. Ibid., 230.

20. On farmers' innovative and adaptive uses of the automobile, see Ronald Kline and Trevor Pinch, "Users as Agents of Technological Change: The Social Construction of the Automobile in the Rural United States," *Technology and Culture* 37 (October 1996): 763–795. Commission on Good Roads, *Hearing*, 352. Vander-

bilt quoted in Tom Lewis, *Divided Highways: Building the Interstate Highways, Transforming American Life* (New York: Viking, 1997), 30.

21. Bullock, "Financial Aspects of Highway Development," 63–66.

22. On nineteenth-century commissions, see William R. Brock, *Investigation and Responsibility: Public Responsibility in the United States, 1865–1900* (Cambridge: Cambridge University Press, 1984).

23. *NYT*, March 16, 1908.

24. *NYT*, January 12, 1908.

25. *NYT*, February 14, 1909, and September 26, 1909.

26. The course of the trial can be followed in *NYT*, August 3, 1910; August 30, 1910; September 6, 1910; September 8, 1910; and September 9, 1910.

27. Bullock, "Financial Aspects of Highway Development," 91. Anecdotal evidence suggests that Westchester's highways might have been of a superior quality. See *NYT*, October 2, 1909.

28. Bullock, "Financial Aspects of Highway Development," 91, 97–100.

29. Originally only 2,800 miles of state highways were authorized, but the system was later enlarged to 3,600 miles. *RCH*, 1910; *RCH*, 1916.

30. *RCH*, 1909.

31. Macadamized roads (named for the Scottish road builder John Loudon McAdam) are constructed by compacting small broken stones into a dense mass over a crowned subgrade, held together by a binder, such as water, tar, or asphalt. Early roads were water-bound, while roads designed for automobiles used tar or asphalt as a binder in order to preserve the roads surface and minimize dust.

32. *RCH*, 1910, 1911.

33. *NYT*, January 18, 1914; Robert Earl to Franklin Delano Roosevelt, June 5, 1911, "Robert Earl," FDRNYSS. On the governorship of John Dix, see Robert F. Wesser, *A Response to Progressivism: The Democratic Party and New York Politics, 1902–1918* (New York: New York University Press, 1986), ch. 3.

34. This story can be traced in the *NYT*, January 8, 1911; January 10, 1911; January 12, 1911; January 14, 1911; and February 1, 1911.

35. *RCH*, 1911.

36. See assessment in *RCH*, 1910.

37. *NYT*, February 1, 1912; March 14, 1912; and March 20, 1912. Paul Barrett, *The Automobile and Urban Transit: The Formation of Public Policy in Chicago, 1900–1930* (Philadelphia: Temple University Press, 1983); Charles W. Cheape, *Moving the Masses: Urban Public Transit in New York, Boston, and Philadelphia, 1880–1912* (Cambridge, Mass.: Harvard University Press, 1980). For an international perspective on streetcar battles see Daniel T. Rodgers, *Atlantic Crossings: Social Politics in a Progressive Age* (Cambridge, Mass.: Harvard University Press, 1998), 132–159.

38. *New York World*, cited in *NYT*, June 7, 1912.

39. *NYT*, September 18, 1912, and October 14, 1912.

40. *NYT*, November 10, 1912; December 27, 1912; January 18, 1914; and January 26, 1914.

41. New York State, *RSCH*, 1913

42. *NYT*, January 2, 1913; January 4, 1913; January 15, 1913; February 2, 1913; February 3, 1913; February 21, 1913; February 27, 1913; March 6, 1913; and March 8, 1913. Jay W. Forrest, *Tammany's Treason* (Albany, N.Y.: Fort Orange, 1913), 57–

66; Wesser, *Response to Progressivism*, 105–107. Roe B. Smith, *History of New York State: Vol. 4: Political and Governmental* (Syracuse, N.Y.: Syracuse University Press, 1922), 230.

43. "Another Sulzerism Nailed," *Highway Contractor* (Official Bulletin of the New York State Road Builders Association and Connecticut General Contractors Association) 1, no. 2 (1914): 50. William L. Riordon, *Plunkitt of Tammany Hall* (New York: Meridian, 1991 [orig. pub. 1905]).

44. Robert Earl to Franklin D. Roosevelt, November 9, 1912, "Robert Earl," FDRNYSS; *NYT*, March 25, 1913; June 10, 1913; and September 11, 1913.

45. David M. Ellis, James A. Frost, Harold C. Syrett, and Harry J. Carman, *A Short History of New York State* (Ithaca, N.Y.: Cornell University Press, 1957), 388. Murphy insisted, "It will be Gaffney or war." Forrest, *Tammany's Treason*, 57–66.

46. *Engineering News*, October 23, 1913, p. 829. On the engineering press's criticism of politics in New York road building, see the following articles and editorials in *Engineering News*: "The Prospects of State Highway Administration in New York," October 23, 1913, p. 829; "The Investigation of the New York State Highway Work," December 4, 1913, p. 1142; "The New York State Highway Department: After Investigation, What?" February 19, 1914, pp. 423–425; "Politics vs. Business in New York State Road Work," March 26, 1914, p. 686; "Governor Glynn's Investigation of Highway Work," March 26, 1914, pp. 694–695.

47. *NYT*, October 30, 1913, and November 4, 1913.

48. *NYT*, November 4, 1913, and November 14, 1913; Forrest, *Tammany's Treason*, 295–302.

49. Smith, *History of New York State: Vol. 4*, 246.

50. *NYT*, December 1, 1914.

51. "The New York Highway Department: After Investigation, What?" *Engineering News*, February 19, 1914, pp. 423–425.

52. In a bitter conclusion to Carlisle's career in the highway department, some nasty weather added injury to insult. On the way to the capitol to tender his resignation in the aftermath of a debilitating winter storm, he took a spill on the ice, suffering serious sprains in both arms and sending him to the hospital. *NYT*, January 7, 1915; January 9, 1915; January 23, 1915; and February 3, 1915.

53. *Better Roads and Streets*, July 1915, p. 22. On the world of patronage politics in Chenango County, New York, see James Flanagan to Assemblyman Bert Lord, March 7, 1915; Harrison Beatty to Lord, September 22, 1915; Lord to Beatty, September 24, 1915; Republican State Committeeman Judge James Hill to Lord, December 2, 1915; and Lord to Fred W. Hammond, December 30, 1915, Bert Lord Papers, Boxes 3–4, Cornell University, Ithaca, New York. Unfortunately for the author, ten highway department employees who had been engaged in writing the history of New York's early efforts to construct state highways were dismissed in the shakeup, saving the state $20,000. *NYT*, January 9, 1915; February 14, 1915; and March 6, 1915.

54. Throughout the late nineteenth century, most maps of New York State listed railway routes but not roads. Roads appeared on local and regional maps for use by railroad and horse-and-carriage travelers. Early twentieth-century road maps included railroad stations, bicycle routes, topography, and notes on the quality of

roads. David Yehling Allen, *Long Island Maps and Their Makers: Five Centuries of Cartographic History* (Mattituck, N.Y.: Amereon House, 1997), 119–121.

55. As of January 1, 1916, New York State had 6,250 miles of surfaced state and state-aid highways, or 12 percent of all improved state and state-aid highways, more than any other state. New York State had 17,500 miles of total surfaced highways (6 percent of the nation's surfaced roads), ranking third behind Ohio and Indiana. New York State surfaced 21.8 percent of its public roads, ranking ninth behind Rhode Island (58.8 percent), Massachusetts (46.6 percent), Indiana (42.6 percent), Ohio (35.8 percent), New Jersey (31.0 percent), Vermont (23.1 percent), Connecticut (22.7 percent), and Kentucky (22.1 percent). Comparisons across states are difficult, however, because of nonstandard reporting techniques that do not differentiate between a mile of narrow gravel road and a mile of high-grade cement highway. Following the money provides a clearer picture of New York State's leadership role. In 1915, New York led the nation in highway expenditures, spending over $16.5 million ($14 million from the state, $2.5 million from local sources). New York's closest competitor, California, spent $8.3 million, or about half that of New York. Total public highway expenditures from all states tallied $80.5 million. Thus one in five U.S. highway dollars was spent in New York. All state money spent on highways from the passage of each state's state-aid law to January 1, 1916, totaled $265.4 million. New York spent $96.6 million of that, or more than one of every three dollars. See Historical Statistics of the U.S., 1916, pp. 275–278.

56. Bruce Seely, *Building the American Highway System: Engineers as Policy Makers* (Philadelphia: Temple University Press, 1987), 15.

57. On ORI and OPRI leadership, see ibid., 9–23. On the history of the Bureau of Public Roads and its earlier incarnations (ORI, OPRI, OPR), see William Stull Holt, *The Bureau of Public Roads: Its History, Activities, and Organizations* (Baltimore: Johns Hopkins University Press, 1923).

58. Seely, *Building the American Highway System*, 19.

59. On Page and the OPR, see ibid., 24–45.

60. The definition of what constituted state aid varied widely and could include such minimal state intervention as dispensing information about road-building technology. Likewise, many state highway commissions had exceedingly limited powers. Charles Dearing, *American Highway Policy* (Washington, D.C.: Brookings Institution, 1941), 54–55.

61. Seely, *Building the American Highway System*, 36–45; Howard Lawrence Preston, *Dirt Roads to Dixie: Accessibility and Modernization in the South, 1885–1935* (Knoxville: University of Tennessee Press, 1991), 39–68.

62. Paul Douglas, "The Development of a System of Federal Grants-in-Aid," *Political Science Quarterly* 35 (1920): 255–271, 522–544, especially 270–271. On rural free delivery, see Wayne Fuller, *RFD: The Changing Face of Rural America* (Bloomington: Indiana University Press, 1964).

63. Seely, *Building the American Highway System*, 36–45. Edward Taylor Bullock lists among contemporary federal subsidy legislation the Smith-Lever (agricultural extension) Act of 1914, the Vocational Education Act of 1917, the Industrial Rehabilitation Act of 1920, and the Maternity and Infancy Hygiene Act of 1921. Bullock, "Financial Aspects," 206.

64. Martha Derthick, "How Many Communities: The Evolution of American

Federalism," in Derthick, ed., *Dilemmas of Scale in America's Federal Democracy* (Cambridge: Cambridge University Press, 1999), especially 130–135; Derthick, *The Influence of Federal Grants: Public Assistance in Massachusetts* (Cambridge, Mass.: Harvard University Press, 1970); V. O. Key Jr., *The Administration of Federal Grants to the States* (Chicago: Public Administration Service, 1937 [reprint New York: Johnson Reprint, 1972]), 1–41; Douglas, "The Development of a System of Federal Grants-in-Aid," 255–271, 522–544.

65. Derthick, *Influence of Federal Grants,* 220. On the emergence of a complex federalism, see also Terrence McDonald, "Building the Impossible State," in John E. Jackson, ed., *Institutions in American Society* (Ann Arbor: University of Michigan Press, 1990), 217–239.

66. *Congressional Record,* 64th Congress, 1st session, 1380–1381, 1473–1474, 1536–1537, 7570. Senator James W. Wadsworth of Groveland and Representatives Charles B. Smith and David A. Driscoll, both of Buffalo, supported the bill. None of the three publicly recorded why he voted for the bill, though it seems important that each was a western New Yorker whose constituents perhaps had more to gain from a national highway program than their eastern counterparts.

67. New York State was one of twelve states that would pay a greater proportion of taxes than it would receive back in federal aid.

68. *Congressional Record,* 64th Congress, 1st session, 1381, 7570. The apportionment was based on the following formula: one-third population, one-third area, one-third mileage. I. J. Morris, secretary of the New York State Highway Commission, explained to former New York highway engineer and then federal district engineer Guy H. Miller that "we have already received quite a little feeling along the lines that New York gets only $4,000,000 where it would pay into the fund some $25,000,000 or $30,000,000." March 30, 1917, FFHCP, 1917–1933.

69. D. F. Houston, Secretary, Bureau of Public Roads, to Governor Charles S. Whitman, n.d. (near February 24, 1917), FFHCP.

70. *RSCH,* 1916; *Better Roads and Streets,* October 1916, p. 18. State Engineer Skene acknowledged in 1907 that the state also used (then cheaper) immigrant labor on force account: "We buy the stone direct from the quarryman, and then we put on a gang of laborers—Italians—(anybody we can pick up) and do the work ourselves." Commission on Good Roads, *Hearings,* 23a.

71. Even as more expensive pavements were used and new labor-saving machinery was introduced, highway construction remained labor intensive. In the early years of state highway construction, road excavation was done entirely with pick and shovel, concrete for culverts was mixed by hand, two-horse teams transported crushed stone in bottom-dump wagons, and steam rollers, followed by vigorous hand brooming, finished the top layer. By the 1910s early power drills and shovels, steam engines (for pulling loaded wagons), traction engines (for grading), and crude pavers appeared, but "hand work still dominated" the profession. Charles T. Fisher, "Road Building in the Good Old Days," *Engineering News Record,* May 21, 1942, pp. 69–72; *Better Roads and Streets,* October 1916, p. 19.

72. *RSCH,* 1917.

73. See, among other works that have addressed this broad historical question, Richard Hofstadter, *The Age of Reform* (New York: Vintage, 1955); Robert H. Wiebe, *The Search for Order, 1877–1920* (New York: Hill & Wang, 1967); McCormick, *From*

Realignment to Reform (1981); Stephen Skowronek, *Building a New American State: The Expansion of National Administrative Capacities, 1877–1920* (Cambridge: Cambridge University Press, 1982); Morton Keller, *Regulating a New Economy: Public Policy and Economic Change in America, 1900–1933* (Cambridge, Mass.: Harvard University Press, 1990); and Theda Skocpol, *Protecting Soldiers and Mothers: The Political Origins of Social Policy in the United States* (Cambridge, Mass.: Harvard University Press, 1992).

Chapter Three. Highways: State-Centered Bureaucracy and the Elevation of Engineer-Administrators, 1919–1931

1. Importantly, in highway politics it was Al Smith, uniquely positioned between the worlds of patronage politics and administrative reformers, who supported Greene's claims to bureaucratic autonomy. For other accounts of the development of bureaucratic autonomy, see Daniel Carpenter, *The Forging of Bureaucratic Autonomy: Reputations, Networks, and Policy Innovations in Executive Agencies, 1862–1928* (Princeton, N.J.: Princeton University Press, 2001).

2. This point is well documented in Mark H. Rose, Bruce E. Seely, and Paul F. Barrett, *The Best Transportation System in the World: Railroads, Trucks, Airlines, and American Public Policy in the Twentieth Century* (Columbus: Ohio State University Press, 2006).

3. Edwin R. A. Seligman, "The New York Income Tax," *Political Science Quarterly* 34 (December 1919): 524; Clarence Heer, *The Post-War Expansion of State Expenditures: An Analysis of the Increase between 1917 and 1923 of the Cost of State Government in New York* (New York: National Institute of Public Administration, 1926), 50; Edward Taylor Bullock, "Financial Aspects of Highway Development with Special Reference to New York State," Ph.D. diss., Harvard University, 1926, p. 132; Arthur D. Gayer, *Public Works in Prosperity and Depression* (New York: National Bureau of Economic Research, 1935), 126.

4. This study echoes Bruce Seely's conclusions regarding the rise of engineers as policy makers, a development that was broadly consistent with the greater reliance on expertise exhibited in many aspects of American governance during the early twentieth century. In contrast to Seely, however, I ascribe greater weight in the New York context to state-level engineering leadership than to that of the federal Bureau of Public Roads. Seely, *Building the American Highway System: Engineers as Policy Makers* (Philadelphia: Temple University Press, 1987).

5. On Greene, see "The Man Who Builds Our State Roads," *NYT*, January 27, 1929; retirement, *NYT*, March 24, 1939, March 25, 1939; obituary, *NYT*, March 27, 1939; "Frederick Stuart Greene," *National Cyclopedia of American Biography*, Vol. 37, pp. 274–275. Greene's award-winning short stories included "The Cat and the Canebrake" and "The Bunker Mouse." He also edited a collection of stories called *The Grim 13*, which included works by other authors not published elsewhere because of their upsetting endings.

6. On Greene's party affiliation, see *NYT*, January 25, 1939. Greene's account of his early meeting with Governor Smith comes from his anonymous, semifictionalized "Highways and Highwaymen," published in the *Saturday Evening Post*, May 20, 1922. The exchange is further documented in repeated newspaper accounts, including one in the *New York Times* on August 31, 1923. See also Henry F. Pringle,

Alfred E. Smith: A Critical Study (New York: Macy-Masius, 1927), 258–261. On the popular support of engineering rhetoric, see John M. Jordan, *Machine-Age Ideology: Social Engineering and American Liberalism, 1911–1939* (Chapel Hill: University of North Carolina Press, 1994), 116.

7. Robert A. Slayton, *Empire Statesman: The Rise and Redemption of Al Smith* (New York: Free Press, 2001), 167.

8. Ibid., 57–61, 84–88, 111–117.

9. *NYT*, December 27, 1938.

10. "Highways and Highwaymen," *Saturday Evening Post*; *NYT*, March 11, 1919; April 4, 1919; and February 7, 1923.

11. *RSCH*, 1919; Heer, *Post-War Expansion*, 93; Bullock, "Financial Aspects," 132; Arthur D. Gayer, *Public Works in Prosperity and Depression* (New York: National Bureau of Economic Research, 1935), 129–144.

12. Ellis L. Armstrong, Michael C. Robinson, and Suellen M. Hoy, eds., *History of Public Works in the United States, 1776–1976* (Chicago: American Public Works Association, 1976), 78.

13. *RSCH*, 1919; *NYT*, August 10, 1919.

14. *RSCH*, 1920; *NYT*, February 29, 1920; March 3, 1920; and May 2, 1920.

15. *NYT*, January 14, 1921; *RSCH*, 1921.

16. *NYT*, January 8, 1922; and September 5, 1922.

17. In 1911, New York State Senators Franklin D. Roosevelt and John F. Schlosser both inquired about the use of political influence in appointing road patrols in their Dutchess County senatorial district, Roosevelt charging that there were too few Democrats and Schlosser too few Republicans. As it turned out, an investigation revealed that the road crew reflected a mix of political affiliations, some recommended by local supervisors, others by county engineers, one by Senator Schlosser himself. Highway Commissioner S. Percy Hooker to Franklin D. Roosevelt, May 25, 1911; Superintendent of Repairs E. M. Sylvester [?] to Hooker, May 9, 1911, "Highway Bills," FDRNYSS.

18. *RSCH*, 1919; *NYT*, October 24, 1920.

19. Al Smith, *Up to Now: An Autobiography* (New York: Viking, 1929), 242–243; *RSCH*, 1920; *NYT*, January 8, 1921; January 20, 1921; February 2, 1921; and October 15, 1922. On the persistence of boss politics in highway building, see the request for a road-building "favor" from Benjamin B. Odell (former governor and Republican party chairman) to Governor Nathan Miller, January 31, 1921, in which he states that "aside from [the new road's] usefulness, [it] would be good politics for the Republican legislature to father." NMP.

20. Heavy trucks consistently caused heavy damage to weak roadways during the first thaw of what highway engineers called "spring break-up." *NYT*, February 12, 1922.

21. In 1917, 83 percent of the trucks operating in New York State weighed less than five tons. Most trucks weighing over five tons operated within New York City. On the origin and growth of early trucking, see William R. Childs, *Trucking and the Public Interest: The Emergence of Federal Regulation, 1914–1940* (Knoxville: University of Tennessee Press, 1985). *NYT*, February 9, 1921; February 10, 1921; February 13, 1921; February 15, 1921; February 26, 1921; March 18, 1921; March 20, 1921; March 24, 1921; January 8, 1922; and August 16, 1922.

22. I. J. Morris, Secretary of the New York State Commission of Highways to Guy H. Miller, Federal District Engineer, March 30, 1917, Department of Transportation, FFHCP.

23. Finch to Guy H. Miller, March 4, 1921, and March 8, 1921, FFHCP.

24. Guy H. Miller to I. J. Morris, February 26, 1917; W. A. Treadwell, Assistant Engineer, New York State Highway Commission, to J. H. Huber, BPR, May 18, 1920, FFHCP.

25. *RSCH*, 1921, p.30.

26. Finch to William G. McCarthy, Acting Secretary to Governor Miller, August 22, 1922, NMP.

27. *NYT*, October 15, 1922; October 18, 1922; October 19, 1922; October 23, 1922; and October 24, 1922; Benjamin Odell to Miller, January 31, 1921, and March 11, 1921, NMP.

28. Robert F. Wesser, *A Response to Progressivism: The Democratic Party and New York Politics, 1902–1918* (New York: New York University Press, 1986), 215–217.

29. *NYT*, December 7, 1922; December 28, 1922; December 31, 1922; January 10, 1923; February 1, 1923; February 2, 1923; and February 2, 1923.

30. "Highways and Highwaymen," *Saturday Evening Post.*

31. *NYT*, February 4, 1923; February 6, 1923; February 7, 1923; and February 8, 1923.

32. Lowman quoted in *NYT*, February 8, 1923.

33. Resolution of Greene County Grange #1413, n.d. [1918?]; W. S. Peck to Lord, March 18, 1919, Bert Lord Papers, Box 8, Cornell University, Ithaca, New York; Paula Baker, *The Moral Frameworks of Public Life* (New York: Oxford University Press, 1991), 137–138. Significantly, some of the proposed benefits of better roads, like school centralization, were steadfastly opposed.

34. Fred M. Baucus, Troy Automobile Club, to Governor Nathan Miller, November 29, 1920; Charles J. Servoss to Miller, September 7, 1922; H. G. Hotchkiss, Second Deputy Commissioner of Highways, to Major William C. Coogan, Secretary to Governor Miller, September 16, 1922, all NMP; *NYT*, October 15, 1922; and February 13, 1923.

35. Baucus to Miller, November 29, 1920, NMP; *NYT*, March 1, 1923.

36. *NYT*, May 21, 1923.

37. *NYT*, May 31, 1923; and June 1, 1923.

38. *NYT*, February 11, 1923.

39. Slayton, *Empire Statesman*, 156–163.

40. Ibid., 161–162; David M. Ellis et al., *A Short History of New York State* (Ithaca, N.Y.: Cornell University Press, 1957), 390; *NYT*, November 3, 1915.

41. Though Smith has been given much credit for reorganizing state government, Charles Evans Hughes, who chaired Smith's Reconstruction Commission, had advocated reorganization in 1909. *Report of the Reconstruction Commission to Governor Alfred E. Smith on Retrenchment and Reorganization in the State Government*, October 10, 1919 (Albany, N.Y.: J. B. Lyon, 1919), 85–97; Ellis et al., *A Short History of New York State*, 401; *NYT*, April 24, 1923, and May 5, 1923.

42. Carpenter, *Forging of Bureaucratic Autonomy*, 3–4.

43. *NYT*, June 9, 1923, and July 3, 1923.

44. *NYT*, August 31, 1923, and September 1, 1923.

45. *NYT*, March 30, 1924.

46. *NYT*, January 16, 1924; January 17, 1924; and March 30, 1924.

47. Press release, May 7, 1924, in Alfred E. Smith, Official Papers, New York State Executive Department Correspondence, New York State Archive, Albany; *NYT*, December 16, 1923, and May 7, 1924.

48. *NYT*, April 19, 1925.

49. DPWAR, 1925.

50. *NYT*, January 30, 1920; January 5, 1928; February 2, 1928; and June 14, 1930; Heer, *Post-War Expansion*, 13; State of New York, *State Expenditures, Tax Burden, and Wealth: A Study of the Growth of the Functions and Expenditures of the State Government and the Relation of Total Tax Burden to the Income of the People of the State*, A Report by the Special Joint Committee on Taxation and Retrenchment, February 11, 1926. See also Gayer, *Public Works in Prosperity and Depression*, 129–133. On rank of highways, see Bullock, "Financial Aspects," 126. (The figure is for 1924.)

51. *NYT*, November 23, 1926; September 6, 1927; October 17, 1927; and January 5, 1928.

52. The large increase in truck registrations, which carried higher fees than passenger vehicles, accounted for the exceptional jump in revenue during this period.

53. *NYT*, July 29, 1921; September 11, 1921; December 3, 1926; January 5, 1928; January 6, 1929; and March 10, 1929; DPWAR, 1925; Bullock, "Financial Aspects," 132; John Chynoweth Burnham, "The Gasoline Tax and the Automobile Revolution," *Mississippi Valley Historical Review* 48 (December 1961): 435–459; Ruth Gillette Hutchinson, *State-Administered Locally-Shared Taxes: Development in the State and Local Tax Systems in the United States*, (New York: Columbia University Press, 1931), 83–92. A federal levy on gasoline was first considered in 1914 but did not pass through Congress. Jon C. Teaford, *Rise of the States: Evolution of American State Government* (Baltimore: Johns Hopkins University Press, 2003), 108; Seely, *Building the American Highway System*, 72–73.

54. *NYT*, December 30, 1928.

55. On Roosevelt as governor, see Bernard Bellush, *Franklin D. Roosevelt as Governor of New York* (New York: AMS, 1968 [orig. Columbia University Press, 1955]). On the map showing the progress of public works, see FDR to FSG, November 4, 1929; Governor's Secretary Guernsey T. Cross to FSG, January 14, 1929; FSG to Cross, January 16, 1929; FDR to FSG, December 29, 1931, "Greene," all in FDRGP-Greene.

56. *NYT*, January 3, 1929; January 11, 1929; February 1, 1929; and February 20, 1929.

57. *NYT*, March 29, 1929; April 9, 1929; and April 11, 1929.

58. *NYT*, January 11, 1930; January 23, 1930; and July 25, 1930.

59. *NYT*, April 6, 1930 (citing the Rome *Sentinel*); July 20, 1930; and July 27, 1930; William Pierrepont White, *Oneida County, New York, and Her Road Building* (Oneida County League for Good Roads, December 1900 [2d ed., January 1902]).

60. DPWAR, 1929, 1930.

61. DPWAR, 1930, p. 89.

62. *NYT*, April 22, 1928; July 5, 1929; and July 25, 1930; DPWAR, 1930.

63. Greene seconded Brandt's opinion in 1931: "It is considered too dangerous

politically to openly advocate the elimination of 933 elected officials." DPWAR, 1931, p. 6.

64. DPWAR, 1928, p. 65.

65. Section 320-b of the state highway law, adopted in 1921 after heavy lobbying by Senator Seymour Lowman, fostered a notable increase in county road construction. Prior to the Lowman Act, most county construction was confined to wealthy areas of the state. William M. Curtiss, "The Development of Highway Administration and Finance in New York," Department of Agricultural Economics and Farm Management, New York State College of Agriculture (Ithaca, N.Y.: Cornell University, 1936), 38–40; DPWAR, 1930.

66. DPWAR, 1930, 1931.

67. DPWAR, 1930, p. 89.

68. *NYT*, March 31, 1925, and November 12, 1925; DPWAR, 1925.

69. FSG to Governor Roosevelt's Secretary Guernsey T. Cross, PERSONAL, March 27, 1929, FDRGP—Greene.

70. On the difficulties in implementing rational top-down public works projects, see James C. Scott, *Seeing Like a State: How Certain Schemes to Improve the Human Condition Have Failed* (New Haven, Conn.: Yale University Press, 1998).

71. Sigurd Grava, "The Bronx River Parkway: A Case Study in Innovation," *New York Affairs* 7 (1981): 15–23.

72. Ibid.; *NYT*, June 14, 1931.

73. *NYT*, January 18, 1925; February 1, 1925; March 17, 1925; and March 18, 1925; Paula Eldot, *Governor Alfred E. Smith: The Politician as Reformer* (New York: Garland, 1983), 115. The quote refers to the *State Park Plan for New York* but is equally true of the Westchester commission. On Westchester's development, see George A. Lundberg, Mirra Komarovsky, and Mary Alice McInerny, *Leisure: A Suburban Study* (New York: Columbia University Press, 1934); Ernest F. Griffin, ed., *Westchester County and Its People: A Record, Vol. 1* (New York: Lewis Historical Publishing, 1946), 461–466; and Roger Panetta, ed., *Westchester: The American Suburb* (New York and Yonkers: Fordham University Press and the Hudson River Museum, 2006).

74. *NYT*, June 14, 1925, and August 21, 1927. The Briarcliff-Peekskill Parkway roughly parallels the Hudson River inland from Route 9. The Pelham-Portchester Parkway ran along Long Island Sound and is now part of the New England Expressway. The Croton River Parkway was eventually abandoned because of prohibitive real estate costs. *NYT*, March 16, 1926.

75. Eldot, *Governor Alfred E. Smith*; *NYT*, January 23, 1924; January 5, 1926; January 16, 1927; and March 18, 1928; *Westchester County and the Regional Plan: Just What This Great Enterprise Means to the County and Particularly to the Community in Which You Live* (New York: Regional Plan Association, 1932).

76. Regional Plan Association, Report, "Control of Amenities," quoted in *NYT*, November 7, 1930.

77. *NYT*, August 21, 1927; March 11, 1928; and April 29, 1928.

78. Robert A. Caro, *The Power Broker: Robert Moses and the Fall of New York* (New York: Vintage, 1975); Joann P. Krieg, ed., *Robert Moses: Single-Minded Genius* (Interlaken, N.Y.: Heart of the Lakes, 1989); *NYT*, November 30, 1924; May 10, 1925; June 14, 1925; and February 6, 1926.

79. *NYT*, April 1, 1928; April 29, 1928; and June 7, 1929.

80. Caro, *Power Broker*, 299–301; *NYT*, November 8, 1928; July 29, 1929; November 9, 1929; December 20, 1929.

81. This was the motive behind a 1929 bill, which Governor Roosevelt vetoed, authorizing Nassau County highway contracts under $3,000 to be let without competitive bidding. *NYT*, April 4, 1929.

82. *NYT*, May 2, 1926; May 9, 1926; January 21, 1926; June 16, 1928; June 9, 1929; and April 27, 1930.

83. *NYT*, April 29, 1928, and May 3, 1930.

84. Kenneth T. Jackson, *Crabgrass Frontier: The Suburbanization of the United States* (New York: Oxford University Press, 1985), 234.

85. Roosevelt quoted in Caro, *Power Broker*, 290.

86. Caro, *Power Broker*; *NYT*, January 7, 1926; January 6, 1927; January 29, 1929; and September 15, 1930; Governor Franklin D. Roosevelt to FSG, December 28, 1929, FDRGP—Greene. Roosevelt thought Nassau County highway appropriations ought to be kept separate "or else in future years it will be wholly lost in the scuffle." DPWAR, 1926; Niagara Frontier Planning Board, *Annual Reports*, 1925–1928, Loeb Library, Harvard University, Cambridge, Massachusetts.

87. *NYT*, January 10, 1926, and December 3, 1926; New York State Association of Real Estate Boards, Service Letter, Summary of Answers Received to Questionnaire on City and Suburban Planning, June 30, 1924, Loeb Library, Harvard University, Cambridge, Massachusetts.

88. DPWAR, 1925, 1926; *NYT*, January 9, 1927, and February 1, 1927.

89. On railroad crossings and the evolution of motorist liability law, see Morton Keller, *Regulating a New Economy: Public Policy and Economic Change in America, 1900–1933* (Cambridge, Mass.: Harvard University Press, 1990), 73. *NYT*, December 9, 1923; December 14, 1923; November 1, 1925; October 29, 1926; and November 4, 1928; DPWAR, 1924, p. 24; see also Oscar Handlin, *Al Smith and His America* (Boston: Little Brown, 1958), 101.

90. Richard F. Weingroff, "Moving the Goods: As the Interstate Era Begins: An Introduction to Web Site Information on Freight Transportation," Federal Highway Administration, http://www.fhwa.dot.gov/infrastructure/freight.cfm (accessed August 16, 2006); Stephen B. Goddard, *Getting There: The Epic Struggle between Road and Rail in the American Century* (New York: Basic, 1994), 84–101.

91. DPWAR, 1929, p. 74; DPWAR, 1925–1929; *NYT*, January 10, 1926, and March 23, 1930.

92. *NYT*, January 15, 1930; March 13, 1930; and March 25, 1930. The Regional Plan of New York and Its Environs was organized in 1922 under a million-dollar grant from the Russell Sage Foundation. In 1925 the state authorized the creation of statewide regional planning boards composed of clusters of municipal and county planners. The following year the state conferred on the towns enlarged zoning powers. United Civic Bodies of Suffolk County and Long Island Chamber of Commerce, "Planning and Zoning for Suffolk County: A Brief on the Subject with Recommendations presented to the Board of Supervisors of Suffolk County, Long Island, New York," March 26, 1928, pp. 7–8, Loeb Library, Harvard University, Cambridge, Massachusetts.

93. *NYT*, November 6, 1928, and January 5, 1930.

94. On suburban development, see Sam Bass Warner Jr., *Streetcar Suburbs: The Process of Growth in Boston (1870–1900)* (Cambridge, Mass.: Harvard University Press, 1962); Jackson, *Crabgrass Frontier*; Jon C. Teaford, *City and Suburb: The Political Fragmentation of Metropolitan America, 1850–1970* (Baltimore: Johns Hopkins University Press, 1979); and W. A. Anderson, "Population Trends in New York State, 1900–1930," Cornell University Agricultural Experiment Station, Ithaca, New York, 1932, 48–50.

95. DPWAR, 1930.

96. *NYT*, August 31, 1930.

97. Anderson, "Population Trends in New York State."

98. *NYT*, November 22, 1916; January 10, 1914; and January 20, 1914.

99. A "heeler" is defined in *NYT*, January 6, 1914.

100. Accurately assessing the changing size and composition of the construction industry in the period 1910–1930 is challenging for many reasons: (1) Changes in census reporting make cross-census comparisons difficult. The 1910 and 1920 censuses list only two categories: road foreman and road laborers. The 1930 census reflects industry specialization. It lists general highway contractors, bridge and culvert contractors, grading contractors, and street pavers, and it records the number of establishments, proprietors, salaried employees, wage earners, equipment valuation, and subcontracting expenditures. (2) Rapidly changing technology made highway work less labor intensive—there were more highway laborers in 1910 than in 1930, even though the industry had grown tremendously. (3) Atypically low figures were posted during the postwar depression, when the 1920 enumeration took place. These numbers do not bear out the early growth of the highway construction industry. Nonetheless, a conservative reading of the census figures corroborates growing competition within the industry during the 1920s. That decade saw a rise in the number of contractors, increased specialization, and greater investment in expensive equipment. U.S. Department of Commerce, Bureau of the Census, *13th Census of the United States: 1910—Population-Occupation Statistics, Vol. 4* (Washington, D.C.: Government Printing Office, 1914), pp. 410–413, 496; U.S. Department of Commerce, Bureau of the Census, *14th Census of the United States: 1920—Population-Occupations, Vol. 4* (Washington, D.C.: Government Printing Office, 1923), pp. 39–40, 100–103; U.S. Department of Commerce, Bureau of the Census, *15th Census of the United States: 1930—Construction Industry* (Washington, D.C.: Government Printing Office, 1933), pp. 88, 96, 101, 112, 831, 836, 840, 848.

101. William L. Collins, Chapter President, "A Message to Highway Contractors of New York State," *Low Bidder*, Official Publication of the New York State Highway Chapter of the Associated General Contractors of America (first published in 1927), September 1927; "Financing Road Contractors," *Low Bidder*, October, 1927; "The Irresponsible Contractor and His Allies, the Equipment Distributor and the Material Man," *Low Bidder*, April 1928; "Association of General Contractors Launches Attack on False Credit Extended by Motor Truck Manufacturers," ibid., May 1928.

102. Sometimes state officials inadvertently added to this destructive competition. Distressed by the differential between low bids and the DPW's project cost estimations, Governor Roosevelt, claiming that the figures did not "show good business practice," demanded that the department bring its estimates in line with actual costs. As Greene predicted, this sent a shockwave through the highway industry:

contractors drastically reduced their bids, offsetting the department's cuts and maintaining the same wide margin of difference. Roosevelt was not satisfied and asked for further cuts. This time Greene resisted. "According to some of the older and better contractors," he argued, "the work cannot be done for the prices bid." Greene settled on "arbitrarily" cutting 10 percent more from every engineering estimate, and he agreed to "continue at this level unless the contractors refuse to bid for our work." Roosevelt to FSG, September 6, 1929; FSG to Roosevelt, May 28, 1930, FDRGP—Greene.

103. *RSCH*, 1921, p. 17. In 1917 the Highway Commission requested and the legislature allowed for an alternative to the surety bonds. Contractors could choose to dispense with the bond if they authorized the state to hold on to 20 percent of the monthly estimates. Such an experiment was designed to lower the total cost to the state and to keep surety companies from "taking an unreasonable attitude"—that is, collectively raising the cost of premiums on surety bonds, knowing that contractors would have no choice but to pay it. In 1921, however, the Highway Commission requested that the law be repealed since it allowed incompetent contractors to make unreasonably low bids.

104. *NYT*, February 19, 1928; F. P. Kimball to William P. White, February 21, 1928, William Pierrepont White Papers, "Good Roads Correspondence," #399, Box 65, Cornell University, Ithaca, New York.

105. William H. Connell, chairman, et al., "Report of the Investigation of Paving and General Highway Conditions by the Engineering Commission appointed by the National Paving Brick Manufacturers Association," 1928, p. 32, Science, Industry, and Business Library, New York Public Library, New York City.

106. Ellis Hawley, "Herbert Hoover, the Commerce Secretariat, and the Vision of an 'Associative' State, 1921–1928," *Journal of American History* 61 (June 1974): 116–140, especially 131; Richard F. Weingroff, "From Names to Numbers: The Origins of the U.S. Numbered Highway System," Federal Highway Administration, https://www.fhwa.dot.gov/infrastructure/numbers.htm (accessed August 16, 2006).

107. DPWAR, 1924; *NYT*, December 21, 1924, and August 16, 1928; *Official Automobile Blue Book 1919: Standard Road Guide of America*, Vol. 1: New York State and Adjacent Canada (New York: Automobile Blue Book., 1919).

108. DPWAR, 1927; *Cherry Valley Gazette and Richmond Tribune*, September 9, 1927; *Literary Digest*, November 12, 1927. Both newspapers quoted in *New York History* 63 (1982): 470–471.

109. U.S. Bureau of the Census, *Historical Statistics of the United States, Colonial Times to 1970*, Part 1 (Washington, D.C., 1975), Series B 163, p. 58. *NYT*, April 24, 1921, and June 8, 1921.

110. DPWAR, 1922, p. 5.

111. *NYT*, January 4, 1923; July 21, 1929; and May 13, 1930.

112. A limited state highway map had been introduced in 1907, and the Hewitt Map had been adopted in 1921. Greene's map, the basis for the state's modern highway system, was first laid out in 1919 and finally approved in 1925.

113. DPWAR, 1928, 1931; Alfred E. Smith, *Progress of Public Improvements: A Report to the People of the State of New York*, October 1927.

114. Stephen Skowronek, *Building a New American State: The Expansion of Na-*

tional Administrative Capacities, 1877–1920 (Cambridge: Cambridge University Press, 1982); Gary Alchon, *The Invisible Hand of Planning: Capitalism, Social Science, and the State in the 1920s* (Princeton, N.J.: Princeton University Press, 1985).

115. FSG to Franklin D. Roosevelt, August 9, 1928, Frederick S. Greene Collection, Small Collections, Series Credit: Mr. and Mrs. Francis Thornton Greene, Warrenton, Virginia, held at FDR Library, Hyde Park, New York.

Chapter Four. Clearing the Way: Depression, War, and the Nationalization of the Bureaucratic Regime, 1931–1945

1. On the importance of the 1920s in laying the "ideological and institutional [and I would add *infrastructural*] foundations" for the postwar years, see Ellis Hawley, *The Great War and the Search for a Modern Order* (New York: St. Martin's Press, 1992), vi. In his valuable new work, Jason Scott Smith cogently argues that the New Deal was a defining moment in the development of American infrastructure, though, as I argue here, the New Deal served primarily to hasten transformations that were already under way. See Smith, *Building New Deal Liberalism: The Political Economy of Public Works, 1933–1956* (New York: Cambridge University Press, 2006).

2. *NYT*, October 9, 1930. On Hoover, the economic strategy of "stabilization," and the publication of public employment data to sustain business confidence, see William J. Barber, *From New Era to New Deal: Herbert Hoover, the Economists, and American Economic Policy, 1921–1933* (Cambridge: Cambridge University Press, 1985), chs. 4–5.

3. *NYT*, January 7, 1931; January 13, 1931; and January 15, 1931. Highway Bureau Chief Arthur W. Brandt suggested that Roosevelt expedite the appropriation of another $4 million, to be reimbursed by the federal government under President Hoover's 1931 Federal-Aid Emergency Highway Act. FDR passed Brandt's letter on verbatim to the legislature, which quickly passed the enabling legislation. AWB to FDR, January 27, 1931; and FDR to New York State Legislature, January 28, 1931, FDRGP-Brandt.

4. *NYT*, January 7, 1931, and February 10, 1931.

5. Arthur D. Gayer, *Public Works in Prosperity and Depression* (New York: National Bureau of Economic Research, 1935), 136; *NYT*, January 17, 1931, and February 11, 1931.

6. *NYT*, May 3, 1931; June 15, 1931; and July 6, 1931.

7. Governor Herbert Lehman considered prohibiting the use of out-of-state contractors in 1933, but Superintendent Frederick Greene advised against this move, citing the high costs involved and the likelihood of retaliatory measures by other states. FSG to Lehman, January 5, 1933, HLP.

8. *NYT*, May 3, 1931; "'Racketeering' in Highway Construction," *Low Bidder*, August 1931; *County Contractor*, April 1931.

9. Compared to other manual work, highway laborers had been well paid; the prevailing wage rate in the area ranged from 30 to 40 cents an hour.

10. Greenburgh had produced a thirty-year plan for highway expansion in 1930 that placed it at the center of Westchester County's road-building activities. *NYT*, November 9, 1930; *Mount Vernon Daily Argus*, July 10, 1931, and July 11, 1931.

11. *NYT*, July 11, 1931, and July 12, 1931.

12. Charles F. Howlett, *Brookwood Labor College and the Struggle for Peace and Social Justice in America* (Lewiston, N.Y.: Edwin Mellen, 1993); Richard J. Altenbaugh, *Education for Struggle: The American Labor Colleges of the 1920s and 1930s* (Philadelphia: Temple University Press, 1990).

13. *NYT*, July 14, 1931.

14. *NYT*, July 16–24, 1931; *Mount Vernon Daily Argus*, July 13–16, 1931. On divisions between Communist, Progressive, and craft union labor organizations, see James O. Morris, *Conflict within the AFL: Craft versus Industrial Unionism, 1901–1938* (Ithaca, N.Y.: Cornell University Press, 1958), 125–135; Louis Francis Budenz, *This Is My Story* (New York: McGraw-Hill, 1947), 97–99.

15. *NYT*, July 18, 1931.

16. *NYT*, July 19, 1931; July 22, 1931; July 23, 1931; and July 28, 1931; *Mount Vernon Daily Argus*, July 23, 1931. In the midst of this labor crisis, Governor Franklin Roosevelt happily completed his motor tour of Long Island highways. Wielding a trowel, the governor symbolically laid the cornerstone connecting Grand Central Parkway in Queens with the Northern State Parkway in Nassau County. To the audience and press he joked that he was an expert bricklayer, with the union card to prove it. "And I get double pay for this," he announced, "because I'm working on a Sunday." *NYT*, July 25, 1931, and July 27, 1931.

17. Concurrent with the Westchester strike, Brookwood and the CPLA organized a union drive among West Virginia miners. This costly, and ultimately unsuccessful, effort drained the union of its strength and resources. Howlett, *Brookwood Labor College*, 264–270.

18. *NYT*, July 31, 1931, and August 2, 1931.

19. *NYT*, August 4, 1931, and August 5, 1931; for contractors' views on union arbitration, see "The Labor Situation," *County Contractor* 3, no. 8 (August 1931): 1. On the alliance with the AFL, see *County Contractor* 3, no. 9 (September 1931).

20. *NYT*, August 7, 1931, and August 23, 1931.

21. Altogether there were 20,000 men working on highway construction: 6,000 worked for the state forces while the remaining 14,000 were hired by contractors. *NYT*, July 13, 1931; July 29, 1931; and August 3, 1931.

22. *NYT*, January 5, 1938.

23. Barber, *New Era to New Deal*, 149–150; James T. Patterson, *The New Deal and the States: Federalism in Transition* (Princeton, N.J.: Princeton University Press, 1969), 40–41.

24. Arthur W. MacMahon et al., *Administration of Federal Work Relief* (New York: Da Capo, 1971 [1941]), 128.

25. Secretary of Interior Harold Ickes to Presidential Secretary Marvin McIntyre, June 14, 1933, "National Recovery Association/Public Works Administration," FDR Papers, OF 466, Box 12, FDR Library, Hyde Park, New York.

26. On New Deal public works programs, see William Leuchtenberg, *Franklin D. Roosevelt and the New Deal* (New York: Harper & Row, 1963); Anthony Badger, *The New Deal: The Depression Years, 1933–1940* (New York: Hill & Wang, 1989); Harold Ickes, *Back to Work* (New York: Da Capo, 1974 [1935]); MacMahon et al., *Administration of Federal Work Relief*; and Gayer, *Public Works in Prosperity and Depression*. On the CWA, see Bonnie Fox Schwartz, *The Civil Works Administration: The Business of*

Emergency Employment in the New Deal (Princeton, N.J.: Princeton University Press, 1984), especially 182.

27. Gill quoted in MacMahon, *Administration of Federal Work Relief*, 68.

28. *NYT*, March 18, 1933.

29. *NYT*, July 24, 1933, and October 11, 1933.

30. At the same time, the national unemployment rate was approximately 25 percent. Robert P. Ingalls, *Herbert H. Lehman and New York's Little New Deal* (New York: New York University Press, 1975), 35; Robert McIlvaine, *The Great Depression* (New York: Times Books, 1985), 75.

31. The BPR's insistence on high construction standards impeded the employment of untrained men on the unemployment rolls, and its never-ending "red tape" was a source of great frustration to New York's DPW. On these issues, see FFHCP, especially folders 15 and 16.

32. *NYT*, January 24, 1933; October 11, 1933; November 13, 1933; November 21, 1933; November 28, 1933; and November 29, 1933; DPWAR, 1939, p. 13; Gayer, *Administration of Federal Work Relief*, 251–252 n2.

33. *NYT*, February 27, 1934, and May 5, 1934.

34. DPWAR, 1937.

35. *NYT*, January 19, 1834; January 21, 1934; January 29, 1934; February 24, 1935; and October 30, 1935; DPWAR, 1937. On the contrast between a Progressive emphasis on measuring productivity through construction and a New Deal emphasis on measuring productivity through employment, see Otis Graham, *An Encore for Reform: The Old Progressives and the New Deal* (New York: Oxford University Press, 1967).

36. *Road Builders' News*, November 24, 1934.

37. MacMahon, *Administration of Federal Work Relief*, 56–57; Leuchtenberg, *Franklin D. Roosevelt*, 124–125; *NYT*, June 16, 1935.

38. FDR to Herbert Lehman, telegram, November 27, 1935, "Herbert Lehman," President's Personal File, FDR Library, Hyde Park, New York.

39. John Joseph Wallis and Wallace E. Oates, "The Impact of the New Deal on American Federalism," in Michael D. Bordo, Claudia Goldin, and Eugene N. White, eds., *The Defining Moment: The Great Depression and the American Economy in the Twentieth Century* (Chicago: University of Chicago Press, 1998), 163–171.

40. *NYT*, August 2, 1935; DPWAR, 1935, p. 5.

41. The original act had authorized $4.8 billion in expenditures with $800 million for roads, highways, and grade crossings. But these figures were based on unrealistic estimates. By the end of 1935 about $400 million had been allocated for highway construction. A year later, highway allocations passed the $500 million mark. MacMahon, *Administration of Work Relief*, 128.

42. Ickes, *Back to Work*, 81–83.

43. *NYT*, July 11, 1936, and March 29, 1935; DPWAR, 1935, pp. 52–55.

44. On New Deal spending, see John Joseph Wallis, "The Birth of the Old Federalism: Financing the New Deal, 1932–1940," *Journal of Economic History* 44 (March 1984): 139–159; Wallis and Wallace E. Oates, "The Impact of the New Deal on American Federalism"; Wallis, "The Political Economy of New Deal Spending Revisited, Again: With and Without Nevada," *Explorations in Economic History* 35 (1998): 140–170; Don C. Reading, "New Deal Activity and the States, 1933–1939,"

Journal of Economic History 33 (1973): 792–810; Edwin Amenta et al., "Bring Back the WPA: Work, Relief, and the Origins of American Social Policy in Welfare Reform," *Studies in American Political Development* 12 (1998): 1–56; and Mark Leff, *The Limits of Symbolic Reform: The New Deal and Taxation* (Cambridge: Cambridge University Press, 1984). On the gasoline tax, see James A. Dunn Jr., "The Importance of Being Earmarked: Transport Policy and Highway Finance in Great Britain and the United States," *Comparative Studies in Society and History* 20 (1978): 29–53; and John Chynoweth Burnham, "The Gasoline Tax and the Automobile Revolution," *Mississippi Valley Historical Review* 48 (1961): 435–459.

45. State of New York, *Executive Budget*, 1931–1932, p. vii.

46. *NYT*, February 27, 1934; April 21, 1934; and November 3, 1935.

47. Robert Caro suggests that Moses wrote the platform himself. Robert A. Caro, *The Power Broker: Robert Moses and the Fall of New York* (New York: Vintage, 1974), 407.

48. *NYT*, April 23, 1934.

49. *NYT*, January 10, 1935.

50. *NYT*, February 5, 1936.

51. During the period 1923–1936, New York State spent a total of $601 million on its highways, including $124 million in federal aid. Over the fourteen-year period, the federal government covered about 20 percent of state highway costs. In 1936 the federal government covered two-thirds of the costs; *NYT*, February 2, 1937. Nationally, federal disbursements to states rose from an average of 8 percent in 1928 to 45 percent in 1936; see *Road Builders' News*, January 1936, p. 2.

52. *NYT*, February 15, 1937, and February 18, 1937.

53. *NYT*, March 4, 1937.

54. *NYT*, April 23, 1937.

55. Hayden-Cartwright Act of 1934, 48 Stat. 993, Sec. 12: "Since it is unfair and unjust to tax motor-vehicle transportation unless the proceeds of such taxation are applied to the construction, improvement, or maintenance of highways, after June 30, 1935, Federal Aid for highway construction shall be extended only to those States that use at least the amounts now provided by law for such purposes in each State from State motor vehicle registration fees, licenses, gasoline taxes, and other special taxes on motor-vehicle owners and operators of all kinds for the construction, improvement and maintenance of highways and administrative expenses in connection therewith, including the retirement of bonds for the payment of which such revenues have been pledged, and for no other purposes, under such regulations as the Secretary of Agriculture shall promulgate from time to time: Provided, That in no case shall the provisions of this section operate to deprive any State of more than one-third of the amount to which that State would be entitled under any apportionment hereafter made, for the fiscal year for which the apportionment is made."

56. *NYT*, April 6, 1937; May 2, 1937; and January 12, 1938. The two states were New Jersey in 1937 ($200,000) and Massachusetts in 1938 ($472,000). Richard Weingroff, "Clearly Vicious as a Matter of Policy: The Fight against Federal Aid," Federal Highway Administration, http://www.fhwa.dot.gov/infrastructure/hwyhist01.cfm (accessed August 25, 2006); Thomas MacDonald, chief of the Bureau of Public Roads, "Highway Progress Responsibility," paper presented before American Association of State Highway Officials, February 12, 1936; MacDonald, "Future of

Our Highways," prepared for Chamber of Commerce monthly magazine, Kansas City, Missouri, October 19, 1936; MacDonald, "Talk before Michigan Good Roads Federation," October 20, 1938. MacDonald speeches available at Department of Transportation Library, http://dotlibrary1.specialcollection.net/scripts/ws .dll?websearch&site=dot_Turner (accessed August 25, 2006).

57. Highway Commissioner Arthur W. Brandt to members of the U.S. House of Representatives, draft letter, June 9, 1934, HLP (emphasis in the original).

58. Using 1934 as a benchmark allowed states exceptional leeway in diverting funds away from highways. Diversion in New York had already increased dramatically between 1932 and 1934. Arthur W. Brandt to Nathan R. Sobel, Counsel to the Governor, April 21, 1938, HLP.

59. The committee was chaired by Senator George Fearon and thus often referred to as the Fearon Committee.

60. As of January 1, 1935, only 56 percent of the state's roads were improved. Though most of the state highway system was classified as improved, traffic surveys completed in 1934 reinforced DPW arguments that the entire system required widening. These surveys also revealed that two-thirds of New York's town highways (local roads, which were the town's responsibility and constituted half of the state's total road mileage) remained unimproved. State of New York, Legislative Document (1936) No. 89, *Report of the State Highway Survey Committee.*

61. State of New York, *Report of the State Highway Survey Committee*, 1936; *NYT*, March 13, 1936; March 22, 1936; and February 9, 1937.

62. *NYT*, March 22, 1923.

63. On contemporary privatization schemes, see Colleen Marie O'Connor, "A New Breed of Toll Collector; Wall Street's Cruising for Toll Road Deals as Cash-Strapped States Seek Big Money from Private Investors," *Investment Dealers Digest*, May 15, 2006.

64. According to 1930 census data there were 187.2 cars per 1,000 people in 1930, or 1 car per 5.34 people. Using 1930 census data that lists 4.1 people per household, it appears that more than 3 out 4 households owned cars. U.S. Census Bureau, *Historical Abstract*, "Transportation Indicators for Motor Vehicles and Airlines," http://www.census.gov/statab/hist/02HS0041.xls (accessed February 7, 2007); U.S. Census Bureau, "How the Nation Has Changed since the 1930 Census," http://www.census.gov/pubinfo/www/1930_factsheet.html (accessed February 7, 2007).

65. This tension between citizen-motorists and motorist-consumers parallels Lizabeth Cohen's discussion of citizen-consumers and purchaser-consumers in Cohen's *A Consumers' Republic: The Politics of Mass Consumption in Postwar America* (New York: Knopf, 2003).

66. Despite the increasing power of automobile associations, the New York auto clubs were unable to secure an antidiversion amendment to the state constitution. By 1940 only eleven states had such amendments. Charles Dearing, *American Highway Policy* (Washington, D.C.: Brookings Institution, 1941), 180. On California's earmarking amendment, see Paul E. Sabin, "Petroleum Polity: Law and Politics in the California Oil Economy, 1900–1940," Ph.D. diss., University of California, Berkeley, 2000.

67. *NYT*, September 1, 1923, and December 27, 1935.

68. Greene's appointment had also been held up in 1935 by Jeremiah F. Twomey, Senate Finance chairman. *NYT*, January 3, 1935, and January 16, 1935.

69. Greene's offending remark accused several unnamed legislators of "sheer dishonesty—nothing that will put you in jail, but dishonesty just the same." *NYT*, January 25, 1939, and January 26, 1939.

70. FSG to FDR, January 5, 1939; and FDR to Frederic A. Delano, Memorandum, December 21, 1938, FDRPPF-Greene.

71. Grace C. Greene to FDR, n.d. [March 1939?], FDRPPF-Greene; *NYT*, March 9, 1939; March 24, 1939; and March 25, 1939.

72. The legislature at this time made a practice of passing every name through committee. *NYT*, March 26, 1939, and March 31, 1939.

73. On visible politics and local government, see Arthur J. Vidich and Joseph Bensman, *Small Town in Mass Society: Class, Power, and Religion in a Rural Community* (Princeton, N.J.: Princeton University Press, 1958, rev. 1968), 137–170. This study of "Springdale," actually the rural community of Candor, New York, was conducted in the mid-1950s. Charlotte Allen, "Spies Like Us: When Sociologists Deceive Their Subjects," *Lingua Franca* 7 (November 1997): 30–39.

74. Norman Bel Geddes, *Magic Motorways* (New York: Random House, 1940); David Gelernter, *1939: The Lost World of the Fair* (New York: Free Press, 1995); Robert Rydell, *World of Fairs: The Century of Progress Exhibitions* (Chicago: University of Chicago Press, 1993); Roland Marchand, "The Designers Go to the Fair II: Norman Bel Geddes, General Motor's Futurama, and the Visit to the Factory Transformed," *Design Issues* 8 (Spring 1992): 23–40; Christine Cogdell, "The Futurama Recontextualized: Norman Bel Geddes's Eugenic 'World of Tomorrow,'" *America Quarterly* 52 (June 2000): 193–245; Folke Kihlstedt, "Utopia Realized: The World's Fairs of the 1930s," in Joseph Corn, ed., *Imagining Tomorrow: History, Technology, and the American Future* (Cambridge, Mass.: MIT Press, 1986). On styling and the automotive industry, see Flink, *Automobile Age*, 235–241. For video footage of the Futurama exhibit, see "The Iconography of Hope: The 1939–40 New York World's Fair," *America in the 1930s*, online exhibit, American Studies Department, University of Virginia, http://xroads.virginia.edu/~1930s/DISPLAY/39wf/front.htm (accessed February 5, 2007).

75. Robert Moses, "Tomorrow's Cars and Roads," reprint from *Liberty Magazine*, n.d. [January 1944?)], 3, Science, Industry, and Business Library, New York Public Library, New York City.

76. Governor Herbert Lehman prioritized local unemployment relief in proposing new public road construction: "As far as possible," he instructed Superintendent of Public Works Frederick S. Greene, "all unskilled labor employed shall be citizens who have resided for a substantial period of time in the immediate vicinity in which the work is to be done. In other words, I want to see local labor employed so far as possible." Lehman to FSG, January 21, 1933, HLP.

77. The construction of a major national defense highway in New York, roughly paralleling today's Thruway, was a top priority according to the FWA survey. FDR to Henry B. Brewster, Syracuse Chamber of Commerce, New York State Defense Highway Committee, June 10, 1941, Henry B. Brewster to Herbert Lehman,

March 17, 1941, Pres OF 129, "Roads and Highways," FDR Library, Hyde Park, New York; Mark Rose, *Interstate: Express Highway Politics, 1939–1989* (Knoxville: University of Tennessee Press, 1990), 12, 17; *NYT*, January 8, 1941; January 26, 1941; January 29, 1941; and February 7, 1941.

78. *NYT*, February 28, 1941.

79. *NYT*, January 6, 1944.

80. *NYT*, April 9, 1933; April 20, 1933; February 27, 1934; January 16, 1934; April 20, 1934; and April 18, 1939; New York State Association of Town Superintendents of Highways, "1939 Convention Highlights," at New York Public Library, Science, Industry, and Business Library. Governor Dewey, facing the first budgetary surplus since 1931, authorized the full reinstatement of state aid to towns and counties in 1943. New York State, *Executive Budget*, 1943. On the lack of balance between state and local highway construction during the depression, see State Highway Commissioner Arthur W. Brandt to Governor Herbert Lehman, Memorandum, June 19, 1934, HLP.

81. *NYT*, July 3, 1934; July 8, 1934; August 22, 1934; and October 13, 1935.

82. *Road Builders' News*, September 17, 1935.

83. Greene and Brandt repeatedly—and unsuccessfully—sought the eradication of the position of town highway commissioner.

84. *NYT*, December 30, 1932.

85. *NYT*, March 31, 1932, and April 18, 1934; DPWAR, 1938, pp. 48–50; DPWAR, 1939, pp. 14–15; DPWAR, 1940, p. 61.

86. Highway Commissioner Arthur W. Brandt to Governor Herbert Lehman, September 22, 1938; District Engineer James S. Bixby to AWB, September 20, 1938, HLP.

87. *NYT*, February 2, 1941; May 3, 1941; and June 17, 1941.

88. *NYT*, May 8, 1942; April 18, 1943; February 2, 1944; March 9, 1944; and April 8, 1944.

89. *NYT*, January 6, 1944, and May 20, 1944.

90. Arthur Brandt to John H. Ayers, Senior Highway Engineer, Bureau of Public Roads, October 20, 1932, FFHCP.

91. *NYT*, June 28, 1933 (copy in HLP); *NYT*, June 29, 1933; July 1, 1933; and July 2, 1933. The Highway Survey Committee's 1936 report (which was not acted upon) recommended increased aid to cities. *NYT*, March 13, 1937.

92. See daily coverage in the *New York Times* from March 9, 1944, through March 18, 1944; quote from March 12, 1944.

93. *NYT*, March 8, 1944.

94. DPWAR, 1944; Mark Rose, *Interstate: Express Highway Politics, 1939–1989* (Knoxville: University of Tennessee Press, 1990), ch. 2.

95. On the policy shift from unemployment relief to economic development, see Jordan Schwarz, *The New Dealers: Power Politics in the Age of Roosevelt* (New York: Knopf, 1993).

96. *NYT*, January 12, 1933. On Westchester's development as a commuter community, see George A. Lundberg, Mirra Komarovsky, and Mary Alice McInerny, *Leisure: A Suburban Study* (New York: Columbia University Press, 1934); Ernest F. Griffin, ed., *Westchester County and Its People: A Record*, Vol. 1 (New York: Lewis Historical Publishing, 1946), 461–466; Roger Panetta, ed., *Westchester: The American*

Suburb (New York and Yonkers: Fordham University Press and the Hudson River Museum, 2006), 291–326.

97. *NYT*, December 10, 1933.

98. Marilyn E. Weigold, "Pioneering in Parks and Parkways: Westchester County, New York, 1895–1945," *Essays in Public Works History* 9 (February 1980): 1–43; *NYT*, August 19, 1934.

99. The town of Amherst (near Buffalo) had also threatened to charge tolls on its Sheridan Drive unless the state picked up its bonded debt of $1.8 million. During the 1920s' age of easy finance, the town had constructed the marginal road on the outskirts of Buffalo as part of a belt system that linked Buffalo and its suburbs to Main Street (U.S. Route 5). The route once traversed undeveloped farmland, but now it figured into the state's plan to construct an approach to the Grand Island Bridge near the Canadian border. *NYT*, November 18, 1934.

100. *NYT*, January 13, 1935; January 26, 1936; June 6, 1936; November 3, 1936; December 20, 1936; December 28, 1936; and December 29, 1936.

101. *NYT*, January 12, 1937; April 6, 1937; April 11, 1937; March 9, 1938; March 27, 1938; and April 3, 1938. The Bronx River Parkway fell into such disrepair that it was nearly shut down entirely in 1942 when wartime material shortages further curtailed reconstruction; *NYT*, March 14, 1942.

102. This route eventually became the New England Expressway (I-95).

103. *NYT*, May 6, 1937; February 6, 1938; February 7, 1938; February 11, 1938; February 13, 1938; February 22, 1938; April 3, 1938; April 5, 1938; and April 22, 1938.

104. DPWAR, 1938; *NYT*, August 2, 1938; September 12, 1938; October 23, 1938; December 18, 1938; and December 22, 1938.

105. *NYT*, January 3, 1939.

106. *NYT*, May 3, 1938, and June 13, 1938.

107. These findings were no great surprise, though the census, taken on a Saturday in August, reflected the draw of Manhattan shopping more than weekday commuting.

108. *NYT*, July 28, 1938.

109. *NYT*, March 17, 1940.

110. Wilfred Owen and Charles L. Dearing, *Toll Roads and the Problem of Highway Modernization* (Washington, D.C.: Brookings Institution, 1951), 4–21; Owen Gutfreund, *Twentieth-Century Sprawl* (New York: Oxford University Press, 2004), 37–42.

111. The old Bronx Valley viaduct had been condemned in 1932 as unsafe and inadequate to traffic. Lehman vetoed a bill that would have passed the reconstruction costs off to the state. *NYT*, May 8, 1937; May 24, 1937; September 19, 1937; February 6, 1938; and April 3, 1938.

112. *NYT*, March 7, 1940; March 12, 1940; March 14, 1940; March 15, 1940; March 17, 1940; and March 19, 1940.

113. *NYT*, April 11, 1940; April 27, 1940; and November 24, 1940.

114. Westchester County Parks Commission, "The Needs of Westchester County Parkways from a Through Traffic Perspective," 1940, at New York Public Library, Science, Industry, and Business Collection; *NYT*, November 8, 1940.

115. *NYT*, November 10, 1941.

116. *NYT*, February 3, 1942, March 10, 1944.

117. *NYT*, February 1, 1944; February 8, 1944; March 21, 1944; March 24, 1944; April 14, 1944; and April 15, 1944.

118. An August 17, 1940, traffic count revealed that 85 percent of traffic on the Hutchinson River Parkway was from outside Westchester County. Westchester County Parks Commission, "Needs of Westchester County Parkways."

119. Bruce Seely, *Building the American Highway System: Engineers as Policy Makers* (Philadelphia: Temple University Press, 1987), 39.

120. *NYT*, January 28, 1932; January 13, 1934; and September 30, 1934.

121. Moses, "Tomorrow's Cars and Roads"; *NYT*, September 20, 1936, and December 1, 1940. The Eastern State Parkway is now known as the Taconic Parkway. For other remarks on parkways and superhighways, see Public Hearings before the New York State Joint Legislative Highway Survey Committee, Rochester, New York, October 21, 1940, New York State Library, Albany, New York.

122. *NYT*, December 16, 1936; DPWAR, 1936.

123. On Roosevelt's reaction to the highway, see FDR to FSG, June 28, 1938; FDR to FSG, September 28, 1938, Frederick S. Greene Collection, Small Collections, Series Credit: Mr. and Mrs. Francis Thornton Greene, Warrenton, Virginia, held at FDR Library, Hyde Park, New York; FSG to FDR, September 29, 1938, FDRPPF-Greene. Greene made special note of the fact that Roosevelt took the time to write him over New York highway affairs just hours after the president had sent an important telegram to Adolph Hitler in Munich regarding the fate of Czechoslovakia on the evening of September 27, 1938.

124. *NYT*, February 4, 1938; February 5, 1938; February 9, 1938; and February 10, 1938.

125. Assemblyman Abbot Low Moffat "hit upon the word [Thruway] in the summer of 1941 while he was Chairman of the Assembly Ways and Means Committee and was drafting legislation to place upon the State highway map a great new highway running from New York City to Buffalo and the Pennsylvania border. . . . He believed it desirable to enact a legal definition of the type of highway contemplated to insure its construction without compromise of its speed or safety factors. . . . He wanted a word which would indicate the true nature and function of the highway. . . . After considering and discarding 'Throughway' and 'Thro'way' Mr. Moffat devised 'Thruway' which had only seven letters and described the highway accurately. The new word, in fact, is a modern version of the word 'Thorofare.'" Director of Public Relations [Robert Monahan?] to Joseph C. Ingraham, of the *New York Times*, May 19, 1954. New York State Thruway, Public Relations and Planning Files, Box 1, New York State Archives, Albany.

126. *NYT*, March 14, 1942, and May 24, 1942.

127. *NYT*, March 3, 1943; March 25, 1943; April 24, 1943; and August 27, 1944.

128. DPWAR, 1943, 1944.

129. Between 1930 and 1945, vehicular travel increased by 38 percent, from 19.5 to 27 million car miles per year. DPWAR, 1946.

130. As James Patterson has argued, the expansion of federal power during the New Deal was constrained by a wide range of limitations and ultimately yielded "a rather flat mixture of achievement, mediocrity, and confusion." "Far from serving

as a flexible medium for change," the system of federalism proved "better suited to preserving diversity than to encouraging strong and coordinated national action." James T. Patterson, *The New Deal and the States: Federalism in Transition* (Princeton, N.J.: Princeton University Press, 1969), 202, 207.

Chapter Five. Authority: The Thruway and the Consolidation of the Bureaucratic Regime, 1945–1956

1. DPWAR, 1932; New York State Governor's Office, Executive Budget, "Highways and Bridges," 1957. The DPW let $50 million in highway contracts in 1931, or just under $90 million in 1956 dollars. It let $195 million in 1956.

2. Greene's own political leanings were toward the Republican Party, but this "Al Smith Republican" served exclusively in Democratic administrations.

3. The 1953 highway program cost a total of $362 million, including $253 million for the Thruway. DPWAR, 1953.

4. Editorial on the postwar reconstruction program, *NYT*, January 5, 1945.

5. On the development of Dewey's political position, see Milton Klein, ed., *The Empire State: A History of New York* (Ithaca, N.Y.: Cornell University Press, 2001), 611–612.

6. Dewey thought "financial history" had been made in establishing the fund in 1944. Quoted in speech to legislature, *NYT*, February 1, 1946.

7. *NYT*, January 4, 1945; February 1, 1945; May 12, 1945; and May 13, 1945.

8. *NYT*, September 7, 1945.

9. Dewey in speech to legislature, *NYT*, February 1, 1946.

10. *NYT*, January 10, 1946.

11. DPWAR, 1946.

12. *NYT*, July 12, 1946.

13. DPWAR, 1946.

14. *NYT*, September 8, 1945; DPWAR, 1946.

15. DPWAR, 1946; Superintendent of Public Works Bertram D. Tallamy to T. N. Hurd, Division of the Budget, August 13, 1954, in SPW.

16. On the triumph of the modern business firm and the origins of public relations management, see Louis Galambos and Joseph Pratt, *The Rise of the Corporate Commonwealth: United States Business and Public Policy in the 20th Century* (New York: Basic, 1988), especially 96–99. On public relations and commercial imitation in New York government, see Bernard Rubin, *Public Relations in the Empire State: A Case Study of New York Administration* (New Brunswick, N.J.: Rutgers University Press, 1958), especially 61–65.

17. Paul Barrett and Mark Rose, "Street Smarts: The Politics of Transportation Statistics in the American City, 1900–1990," *Journal of Urban History* 25 (March 1999): 405–433, especially 417.

18. DPWAR, 1946.

19. As the number of motor vehicles and their average amount of travel increased, even the twenty-year life span was not assured. Department of Public Works, *Report Pertaining to the Condition of the State Highway System*, September 15, 1947, pp. 3–4.

20. Department of Public Works, *Report Pertaining to the Condition of the State Highway System*, September 15, 1947. *NYT*, February 2, 1947; February 28, 1947; April 12, 1947; April 25, 1947; May 16, 1947; and May 23, 1947. On wartime insta-

bility in the construction industry, which continued to plague New York contractors into the late 1940s, see William Haycraft, *Yellow Steel: The Story of the Earthmoving Equipment Industry* (Urbana: University of Illinois Press, 2000), 100–108.

21. DPWAR, 1944. On closed versus open engineering systems, see Thomas Hughes, *Rescuing Prometheus* (New York: Pantheon, 1998).

22. DPWAR, 1946, 1949.

23. DPWAR, 1947, 1953; Rose and Barrett, "Street Smarts."

24. *NYT*, September 23, 1947. On the link between early twentieth-century policy choices and mid-twentieth-century urban highway crises, see Matthew Roth, "Whittier Boulevard, Sixth Street Bridge, and the Origins of Transportation Exploitation in East Los Angeles," *Journal of Urban History* 30 (July 2004): 729–748. On the explosion of community protests in the 1960s, see Alan Lupo, Frank Colcord, and Edmund P. Fowler, *Rites of Way: The Politics of Transportation in Boston and the U.S. City* (Boston: Little, Brown, 1971); Raymond Mohl, "Stop the Road: Freeway Revolts in American Cities," *Journal of Urban History* 30 (July 2004): 674–706; Zachary Schrag, "The Freeway Fight in Washington, D.C.: The Three Sisters Bridge in Three Administrations," *Journal of Urban History* 30 (July 2004): 648–673; Michael N. Danielson and Jameson W. Doig, *New York: The Politics of Urban Regional Development* (Berkeley: University of California Press, 1982); Helen Leavitt, *Superhighway-Superhoax* (New York: Doubleday, 1970); and Ben Kelley, *The Pavers and the Paved* (New York: Charles Scribner's Sons, 1971).

25. DPWAR, 1946; Superintendent of Public Works Bertram D. Tallamy [hereafter BDT] to C. Fichtner, Executive Vice President, Buffalo Chamber of Commerce, April 30, 1954, SPW.

26. This section of Buffalo's arterial system was eventually incorporated into the Thruway.

27. BDT to A. H. Kirchoffer, *Buffalo Evening News*, August 9, 1954, SPW. On continuing problems with the Buffalo program, see also Superintendent of Public Works John W. Johnson [hereafter JWJ] to John Naples, Corporation Council, Department of Law, City of Buffalo, n.d. [January or February 1955?], SPW; JWJ to K. B. Foster, District Engineer, Bureau of Public Roads, January 12, 1956, SPW. On the skyway, see also *Buffalo Evening News*, September 4, 1955; on the "Aud," see Mike Vogel, "Buffalo's Town Hall," *Buffalo Magazine* (March 13, 1994): 4–7, clippings file, Buffalo and Erie County Historical Society Research Library, Buffalo, New York. As of 2005, support has been growing to tear down the skyway and revitalize the waterfront.

28. Address by JWJ to New York State Waterways Association, January 21, 1955, SPW.

29. JWJ quoting an alternate proposal for Syracuse's highways to William A. Maloney, March 11, 1955, SPW.

30. JWJ to William A. Maloney, March 11, 1955, SPW.

31. JWJ to Daniel Patrick Moynihan, Assistant Secretary to Governor Averell Harriman, March 30, 1955, SPW.

32. JWJ to Charles H. Tuttle, Chairman, Metropolitan Rapid Transit Commission, New York City, May 2, 1955, SPW. Tuttle persisted, and in a follow-up letter, Johnson reiterated his point. He conceded that "planning agencies should cooperate in the study of all phases of transportation. However, such planning must

be related to accomplishments. . . . Highway monies used for rapid transit purposes would automatically reduce our already limited highway funds. . . . Further planning to accommodate future rapid transit lines would only tend to delay." JWJ to Tuttle, June 6, 1955, SPW.

33. Kenneth T. Jackson, *Crabgrass Frontier: The Suburbanization of the United States* (New York: Oxford University Press, 1985); Jon C. Teaford, *City and Suburb: The Political Fragmentation of Metropolitan America, 1850–1970* (Baltimore: Johns Hopkins University Press, 1979); Sam Bass Warner Jr., *Streetcar Suburbs: The Process of Growth in Boston (1870–1900)* (Cambridge, Mass.: Harvard University Press, 1962).

34. Farm leaders had been calling for a ten-year program since the late 1940s. New York State Conference Board of Farm Organizations, "Secondary Roads," June 1, 1948, Farm Bureau Records, #2714, Box 8, Cornell University, Ithaca, New York.

35. *NYT*, February 18, 1950; JWJ to James E. Treux, Director of Public Relations, June 11, 1955, SPW.

36. *NYT*, January 27, 1952.

37. *NYT*, January 25, 1954; DPW Memo to Town Supervisors and Members of Town Boards re: Erwin Act, March 15, 1954, SPW; JWJ to F. Theodore Jenzen, Executive Secretary of the New York State Association of Town Superintendents of Highways, September 7, 1956, SPW.

38. Arthur J. Vidich and Joseph Bensman, *Small Town in Mass Society: Class, Power, and Religion in a Rural Community* (Princeton, N.J.: Princeton University Press, 1958, rev. 1968), 151–152. Candor, New York, is fictionalized as "Springdale" in Vidich and Bensman's study. Charlotte Allen, "Spies Like Us: When Sociologists Deceive Their Subjects," *Lingua Franca* 7 (November 1997): 30–39.

39. *Elmira Sunday Telegram*, December 23, 1956, Chemung County Historical Society.

40. JWJ Report on Closing of Farm Crossings on Route 17, n.d. [January 1957?], SPW; JWJ to J. Sloat Welles, January 14, 1957, SPW.

41. Stanley I. Kutler, *Privilege and Creative Destruction: The Charles River Bridge Case* (Philadelphia: Lippincott, 1971).

42. The Thruway, which was eventually incorporated into the Interstate Highway System, linked New York City and Buffalo by 1956. Extensions to neighboring states and Canada were in place by 1960; two more Grand Island bridges to Canada opened in 1962. The Thruway system remained static until the acquisition of I-287 (the Cross Westchester Expressway) and I-84 in 1991. See New York State Thruway Factbook, http://www.thruway.state.ny.us (accessed February 5, 2007).

43. Dewey quoted in *NYT*, July 12, 1946.

44. *NYT*, October 13, 1946; October 24, 1946; February 26, 1946; March 2, 1946; January 21, 1949; January 28, 1949; and March 9, 1950.

45. *NYT*, October 3, 1946.

46. *NYT*, July 12, 1946.

47. *NYT*, July 14, 1946. On postwar growth liberalism, see Alan Brinkley, *The End of Reform: New Deal Liberalism in Recession and War* (New York: Vintage, 1995).

48. *NYT*, September 13, 1947, and November 15, 1947.

49. *NYT*, February 1, 1945.

50. *NYT*, October 24, 1945.

51. *NYT*, February 2, 1950.

52. *NYT*, November 24, 1947, and January 23, 1948.

53. *NYT*, July 25, 1948.

54. *NYT*, February 9, 1945.

55. *NYT*, July 21, 1948, and February 28, 1949.

56. Brinkley, *End of Reform*, ch. 4; Lizabeth Cohen, *A Consumers' Republic: The Politics of Mass Consumption in Postwar America* (New York: Knopf, 2003).; Robert M. Collins, *More: The Politics of Economic Growth in Postwar America* (Oxford: Oxford University Press, 2000).

57. William H. Chafe, *The Unfinished Journey: America since World War II* (New York: Oxford University Press, 1991), 117–119.

58. "Current Highway Problems," BDT address to Empire State Association of Commerce, October 19, 1951, TPIF.

59. *NYT*, February 10, 1950.

60. *NYT*, February 20, 1950, and February 21, 1950.

61. Report of the Governor's Thruway Committee, March 5, 1950, held in Loeb Library, Harvard University, Cambridge, Massachusetts.

62. *NYT*, March 11, 1898.

63. The switch from a toll-free to a toll road required some redesign. For instance, the trumpet exchange at Victor had to be torn down and reconstructed in cloverleaf-style in order to accommodate toll collection. See David Beetle's coverage of the Thruway, "Beetle Series," TSNRF; *Rochester Times-Union* [June 25?] 1954, clippings collection from Rochester Historical Society, Rochester, New York; New York State Thruway Authority, *Annual Report*, 1953. The flat-fee permits were successful for many years, then phased out in 1970, following toll increases and procedural changes in permit use. E-mail correspondence with the Thruway Authority, Department of Public Affairs, February 28, 2002, in author's possession.

64. On public authorities, see Alan G. Hevesi, New York State Office of the Comptroller, *Public Authorities: Reining in New York's Secret Government* (Albany, February 2004); Gail Radford, "From Municipal Socialism to Public Authorities: Institutional Factors in the Shaping of Public Enterprise," *Journal of American History* 90 (December 2003): 867–890; Jameson W. Doig, *Empire on the Hudson: Entrepreneurial Vision and Political Power at the Port of New York Authority* (New York: Columbia University Press, 2001); Doig and Jerry Mitchell, "Expertise, Democracy, and the Public Authority Model: Groping toward Accommodation," in Mitchell, ed., *Public Authorities and Public Policy: The Business of Government* (Westport, Conn.: Greenwood, 1992); Jon J. Lines, Ellen L. Parker, and David C. Perry, "Building the Twentieth-Century Public Works Machine: Robert Moses and the Public Authority," in "Planning and Financing Public Works: Three Historical Cases," *Essays in Public Works History* 15 (September 1987): 47–69; Annmarie Hauck Walsh, *The Public's Business: The Politics and Practices of Government Corporations* (Cambridge, Mass.: MIT Press, 1978); Robert G. Smith, *Ad Hoc Governments: Special Purpose Transportation Authorities in Britain and the United States* (Beverly Hills, Calif.: Sage, 1974); Thomas K. McCraw, *TVA and the Power Fight, 1933–1939* (Philadelphia: Lippincott, 1971); Robert C. Wood, *1400 Governments: The Political Economy of the New York Metropolitan Region* (Cambridge, Mass.: Harvard University Press, 1961).

65. Walsh, *Public's Business*, 27–29. New York authorities include the New York Power Authority (1931), the New York State Bridge Authority (1932), and the New York Dormitory Authority (1944). Federal corporations created at this time were largely geared toward finance or war-related materials production.

66. McCraw, *TVA*, 140–161.

67. Doig, *Empire on the Hudson*, 374–402.

68. Still, toll-collecting authorities were a popular model. Between 1950 and 1954, nineteen states created independent toll road authorities or authorized state highway departments to collect tolls. U.S. Federal Highway Administration, *America's Highways, 1776–1976: A History of the Federal-aid Program* (Washington, D.C.: Government Printing Office, 1977).

69. Another plum for Manhattan: Dewey announced a route shift that would have the Thruway cross the Hudson above the city and enter it from the north. Originally the Thruway was to run along the west shore of the Hudson, entering New York from New Jersey and allowing the Garden State to siphon away commerce.

70. Press Release, June 1954, TPRPF; *NYT*, February 6, 1951; March 6, 1951; March 7, 1951; March 9, 1951; and March 26, 1951.

71. *NYT*, August 15, 1951.

72. *NYT*, November 5, 1951, and November 8, 1951. The financial soundness of the proposal appealed to the *New York Times*, which recorded that the Democratic Party has "little to be proud of in its opposition."

73. BDT to Association of New York State Highway Employees, August 12, 1950, TPIF.

74. *NYT*, October 31, 1951, and April 1, 1952; BDT to Thomas H. MacDonald, Former Chief of the Federal Bureau of Public Roads, March, 29, 1954, SPW; BDT to Francis W. DuPont, Commissioner of the Bureau of Public Roads, confidential letter, February 23, 1954, SPW.

75. Economic historians Peter D. McClelland and Alan L. Magdovitz argue in their tellingly titled study, *Crisis in the Making*, that heavily partisan debate left "neither side winning any laurels for cogent justification" for passing off the Thruway to a quasi-public agency, nor for providing it with the state's excellent credit rating. Writing in the aftermath of New York City's fiscal collapse in the 1970s, they found little evidence to suggest that public authorities operate more efficiently than traditional government agencies, or that insulating projects like the Thruway from the political arena did any more than substitute the "vested interests of the bureaucrats" for those of the people. McClelland and Magdovitz, *Crisis in the Making: The Political Economy of New York State since 1945* (Cambridge: Cambridge University Press, 1981), chs. 5 and 6, quoted on p. 218. McClelland and Magdovitz joined other scholars, such as political scientists Robert Wood and Annmarie Hauck Walsh, in condemning public authorities, though Wood faults authorities for contributing to the fragmentation of government while Walsh criticizes them for replacing political imperatives with economic ones. Wood, *1400 Governments*, 123–144; Walsh, *The Public's Business*, passim.

76. Lines, Parker, and Perry, "Building the Twentieth-Century Public Works Machine."

77. New York State Thruway Authority pamphlet, "Forging Ahead—the New

York State Thruway," Fall 1951, held in Loeb Library, Harvard University, Cambridge, Massachusetts.

78. JWJ to William M. Ringle, June 20, 1955, SPW; H. Floyd Burd quoted in New York *Herald Tribune*, October 24, 1954, TPRPF.

79. BDT to Director of Public Relations Bob Monahan, April 16, 1954, SPW.

80. On the "financial independence" argument and the substitution of legislative dependence for bond market dependence, see Walsh, *Public's Business*, 116–117.

81. *NYT*, February 2, 1954.

82. *NYT*, November 4, 1951.

83. *NYT*, July 9, 1950.

84. Dewey speech at Catskill-Saugerties opening ceremonies, July 14, 1950, "Early Thruway Releases," Speech and News Release File, TPIF.

85. *NYT*, June 17, 1950, and September 14, 1952.

86. Mark Rose, *Interstate: Express Highway Politics, 1939–1989* (Knoxville: University of Tennessee Press, 1990).

87. BDT to PR Director Bob Monahan, May 25, 1954, SPW.

88. Remarks of BDT at the opening of the Rochester-Buffalo Thruway section, August 26, 1954, TPRPF.

89. *New York News*, June 25, 1954, TPCF.

90. *NYT*, December 5, 1954.

91. *NYT*, December 24, 1953. *In the Matter of Alexander's Department Stores, Inc., et al. v. New York State Thruway Authority*, 127 NYS 2d 146 (1954).

92. JWJ to Newman E. Argraves, Connecticut State Highway Commissioner, January 4, 1956, SPW.

93. *NYT*, October 31, 1953, and November 5, 1953.

94. *NYT*, June 20, 1954; BDT speech, "The Thruway and the Economy of New York State," June 8, 1955, TPIF.

95. *NYT*, March 7, 1950; March 8, 1950; and August 10, 1950.

96. *NYT*, February 26, 1951.

97. *NYT*, July 24, 1951; January 13, 1953; and February 14, 1954. On the DPW's policy of shifting work to less contentious upstate projects, see District Engineer James S. Bixby to AWB, September 20, 1938, "Department of Public Works, Division of Highways," Herbert Lehman Papers, Governor's Correspondence, New York State Archives, Albany.

98. *NYT*, January 7, 1954, and June 4, 1954.

99. *NYT*, December 22, 1950.

100. *NYT*, January 2, 1951.

101. *NYT*, December 22, 1950.

102. "Beetle Series," TSNRF.

103. *NYT*, February 23, 1954.

104. "The Thruways and Westchester County," BDT speech to Westchester County Association, May 19, 1953, TPIF.

105. *NYT*, July 24, 1953.

106. *NYT*, August 4, 1953; Bartholomew Bland, "Market in the Meadows: The Development and Impact of Westchester's Cross County Shopping Center, 1947–1956," in Roger Panetta, ed., *Westchester: The American Suburb* (New York and Yonkers: Fordham University Press and the Hudson River Museum, 2006), 291–326.

107. BDT remarks at Suffern-Yonkers barrier opening, December 15, 1955, TPRPF. On the growth of shopping malls in the 1950s, see Lizabeth Cohen, *A Consumers' Republic* (New York: Knopf, 2003), ch. 6; Cohen, "From Town Center to Shopping Center: The Reconfiguration of Community Marketplaces in Postwar America," *American Historical Review*, 101 (October 1996): 1050–1081; and Kenneth T. Jackson, "All the World's a Mall: Reflections on the Social and Economic Consequences of the American Shopping Center," *American Historical Review* 101 (October 1996): 1111–1121.

108. Director of Public Relations, Thruway Authority, Robert M. Monahan, to BDT, May 19, 1953, TPIF.

109. *Buffalo Courier Express*, June 11, 1950; *Buffalo News*, August 6, 1953, in TPCF.

110. ASCE Code of Ethics, January 1, 1953, SPW; BDT to Hal Hale, Executive Secretary of the American Association of State Highway Officials, April 23, 1954, SPW.

111. Jim Power, "Thruway Memorandum #1–8," n.p., May 19–June 17, 1954, TPRPF. Michael. J. "Jack" Madigan had also served as a longtime aide and contractor under Robert Moses. Robert A. Caro, *The Power Broker: Robert Moses and the Fall of New York* (New York: Vintage, 1974), 536.

112. As Lizabeth Cohen has ably demonstrated, postwar economic liberalism offered Americans the opportunity to spend their way to better living, but at the expense of sustaining long-standing inequalities. See Cohen, *A Consumers' Republic*.

113. *NYT*, August 23, 1953.

114. *NYT*, January 8, 1950.

115. *NYT*, January 25, 1951; January 26, 1951; September 23, 1951; and January 11, 1953; JWJ to C. D. Curtis, Commissioner, Bureau of Public Roads, September 21, 1955, SPW.

116. Proposed Public Works Plank, DPW to Governor Dewey, August 12, 1954, SPW.

117. JWJ to Director of Public Relations, DPW, James E. Treux, July 8, 1955, SPW. The difficulties in building the LIE had long been recognized: "For sometime it has been recognized by responsible public officials in New York City, Nassau and Suffolk counties, and our New York State DPW that an all-purpose expressway . . . through Long Island is necessary to meet the unprecedented growth of vehicular traffic in that area of the state. . . . I believe it is important to commence, without delay, the construction of this route across Nassau county and to obtain as much of the right of way in Suffolk county as is necessary to assure economic and prompt construction of the route all the way to the vicinity of Riverhead as traffic in that section of the island requires. Private property is developing so rapidly here that if that is not done it may make impossible the extension of the expressway because of exorbitant right-of-way costs and economic losses to the communities through which it would extend." BDT to E. B. Hughes, Deputy Superintendent of Public Works, January 29, 1954, SPW. See also Caro, *The Power Broker*, 940–950.

118. JWJ to Senator Herbert Lehman, September 28, 1956, SPW.

119. *NYT*, February 10, 1954.

120. BDT speech to the Society of Business Magazine Editors, September 17, 1953, TPIF (emphasis in the original).

121. Statement of BDT to U.S. Congress, House Committee on Public Works, March 1950, reprinted in "Thruway: Ends and Means," *Professional Engineer*, December 1950, TPIF.

122. "A Plan for the State of New York," Speech of Clarence S. Stein, Chairman, New York State Commission of Housing and Regional Planning, before the International City and Town Planning Congress, April 22, 1925, Loeb Library, Harvard University, Cambridge, Massachusetts.

123. *NYT*, June 20, 1954.

124. BDT speech to Municipal Forum of New York, May 9, 1952, TPRPF.

125. The commission remained active from 1953 to 1959 under the chairmanship of Charles Diefendorf, president of Marine Midland Trust. That institution's name adorned the new home of the Buffalo Sabers: the Marine Midland Arena. The sports center was built in 1995 to replace the aging Memorial Auditorium that had suffered after the construction of the elevated expressway in 1954.

126. *NYT*, January 4, 1955; January 6, 1955; and April 4, 1955.

127. New York State Good Roads Association Bulletin, August 1954. By the end of 1955 the Thruway was opened from Buffalo to Yonkers. The Yonkers to New York City section opened the following year, and the remaining extensions handled traffic by 1960.

128. *NYT*, June 19, 1955, and April 13, 1955.

129. New York City and upstate voters rejected the proposal in roughly equal proportions. New York City residents opposed it by 58 percent, upstate residents by 56 percent. *NYT*, September 10, 1955.

130. McClelland and Magdovitz, *Crisis in the Making*.

131. *NYT*, January 2, 1955, and November 9–13, 1955.

132. *NYT*, November 13, 1955; November 10, 1955; and November 7, 1956. McClelland and Magdovitz claimed that the bond issue defeat suggested that "voters' tolerance for highway spending proved to be rather low." [*Crisis in the Making*, 156.] But the passage of a modified bond authorization amendment the following year supports the argument that interest-group lobbying by hard-line highway advocates, rather than true antihighway sentiment, was at the source of the 1955 bond rejection.

133. Statement of BDT to U.S. Congress, House Committee on Public Works, March 1950, reprinted in "Thruway: Ends and Means," *Professional Engineer*, December 1950, TPIF.

134. On highway opposition after 1956, see especially Mark Rose and Bruce Seely, "Getting the Interstate System Built," *Journal of Policy History* 2 (1990): 23–56; Mark Rose, "Reframing American Highway Politics, 1956–1995," *Journal of Planning History* 2 (August 2003): 212–236; and Raymond Mohl, "Stop the Road: Freeway Revolts in American Cities," *Journal of Urban History* 30 (July 2004): 674–706.

135. Minutes, Meeting of District Engineers, January 19, 1955, SPW.

136. Quoted in Rose, *Interstate*, 5. This section draws heavily on Rose's insightful analysis of interstate highway politics.

137. Ibid., ch. 2.

138. Ibid., 74; BDT to Francis W. DuPont, Commissioner of the Bureau of Public Roads, confidential letter, February 23, 1954, SPW.

139. JWJ to Senators Herbert Lehman, Irving Ives, and Dennis Chavez, May 21, 1956, SPW.

140. Bruce Seely's *Building the American Highway System: Engineers as Policy Makers* (Philadelphia: Temple University Press, 1987), 39.

141. John A. Volpe served as temporary highway administrator until Tallamy's appointment.

142. Deil S. Wright explains that by the mid-1950s, the shift in power from "governing generalists" to "program specialists" had created a series of "vertical functional autocracies," in which program professionals (in this case engineers) competed against governing generalists and other program specialists for resources. These intergovernmental relationships have been aptly described by Terry Sanford as "picket-fence federalism," with each vertical picket representing an alliance of experts and professionals, regardless of the level of government in which they serve. Wright, "Intergovernmental Relations: An Analytical Overview," *Annals of the American Academy of Political and Social Science* 416 (November 1974): 1–16; Wright, "Revenue Sharing and Structural Features of American Federalism," *Annals of the American Academy of Political and Social Science* 419 (May 1975): 100–119; Wright, "Policy Shifts in the Politics and Administration of Intergovernmental Relations, 1930s–1990s," *Annals of the American Academy of Political and Social Science* 509 (May 1990): 60–72; Terry Sanford, *Storm over the States* (New York: McGraw-Hill, 1967), 80.

143. Jon C. Teaford, *The Rise of the States: Evolution of American State Government* (Baltimore: Johns Hopkins University Press, 2003).

144. Rose, *Interstate*, epilogue.

Conclusion

1. Mark Rose, "Reframing American Highway Politics, 1956–1995," *Journal of Planning History* 2 (August 2003): 212–236; Raymond Mohl, "Stop the Road: Freeway Revolts in American Cities," *Journal of Urban History* 30 (July 2004): 674–706; Mohl, "Ike and the Interstates: Creeping toward Comprehensive Planning," *Journal of Planning History* 2 (August 2003): 237–262.

2. Mark H. Rose and Bruce E. Seely, "Getting the Interstate System Built: Road Engineers and the Implementation of Public Policy, 1955–1985," *Journal of Policy History* 2 (1990): 23–56 at 33–34.

3. Thomas P. Hughes, *Rescuing Prometheus* (New York: Pantheon, 1998), 303.

4. Deil Wright, *Understanding Intergovernmental Relations* (Belmont, Calif.: Duxbury, 1978).

5. For a competing perspective on the importance of the New Deal public works projects to the American political economy, see Jason Scott Smith, *Building New Deal Liberalism: The Political Economy of Public Works, 1933–1956* (New York: Cambridge University Press, 2006).

6. Daniel Carpenter, *The Forging of Bureaucratic Autonomy: Reputations, Networks, and Policy Innovations in Executive Agencies, 1862–1928* (Princeton, N.J.: Princeton University Press, 2001).

7. *NYT*, December 16, 1955.

8. Zachary M. Schrag, "The Freeway Fight in Washington, D.C.: The Three

Sisters Bridge in Three Administrations," *Journal of Urban History* 30 (July 2004): 661.

9. Hugh Pomeroy, "Plans, Planners, and People: Case Reports from Westchester County on Some Human Aspects of Thoroughfare Planning," n.d. (c. 1955), HRPC.

10. "Statement of the Westchester County Planning Commission, Re: Resolution Adopted by the Town Board of Lewisboro, September 24, 1956, Relative to the Preliminary Plan for Major Thoroughfares in Northern Westchester," October 30, 1956, HRPC.

11. Pomeroy, "Is the Turnpike a Good Neighbor?" presented at the 23rd Annual Meeting of the American Bridge, Tunnel, and Turnpike Association, Atlantic City, New Jersey, October 12, 1955, HRPC.

12. Pomeroy, Comments on Procedure for Thoroughfare Planning in Westchester County, Minutes of the Westchester County Planning Board, August 11, 1950, HRPC; Pomeroy, "The Planning Process and Public Participation," presented at the first session of the Urban Planning Forum, conducted by the Bureau of Urban Research, Princeton University, New Jersey, October 22, 1951, HRPC.

13. Pomeroy, "Is the Turnpike a Good Neighbor?"

14. Bertram Tallamy, interview by Lee Mertz for the Public Works Historical Society, AASHTO Interstate Highway Research Project, Institute of Transportation Studies, University of California, Berkeley, 1987.

15. Rose, "Reframing American Highway Politics."

16. Hughes, *Rescuing Prometheus*, ch. 5; James Tobin, *Great Projects: The Epic Story of the Building of America, from the Taming of the Mississippi to the Invention of the Internet* (New York: Free Press, 2001), ch. 7; Alan A. Altshuler and David E. Luberoff, *Mega-Projects: The Changing Politics of Urban Public Investment* (Washington, D.C.: Brookings Institution, 2003); Altshuler and Luberoff, "Big Dig Projects: Are They Worth It?" *Boston Globe*, March 27, 2003.

17. Altshuler and Luberoff, *Mega-Projects*; Michael R. Fein, "Tunnel Vision: The 'Big Dig,' Invisible Highways and the Politics of Planning," paper presented at the Fourth International Conference on the History of Traffic, Transport, and Mobility, Paris, 2006.

18. Colleen Marie O'Connor, "A New Breed of Toll Collector; Wall Street's Cruising for Toll Road Deals as Cash-Strapped States Seek Big Money from Private Investors," *Investment Dealers Digest*, May 15, 2006.

19. Karen Orren and Stephen Skowronek, *The Search for American Political Development* (Cambridge: Cambridge University Press, 2004).

20. *NYT*, June 24, 1954.

BIBLIOGRAPHY

Archival Sources

Buffalo and Erie County Historical Society and Research Library. Clippings File. Buffalo, N.Y.

Bureau of Public Roads. Record Group 30. Archives II, Library of Congress, Suitland, Md.

Greene, Frederick S. Small Collections. Series Credit: Mr. and Mrs. Francis Thornton Greene, Warrenton, Va. Collection held at Franklin D. Roosevelt Library, Hyde Park, N.Y.

Lehman, Herbert. Governor's Correspondence. "Department of Public Works." New York State Archives, Albany.

——. Governor's Correspondence. "Department of Public Works, Division of Highways." New York State Archives, Albany.

Lord, Bert. Papers. #1776, Boxes 3, 4, 8. Kroch Rare and Manuscript Library. Cornell University, Ithaca, N.Y.

Miller, Nathan. Governor's Correspondence. "Highway Commission." New York State Archives, Albany.

New York State Department of Transportation. Correspondence Files of Division of Highways Regarding Federally Funded Highway Construction Projects, 1917–1933. B0228. New York State Archives, Albany.

New York State Engineer and Surveyor. Record of Contracts Awarded for Improvement of Public Highways, 1898–1908. B0272. New York State Archives, Albany.

New York State Farm Bureau. Records. #2714, Box 8. Kroch Rare and Manuscript Library. Cornell University, Ithaca, N.Y.

New York State Legislature, Joint Legislative Commission on Good Roads. Hearing Testimony. 1907. New York State Library, Albany.

New York State Thruway Authority. Press Clippings File. New York State Archives, Albany.

——. Public Information File. New York State Archives, Albany.

——. Public Relations and Planning Files. New York State Archives, Albany.

——. Speech and News Release File. "Beetle Series." New York State Archives, Albany.

Pomeroy, Hugh. Hugh R. Pomeroy Collection, 1926–1966, Series 21. Westchester County Archives, Elmsford, N.Y.

Rochester Historical Society. Clippings Collection. Rochester, N.Y.

Roosevelt, Franklin D. Governor's Papers. "Brandt, Arthur W." Franklin D. Roosevelt Library, Hyde Park, N.Y.

——. Governor's Papers. "Greene, Frederick S." Franklin D. Roosevelt Library, Hyde Park, N.Y.

——. Governor's Papers. "Public Works: Route 17." Franklin D. Roosevelt Library, Hyde Park, N.Y.

——. New York State Senator's Papers. "Earl, Robert." Franklin D. Roosevelt Library, Hyde Park, N.Y.

——. New York State Senator's Papers. "Highway Bills." Franklin D. Roosevelt Library, Hyde Park, N.Y.

——. President's Official File 129. "Roads and Highways." Franklin D. Roosevelt Library, Hyde Park, N.Y.

——. President's Official File 466. "National Recovery Association/Public Works Administration." Franklin D. Roosevelt Library, Hyde Park, N.Y.

——. President's Personal File 93. "Lehman, Herbert." Franklin D. Roosevelt Library, Hyde Park, N.Y.

——. President's Personal File 3041. "Greene, Frederick S." Franklin D. Roosevelt Library, Hyde Park, N.Y.

Shaw, S. F. Account Book. #745. Kroch Rare and Manuscript Library. Cornell University, Ithaca, N.Y.

Smith, Alfred E. Official Papers. "Highway Commission." New York State Executive Department Correspondence. New York State Archives, Albany.

Superintendent of Public Works. Correspondence and Subject Files, 1943–64. New York State Archives, Albany.

Tallamy, Bertram. Interview by Lee Mertz for the Public Works Historical Society. AASHTO Interstate Highway Research Project. Institute of Transportation Studies. University of California, Berkeley. 1987.

White, William Pierrepont. Papers. "Good Roads Correspondence." #399, Box 65. Kroch Rare and Manuscript Library. Cornell University, Ithaca, N.Y.

Books, Articles, and Dissertations

Alchon, Gary. *The Invisible Hand of Planning: Capitalism, Social Science, and the State in the 1920s.* Princeton, N.J.: Princeton University Press, 1985.

Allen, Charlotte. "Spies Like Us: When Sociologists Deceive Their Subjects." *Lingua Franca* 7 (November 1997): 30–39.

Allen, David Yehling. *Long Island Maps and Their Makers: Five Centuries of Cartographic History.* Mattituck, N.Y.: Amereon House, 1997.

Altenbaugh, Richard J. *Education for Struggle: The American Labor Colleges of the 1920s and 1930s.* Philadelphia: Temple University Press, 1990.

Altshuler, Alan A., and David E. Luberoff. "Big Dig Projects: Are They Worth It?" *Boston Globe.* March 27, 2003.

——. *Mega-Projects: The Changing Politics of Urban Public Investment.* Washington, D.C.: Brookings Institution, 2003.

Amenta, Edwin, et al. "Bring Back the WPA: Work, Relief, and the Origins of American Social Policy in Welfare Reform." *Studies in American Political Development* 12 (1998): 1–56.

Anderson, W. A. "Population Trends in New York State, 1900–1930." Ithaca, N.Y.: Cornell University Agricultural Experiment Station, 1932.

Armstrong, Ellis L., Michael C. Robinson, and Suellen M. Hoy, eds. *History of Public Works in the United States, 1776–1976.* Chicago: American Public Works Association, 1976.

Badger, Anthony. *The New Deal: The Depression Years, 1933–1940.* New York: Hill & Wang, 1989.

Baer, Christopher, Daniel B. Klein, and John Majewski. "From Trunk to Branch: Toll Roads in New York, 1800–1860." *Essays in Economic and Business History* 11 (1993): 191–209.

Baker, Paula. *The Moral Frameworks of Public Life: Gender, Politics, and the State in Rural New York, 1870–1930.* New York: Oxford University Press, 1991.

Balogh, Brian. *Chain Reaction: Expert Debate and Public Participation in American Commercial Nuclear Power, 1945–1975.* Cambridge: Cambridge University Press, 1991.

———. "Reorganizing the Organizational Synthesis: Federal-Professional Relations in Modern America." *Studies in American Political Development* 5 (1991): 119–172.

Bankson, Paul A. "The Challenge of the Gasoline Filling Station: Have Zoning Boards of Appeals Failed to Meet It?" In Westchester County Planning Federation, *Planning and Zoning Problems.* Paper presented at the Conference of the Westchester County Planning Federation, White Plains, N.Y., 1931.

Barber, William J. *From New Era to New Deal: Herbert Hoover, the Economists, and American Economic Policy, 1921–1933.* Cambridge: Cambridge University Press, 1985.

Barrett, Paul. *The Automobile and Urban Transit: The Formation of Public Policy in Chicago, 1900–1930.* Philadelphia: Temple University Press, 1983.

Barron, Hal S. *Mixed Harvest: The Second Great Transformation in the Rural North, 1870–1930.* Chapel Hill: University of North Carolina Press, 1997.

———. *Those Who Stayed Behind: Rural Society in Nineteenth-Century New England.* Cambridge: Cambridge University Press, 1984.

Bass, Herbert J. *"I Am a Democrat": The Political Career of David Bennett Hill.* Syracuse, N.Y.: Syracuse University Press, 1961.

Bednarek, Janet R. Daly. *America's Airports: Airfield Development, 1918–1947.* College Station: Texas A&M Press, 2001.

Bellush, Bernard. *Franklin D. Roosevelt as Governor of New York.* New York: AMS, 1968 [orig. Columbia University Press, 1955].

Bensel, Richard F. *The Political Economy of Industrialization, 1877–1900.* Cambridge: Cambridge University Press, 2000.

Benson, Lee. *Merchants, Farmers, and Railroads: Railroad Regulation and New York Politics, 1880–1887.* Cambridge, Mass.: Harvard University Press, 1955.

Billings, Henry. *Construction Ahead.* New York: Viking, 1951.

Bouton, Terry. "A Road Closed: Rural Insurgency in Post-Independence Pennsylvania." *Journal of American History* 87 (December 2000): 855–887.

Brandt, Arthur W. "DPW," in Charles A. Brind and Arthur K. Gitman, eds., *Story of State Government, State of New York*. Albany: Association of State Civil Service Employees of the State of New York, 1942.

Brinkley, Alan. *The End of Reform: New Deal Liberalism in Depression and War.* New York: Vintage, 1995.

Brock, William R. *Investigation and Responsibility: Public Responsibility in the United States, 1865–1900.* Cambridge: Cambridge University Press, 1984.

Brown, M. Craig, and Charles N. Halaby. "Bosses, Reform, and the Socioeconomic Bases of Urban Expenditure, 1890–1940." In Terrence J. McDonald and Sally K. Ward, eds., *The Politics of Urban Fiscal Policy*. Beverly Hills, Calif.: Sage, 1984.

Brownlee, W. Elliot. "The Public Sector." In Stanley Engerman and Robert Gallman, eds., *The Cambridge Economic History of the United States, Vol. 3: The Twentieth Century*. Cambridge: Cambridge University Press, 2000.

Budenz, Louis Francis. *This Is My Story.* New York: McGraw-Hill, 1947.

Bullock, Edward Taylor. "Financial Aspects of Highway Development with Special Reference to New York State." Ph.D. diss., Harvard University, 1926.

Burnham, John Chynoweth. "The Gasoline Tax and the Automobile Revolution." *Mississippi Valley Historical Review* 48 (December 1961): 435–459.

Campbell, Ballard. *The Growth of American Government: Governance from the Cleveland Era to the Present.* Bloomington: Indiana University Press, 1995.

Caro, Robert A. *The Power Broker: Robert Moses and the Fall of New York.* New York: Vintage, 1975 [orig. Knopf, 1974].

Carpenter, Daniel. *The Forging of Bureaucratic Autonomy: Reputations, Networks, and Policy Innovations in Executive Agencies, 1862–1928.* Princeton, N.J.: Princeton University Press, 2001.

Chafe, William H. *The Unfinished Journey: America since World War II.* New York: Oxford University Press, 1991.

Chandler, Alfred D. *The Visible Hand: The Managerial Revolution in American Business.* Cambridge, Mass.: Harvard University Press, 1977.

Cheape, Charles W. *Moving the Masses: Urban Public Transit in New York, Boston, and Philadelphia, 1880–1912.* Cambridge, Mass.: Harvard University Press, 1980.

Childs, William R. *Trucking and the Public Interest: The Emergence of Federal Regulation, 1914–1940.* Knoxville: University of Tennessee Press, 1985.

Churchill, Henry. "Henry Wright: 1878–1936." In Donald A. Krueckeberg, ed., *The American Planner: Biographies and Recollections,* 2d ed. New Brunswick, N.J.: Center for Urban Policy Research, 1994.

Clemens, Elisabeth S. *The People's Lobby: Organizational Innovation and the Rise of Interest Group Politics in the United States, 1890–1925.* Chicago: University of Chicago Press, 1997.

Cochran, Thomas. *Railroad Leaders: The Business Mind in Action, 1845–1890.* Cambridge, Mass.: Harvard University Press, 1951.

Cogdell, Christine. "The Futurama Recontextualized: Norman Bel Geddes's Eugenic 'World of Tomorrow.'" *America Quarterly* 52 (June 2000): 193–245.

Cohen, Lizabeth. *A Consumers' Republic: The Politics of Mass Consumption in Postwar America.* New York: Knopf, 2003.

———. "From Town Center to Shopping Center: The Reconfiguration of Community Marketplaces in Postwar America." *American Historical Review* 101 (October 1996): 1050–1081.

Collins, Robert M. *More: The Politics of Economic Growth in Postwar America.* New York: Oxford University Press, 2000.

Cross, Whitney. *The Burned-Over District: The Social and Intellectual History of Enthusiastic Religion in Western New York, 1800–1850.* Ithaca, N.Y.: Cornell University Press, 1950.

Curtiss, William M. "The Development of Highway Administration and Finance in New York." Department of Agricultural Economics and Farm Management, New York State College of Agriculture. Ithaca, N.Y.: Cornell University Press, March 1936.

Danielson, Michael N., and Jameson W. Doig. *New York: The Politics of Urban Regional Development.* Berkeley: University of California Press, 1982.

Dearing, Charles L. *American Highway Policy.* Washington, D.C.: Brookings Institution, 1941.

Derthick, Martha. "How Many Communities: The Evolution of American Federalism." In Martha Derthick, ed., *Dilemmas of Scale in America's Federal Democracy.* Cambridge, Mass.: Cambridge University Press, 1999.

———. *The Influence of Federal Grants: Public Assistance in Massachusetts.* Cambridge, Mass.: Harvard University Press, 1970.

———. *Keeping the Compound Republic: Essays on American Federalism.* Washington, D.C.: Brookings Institution, 2001.

Doig, Jameson W. *Empire on the Hudson: Entrepreneurial Vision and Political Power at the Port of New York Authority.* New York: Columbia University Press, 2001.

Doig, Jameson W., and Jerry Mitchell. "Expertise, Democracy, and the Public Authority Model: Groping toward Accommodation." In Jerry Mitchell, ed., *Public Authorities and Public Policy: The Business of Government.* Westport, Conn.: Greenwood, 1992.

Douglas, Paul. "The Development of a System of Federal Grants-in-Aid." *Political Science Quarterly* 35 (1920): 255–271, 522–544.

Dunlavy, Colleen A. *Politics and Industrialization: Early Railroads in the United States and Prussia.* Princeton, N.J.: Princeton University Press, 1994.

Dunn, James A., Jr. "The Importance of Being Earmarked: Transport Policy and Highway Finance in Great Britain and the United States." *Comparative Studies in Society and History* 20 (1978): 29–53.

Dye, Thomas R. *Politics in States and Communities.* Englewood Cliffs, N.J.: Prentice Hall, 1969, 1973.

Eldot, Paula. *Governor Alfred E. Smith: The Politician as Reformer.* New York: Garland, 1983.

Ellis, David M., et al. *A Short History of New York State.* Ithaca, N.Y.: Cornell University Press, 1957.

Faulkner, Harold U. *The Decline of Laissez-Faire, 1897–1917.* Vol. 7 of *The Economic History of the United States.* New York: Holt, Rinehart & Winston, 1951.

———. *The Quest for Social Justice, 1898–1914.* New York: Macmillan, 1931.

Ferleger, Lou. "Uplifting American Agriculture." *Agricultural History* 64 (Spring 1990): 5–23.

Finan, Christopher M. *Alfred E. Smith: The Happy Warrior.* New York: Hill & Wang, 2002.

Finegold, Kenneth. *Experts and Politicians: Reform Challenges to Machine Politics in New York, Cleveland, and Chicago.* Princeton, N.J.: Princeton University Press, 1995.

Fisher, Charles T. "Road Building in the Good Old Days." *Engineering News Record* (May 21, 1942): 69–72.

Flink, James J. *The Automobile Age.* Cambridge, Mass.: MIT Press, 1988.

———. *The Car Culture.* Cambridge, Mass.: MIT Press, 1975.

Forrest, Jay W. *Tammany's Treason.* Albany, N.Y.: Fort Orange, 1913.

Fuller, Wayne E. "Good Roads and Rural Free Delivery of Mail." *Mississippi Valley Historical Review* 42 (June 1955): 67–83.

———. *RFD: The Changing Face of Rural America.* Bloomington: Indiana University Press, 1964.

Galambos, Louis. "The Emerging Organizational Synthesis in Modern American History." *Business History Review* 44 (Autumn 1970): 279–290.

———. "Technology, Political Economy, and Professionalization: Central Themes of the Organizational Synthesis." *Business History Review* 57 (Winter 1983): 471–493.

Galambos, Louis, and Joseph Pratt. *The Rise of the Corporate Commonwealth: United States Business and Public Policy in the 20th Century.* New York: Basic, 1988.

Gamm, Gerald. Review of Jon Teaford's *Rise of the States. Journal of American History* 91 (September 2004): 676.

Gayer, Arthur D. *Public Works in Prosperity and Depression.* New York: National Bureau of Economic Research, 1935.

Geddes, Norman Bel. *Magic Motorways.* New York: Random House, 1940.

Gelernter, David. *1939: The Lost World of the Fair.* New York: Free Press, 1995.

Gladwell, Malcolm. "Clicks and Mortar." *New Yorker.* December 6, 1999.

Goddard, Stephen B. *Getting There: The Epic Struggle between Road and Rail in the American Century.* New York: Basic, 1994.

Goodrich, Carter. *Government Promotion of American Canals and Railroads, 1800–1890.* New York: Columbia University Press, 1960.

Goodrich, Carter, et al., eds. *Canals and American Economic Development.* New York: Columbia University Press, 1961.

Goodwyn, Lawrence. *Democratic Promise: The Populist Moment in America.* New York: Oxford University Press, 1976.

Gosnell, Harold F. *Boss Platt and His New York Machine.* Chicago: University of Chicago Press, 1924.

Graham, Otis. *An Encore for Reform: The Old Progressives and the New Deal.* New York: Oxford University Press, 1967.

Grava, Sigurd. "The Bronx River Parkway: A Case Study in Innovation." *New York Affairs* 7 (1981): 15–23.

Griffin, Ernest F., ed. *Westchester County and Its People: A Record.* New York: Lewis Historical Publishing, 1946.

Gunn, L. Ray. *The Decline of Authority: Public Economic Policy and Political Development in New York, 1800–1860.* Ithaca, N.Y.: Cornell University Press, 1988.

Gutfreund, Owen. *Twentieth-Century Sprawl: Highways and the Reshaping of the American Landscape.* New York: Oxford University Press, 2004.

Handlin, Oscar. *Al Smith and His America.* Boston: Little, Brown, 1958.

Harmond, Richard. "Progress and Flight: An Interpretation of the American Cycling Craze." *Journal of Social History* 5 (1971–1972): 235–257.

Hawley, Ellis. *The Great War and the Search for a Modern Order.* New York: St. Martin's, 1992.

———. "Herbert Hoover and Economic Stabilization, 1921–22." In Ellis Hawley, ed., *Herbert Hoover as Secretary of Commerce: Studies in New Era Thought and Practice.* Iowa City: University of Iowa Press, 1981.

Haycraft, William R. *Yellow Steel: The Story of the Earthmoving Equipment Industry.* Urbana: University of Illinois Press, 2000.

Hays, Samuel P. *The Response to Industrialism, 1885–1914.* Chicago: University of Chicago Press, 1957.

Hazelton, Henry Isham. *The Boroughs of Brooklyn and Queens, Counties of Nassau and Suffolk, Long Island, New York, 1609–1924.* New York: Lewis Historical Publishing, 1925.

Heer, Clarence. *The Postwar Expansion of State Expenditures: An Analysis of the Increase between 1917 and 1923 in the Cost of State Government in New York.* New York: National Institute of Public Administration, 1926.

Higgens-Evenson, R. Rudy. *The Price of Progress: Public Services, Taxation, and the American Corporate State, 1877 to 1929.* Baltimore: Johns Hopkins University Press, 2003.

Higham, John. "The Reorientation of American Culture in the 1890s." In John Weiss, ed., *The Origins of Modern Consciousness.* Detroit: Wayne State Press, 1965.

Hilton, George W., and John F. Due. *The Electric Interurban Railways in America.* Stanford, Calif.: Stanford University Press, 1960.

Hirsch, Richard, and Joseph John Trento. *The National Aeronautics and Space Administration.* New York: Praeger, 1973.

Hofstadter, Richard. *The Age of Reform.* New York: Vintage, 1955.

Holt, Richard. "The Bicycle, the Bourgeoisie, and the Discovery of Rural France, 1880–1914." *British Journal of Sports History* 2 (September 1985): 127–139.

Holt, William Stull. *The Bureau of Public Roads: Its History, Activities, and Organizations.* Baltimore: Johns Hopkins University Press, 1923.

Holtz, Jane Kay. *Asphalt Nation: How the Automobile Took over America and How We Can Take It Back.* New York: Crown, 1997.

Hoover, Dwight W. "Roller Skating toward Industrialism." In Kathryn Grover, ed., *Hard at Play: Leisure in America, 1840–1940.* Amherst: University of Massachusetts Press, 1992.

Horwitz, Morton J. *The Transformation of American Law, 1870–1960.* New York: Oxford University Press, 1992.

Howlett, Charles F. *Brookwood Labor College and the Struggle for Peace and Social Justice in America.* Lewiston, N.Y.: Edwin Mellen, 1993.

Hughes, Thomas P. *Networks of Power: Electrification in Western Society, 1880–1930.* Baltimore: Johns Hopkins University Press, 1983.

———. *Rescuing Prometheus.* New York: Pantheon, 1998.

Hugill, Peter J. "Good Roads and the Automobile in the United States, 1880–1929." *Geographical Review* 72 (1982): 327–349.

Hutchinson, Ruth Gillette. *State-Administered Locally-Shared Taxes: Development in the State and Local Tax Systems in the United States.* New York: Columbia University Press, 1931.

Ickes, Harold. *Back to Work.* New York: Da Capo, 1974 [1935].

Ingalls, Robert P. *Herbert H. Lehman and New York's Little New Deal.* New York: New York University Press, 1975.

Jackson, Donald C. "Roads Most Traveled: Turnpikes in Southeastern Pennsylvania in the Early Republic." In Judith A. McGaw, ed., *Early American Technology: Making and Doing Things from the Colonial Era to 1850.* Chapel Hill: University of North Carolina Press, 1994.

Jackson, John Brinckerhoff. *American Space: The Centennial Years, 1865–1876.* New York: W. W. Norton, 1972.

———. *Discovering the Vernacular Landscape.* New Haven, Conn.: Yale University Press, 1984.

Jackson, Kenneth T. "All the World's a Mall: Reflections on the Social and Economic Consequences of the American Shopping Center." *American Historical Review* 101 (October 1996): 1111–1121.

———. *Crabgrass Frontier: The Suburbanization of the United States.* New York: Oxford University Press, 1985.

Jacoby, Karl. *Crimes against Nature: Squatters, Poachers, Thieves, and the Hidden History of American Conservation.* Berkeley: University of California Press, 2001.

John, Richard R. "Elaborations, Revisions, Dissents: Alfred D. Chandler Jr.'s *The Visible Hand* after Twenty Years." *Business History Review* 71 (Summer 1997): 151–200.

———. "The Politics of Innovation." *Daedalus* 127 (Fall 1998): 187–214.

———. "Recasting the Information Infrastructure for the Industrial Age." In Alfred D. Chandler Jr. and James W. Cortada, eds., *A Nation Transformed by Information: How Information Has Shaped the United States from Colonial Times to the Present.* New York: Oxford University Press, 2000.

———. *Spreading the News: The American Postal System from Franklin to Morse.* Cambridge, Mass.: Harvard University Press, 1995.

Johnson, Katherine M. "Federalism and the Origins of the Urban Crisis: The Geo-Politics of Housing and Highways, 1916–1956." Ph.D. diss., University of California, Berkeley, 2002.

Jordan, John M. *Machine-Age Ideology: Social Engineering and American Liberalism, 1911–1939.* Chapel Hill: University of North Carolina Press, 1994.

Kantor, Harvey A. "Charles Dyer Norton and the Origins of the Regional Plan Association of New York." In Donald A. Krueckeberg, ed., *The American Planner: Biographies and Recollections,* 2d ed. New Brunswick, N.J.: Center for Urban Policy Research, 1994.

Katz, Michael B. *In the Shadow of the Poorhouse: A Social History of Welfare*, rev. ed. New York: Basic, 1996.

Keller, Morton. *The Life Insurance Enterprise, 1885–1910: A Study in the Limitations of Corporate Power.* Cambridge, Mass.: Harvard University Press, 1963.

———. "Looking at the State: An American Perspective." *American Historical Review* 106 (February 2001): 114–118.

———. *Regulating a New Economy: Public Policy and Economic Change in America, 1900–1933.* Cambridge, Mass.: Harvard University Press, 1990.

———. *Regulating a New Society: Public Policy and Social Change in America, 1900–1933.* Cambridge, Mass.: Harvard University Press, 1994.

Kelley, Ben. *The Pavers and the Paved.* New York: Charles Scribner's Sons, 1971.

Key, V. O., Jr. *The Administration of Federal Grants to the States.* Chicago: Public Administration Service, 1937 [reprint New York: Johnson Reprint, 1972].

Kihlstedt, Folke. "Utopia Realized: The World's Fairs of the 1930s." In Joseph Corn, ed., *Imagining Tomorrow: History, Technology, and the American Future.* Cambridge, Mass.: MIT Press, 1986.

Klein, Maury. *The Life and Legend of Jay Gould.* Baltimore: Johns Hopkins University Press, 1986.

———. *Unfinished Business: The Railroad in American Life.* Hanover, N.H.: University Press of New England, 1994.

Klein, Milton M., ed. *The Empire State: A History of New York.* Ithaca, N.Y.: Cornell University Press, 2001.

Kline, Ronald, and Trevor Pinch. "Users as Agents of Technological Change: The Social Construction of the Automobile in the Rural United States." *Technology and Culture* 37 (October 1996): 763–795.

Krieg, Joann P., ed. *Robert Moses: Single-Minded Genius.* Interlaken, N.Y.: Heart of the Lakes, 1989.

Kutler, Stanley I. *Privilege and Creative Destruction: The Charles River Bridge Case.* Philadelphia: Lippincott, 1971.

Labatut, Jean, and Wheaton J. Lane. *Highways in Our National Life: A Symposium.* Princeton, N.J.: Princeton University Press, 1950.

Lacey, Michael. "Federalism and National Planning: The Nineteenth-Century Legacy." In Robert Fishman, ed., *The American Planning Tradition.* Washington, D.C.: Woodrow Wilson Center, 2000.

Lambright, W. Henry. *Powering Apollo: James E. Webb of NASA.* Baltimore: Johns Hopkins University Press, 1995.

Larson, John Lauritz. *Internal Improvement: National Public Works and the Promise of Popular Government in the Early United States.* Chapel Hill: University of North Carolina Press, 2001.

———. "Liberty by Design: Freedom, Planning, and John Quincy Adams's American System." In Mary O. Furner and Barry Supple, eds., *The State and Economic Knowledge.* Cambridge: Cambridge University Press, 1990.

Leavitt, Helen. *Superhighway—Superhoax.* New York: Doubleday, 1970.

Leff, Mark. *The Limits of Symbolic Reform: The New Deal and Taxation.* Cambridge: Cambridge University Press, 1984.

Leuchtenberg, William. *Franklin D. Roosevelt and the New Deal.* New York: Harper & Row, 1963.

Lewis, Eugene. *Public Entrepreneurship: Toward a Theory of Bureaucratic Political Power.* Bloomington: Indiana University Press, 1980.

Lewis, Tom. *Divided Highways: Building the Interstate Highways, Transforming American Life.* New York: Viking, 1997.

Lines, Jon J., Ellen L. Parker, and David C. Perry. "Building the Twentieth-Century Public Works Machine: Robert Moses and the Public Authority." In "Planning and Financing Public Works: Three Historical Cases." *Essays in Public Works History* 15 (September 1987): 47–70.

Ling, Peter J. *America and the Automobile: Technology, Reform, and Social Change, 1893–1923.* Manchester, UK: Manchester University Press, 1990.

Lowi, Theodore J. "Distribution, Regulation, Redistribution: The Functions of Government." In Stella Z. Theodoulou and Matthew A. Cahn, eds., *Public Policy: The Essential Readings.* Upper Saddle River, N.J.: Pearson Education, 1994.

Lundberg, George A., Mirra Komarovsky, and Mary Alice McInerny. *Leisure: A Suburban Study.* New York: Columbia University Press, 1934.

Lupo, Alan, Frank Colcord, and Edmund P. Fowler. *Rites of Way: The Politics of Transportation in Boston and the U.S. City.* Boston: Little, Brown, 1971.

MacMahon, Arthur W., et al. *Administration of Federal Work Relief.* New York: Da Capo, 1971 [1941].

Majewski, John, Christopher Baer, and Daniel B. Klein. "Responding to Relative Decline: The Plank Road Boom of Antebellum New York." *Journal of Economic History* 53 (March 1993): 106–122.

Marchand, Roland. "The Designers Go to the Fair II: Norman Bel Geddes, General Motor's Futurama, and the Visit to the Factory Transformed." *Design Issues* 8 (Spring 1992): 23–40.

Martin, Albro. *Enterprise Denied: The Origins of the Decline of American Railroads, 1897–1917.* New York: Columbia University Press, 1971.

———. *Railroads Triumphant: The Growth, Rejection, and Rebirth of a Vital American Force.* New York: Oxford University Press, 1992.

Mason, Philip Parker. "The League of American Wheelmen and the Good Roads Movement, 1880–1905." Ph.D. diss., University of Michigan, 1957.

Mazlish, Bruce, ed. *The Railroad and the Space Program: An Exploration in Historical Analogy.* Cambridge, Mass.: MIT Press, 1965.

McClelland, Peter D., and Alan L. Magdovitz. *Crisis in the Making: The Political Economy of New York State since 1945.* Cambridge: Cambridge University Press, 1981.

McCormick, Richard L. *From Realignment to Reform: Political Change in New York State, 1893–1910.* Ithaca, N.Y.: Cornell University Press, 1981.

McCraw, Thomas K. *TVA and the Power Fight, 1933–1939.* Philadelphia: Lippincott, 1971.

McDonald, Terrence. "Building the Impossible State." In John E. Jackson, ed. *Institutions in American Society.* Ann Arbor: University of Michigan Press, 1990.

McDonald, Terrence J., and Sally K. Ward. "San Francisco: Socioeconomic Change,

Political Culture, and Fiscal Politics, 1870–1906." In Terrence J. McDonald and Sally K. Ward, eds., *The Politics of Urban Fiscal Policy*. Beverly Hills, Calif.: Sage, 1984.

McDougall, Walter M. *The Heavens and the Earth: A Political History of the Space Race*. New York: Johns Hopkins University Press, 1995.

McGuinn, Patrick, and Frederick Hess. "Freedom from Ignorance? The Great Society and the Evolution of the Elementary and Secondary Education Act." In Sidney Milkis and Jerome Mileur, eds., *The Great Society and the High Tide of Liberalism*. Amherst: University of Massachusetts Press, 2005.

McIlvaine, Robert. *The Great Depression*. New York: Times Books, 1985.

McLennan, Rebecca Mary. "Citizens and Criminals: The Rise of the American Carcereal State, 1890–1935." Ph.D. diss., Columbia University, New York, 1999.

McSeveney, Samuel T. *The Politics of Depression: Political Behavior in the Northeast, 1893–1896*. New York: Oxford University Press, 1972.

McShane, Clay. *Down the Asphalt Path: The Automobile and the American City*. New York: Columbia University Press, 1994.

Meinert, Charles. "Bicycling in the Hudson-Mohawk Region of New York State, 1870–1900." *The Wheelmen*, part 2, 51 (November 1997): 2–7.

Meyers, Marvin. *The Jacksonian Persuasion*. Stanford, Calif.: Stanford University Press, 1957 [rev. 1960].

Milkis, Sidney M., and Jerome M. Mileur, eds. *The New Deal and the Triumph of Liberalism*. Amherst: University of Massachusetts Press, 2002.

Mohl, Raymond. "Ike and the Interstates: Creeping toward Comprehensive Planning." *Journal of Planning History* 2 (Summer 2003): 237–262.

———. "Stop the Road: Freeway Revolts in American Cities." *Journal of Urban History* 30 (July 2004): 674–706.

Mom, Gijs, and Laurent Tissot, eds. *Road History: Planning, Building and Use*. Neuchâtel, Switzerland: Alphil, 2007.

Morris, James O. *Conflict within the AFL: Craft Versus Industrial Unionism, 1901–1938*. Ithaca, N.Y.: Cornell University Press, 1958.

Moscow, Warren. *Politics in the Empire State*. New York: Knopf, 1948.

Moses, Robert. *Public Works: A Dangerous Trade*. New York: McGraw-Hill, 1970.

———. "Tomorrow's Cars and Roads." Reprint from *Liberty Magazine*. n.d. (January 1944?). New York Public Library, Science, Industry, and Business Library, New York.

Murray, Robert K. "Herbert Hoover and the Harding Cabinet." In Ellis Hawley, ed., *Herbert Hoover as Secretary of Commerce: Studies in New Era Thought and Practice*. Iowa City: University of Iowa Press, 1981.

National Industrial Conference Board. *Taxation of Motor Vehicle Transportation*. New York: National Industrial Conference Board, 1932.

Nelson, Robert. "The Economics Profession and the Making of Public Policy." *Journal of Economic Literature* 25 (March 1987): 49–91.

New York Regional Plan Association. *Westchester County and the Regional Plan: Just What This Great Enterprise Means to the County and Particularly to the Community in Which You Live*. New York: Regional Plan Association, 1932.

Noble, David F. *America by Design: Science, Technology, and the Rise of Corporate Capitalism.* Oxford: Oxford University Press, 1977.

Novak, William J. *The People's Welfare: Law and Regulation in Nineteenth-Century America.* Chapel Hill: University of North Carolina Press, 1996.

Nye, David E. *American Technological Sublime.* Cambridge, Mass.: MIT Press, 1994.

Official Automobile Blue Book 1919: Standard Road Guide of America, vol. 1: New York State and Adjacent Canada. New York: Automobile Blue Book, 1919.

Orren, Karen, and Stephen Skowronek. *The Search for American Political Development.* New York: Cambridge University Press, 2004.

Owen, Wilfred, and Charles L. Dearing. *Toll Roads and the Problem of Highway Modernization.* Washington, D.C.: Brookings Institution, 1951.

Panetta, Roger, ed. *Westchester: The American Suburb.* New York and Yonkers: Fordham University Press and Hudson River Museum, 2006.

Parkerson, Donald H. *The Agricultural Transition in New York State: Markets and Migration in Mid-Nineteenth-Century America.* Ames: Iowa State University Press, 1995.

Patterson, James T. *The New Deal and the States: Federalism in Transition.* Princeton, N.J.: Princeton University Press, 1969.

Paxson, Frederic L. "The Highway Movement, 1916–1935." *American Historical Review* 51 (1946): 236–253.

———. "The Rise of Sport." *Mississippi Valley Historical Review* 4 (September 1917): 143–168.

Preston, Howard Lawrence. *Dirt Roads to Dixie: Accessibility and Modernization in the South, 1885–1935.* Knoxville: University of Tennessee Press, 1991.

Pringle, Henry F. *Alfred E. Smith: A Critical Study.* New York: Macy-Masius, 1927.

Radford, Gail. "From Municipal Socialism to Public Authorities: Institutional Factors in the Shaping of Public Enterprise." *Journal of American History* 90 (December 2003): 863–890.

Rae, John B. "Coleman du Pont and His Road." *Delaware History* 16 (1975): 171–183.

———. *The Road and the Car in American Life.* Cambridge, Mass.: MIT Press, 1971.

Reading, Don C. "New Deal Activity and the States, 1933–1939." *Journal of Economic History* 33 (1973): 792–810.

Riordon, William L. *Plunkitt of Tammany Hall.* New York: Meridian, 1991 [1905].

Rockwood, Nathan C. *One Hundred and Fifty Years of Roadbuilding in America.* New York: Engineering News, 1914.

Rodgers, Cleveland. *Robert Moses: Builder for Democracy.* New York: Henry Holt, 1952.

Rodgers, Daniel T. *Atlantic Crossings: Social Politics in a Progressive Age.* Cambridge, Mass.: Harvard University Press, 1998.

Rose, Mark H. *Interstate: Express Highway Politics, 1939–1989,* rev. ed. Knoxville: University of Tennessee Press, 1990.

———. "Reframing American Highway Politics, 1956–1995." *Journal of Planning History* 2 (August 2003): 212–236.

Rose, Mark H., and Paul Barrett. "Street Smarts: The Politics of Transportation

Statistics in the American City, 1900–1990." *Journal of Urban History* 25 (March 1999): 405–433.

Rose, Mark H., and Bruce E. Seely. "Getting the Interstate System Built: Road Engineers and the Implementation of Public Policy, 1955–1985." *Journal of Policy History* 2 (1990): 23–56.

Rose, Mark H., Bruce E. Seely, and Paul F. Barrett. *The Best Transportation System in the World: Railroads, Trucks, Airlines, and American Public Policy in the Twentieth Century*. Columbus: Ohio State University Press, 2006.

Rossiter, Margaret W. *The Emergence of Agricultural Science: Justus Leibig and the Americans, 1840–1880*. New Haven, Conn.: Yale University Press, 1975.

Roth, Matthew. "Whittier Boulevard, Sixth Street Bridge, and the Origins of Transportation Exploitation in East Los Angeles." *Journal of Urban History* 30 (July 2004): 729–748.

Rubin, Bernard. *Public Relations in the Empire State: A Case Study of New York Administration*. New Brunswick, N.J.: Rutgers University Press, 1958.

Rydell, Robert. *World of Fairs: The Century of Progress Exhibitions*. Chicago: University of Chicago Press, 1993.

Sabin, Paul E. "Petroleum Polity: Law and Politics in the California Oil Economy, 1900–1940." Ph.D. diss. University of California, Berkeley, 2000.

Salsbury, Steven. *The State, the Investor, and the Railroad*. Cambridge, Mass.: Harvard University Press, 1967.

Sanford, Terry. *Storm over the States*. New York: McGraw-Hill, 1967.

Sautter, Udo. "Government and Unemployment: The Use of Public Works before the New Deal." *Journal of American History* 73 (June 1986): 59–86.

Scheiber, Harry. *Ohio Canal System: A Case Study of Government and the Economy*. Athens: Ohio University Press, 1969.

Schlesinger, Arthur M. *The Rise of the City*. New York: Macmillan, 1933.

Schrag, Zachary. "The Freeway Fight in Washington, D.C.: The Three Sisters Bridge in Three Administrations." *Journal of Urban History* 30 (July 2004): 648–673.

Schwartz, Bonnie Fox. *The Civil Works Administration: The Business of Emergency Employment in the New Deal*. Princeton, N.J.: Princeton University Press, 1984.

Schwarz, Jordan. *The New Dealers: Power Politics in the Age of Roosevelt*. New York: Knopf, 1993.

Scott, James C. *Seeing Like a State: How Certain Schemes to Improve the Human Condition Have Failed*. New Haven, Conn.: Yale University Press, 1998.

Scott, Roy V. *The Reluctant Farmer: The Rise of Agricultural Extension to 1914*. Urbana: University of Illinois Press, 1970.

Scranton, Philip. *Endless Novelty: Specialty Production and American Industrialization, 1865–1925*. Princeton, N.J.: Princeton University Press, 1997.

Seely, Bruce E. *Building the American Highway System: Engineers as Policy Makers*. Philadelphia: Temple University Press, 1987.

———. "Engineers and Government-Business Cooperation: Highway Standards and the Bureau of Public Roads." *Business History Review* 58 (Spring 1984): 51–77.

———. "Railroads, Good Roads, and Motor Vehicles: Managing Technological Change." *Railroad History* 155 (Autumn 1986): 35–63.

——. "The Saga of American Infrastructure: A Republic Bound Together." *Wilson Quarterly* 17 (Winter 1993): 19–39.

Seligman, Edwin R. A. "The New York Income Tax." *Political Science Quarterly* 34 (December 1919): 524.

Sheriff, Carol. *The Artificial River: The Erie Canal and the Paradox of Progress, 1817–1862*. New York: Hill & Wang, 1996.

Skocpol, Theda. *Protecting Soldiers and Mothers: The Political Origins of Social Policy in the United States*. Cambridge, Mass.: Harvard University Press, 1992.

Skocpol, Theda, Marshall Ganz, and Ziad Munson. "A Nation of Organizers: The Institutional Origins of Civic Voluntarism in the United States." *American Political Science Review* 94 (September 2000): 527–546.

Skowronek, Steven. *Building a New American State: The Expansion of National Administrative Capacities, 1877–1920*. Cambridge: Cambridge University Press, 1982.

Slayton, Robert A. *Empire Statesman: The Rise and Redemption of Al Smith*. New York: Free Press, 2001.

Smith, Alfred E. *Progress of Public Improvements: A Report to the People of the State of New York*. New York: New York State, 1927.

——. *Up to Now: An Autobiography*. New York: Viking, 1929.

Smith, Jason Scott. *Building New Deal Liberalism: The Political Economy of Public Works, 1933–1956*. New York: Cambridge University Press, 2006.

Smith, Robert G. *Ad Hoc Governments: Special Purpose Transportation Authorities in Britain and the United States*. Beverly Hills, Calif.: Sage, 1974.

Smith, Roe B. *History of New York State, vol. 4: Political and Governmental*. Syracuse, N.Y.: Syracuse University Press, 1922.

Stilgoe, John R. *Common Landscape of America, 1580–1845*. New Haven, Conn.: Yale University Press, 1982.

Sugrue, Thomas. "All Politics Is Local: The Persistence of Localism in Twentieth-Century America." In Meg Jacobs, William J. Novak, and Julian Zelizer, eds., *The Democratic Experiment: New Directions in American Political History*. Princeton, N.J.: Princeton University Press, 2003.

Swansinger, Jacqueline. "From Farmers to Businessmen: The Transformation of Elites in Fredonia, New York, 1898–1907." *New York History* 73 (January 1992): 43–63.

Taylor, George Rogers. *The Transportation Revolution, 1815–1860*. Vol. 4 of *The Economic History of the United States*. New York: Holt, Rinehart & Winston, 1951.

Taylor, George Rogers, and Irene D. Neu. *The American Railroad Network, 1861–1890*. Cambridge, Mass.: Harvard University Press, 1956.

Teaford, Jon C. *City and Suburb: The Political Fragmentation of Metropolitan America, 1850–1970*. Baltimore: Johns Hopkins University Press, 1979.

——. *Rise of the States: Evolution of American State Government*. Baltimore: Johns Hopkins University Press, 2002.

Tobin, Gary Allan. "The Bicycle Boom of the 1890s: The Development of Private Transportation and the Birth of the Modern Tourist." *Journal of Popular Culture* 7 (1974): 838–849.

Tobin, James. *Great Projects: The Epic Story of the Building of America, from the Taming of the Mississippi to the Invention of the Internet.* New York: Free Press, 2001.

Trachtenberg, Alan. *The Incorporation of America: Culture and Society in the Gilded Age.* New York: Hill & Wang, 1982.

Vidich, Arthur J., and Joseph Bensman. *Small Town in Mass Society: Class, Power, and Religion in a Rural Community.* Princeton, N.J.: Princeton University Press, 1958, rev. 1968.

Vogel, Mike. "Buffalo's Town Hall." *Buffalo Magazine*, March 13, 1994, 4–7.

Waldo, Dwight. *The Administrative State: A Study of the Political Theory of American Public Administration.* New York: Ronald, 1948.

Walker, C. S. "The Farmers' Movement." *Annals of the American Academy of Political and Social Science* 4 (March 1894): 94–102.

Wallis, John Joseph. "The Birth of the Old Federalism: Financing the New Deal, 1932–1940." *Journal of Economic History* 44 (March 1984): 139–159.

———. "The Political Economy of New Deal Spending Revisited, Again: With and Without Nevada." *Explorations in Economic History* 35 (1998): 140–170.

Wallis, John Joseph, and Wallace E. Oates. "The Impact of the New Deal on American Federalism." In Michael D. Bordo, Claudia Goldin, and Eugene N. White, eds., *The Defining Moment: The Great Depression and the American Economy in the Twentieth Century.* Chicago: University of Chicago Press, 1998.

Walsh, Annmarie Hauck. *The Public's Business: The Politics and Practices of Government Corporations.* Cambridge, Mass.: MIT Press, 1978.

Warner, Sam Bass, Jr. *Streetcar Suburbs: The Process of Growth in Boston, 1870–1900.* Cambridge, Mass.: Harvard University Press, 1962.

Weigold, Marilyn E. "Pioneering in Parks and Parkways: Westchester County, New York, 1895–1945." *Essays in Public Works History* 9 (February 1980): 1–43.

Wesser, Robert F. *Charles Evans Hughes: Politics and Reform in New York, 1905–1910.* Ithaca, N.Y.: Cornell University Press, 1967.

———. *A Response to Progressivism: The Democratic Party and New York Politics, 1902–1918.* New York: New York University Press, 1986.

White, W. Pierrepont. "Facts and Figures Arranged from Official Records Concerning Highways in New York State." 1906. In "Roads" pamphlet collection, New York Public Library, Science, Industry, and Business Library, New York.

———. *Oneida County, New York, and Her Road Building.* Oneida County League for Good Roads, December 1900 [2d ed., January 1902].

Whitford, Noble E. *History of the Canal System of the State of New York.* Albany: Office of the New York State Engineer and Surveyor, 1906.

Wiebe, Robert H. *The Search for Order, 1877–1920.* New York: Hill & Wang, 1967.

Wood, Robert C. *1400 Governments: The Political Economy of the New York Metropolitan Region.* Cambridge, Mass.: Harvard University Press, 1961.

Works Progress Administration, New York State. *New York: A Guide to the Empire State.* New York: Oxford University Press, 1940.

Worster, Donald. *Rivers of Empire: Water, Aridity, and the Growth of the American West.* New York: Pantheon, 1986.

Wright, Deil S. "Intergovernmental Relations: An Analytical Overview." *Annals of the American Academy of Political and Social Science* 416 (November 1974): 1–16.

——. "Policy Shifts in the Politics and Administration of Intergovernmental Relations, 1930s–1990s." *Annals of the American Academy of Political and Social Science* 509 (May 1990): 60–72.

——. "Revenue Sharing and Structural Features of American Federalism." *Annals of the American Academy of Political and Social Science* 419 (May 1975): 100–119.

——. *Understanding Intergovernmental Relations.* Belmont, Calif.: Duxbury, 1978.

Yearley, Clifton K. *The Money Machines: The Breakdown and Reform of Governmental and Party Finance in the North, 1860–1920.* Albany: State University of New York Press, 1970.

Newspapers and Periodicals

Albany Argus
Albany Times-Union
Better Roads and Streets
Boston Globe
Buffalo Courier Express
Buffalo Evening News
Buffalo Evening News Magazine
Buffalo News
Cherry Valley Gazette and Richmond Tribune
Country Gentleman
County Contractor
Cultivator and Country Gentleman
Elmira Sunday Telegram
Engineering News
Good Roads
Harper's Weekly
Highway Contractor
Horseless Age
Investment Dealers' Digest
Literary Digest
Low Bidder
Middletown Times-Herald
Mount Vernon Daily Argus
New York State Good Roads Association Bulletin
New York Times
New Yorker
Professional Engineer
Public Roads
Road Builders' News
Rochester Times-Union
Rochester Union Advertiser
Saturday Evening Post

Scientific American
Wall Street Journal

Government Documents and Reports

New York State Department of Public Works. *Annual Report.*

———. *Report Pertaining to the Condition of the State Highway System.* September 15, 1947.

New York State Governor's Office. *Executive Budget.*

New York State Highway Commission. *Report of the Commission of Highways.*

———. *Report of the State Commissioner of Highways.*

New York State Highway Survey Committee. Legislative Document (1936) No. 89. *Report of the State Highway Survey Committee.*

———. Legislative Document (1941) No. 44. *Interim Report of the State Highway Survey Committee.*

———. Legislative Document (1941) No. 50. *Report of the State Highway Survey Committee.*

New York State Joint Legislative Highway Survey Committee. *Public Hearings.* Rochester, N.Y., October 21, 1940. New York State Library, Albany.

New York State Office of the Comptroller, Alan G. Hevesi. *Public Authority Reform: Reining in New York's Secret Government.* Albany, February 2004.

New York State Reconstruction Commission. *Report of the Reconstruction Commission to Governor Alfred E. Smith on Retrenchment and Reorganization in the State Government.* Albany, N.Y.: J. B. Lyon, 1919.

New York State Special Joint Committee on Taxation and Retrenchment. Report. *State Expenditures, Tax Burden, and Wealth: A Study of the Growth of the Functions and Expenditures of the State Government and the Relation of Total Tax Burden to the Income of the People of the State.* February 11, 1926.

New York State Thruway Authority. *Annual Report.*

Niagara Frontier Planning Board. *Annual Reports.* Loeb Library, Harvard University, Cambridge, Mass.

U.S. Bureau of the Census. *Historical Statistics of the United States, Colonial Times to 1970.* Part 1. Washington, D. C., 1975.

———. *13th Census of the United States: 1910—Population—Occupation Statistics.* Washington, D.C.: U.S. Government Printing Office, 1914.

———. *14th Census of the United States: 1920—Population—Occupations.* Washington, D.C.: U.S. Government Printing Office, 1923.

———. *15th Census of the United States: 1930—Construction Industry.* Washington, D.C.: U.S. Government Printing Office, 1933.

U.S. Department of Agriculture, Office of Public Roads. Bulletin 21. Washington, D.C.: U.S. Government Printing Office, 1901.

———. Bulletin 22. Washington, D.C.: U.S. Government Printing Office, 1902.

U.S. Department of Agriculture, Office of Road Inquiry. "State Laws Relating to the Management of Roads Enacted in 1894–95." Washington, D.C.: U.S. Government Printing Office, 1895.

U.S. Department of Transportation, Federal Highway Administration. *America's*

Highways, 1776–1967. Washington, D.C.: U.S. Government Printing Office, 1976.

Internet Sources

American Studies Department, University of Virginia. "The Iconography of Hope: The 1939–40 New York World's Fair." *America in the 1930s.* http://xroads.virginia .edu/~1930s/DISPLAY/39wf/front.htm (accessed February 5, 2007).

Department of Transportation Library. Papers By H. S. Fairbank—Frank Turner—T. H. MacDonald. http://dotlibrary1.specialcollection.net/scripts/ws .dll?websearch&site=dot_Turner (accessed August 25, 2006).

New York State. Thruway Authority. *Factbook.* http://www.nysthruway.gov/about/ factbook/index.html (accessed February 5, 2007).

Weingroff, Richard F. "Clearly Vicious as a Matter of Policy: The Fight against Federal Aid." Federal Highway Administration. http://www.fhwa.dot.gov/ infrastructure/hwyhist01.cfm (accessed August 25, 2006).

———. "From Names to Numbers: The Origins of the U.S. Numbered Highway System," Federal Highway Administration. https://www.fhwa.dot.gov/ infrastructure/numbers.htm (accessed August 16, 2006).

———. "Moving the Goods: As the Interstate Era Begins: An Introduction to Web Site Information on Freight Transportation." Federal Highway Administration. http://www.fhwa.dot.gov/infrastructure/freight.cfm (accessed August 16, 2006).

Unpublished Sources

Connell, William H., et al. "Report of the Investigation of Paving and General Highway Conditions by the Engineering Commission Appointed by the National Paving Brick Manufacturers Association." 1928. New York Public Library, Science, Industry, and Business Library, New York.

Fein, Michael R. "Tunnel Vision: The 'Big Dig,' Invisible Highways and the Politics of Planning." Paper presented at the Fourth International Conference on the History of Traffic, Transport, and Mobility. Paris, 2006.

Governor's Thruway Committee. Report. March 5, 1950. Loeb Library, Harvard University, Cambridge, Mass.

New York State Association of Real Estate Boards. Service Letter, Summary of Answers Received to Questionnaire on City and Suburban Planning. June 30, 1924. Loeb Library, Harvard University, Cambridge, Mass.

New York State Association of Town Superintendents of Highways. 1939 Convention Highlights. New York Public Library, Science, Industry, and Business Library, New York.

New York State Thruway Authority. "Forging Ahead—the New York State Thruway." Fall 1951. Loeb Library, Harvard University, Cambridge, Mass.

Stein, Clarence S., chairman, New York State Commission of Housing and Regional Planning. "A Plan for the State of New York." Speech before the International City and Town Planning Congress, April 22, 1925. Loeb Library, Harvard University, Cambridge, Mass.

United Civic Bodies of Suffolk County and the Long Island Chamber of Commerce. "Planning and Zoning Needs for Suffolk County: A Brief on the Subject with Recommendations Presented to the Board of Supervisors of Suffolk, County, Long Island, New York." March 26, 1928. Loeb Library, Harvard University, Cambridge, Mass.

Westchester County Parks Commission. "The Needs of Westchester County Parkways from a Through Traffic Perspective." November 8, 1940. New York Public Library, Science, Industry and Business Library, New York.

INDEX